D1488583

FUNERAL SERVICE:

A bibliography of literature on its past,
present and future, the various means of
disposition, and memorialization

by

BARBARA K. HARRAH

and

DAVID F. HARRAH

The Scarecrow Press, Inc.
Metuchen, N.J.   1976

Library of Congress Cataloging in Publication Data

Harrah, Barbara K
   Funeral service.

   Includes indexes.
   1. Undertakers and undertaking--Bibliography.
2. Undertakers and undertaking--United States--Bibliog-
raphy. 3. Funeral rites and ceremonies--Bibliography.
4. Funeral rites and ceremonies--United States--Bibliog-
raphy. 5. Dead--Bibliography. I. Harrah, David F.,
1949-   joint author. II. Title.
Z5994.H3   [RA619]   016.614'6'0973   76-40340
ISBN 0-8108-0946-X

to

FRANCES T. CAHN

our cousin and friend

TABLE OF CONTENTS

v

PREFACE

Why a reference book on funeral service? Because until now there was no complete, up-to-date reference. The latest, E. H. McClelland's The Literature of Mortuary Science [see 845], was compiled in 1949 and, though mimeographed by the National Association of Mortuary Sciences, was never published. Funeral Service Abstracts (renamed Thanatology Abstracts in 1975), includes selected periodical entries beginning in 1965 and can be profitably used along with the present work. The latest bibliography in book form was printed privately by John Townshend--in 1887. The second reason for a funeral bibliography is that funeral service in America should or does rank with stagflation, environment, energy, and women's rights as one of the major concerns of the 1970's.

We have made our compilation, then, to assist librarians, students, and those professionally interested in researching funeral service, the means of final disposition, and the memorializing of the dead. The criterion used in selecting literature was simply its relevance. Details of organization under the three major categories are outlined in the Introduction (which follows this Preface).

To initiate the layman into the mystery and fascination of American funeral service, we would like to explain, briefly, its present status, how it arrived there, and where it is going.

Disposing of the dead has preoccupied man since prehistoric times; the means are today essentially unchanged since then. In ancient times, the choice of means hinged on mystical or religious beliefs. The early Egyptians, for example, believed in eventual physical resurrection and developed elaborate embalming techniques to restore the body for the great day. Early Christians believed the soul left the body after death, making elaborate funeral rites unnecessary.

Today's decision to bury, cremate, or donate the body to science rests heaviest on economic considerations and social pressures. Social trends, in turn, reflect considerations of public health, costs, and new public attitudes toward land use, particularly of cemeteries as a source of greenery in urban areas.

Until the outbreak of the Civil War in 1861, disposing of the dead in the U.S. was largely a simple, family matter. The ladies of the house prepared the body, viewing took place in the parlor, and friends or relatives opened and closed the grave. The undertaker provided the coffin. On rare occasions for viewing or transit he was asked to preserve the body by packing it in ice--a rather unsatisfactory technique which often resulted in its exploding at some inauspicious moment during the service.

Americans' early resistance to arterial embalming as a "mutilation" gave way to general acceptance during the latter half of the 19th century. Ruth Harmer in an encyclopedia article, "Embalming, Burial, and Cremation" [see 442], describes its promotion by "a newly emerging group of undertaker-businessmen" and how a vigorous salesman like Joseph H. Clarke, aware of its profit potential, pursuaded a Cincinnati medical college to offer a course in embalming. The basis for mortuary education was thereby established and the Golden Age of funeral service began.

During the century that followed, undertaking rocketed toward success, propelled by the uniquely American life styles that blessed other businesses. The first factor was mobility. Far travelers had to be embalmed to be shipped home; embalming techniques improved; major airlines offered air transport service across the country and in foreign countries; and today air hearses are beginning to shuttle bodies back and forth to out-of-the-way places.

Breaking up of large families meant smaller houses which did not lend themselves to displaying the dead: funeral homes expanded to include viewing rooms. Our once religious society secularized; funeral services, once the pastor's forte, became increasingly the mortician's. And now, corporations with their larger salaries and better medical and life insurance plans are pushing the family funeral home into memory. In short, the funeral industry has grown, like other industries, in response to the demands, pressures, and potential of the developing American society. Its story seemed an unadulterated success sage--until The American Way of Death.

What happened?

The same thing that happened to the SST and the penny postcard: consumer awareness and inflation. If Mitford hadn't written "The Book" [see 993] somebody else would have. (Ruth Mulvey Harmer [see 968] and Leroy Bowman [see 921], in effect, did.) People who can no longer afford expensive cars can't afford expensive funerals. Those who prefer Datsun utility to the flash of Cadillac chrome will cotton to plain pine boxes and eschew the solid copper elegance of perma-seal caskets with shell pink velvet side rolls, wings, and overlays. Spartans must remember, however, that a lot of people genuinely like Cadillacs and pink side rolls and will pay handsomely for them. Many religions and ethnic groups see the funeral as a necessary and desirable rite of passage.

Clever car manufacturers put out both the luxury and the stripped down economy models. Funeral service innovators, too, are finding profits lost on splashy extras come back on volume sales. The Humphrey Co. in Chula Vista, Cal., offers a low-priced "unique utility container that enables the funeral director to meet the growing demand for inexpensive direct cremations and interments." M. K. Bates Co. trains practicing directors to arrange and promote the adaptive funeral.

Still, the reverberations from Mitford's book echo longer and louder than for example, Meadow's environmental counterpart, Limits to Growth. Funeral directors do the dirty work that literally 99 per cent (or more) of society would not do. They perform an absolutely vital service. Society might be grateful. Instead, it heaps abuse on him or her higher than on sanitation workers, pornographers, or child molesters. Why?

People tolerate (more or less), pollution, dirty pictures, and rape because they think they can escape them. But death-defying,

death-denying syndromes notwithstanding, deep down, everyone knows
he's going to die and he doesn't like it. Funerals remind him he's
mortal. He doesn't like to shake hands with a mortician.

The funeral business, of course, is not undeserving of cen-
sure. Investigations are going on in many places and unearthing
derogatory information: some directors have agents out picking up
state burial allowances allocated to the poor; some stash cheap
caskets in garages and display only the higher priced items; illegal-
ly, some crematoria insist a body be casketed; directors have been
known to misrepresent the need for embalming.

Fraud in funeral service, however, is restricted to a minority of dishonest directors. In American Funeral: A Study of Guilt,
Extravagance and Sublimity [see 921], Leroy Bowman attacks ma-
terialism and meaningless in the contemporary funeral, not the directors. Ruth Mulvey Harmer, in "Funerals That Make Sense"
[see 967], decries the industry's nurturing the ideas that you can
take it with you and that expensive funerals ease guilt. That's not
illegal. That's how people sell used cars. It's society's ambiva-
lence that puts a man's picture in the paper for selling a million
dollars' worth of life insurance and vilifies the funeral director who
uses the same techniques to sell a casket.

Yet the funeral persists, National Funeral Directors Association Executive Director Howard C. Raether says, because it provides "what most people want, need, and often demand." The results of the Casket Manufacturers of America's study on American
Attitudes Toward Death and Funerals [see 926] concur: the majority of Americans still favor the traditional funeral--but they want to
know what they are paying for.

In response, the funeral industry is itemizing merchandise
and service charges and offering a choice of services with competitive price tags. It is also broadening its base.

One way is by expanding into areas traditionally separate
from funeral service. A Los Angeles mortician/pilot collects the
body, prepares it, holds services, cremates and scatters the remains over the ocean. In ten states across the country, universities

are offering courses on eye enucleation for funeral directors, ena-
bling them to supply corneas for transplanting into the living.   Many
leaders in the field are trying to spot potential problems before they
become major issues.

An Environmental Protection Agency spokesman, for instance,
says emissions from local crematoria and seepage from mausolea
and graves are not yet severe enough to command national attention.
Howard F. Barnard, editor of Casket and Sunnyside, however, ad-
monishes in the June 1975 issue: "You should avoid using for cremation cases not only caskets made entirely of plastic but those which
have plastics incorporated in any form."   Fred L. Bates, National
Selected Morticians assistant executive secretary, responds in private correspondence to a question on wastes from the drainage system in the Rio de Janeiro high-rise mausoleum: "How much waste
would be carried to sewers is something I cannot answer; however
it does seem to pose some very significant problems."   John P.
Danglade, executive vice president of the American Cemetery Association, points out the necessity of trying new ideas, but scrapping
them if they do not work.   In private correspondence he explains the
Rio high-rise is not "nearly the height originally planned.   It may
end up being the one and only, if it is ever finished."   Vanderlyn R.
Pine, National Funeral Directors Association research analysis consultant, believes high-rise mausolea will become "quite popular in a
few areas" but environmental problems can be taken care of by the
combined efforts of "experts in microbiology, hydrodynamics, environmental pollution and other similar fields."

By far the greatest expansion in funeral service, however,
is in service and education.   The focus of funeral directing is shift-
ing from product (and sales) to counseling.   James Frueling, in the
March 1975 NSM Bulletin, explores the professionalizing of funeral
service in the future, the dual role of the director as businessman
and professional, and the potential implications of supplanting product
with professional service as the conceptual basis for funerals.   In
The Funeral--An Experience of Value [see 1171], the Rev. Paul
Irion specifies the funeral's value in providing a means for the

bereaved to express sorrow, actualize their loss, and realize the support of family and friends. Robert Slater, in "The Funeral-- Beginning at the Beginning" [see 1238], says, "We have lost our classroom for death, which was the old-style multi-generational family." The funeral director can't restore the classroom, but with proper education he can provide counseling to help the bereaved recover.

Proper education, R. A. Ebeling defines in "Education" [see 770] as more specialized vocation training and extended study for those already involved in funeral service. William Matthews [see 790] urges that psychology be included in the regular curriculum for would-be funeral directors and that general educational and licensing standards be toughened to ensure funeral service's future.

Funeral service literature of the past decade has been a veritable blizzard of works on how to improve image, preserve value in excoriated traditions, and survive--profitably. But if the last years have been a struggle and the Golden Age is now past, still funeral service has clearly weathered the Age of Mitford and seems bound successfully on a reasonable compromise. Its story should be read, not only to learn the means, costs, and alternatives of final disposition from a practical standpoint, but for the fascinating story of a nationwide business attempting to meet the demands of a society in flux and for the story of the people in the funeral business, the embalmers and directors who every day of their lives deal with death.

In compiling our sources, we received enormous help from many people in funeral service. We would like to thank in particular Howard C. Raether for his advice and comments, and for letting us review the National Funeral Directors Association's extensive publications; Dr. Otto Margolis for lending us the use of the library at the American Academy/McAllister Institute in New York; John P. Danglade of the American Cemetery Association for his interesting comments on various aspects of funeral service and for suggestions on organizing the contents of this volume; Fred L. Bates of National Selected Morticians for his thoughtful ideas on the problems of disposition; John Kastings of the New York Metropolitan Funeral Directors Association for his time, referrals, and introduction to the whole of funeral service; Sarah Cooke of the Stamford, Conn., Memorial Society for explaining the functions of memorial societies and her insights into the growing consumer movement and the need for consumers to organize to get the services they want; Vanderlyn R. Pine, National Funeral Directors Association consultant, for his overview of the present status of funeral service and thoughts on its future; and John B. Reynolds and John J. Hart, Jr., of the Bouton-Reynolds Funeral Home in Stamford, Conn., who showed us a little of what it is like to be in funeral service, living with death and under constant criticism, and trying at the same time to make a living.

For letting us review their materials, we wish also to thank the following: Mrs. M. Cox of the Memorial Association of Canada; William H. Ford of the American Board of Funeral Service Education; Peter Perry, editor/publisher of the Canadian Funeral Director; Anita Doyle, publicity director of the Associated Funeral Directors Service; Priscilla Fox of Casket Manufacturers Association of America; Rebecca Cohen of the Continental Association of Funeral and Memorial Societies, Inc.; Lynn Melby, executive director of the Allied Memorial Council; Charles H. Nichols, director of the National Foundation of Funeral Service; Nina S. Klein of Educational Perspectives Associates; Jean Scribner of National Cremation Magazine; Wendell W. Hahn, president of the Federated Funeral Directors of America; James R. Mulvaney, executive secretary of the National Catholic Cemetery Conference; Howard Barnard, editor of Casket & Sunnyside; Bennett Goldstein, President of the Jewish Funeral Directors of America; and John A. Dunn of the Flying Funeral Directors of America.

We thank also the staffs of the Greenwich, Conn., Public Library, the New York Public Library, and the Ferguson Library in Stamford, Conn., for their great assistance and James Godfrey, director of libraries at Rye Country Day School, Rye, New York, our constant and untiring abettor.

Barbara Harrah
December 1975

INTRODUCTION

In this book funeral literature has been codified under its three basic components: funeral service, disposition, and memorialization. Each of these have been further subdivided, and where a large number of entries made it advisable, these subdivisions, too, have been broken into categories. To avoid further fragmentation, unannotated entries have been listed in sequence along with the annotated ones. Quotation marks indicate titles of magazine articles; underlines are used for books and pamphlets. The latter are distinguishable from books by the number of pages cited or by the word "pamphlet" or "brochure."

All readily obtainable literature has been annotated. For the scholar more difficult to find and out-of-print materials have been included. Late 19th-century titles are generally descriptive of the books' contents and need no further explanation; most highly technical articles do not also. (These appear generally in Part I, Section B2, Embalming and Restorative Art.) Otherwise, listings are non-technical, selected to give laymen as well as funeral service practitioners a reference to literature on the whole of the profession --its history, its counterparts abroad, contemporary practice in the United States, and related industries.

Part I, Funeral Service, comprises the bulk of this volume. After a short historical and comparative section A, Part I breaks down into the following categories of its main section B (Contemporary American Funeral Service): 1. the basic services and responsibilities of the funeral director; 2. the embalming and restorative arts; 3. funeral economics and business techniques; 4. the design, necessary equipment, and zoning of the funeral home; 5. funeral service education (including licensing, school accreditation, and career potentials); 6. the funeral director's relation with doctors and the clergy; 7. professional associations, directories, and biographical material; and 8. the allied industries of casket manufacturing, hearses and ambulances, air transportation, and flowers.

Part I, Section C--analysis, alternatives to the traditional funeral, and the future of funeral service--is divided into four categories: 1. investigations, analyses, statistics, and criticism; 2. mortuary law; 3. memorial societies and consumer education; and 4. the profession's response to society's new demands and its efforts to improve its image.

The second basic industry related to funerals is disposition of the dead. Literature on burial and other means is listed under Part II, which is divided into four sections: A concerns cemeteries and memorial parks, broken into 1. historical (including old cemeteries, mounds, barrows, catacombs, and earthworks); and 2. contemporary (including modern cemeteries and mausolea, columbaria, and related subjects such as vaults and urns, and the movements to conserve land and convert cemeteries into grounds for multiple use by the public), Section B deals with cremation and ash scattering; C with cryonics; and D with other means of disposition (such as organ and whole body donation to science and sea burial).

Memorialization is the last step in disposition; its literature is listed under Part III. Section A comprises historical and foreign aspects (of carvings, epitaphs, rubbings, etc.) and Section B lists modern American monuments, markers, designs and methods of memorialization for traditional cemeteries and the newer memorial parks.

There is an ever-increasing amount of audio-visual material available from a variety of groups. These are described in Part IV, with addresses and phone numbers of distributors.

The appendices include a glossary of some frequently used funeral terminology, acronyms of professional organizations, lists of funeral organizations and cemetery associations, with addresses, phone numbers, purpose, and publications; a list of the most popular trade magazines with their addresses, phone numbers, description and, where possible, frequency of publication; lists of memorial societies, co-op funeral homes, and body donation associations, divided into national, regional, and state, with definition, addresses, and phone numbers; a list of accredited funeral service colleges; a checklist of embalming requirements in each state; and a reprinting of the industry's three main codes of ethics and professional practices.

There are three indices: author, title, and subject. The authors urge that these be consulted in addition to the Table of Contents because many books and articles span more than one of the three basic categories. All works that lay equal or almost equal emphasis on two or more subjects are listed whenever they pertain, cross-referenced to the entry where the full citation and annotation may be found. Books and articles that allude only briefly to other subjects are not so cross-referenced, but the subjects they cover are reflected in the Subject Index.

I. FUNERAL SERVICE

A. HISTORICAL, FOREIGN, ETHNIC, REGIONAL, AND RELIGIOUS CUSTOMS

1 Ablon, Joan. "The Samoan Funeral in Urban America. " Ethnol-
    ogy 9:209-227 (July 1970).
        Samoan funerals are characterized by elaborate Christian
ceremony; changes in traditional customs traced.

2 Ahern, Emily M. The Cult of the Dead in a Chinese Village.
    Stanford, CA: Stanford University Press, 1973. 282pp. ,
    illus. , bibliog. , index.
        Examination of the care and management of the dead in
Ch'inan, a four-lineage northern Taiwanese village. The basis for
their ancestor worship is a belief in the reciprocal obligations between the dead and the living.

3 Alexander, Levy. Alexander's Hebrew Ritual, and Doctrinal Ex-
    planation of the Whole Ceremonial Law, Oral and Traditional
    of the Jewish Community in England and Foreign Parts. Lon-
    don: the Author, 1819. 307pp.

4 "Ancient Body Found Buried in China. " The American Funeral
    Director 98(8):42-43 (Aug. 1975).
        A body of a man believed dead since 167 B.C. has been
found in Hupeh Province in Central China. The skin is elastic, the
joints moveable. The body had been immersed in a preservative
fluid and buried inside a series of caskets. The caskets and over
three hundred burial objects were laid at the bottom of a thirty-foot
pit.

5 Anderson, Joseph. Notes on the Survival of Pagan Customs in
    Christian Burial. Ann Arbor, MI: Finch Press, 1974
    (repr. of 1876 ed.).

6 Anderson, Raymond H. "Funeral Customs Decried in Soviet. "
    New York Times cxvi(39, 893):8 (April 15, 1967).
        Plea for opening of funeral homes in U. S. S. R. made in
Ekonomicheskaya Gazeta.

7 Asbell, Bernard. When F. D. R. Died. New York: Holt,
    Rinehart and Winston, 1961.
        Descriptions of President Franklin D. Roosevelt's funeral.

8   Atwater, Caleb. Description of the Antiquities Discovered in
     the State of Ohio and Other Western States. New York:
     AMS Press, 1974 (repr. of 1820 ed.). Illus. (also in paper).
         Burial objects give clues to burial customs of the early
American Indians.

9   Basevi, William H. F. The Burial of the Dead. Ann Arbor,
     MI: Finch Press, 1974 (repr. of 1920 ed.).
         Detailed historical and cultural study of burial and crema-
tion from prehistoric times to the 20th century.

10   Bellush, Bernard. He Walked Alone: A Biography of John Gil-
     bert Winant. Atlantic Highlands, NJ: Humanities, 1968.

11   Bendann, Effie. Death Customs; An Analytical Study of Burial
     Rites (repr. of 1930 Knopf ed.). New York: Gordon Press,
     1974; Atlantic Highlands, NJ: Humanities (text ed.); Detroit:
     Gale, 1974. 304pp., biblio.
         Detailed and well-documented survey of mortuary practices
of pre-literate groups of Australia, Melanesia, India, and Northeast
Siberia. In two parts: the first analyzes the similarities of the
groups' customs; the second describes the origin of death, causes of
death, disposal of the dead, spirits, attitudes toward the corpse,
mourning, grave huts, purification feasts after death, taboos, the
role of women, the destruction of property and cults of the dead.

12   Benet, Sula. Song, Dance and Custom of Peasant Poland. New
     York: Roy Publishers, 1951.
         Polish peasant funeral customs.

13   Berg, Charles W. Confessions of an Undertaker. Wichita, KA:
     The Author, 1919. 116pp.

14   Best, Elsdon. The Maori: Memoirs of the Polynesian Society
     (vols. 2 and 5). New Zealand, 1924.

15   Bibby, Geoffrey. "The Body in the Bog: Archeological Detec-
     tive Story." Horizon 19(1):44-51 (winter 1968). Photos.
         Well-preserved bodies recently discovered in Danish peat
bogs with discussion of early Scandinavian funeral practices.

16   Biesanz, John, and Biesanz, Mavis. The People of Panama.
     New York: Columbia University Press, 1955.
         Funeral customs and funeral literature on Cunas.

17   Bishop, John P., and Wilson, Edmund. Undertaker's Garland.
     New York: Haskell, 1974 (repr. of 1922 Knopf ed.).

18   Blair, Robert. The Grave: To Which Is Added Gray's Elegy
     (written) In a Country Church Yard. With Notes Moral, Crit-
     ical, and Explanatory by G. Wright. London: Scatcherd &
     Whitaker, 1785.
         Minor details of historical burial customs.

19 Boase, T. S. <u>Death in the Middle Ages: Mortality, Judgment</u>
    <u>and Remembrance.</u> New York: McGraw-Hill, 1972. 144pp.,
    illus. (also in paper). (Library of Medieval Civilization
    series.)

20 "The Bog People: Preserved in Peat for Thousands of Years. "
    <u>American Funeral Director</u> 98(5):33-40 (May 1975). Photo.
           Bog people are human remains preserved in peat bogs.
    Recent finds in Europe date back 5000 years. The acid in the water
    and almost total absence of air tans the skin and hair, preserving
    them.

21 Borlase, William C. <u>Naenia Cornubiae; A Descriptive Essay</u>
    <u>Illustrative of the Sepulchres and Funeral Customs of the</u>
    <u>Early Inhabitants of Cornwall.</u> London: Longmans, 1872.
    287pp.

22 Bossard, James, and Boll, Eleanor. <u>Ritual in Family Living.</u>
    Philadelphia: University of Pennsylvania Press, 1950.

23 "Bound in Skin. " <u>The American Funeral Director</u> 98(8):6
    (March 1975).
           The ultimate in body recycling: novelist Eugene Sue's
    mistress out-sensationalized the notorious author of <u>The Wandering</u>
    <u>Jew</u> (1844). In pursuance of her wishes, a set of his books was
    bound with skin taken from her shoulders after death. In 1951
    Foyles bookshop sold it for $29.

24 Bowra, C. M. <u>The Greek Experience.</u> New York, 1959.
           Shows the profound influence Greek customs have had on
    western funeral practice.

25 Branson, Helen K. "Burial Customs Modified by Cultural Back-
    ground in Hawaii. " <u>Mortuary Management</u> 58(1):20+ (1971).
           Member of the Family Services Division of the Hawaiian
    Memorial Park discusses Hawaiian funeral customs, the present
    trend towards cremation, cultural reasons for practice of cremation
    and historical background for Hawaiian burial practices.

26 Breasted, James H. <u>A History of the Ancient Egyptians.</u> New
    York: 1903.
           Material on ancient Egyptian preservation techniques, fun-
    eral customs, etc.

27 Breed, William P. <u>Handbook for Funerals.</u> Philadelphia:
    Presbyterian Board of Publication, 1871. 95pp.
           Nineteenth century funeral practices.

28 "British Coffins Average $47. " <u>American Funeral Director</u>
    98(7):36 (July 1975).
           Officials of Kent Funeral Supplies, Ltd. , Faversham, Eng-
    land, in a letter to <u>The Observer</u>, refute allegation that funeral costs
    are too high: 95% of British coffins are made of 12-15mm chipboard

faced with wood veneer. Cost of labor and materials averages approximately $47.

29 Bruce, Philip Alexander. Social Life of Virginia in the Seventeenth Century. Richmond, VA: Whittet and Shepperson, 1907. p. 218-22.
     Early Virginia funeral ceremonies were important social events.

30 Bruning, Leslie D. "Funerals in Venice ... as Unique as the City Itself." The American Funeral Director 98(8):22-25 (Aug. 1975).
     The cemetery is separated from the city, necessitating a unique funeral procession by gondola or motorboat. Old families and celebrities rate an "exceptional funeral"; the majority enjoy few options to the "standard funeral," which includes filling out documents and selecting the casket. All are zinc-lined wood, the only difference being in the amount of "sculptural intricacy." There is no embalming; no open viewing; bodies are buried within two days. Caskets are inexpensive, as there is no padding. Boat, driver, and pallbearers cost $100. City pays one-third of total funeral expense. Brief description of typical funeral rites and of Igor Stravinsky's elaborate funeral.

31 Budge, E. A. Wallis. The Liturgy of Funerary Offerings: The Egyptian Texts with English Translations. New York: Benjamin Blom, 1974 (repr. of 1909 ed.). Illus.

32 _____. The Mummy: A Handbook of Egyptian Funerary Archaeology. Cambridge, England: Cambridge University Press, 1925, 513pp., drawings, photos, index; New York: Macmillan, 1926; New York: Biblio & Tanner, 1964, 404pp., illus.; New York: Collier, 1972, 404pp., illus. (in paper).
     Definitive work on every aspect of Egyptian disposal of the dead amply illustrated by drawings and photographs. The process of mummification; paraphernalia of the tomb; long section on scarabs, amulets, and various Egyptian funeral ceremonies; tombs, coffins, sarcophagi, and pyramids.

33 Buechel, William W. "Christian Burial--What It Means." The Ave Maria 80(19):8-9 (Nov. 6, 1954).

34 "Burial Customs." American Funeral Director 95(2):26+ (1972).
     Archeological discoveries in China show burial customs which date back to the first century B.S.

35 "Burial in Kremlin Wall Dates to 1926." American Funeral Director 10(97):98 (Oct. 1974).
     Burial of the cremated remains of Leonid Borisovich Krassin, the first person to be buried in the Kremlin Wall. An advocate of peaceful co-existence, he died in Great Britain while serving there as Soviet envoy. Description of the decorated funeral train, the procession of over 20,000 led by cavalry, the speeches. His final dis-

position was to set a precedent for future burials. "The ashes and memorial tablets of our leaders will redeem the wall of the fortress built to protect tyrants. "

36 "Burial in the British Style. " Casket & Sunnyside 101(13[cen-
        tennial issue]):18-22 (1972). Photos.
            British customs have changed slowly in the past century.
Then, as now, cremations were popular, burial ground at a pre-
mium--bodies were tiered underground, and profits low because
clients' incomes were low. Morticians became wealthy because
volume of business was high. There are ten times fewer mortuaries now; body snatching has ceased; and transportation is motorized.

37 "Burial Problems Abound in Asia. " American Funeral Director
        95(11):22+ (1972).
            Increased foreign travel has meant increasing number of
Americans are dying in Asia where there is a lack of facilities such
as morgues, embalmers, caskets, and cemetery space. U.S. Con-
sular officials must dispose of them there or return them to the
States. Cases quoted.

38 Carson, Steven Lee. "The Civil War Mortician. " American
        Funeral Director 93(4):28-32 (1970).
            Lists woes and problems of the embalmer and mortician
passing through enemy lines and collecting mutilated bodies to be
patched up and sent home. Good anecdotes.

39 Chadwick, Edwin Sir. Sanitary Conditions of the Labouring
        Population in England, ed. by M. W. Flinn. Chicago: Al-
        dine, 1974 (repr. of 1842 ed.).
            Sections on burial customs; their effect on public
health.

40 Christensen, James B. Double Descent Among the Fanti. New
        Haven, CT: Human Relations Area Files, 1954.
            Doctoral thesis presented to Northwestern University based
on field work in the Fanti states of Anomabu, Abura, and Esiam.
Detailed information on funeral rites.

41 Cockburn, T. Aidan. "Death and Disease in Ancient Egypt. "
        Science 181(4098):470-71 (1973).
            Climatic conditions in Egypt helped preserve remains nat-
urally; advanced techniques of drying, wrapping, and eviscerating
practiced later when funerals became more elaborate. Autopsy of
a 700 B. C. mummy found bone, cartilage, connective tissue, muscle,
and epithelial tissues well preserved.

42 Consumers' Association. What to Do When Someone Dies, ed.
        by Edith Rudinger. London: Consumers Association, Ltd.
        (14 Buckingham St. , London W. C. 2), 1969. 125pp. , illus.
        (in paper).

43 Cooney, Larry. "Funeral Service by 1985 ... A Look Into the
      Crystal Ball. Canadian Funeral Service 51(2):7-10 (1973).
      A speech before the Ontario Funeral Service Association
Convention. Predicts more mergers, varied contracts, cost analyses
and planning, simpler services, higher wages, better working conditions, more metal caskets and fewer wood, more sophisticated counseling, flexible pricing systems, better educated personnel.

44 Cooper, Gordon. I Searched the World for Death. London:
      J. Long, 1940. 287pp., plates.

45 Cormack, Annie. Chinese Birthday, Wedding, Funeral and
      Other Customs. Peking: La Librairie Française, 1923.
      209pp.

46 "The Coroner, the Pathologist, the Physician, the Registrar,
      and the Funeral Director." Canadian Funeral Director 3(6):
      17-23 (June 1975).
      Medical-Legal panel at the post graduate course held in
Toronto, April 23-24, 1975, answers questions of attending funeral
directors.

47 "Court Mourning: The Panoply of Grief." Economist 243(6719):
      18 (June 3, 1972). Photo.
      The funeral of Edward VIII and the various degrees of
British court mourning.

48 Covarrubias, Miguel. Island of Bali. New York: Knopf, 1937.
      Chapter XI, "Death and Cremation," valuable reference on
Balinese funeral customs.

49 Covey, Cyclone. American Pilgrimage: The Roots of American
      History, Culture, and Religion. New York: Macmillan,
      n.d. (in paper); Gloucester, MA: Peter Smith, n.d.
      References to early American funeral customs.

50 Crispo, John. Fee-Setting by Independent Practitioners: A Study
      for the Prices and Incomes Commission of Canada, The
      Commission, 1972.

51 Cunnington, Phillis, and Lucas, Catherin. Costume for Births,
      Marriages, and Deaths. New York: Barnes and Noble, 1972.
      331pp., index, drawings, photos, appendices, ref., biblio.
      Scholarly, well illustrated with photographs and drawings;
customs; descriptions of memorable funerals such as those of Gladstone and Catharine of Aragon; common peoples' and royal funerals;
widows' clothes; children's mourning wear; and dress for the corpse.

52 Curl, James S. The Victorian Celebration of Death. Detroit:
      Partridge Press, 1972. 222pp., index, notes, biblio., photos.

53/4 Davey, Richard. A History of Mourning. London: Jay's,
      1890. 111p.; Ann Arbor, MI: Finch Press, 1974 (repr. of
      1890 ed.).

Davidson, H. R. <u>The Road to Hel</u>. See entry 63.

55 Davis, N. "Two Early Sixteenth Century Accounts of Royal Occasions. " <u>Notes and Queries</u> 20:122-30 (April 1973).

56 Dawson, Warren Royal. <u>Bibliography of Works Relating to Mummification in Egypt; With Exerpts, Epitomes, Critical and Bibliographical Notes</u>. Cairo: Institut d'Egypte, 1929.

57 "Death in Chamula. " <u>Natural History</u>, Jan. 1968, p. 48-57.

58 De Groot, J. J. M. <u>Religion in China</u>. New York: G. P. Putnam's, 1912.

59 _____. <u>Religious System of China</u>. New York: Paragon, 1964. 6 vols.

60 Douglass, William A. <u>Death in Murelaga: Funerary Rituals in a Spanish Basque Village</u>. Seattle: University of Washington Press, 1969. 240pp. (American Ethnological Society Monograph, no. 49.)

61 Earle, Alice Morse. <u>Customs and Fashions in Old New England</u>. New York: Scribner's, 1893.
   Early American funeral customs.

62 Edwards, I. E. S. <u>The Treasures of Tutankhamun</u>. New York: Viking, 1973. 47pp. of text+ 50 illus., biblio.
   Catalogue from the British Museum's 1972 exhibition of the contents of Tutankhamun's tomb; short introduction to Tutankhamun, the discovery of the tomb; detailed descriptions of items on display.

63 Ellis, Hilda R. <u>Road to Hel: A Study of the Conception of the Dead in Old Norse Literature</u>. Westport, CT: Greenwood Press, 1968 (repr. of a 1943 ed.). Illus.
   Norse funeral beliefs and cemeteries.

64 Erskine, William H. <u>Japanese Customs</u>. Tokyo: Kyo Bun Kwan, 1925.
   Description of traditional death customs of urban Japanese: chapters 7, 8, 9, and 10.

65 Evelyn, John. <u>Diary</u>. New York: Oxford University Press, 1955.
   Rich source of information on 17th-century funerals.

66 Fearnley, Leonard. "Funeral Procedure in England. " <u>The Director</u> (Milwaukee), Aug. 1950.

67 Fellows, Alfred. <u>Law of Burial and Generally of the Disposal of the Dead</u>. London: Hadden, Best, 1940. 620pp.

68 Fletcher, Ronald. <u>The Akenham Burial Case</u>. New York: British Book Center, 1974. 280pp., illus.

69 Frazer, James G. Belief in Immortality and the Worship of the Dead. New York: Barnes and Noble, 1968 (repr.). 3 vols. Vol. 1: The Belief Among the Aborigines of Australia, the Torres Straits Islands, New Guinea and Melanesia (repr. of 1913 ed.); Vol. 2: The Belief Among the Polynesians (repr. of 1922 ed.); Vol. 3: The Belief Among the Micronesians (repr. of 1924 ed.).

70 _____. Fear of the Dead in Primitive Religion. New York: Biblo, 1933.

Freeman, Albert C. Antiquity of Cremation and Curious Funeral Customs. See entry 1674.

71 Friedlander, Ludwig. Roman Life and Manners Under the Early Empire, 7th ed. Freese, J. H., translator. London: George Routledge & Sons, 1913. 3 vols.
Of special note is "Luxury in Funerals," vol. II, pp. 210-18, Roman funerals for rich were grander and more extravagant than contemporary displays.

72 Frothingham, O. B. The Disposal of Our Dead. New York: D. G. Francis, 1874.

73 Funeral Customs Through the Ages. St. Louis: F. C. Riddle & Bro. Casket Co., 1929.

74 Garstang, John. Burial Customs of Ancient Egypt as Illustrated by Tombs of Middle Kingdom. London: A. Constable, 1907. 250pp.

75 Gasquet, Cardinal Francis. The Black Death. London: George Bell & Sons, 1908.

76 Giesey, Ralph E. Royal Funeral Ceremony in Renaissance France. Geneva: Librairie E. Droz, 1960. 236pp.

77 Glob, P. V. The Bog People: Iron Age Man Preserved, tr. by R. L. S. Bruce-Mitford. Ithaca, NY: Cornell University Press, 1969. Illus.
Director General of Museums and Antiquities in Denmark gives the whole story of the bog people. Two finds inspired the book, the so-called Tollund Man, dead 2000 years, and the Nebelgard man, dead since about 310 A.D.

78 Good, Edward R. "Foreign Ownership of Canadian Funeral Homes." Canadian Funeral Service 48(10):12+ (1970).
Speech made at the 1970 Ontario Funeral Service Association's annual convention about the increasing foreign investment, ownership, and control over Canadian funeral industry, especially the Americanization of it in Ontario. Legislative proposals call for concerted action to preserve Canadian methods which are more widely accepted with Canadian public than American methods are accepted in the U.S.

79 Goody, John R. Death, Property and the Ancestors; A Study of the Mortuary Customs of the LoDagaa of West Africa. Stanford, CA: Stanford University, 1962. 452pp., illus.
Sociological analysis of the mortuary institutions of the Dagari (Dagaba or LoDagaa) of West Africa. Compare Robert Hertz's Death and the Right Hand, entry 94.

79a Gorer, Geoffrey. Death, Grief and Mourning. New York: Doubleday, 1965, 205pp.; 1967 (paper), 205pp.
Anthropologist's research on, among other topics, styles of mourning.

80 "A Grand Wake in the Ireland of Yesterday." American Funeral Director 98(6):10-12 (June 1975).
Description of 1904 Irish wake taken from contemporary papers and receipts--whiskey, porter and "budeens"--pipes, and tobacco for the men, wine and biscuits, lashings of tea, bread and jam for the ladies. "Caoine," or crying women, stood around the death bed wailing for a prescribed time.

80a Graver, Elizabeth. "Amish Bury the Dead as Their Ancestors Did 250 Years Ago." Casket & Sunnyside 103(4):44-47 (1973).
Funeral customs of the Amish, who settled in Pennsylvania in the 1730's, follow strict biblical funeral descriptions. Key characteristic is simplicity: Plain hardwood casket, body clothed by family, two-day viewing in the home, gravesite viewing and committal. Funeral procession is led by a horse-drawn hearse.

81 Graves, Frank P. The Burial Customs of the Ancient Greeks. Brooklyn, NY: Roche and Hawkins, 1891. 87pp.
Scholarly, detailed, single-purposed study of Greek death customs.

82 Greene, Joseph N. Funeral, Its Conduct and Proprieties. New York: Methodist Book Concern, 1905; Cincinnati: Jennings and Graham, 1905. 109pp.

83 Griffin, Ernest A. "The Elijah Muhammad Funeral." American Funeral Director 98(5):24ff [4pp.] (May 1975). Photos.
Head of the Griffin Funeral Home in Chicago describes the funeral of Mr. Muhammad, head of the Nation of Islam. Explicit detail of arrangements, choosing the casket, materials selected, funeral procession, the services, helicopter police escort, cortege, final disposition in the Mount Glenwood Cemetery, disinterment and removal to a vault in Muhammad's Temple Number 2.

84 _____. "Funeral Rites of the Late Elijah Muhammad." The Director XLV(5):89 (May 1975). Illus.
Director of Chicago funeral home tells of the funeral and services for the founder and leader of the Nation of Islam. The lesson he draws from the events, which were unusual by traditional standards, is that the funeral "can be adaptive and as it is, meets the needs of those who mourn."

85 Habenstein, Robert, and Lamers, William M., Jr. Funeral
Customs the World Over. Milwaukee, WI: Bulfin Printers,
1960; rev. ed., 1974 (in paper). 866pp., index, illus.
Richly illustrated and excellent detailed description of
funeral and burial practices of all nations and cultures, primitive,
folk, urban and rural. The total process in each culture is described, the meaning of death, immediate care of the body, funeralization,
mourning, burial, memorialization, and post-funeral rites and
practices. The basic culture of a people is reflected in its funeral
practices according to Habenstein, a sociologist, and Lamers, an
historian-educator. Last chapter draws universal conclusions on
death, care of dead and readjustment of those left behind: funerals
and burial rites satisfy basic needs of all people to see meaning in
death and to lessen its horror. Appendices include brief histories
of state funeral directors' associations and rules and procedures of
specific religious groups and fraternal organizations in the U.S. regarding funeral services.

86 _____. The History of American Funeral Directing, rev. ed.
Milwaukee, WI: Bulfin Printers, 1962. 638pp., index, illus.
(in paper). Available from the NFDA.
Detailed survey. Part I: early mortuary behavior, including the pagan roots of modern practices--those of the ancient
Egyptians, Greeks, Romans and the early Christians, Hebrews, and
Scandinavians. "Their burial customs, death beliefs, religious beliefs affecting various customs such as burial, cremation, etc.,
and health considerations as a motive for cremation. Death and
burial through the Middle Ages and Renaissance, the Christian in-
fluences, the Plagues, cemetery overloads, funeral ostentation among
the English middle classes and social developments and funeral practice. Fees, embalmers, the rise of English undertakers, clergy,
sanitary reform. Part II: the rise of American funeral undertaking;
colonial customs through the late 19th century. Part III: modern
funeral practice, institutional growth, mortuary education, law, the
growth of associations.

87 Haestier, Richard E. Dead Men Tell Tales; A Survey of Exhumations from Earliest Antiquity to the Present Day. London: J. Long, 1934. 288pp.

88 Hall, Alice J. "A Lady from China's Past." National Geographic 145(5):661-81 (May 1974). Illus.
Body of a highly placed Chinese aristocrat reveals details
of funeral rituals observed in China early in the Han Dynasty more
than 2100 years ago. Then people believed immortality hinged on
proper observation of funeral rituals and the preservation of the
mortal body. Buried with body in a series of outer coffins were
silks, lacquer ware, musical instruments, paintings, perishable
goods such as eggs, funeral statuettes representing servants and
musicians--all in concordance with instructions of the Book of Rites,
a collection of funeral customs compiled by Han scholars. See
entry 226.

89 Hare, Burt. "Mummies: Man's Drive for Immortality. " Science Digest 66:17-22 (Dec. 1969).
        Egyptian mummification, method and purpose, factors such as climate aiding preservation.   Natural mummies in other parts of the world: Scythian kings (5th and 6th centuries B. C.) and South American Inca kings.   Inca funeral practices; present techniques of cryonic preservation are the newest development in man's search for immortality.

90 Harris, James E. , and Weeks, Kent R.   X-Raying the Pharaohs. New York: Scribner's, 1972.   Illus.

91 _____ . "X-Raying the Pharaohs. " Natural History p54-63+ (Aug. -Sept. 1972).
        Last section of the article describes the 13 mummification steps Egyptians of the New Kingdom (1570-1080 B. C.) practiced.

92 Hastings, John, ed.   "Death and Disposal of the Dead. " In: Encyclopedia of Religion and Ethics, vol. 4, (New York: Scribner's, 1912), p411-511.
        Detailed review of the practices and rationales of the great religions' funeral practices, ancient and modern.

93 Herodotus, The Persian Wars.   New York, 1942.
        Egyptian funeral practices.

94 Hertz, Robert.   Death and the Right Hand, tr. by Rodney Needham (from orig. 1928 French ed. titled La Prééminence de la main droite).   Detroit: Gale, 1974 (repr. of 1960 ed.).
        Sociological study which focuses on the double burial practices of the Dayak of Borneo.   Compare Goody's Death, Property and the Ancestors, entry 79.

95 Heywood, Frank A.   "The Etiquette of Mourning. " American Funeral Director 96(4):42-43 (1973).
        Reprint of a 1917 article describing dress and behavioral customs of that era.

96 Holbrook, Leslie.   "Mary Thompson Leads Business Into 2nd Century of Service. " Canadian Funeral Director 1(2):24-26 (1973).   Photos.
        A 101-year-old fourth-generation funeral director in Fergus, Ontario, with tales of the good old days, customs, traditions, lower costs, and theme that funeral service is not for men only.

97 Holgersson, Mrs. Gunnar.   Funerals and Customs in Sweden. Stockholm: Holgersson's Press Service, n. d.
        Text accompanying 13 pictures of Swedish funerary behavior.

98 Holman, James M.   "Burial Customs. " Casket and Sunnyside 100(4):24-25 (1970).

Detailed discussion of old customs, those based on good sense and those on superstition (stopping the clock, mourning bands, funeral coffins, gravestones, hearses, etc.).

99 _____. "The Undertaker's Lot in America Was Far from Pleasant in the Year 1871." Casket & Sunnyside 101(13[centennial issue]):14-15 (1972).
Obstacles for the undertaker in the 1870's: working under the watchful eyes of the family (preparation and services generally were conducted in private homes); ice cooling techniques which often caused the body to explode during the funeral; controversies over flowers. Lasting changes in the past century include a trend away from caustic epitaphs to sentimental and moving "the American funeral from the realm of morbidity to a thing of beauty."

100 Hostetler, John A. Mennonite Life. Scottdale, PA: Herald Press, 1959.
Mennonite funeral customs.

101 "How the Funeral Director Relates to the Coronor, the Pathologist, the Physician, and the Registrar." Canadian Funeral Service 50(5):26-27; 50(6):5-7 (1972).
Ontario Post Graduate Course, Toronto, April 1972 panel discussion report. Panel members included the chief coronor for Ontario, a field inspector from the Registrar General's Office, a Pathologists Association of Ontario representative, and a representative from the Ontario College of Physicians and Surgeons. Discussion; suggestions on how to alleviate problems in areas of mutual concern: death certificates, warrants to bury, autopsy, disposal of remains after autopsy, delays in releasing bodies to directors.

"How the Vikings Buried Their Dead." See entry 1312.

102 Hsu, Francis L. K. Under the Ancestor's Shadow. New York: Columbia University Press, 1948.

103 Hughes, Barry Conn. "Folks on Grand Manan Island Like Their Friendly Funeral Director." Canadian Funeral Service 50(2):15-17 (1972).
The story of Canada's oldest funeral director, Johnny Graham. Heart-warming and nostalgic and good reading for veteran directors and others as well.

104 Jackson, Edgar N. The Christian Funeral: Its Meaning, Its Purpose, and Its Practice. New York: Channel Press, 1966. 184pp. See Jackson's The Significance of the Christian Funeral, entry 105.

105 _____. The Significance of the Christian Funeral. Complete reproduction of Part 1 of The Christian Funeral--Its Meaning, Its Purpose and Its Practice (entry 104). Available from the NFDA, 36pp. (in paper).
For early Christians, death customs which prepared the

corpse for entombment were as much for the living as for the dead. Church's greater concern was that grief would not overwhelm the faith of the bereaved. Dichotomous views on death administrations in modern society--secular intrusion into religious values; the criterion of good and bad based on monetary considerations; the funeral director's dilemma (vested financial interests versus the need to serve the community); faith in technology and science's ability to solve all problems obscures man's idea of himself as mortal (as a result he denies death and holds those he associates with it--funeral directors--in contempt). Christian funerals should dignify and give meaning to life, meet social, psychological and spiritual needs of mourners, help them to admit their mortality, the reality of the deceased's death; provide them an outlet for grief, an opportunity to feel support from friends, relatives, and the community; and an affirmation of faith.

106   James, E. O.   Prehistoric Religion.   London: Thames & Hudson, 1957.
        Ways that prehistoric man's religion and his attitude towards death are manifest in his funeral customs.

107   Jenkins, Ray.   "An Old-Time Funeral."   New York Times cxxi (41,706):23 (April 1, 1972).
        Rural Georgia funeral.

108   Jenness, Diamond.   The Life of the Copper Eskimos, Report of the Canadian Arctic Expedition, 1913-18.   Vol. 12.   Ottawa: F. A. Acland, 1922.
        Funeral customs, burial methods, etc., included.

109   Jentsch, Dr. Theodore W.   "The End of a Pilgrimage: Death and Burial Among the Old Order Mennonites."   American Funeral Director 98(4):36-38 (April 1975).   Illus.
        Sociology professor at Kutztown State College describes the burial customs of the Mennonites, descendants of the Anabaptists founded in 1525 in Zurich, Switzerland.   The first Mennonite colonists settled in Germantown, in 1683.   Body preparation, simple coffin, services, funeral procession, graveside services, burial, and post-burial customs detailed.

110   Johnson, Edward C.   "Funeral Customs in Europe."   A report prepared for the National Funeral Directors Association, 1959.

111   Johnston, Harold W.   The Private Life of the Romans.   Chicago: Scott, Foresmen, 1932.
        Chapter 14, especially, gives good description of the Roman view of death and the importance of burial.   Early Romans held the animistic view, believing that at death, man's soul separated from the body and hovered around the place of burial.   It required constant attention from its descendants, food and drink for its peace and happiness.   If neglected it would become unhappy and might bring harm to the living.

Kaganoff, Benzion C. "From Machpelah ... to Beth She'arim." American Cemetery 46(9):32-33 (1973). See entry 1317.

112 Kane, John J. "The Irish Wake: A Sociological Appraisal." Sociological Symposium I:10-16 (1968). Biblio.
Analysis of the Irish wake abroad and among immigrant Irish in the U.S. Functions, descriptions, extensive bibliography, the "American Wake" for young Irish emigrants to the U.S. during the 19th and early 20th centuries.

113 Kelemen, Pál. "Mexican Colonial Catafalque." Américas 20 (4):26-33 (April 1968). Illus.
History of the catafalque in general and its importation into the New World. Detailed analysis of the Toluca (Mexico) catafalque, the only surviving Spanish colonial catafalque.

Kerin, Charles A. Privation of Christian Burial; An Historical Synopsis and Commentary. See entry 1320.

114 King, S. G. Douglas. "Austins of Stevenage." American Funeral Director 94(8):30+ (1971).
Report of a funeral service firm near a small English town.

115 Kler, Joseph. "Sickness, Death, and Burial Among the Mongols of the Ordon Desert." In: Catholic Anthropological Conference, Primitive Man, 1936.

116 Kurtz, Donna C., and Boardman, John. Greek Burial Customs. Ithaca, NY: Cornell University Press, 1971. 384pp., maps, index, notes, gazetteer, photos, drawings, diagrs.
Thorough, well-illustrated analysis of Greek burial in Athens, Attica, Crete, Rhodes, Ionia, Aeolis, and the rest of the Greek world, from the Bronze Age through the Hellenistic period. Discussion of cemeteries, cremation, tombs, offerings, gravestones, sculptures, iconography, funeral rites, ephemera, cenotaphs, chamber tombs, communal graves.

117 Lamm, Maurice. Jewish Way in Death and Mourning, rev. ed. Middle Village, NY: Jonathan David, 1971. (Also in paper.)

118 Landauer, Bella C. "Some American Funeral Ephemera." New York Historical Society Quarterly 36:222-23 (April 1953).

119 Lane, Bernard J. "Funeral Customs in Europe." A talk delivered at the National Selected Morticians' 36th Annual Meeting, Oct. 27, 1953. pp. 41-42.

120 Langan, M. C. "Alaskan Mortuary Makes First Call at 60 Degrees Below Zero." Casket & Sunnyside 103(4):10-12+ (1973).

The Chimes funeral home in Fairbanks, Alaska, is the northernmost mortuary on the Continent. About 40% of their cases are transported to other parts of the U.S. and abroad, mostly by air transit. Eskimos and Indians, however, bury their own. Corpses are stored in mausoleums over the winter until they can be buried after the spring thaw.

121 Leane, Jack. "Funeral Fashions of Old New England." Northeast Funeral Director 22(4):4 (1973).
    Almost forgotten customs such as the exchange of mourn-
ing rings; draping black cloth over pictures, mirrors; black crepe
wreath over the door; burying suicides in a common highway grave
and piling stones above the grave; prohibition of exchange of gifts of
wine, rum, scarves or gloves at a funeral by a 1741 High Court of
Massachusetts order.

122 Lee, John M. "London Garbage Strike Spreads to Other Services." New York Times cxix (40, 800):3 (Oct. 8, 1969).
    London gravediggers' strike.

123 Lee, Reuel P. Burial Customs, Ancient and Modern. Minneapolis: Arya Co., 1929, 74pp., photos, index; Ann Arbor,
MI: Finch Press, 1974 (repr. of 1929 ed.).
    Good summary history of the origin of burial for mortuary
science students from pre-historical burial. The deceased's posses-
sions buried along with the corpse to insure its eternal happiness.
The development of scientific care and preparation of the dead and
modern funeral director education.

124 "Lenin Embalming Process Still Russia's Big Secret." Northeast Funeral Director 21(4):15 (1972).
    Author suggests that the remains displayed in the Lenin
mausoleum in Red Square is a fine wax reproduction.

125 Lewis, Oscar. Death in the Sanchez Family. New York:
Random, 1969.

126 Lockyer, Herbert. The Funeral Sourcebook. Grand Rapids,
MI: Zondervan, 1967. 187pp.

127 Long, C. R. "Wooden Chest from the Third Shaft Grave."
American Journal of Archeology 78:75-78 (Jan. 1974). Illus.

128 Lucas, A. Preservative Materials Used by the Ancient Egyptians in Embalming. Cairo: National Printing Dept., 1911.
59pp.

McCall, Walter M. P. "The Funeral Car Industry in Canada."
See entry 885.

_____. "The Funeral Coach Industry in Canada." See
entry 886.

129 McCormick, John C. "A Soldier's Funeral in Izmir." American Funeral Director 98(4):27ff [3pp.] (April 1975). Photo.
U. S. Air Force Staff Sergeant, stationed in Turkey, gives detailed account of the preparation and burial by Turkish officers and soldiers of one of their own men--preparation, funeral procession, coffin (ordinarily rented at low cost).

130 McCracken, Harold. George Catlin and the Old Frontier. New York: Bonanza Books, 1959. 216pp., illus., index.
Description of the strange mortuary customs of the Indian tribe, the Mandans. After death, the body is "oiled, painted, feasted, and supplied with weapons, pipe and tobacco, provisions, and his personal 'medicine'." The corpse is sewed into a buffalo hide and placed in a scaffold outside the village in an area called The Village of the Dead. After the scaffold rots and the body falls to the ground, relatives bury all bones but the skull which is set with others in a circle on the ground where relatives daily converse with it.

131 McHargue, Georgess. Mummies. Philadelphia: Lippincott, 1972. Illus. (also in paper).
For children in grades five to nine.

132 McKern, Saron. "Radiography: New Tool for Retrieving the Wealth of the Pharaohs." Science Digest 68(1):8-13 (July 1970). Photos.
X-rays are now being used for mummy research in order to leave the body undisturbed.

133 Madden, Richard R. Shrines and Sepulchres of the Old and New World ... Including Notices of the Funeral Customs of the Principal Nations, Ancient and Modern. London: T. Newby, 1851, 2 vols.; Ann Arbor, MI: Finch, 1974 (repr. of 1851 ed. in one vol.).

134 Mann, Joseph. Joseph in Egypt. New York, 1940.
Excellent material on eschatological beliefs of the early Jews, Christians, and significant pagan groups. Evolution of coffins in Jewish and Christian cultures.

135 Manning, John. "Soviet Funeral Service." American Funeral Director 89(1):29, 1966.

136 Mason, Frank H. "Burial System of the French." The Embalmers Monthly 21:59 (March 1908).

137 Masse, Henri. Persian Beliefs and Customs. New Haven, CT: Human Relations Area Files, 1954 (orig. pub. in 1925).
Mortuary customs of the Persians with emphasis on rural and village beliefs and folkways.

138 Mathias, E. "Italian-American Funeral: Persistence Through Change." Western Folklore 33:35-50 (Jan. 1974).

139 Mead, Charles W. Peruvian Mummies and What They Teach. New York: American Museum of Natural History, 1907. 24pp.

140 Mendelsohn, Simon. "The Mortuary Craft of Ancient Egypt." Ciba Symposia 6(2):1795-1804 (Mary 1944).
     Technical treatment of the mummification process from vantage of recent information on chemicals used.

141 Meyer, Pamela, and Meyer, Alfred. "Life and Death in Tana Toradja." National Geographic Magazine 141:792-815 (1972). Illus.
     Lively, color-photo article on the funeral customs of Tana Toradja on the island of Sulawesi in Indonesia. Focus is on the death of two noblemen. Mourning may last for months or even years. The body remains in his own home during the entire period. Wives maintain a constant vigil, provide food. After the death is made officially public, members of the community come with food and payments for past debts, feasting, dancing, sports and water buffalo fights. After specified time, months or years again, the mummified body is removed from the home, placed in a coffin, and buried in a limestone cliff.

142 "Military Funerals in the Continental Army." American Funeral Director 98(6):24 (June 1975).
     Taken from Col. John W. Wright's article in the William and Mary College Quarterly. Slain soldiers were buried where they fell, the most honorable spot. Those who died in camp were buried in front of camp on the color line. Detailed description of the more elaborate services for Lt. Col. Bernard Elliot for whom full burial honors were bestowed Oct. 26, 1778.

143 Modi, Jivanji J. The Religious Ceremonies and Customs of the Parsees. Bombay: J. B. Karanis, 1937. 455pp.

144 Molner, Enrico C. S. Rev. Th. D. [Article in] The Episcopal Review, July 1962.
     Detailed exposition of funerals and the Episcopal Church.

145 Moodie, Roy Lee. Roentgenologic Studies of Egyptian and Peruvian Mummies. Chicago: Field Museum, 1931. 66pp.

146 Moore, Joan. "The Death Culture of Mexico and Mexican Americans." Omega 1(4):271-91 (1970).
     Funeral practices of a Mexican-American family, traditional and with variations. Home culture of Mexico denies the characteristic American denial and resentment of death and its corollary emphasis on mastering the environment, achievement, and power.

147 Mori, Koji. "The Increased Cost of Dying in Japan." American Funeral Director 87(9):35-36 (1964).

148 Morley, John. Death, Heaven and the Victorians. Pittsburgh: University of Pittsburgh Press, 1972; London: Studio Vista, 1971; 208pp., index, biblio., photos, notes, appendices, drawings, charts.

Thorough analysis of the unmatched complexity of Victorian English funeral rites; description of the mortality, gentility, and romanticism which were the underpinnings of the age; funeral rites, cemeteries, sepulture, and commemoration; mourning dress and etiquette; detailed description of the Duke of Wellington's funeral; the means of disposal; preoccupation with angels and spirits; 134 plates help illustrate this excellent analysis.

149 "Moslems Disapprove of Public Grief." American Funeral Director 93(12):22 (1970).

Dr. Muhammed A. Rauf, Moslem theology authority, says public grief displayed at Abdel Gamal Nasser's death was against accepted Moslem death practice. Gives Koran prescripts for proper procedures for caring for the dead.

150 Mossman, B. C., and Stark, M. W. The Last Salute: Civil and Military Funerals 1921-1969. Washington, DC: Department of the Army, 1971. 428pp., diagrs., photos, tables, appendices, biblio. Available from the U.S. Gov. Printing Office.

Twenty-nine state and military funerals from that of the World War I unknown soldier and Pershing to Secretary of State Dulles, Robert Kennedy, and President Eisenhower. Narrative description is accompanied by photos, diagrams, aerial plans for procession, gravesites, etc. Appendices include a table of entitlement (types of funerals and who is eligible; policies on strengths and composition of military escorts; summaries of state funerals, official funerals, special military funerals, combined services full honor funerals, special full honor funeral for Gen. Walter Bedell Smith and R. Adm. Richard Byrd, and funerals without classification.

151 "Most Charges Abolished for Funerals in Milan." New York Times cxviii (40,429):2 (Oct. 2, 1968).

The city of Milan will pay all funeral expenses.

152 "Mourning Plumes Once Signified Royalty." American Funeral Director 98(3):26ff [2pp.] (March 1975).

Sketch of the use of black and white plumes from ancient times through the 19th century. The early Hebrews and Egyptians and later the Roman emperors and Normans used plumes to depict rank as well as a symbol of death. Royalty of the Middle Ages could use plumes on biers; those beneath noble rank could not. Upper classes in the 18th century sent black plumes to the bereaved as 20th-century sympathizers send flowers.

153 Muret, Pierre. Rites of Funerals, Ancient and Modern, In Use Through the Known World, tr. by P. Lorrain. London: R. Royston, 1683. 126pp.

154 National Funeral Directors Assoc. The Funeral from Ancient
     Egypt to Present Day America. Milwaukee, WI: NFDA,
     n. d. Illus. (pamphlet).
        An illustrated historical documentary.

155 Negev, Avraham. Ancient Burial Customs (Digging Up the
     Past: An Introduction to Archaeology). Minneapolis: Lerner
     Publications, 1973.
        For children, fifth grade and up.

156 "Nelson of Trafalgar. " American Funeral Director 96(2):35-36
     (1973).
        For the historian: British hero's funeral ceremonies and
burial in casket made from the mainmast of the French flagship
L'Orient.

157 Nieuw, Angel D. "Funeral Service in Curaçao. " American
     Funeral Director 94(4), 1971.
        Changes in funeral practice and methods in Curaçao.

158 Nilsson, Martin P. Greek Popular Religion. New York: Co-
     lumbia University Press, 1940.

159 _____. A History of Greek Religion, tr. by F. J. Fielden.
     Oxford, England: Clarendon Press, 1925. 310pp.
        Widely recommended writings on ancient Greek burial
customs.

     Nock, Arthur D. "Cremation and Burial in the Roman Empire."
        See entry 1701.

160 Nohl, Johannes. The Black Death, tr. by C. H. Clarke. New
     York, 1960.

161 Oglesby, William B. "The Resurrection and the Funeral. "
     Pastoral Psychology, Nov. 1957, p. 11-16.

162 O'Neil, Kate. "Room at the Top. " Canadian Funeral Director
     3(7):22-23 (July-Aug. 1975).
        Funeral directors should smile, say "Hi!, " drink in public,
become a member of the community and shuck the old image: tall,
clammy fingered, carrying an umbrella.

163 "Onyame Will Give Them a Better Place in Heaven. " American
     Funeral Director 95(2):34+ (1972).
        A Ghanaian casket maker furnishes caskets which commem-
orate the occupation of the deceased. For a taxi driver he made a
casket in the form of a Mercedes Benz.

164 Oppenheim, Roger S. Maori Death Customs. Wellington, New
     Zealand: Reed, 1973. 130pp. , illus.

165 O'Reilly, John A. Ecclesiastical Sepulture in the New Code of

Canon Law. Washington, DC: Catholic University Press, 1923.

166 O'Sulleabhain, Sean. Irish Wake Amusements. Washington, DC: McGrath. c. 1974. $4.95

167 Osuna, Patricia, and Reynolds, David K. "A Funeral in Mexico: Description and Analysis." Omega 1(4):249-69 (1970).
    The respectful treatment of the body in small town Mexican funerals is thought to be symbolic of respect for that person. The three main elements of the post-death period are the relations between survivors and the deceased; the relations among the survivors; and the psycho-philosophical orientation of the survivors. Events and feelings described and evaluated.

168 Pace, Eric. "French Undertakers at Odds on Sharing of Business." New York Times cxix (41,043):12 (June 8, 1970).
    Conflict between small and big funeral businesses.

169 Pace, Mildred M. Wrapped for Eternity: The Story of the Egyptian Mummies. New York: McGraw-Hill, 1974. Illus.
    For children, fifth grade and up.

170 Paton, Lewis B. Spiritism and the Cult of the Dead in Antiquity. New York: Macmillan, 1921, 325pp., bibliographical footnotes; New York: Philosophical Library, 1953.
    Detailed, comprehensive account of death beliefs of pagans, Hebrew burial customs, etc.

171 Peterson, Frederick. Ancient Mexico. London, 1959.
    Mexican funeral customs included.

172 Pettigrew, Thomas J. History of Egyptian Mummies, and an Account of the Worship and Embalming of the Sacred Animals by the Egyptians; With Remarks on the Funeral Ceremonies of Different Nations and Observations on the Mummies of the Canary Islands, of the Ancient Peruvians, Burman Priests, etc. London: Longmans, Rees, Orme, Brown, Green, and Longman, 1834. 264pp.

173 Phillimore, Robert J. Ecclesiastical Law of the Church of England. London: Sweet and Maxwell, 1895.

174 Plank, John. "Funeral Services in Old Madrid." American Funeral Director, June 1959.

175 _____. "Modern Funeral Service in European Countries." American Funeral Director, Feb. 1959.

176 _____. "West Berlin Funeral Firm Operates Fifteen Branches." American Funeral Director, Dec. 1959, p. 39-40.

177 Power, Eileen. Medieval People. New York, 1924.

Varying attitudes towards funerals during the Middle Ages.

178 Prideaux, Tom. "Magic Passage to Eternity." Life 64(23):
       66-79 (June 7, 1968). Photos (by Brian Blake).
       Illustrated commentary on Egyptian funeral practices and
entombment.

179 "Probing the New Kingdom Pharaohs with X-Rays." Science
       News 100:245 (Oct. 9, 1971).
       Walter M. Whitehouse, chairman of the department of
radiology at the University of Michigan, and team conduct the first
radiographic studies of Egyptian pharaohs and queens' mummies
dating from 1600 B.C. to 1000 B.C. Preliminary findings reported.

180 "A Professional Approach to Funeral Service Advertising."
       Canadian Funeral Director 1(5):12-13 (1973).
       The Public Relations and Public Information Committee of
the Ontario Funeral Service Association suggest new advertising
program that would be well planned, discrete, showing advantages
of prearrangement, services, the director's qualifications, etc. The
purpose is to replace the present ads which generally are contra-
dictory, cynical, pompous, expedient and in many other ways un-
savory and counter-productive.

181 Puckle, Bertram S. Funeral Customs: Their Origin and De-
       velopment. London: T. Warner Laurie, 1926; Detroit:
       Singing Tree Press, 1968. 283pp., illus., index, biblio.,
       footnotes.
       Classic, comprehensive, entertaining, but since surpassed
(see Habenstein and Lamers, entry 85) study of the "practices
which surround the physical fact of death." Various customs of
burial preparation, coffins, wakes, mutes, wailers, sin-eating,
totemism, and death taxes; feasts and funeral processions; early
burial places and the origins of tombs and the cemetery, and early
Christian catacombs; churchyards, cemeteries, orientation and other
burial customs including Parsees's dokhmas, the Central Asian no-
mads' practice of delivering the bodies of the dead to wild animals;
body-snatching; flowers; the Black Death (14th century) and the Great
Plague (17th century); state and public funerals, cremation, embalming, memorials, epitaphs, rings and mourning cards.

182 R., H. B. The Burial Question; What Is to Be Done?" Lon-
       don: W. Poole, 1877.

183 Rasmussen, Knud. Intellectual Culture of the Eskimos. Re-
       port of the Fifth Thule Expedition, 1921-24, Vol. 9. Copen-
       hagen, 1932.

184 Raymond, W. B. "An Experience in Mexico." Embalmers'
       Monthly, April 1900.

185 "RCMP Warns: Your Funeral Home Files Could Be Aiding a
       Criminal." Canadian Funeral Director 3(7):5-7 (July-Aug.
       1975).

Article based on a presentation made to the Western Canada Funeral Directors Association Convention by representatives from
the Royal Canadian Mounted Police. Their purpose is to make the
funeral profession aware of criminals' use of their files and urge
their discretion in giving out information.

186   Rech, Edward H.   "Glimpses Into Funeral History. " Unpublished
      ms. , prepared under the auspices of the Hess & Eisenhardt
      Co. , of Cincinnati, n. d.

187   "Red China Forbids Traditional Funerals. " American Funeral
      Director 93(10):42+ (1970).
         Elimination of traditional customs in the interest of creat-
ing an atmosphere of "virtue of modesty, " where people will be as
simple, modest and frugal at death as they are through life. Practices are regulated by decree of the Peoples Government of China.
The effects of current funeral practice and enumeration of specific
provisions.

188   Redfield, Robert, and Villa, Alfonso. Chan Kom; A Maya
      Village. Washington, DC: Carnegie Institution of Washing-
      ton, 1934.
         Ethnological study; description of a Chan Kom funeral,
p. 198-204.

189   Report on the Recognition of Certain Rights Concerning the
      Human Body. Quebec Civil Code Revision Office, 1971.

190   Rice, Charles S. , and Steinmetz, Roland C. The Amish Year.
      New Brunswick, NJ: Rutgers University Press, 1956.

191   Ritter, Bess. "Happy Birthday to Us. " Casket & Sunnyside
      101(13[centennial issue]):2 (1972).
         Profile of Casket & Sunnyside's history, which the author
(editor of C & S), describes as the history of funeral service.
The Undertaker was first published in 1871 and shortly afterward
renamed The Sunnyside. The Casket was independently published
in 1876; in 1925 the two merged. Highlights of funeral service developments in the last 100 years--use of burial vaults, shipment by
air transport, perfection of embalming chemicals, rise of funeral
director associations, higher education for directors, abolishment
of poisonous embalming chemicals, reciprocity of embalmers' licenses between states, automobile funerals.

192   Roscoe, Rev. John. The Baganda: An Account of Their Native
      Customs and Beliefs. London: Macmillan, 1911.
         Chapter 4 on funeral customs.

193   Rush, Alfred C. Death and Burial in Christian Antiquity.
      Washington, DC: Catholic University of America Press,
      1941, 282pp. , biblio. , photos, footnotes; New York: Gordon
      Press, 1974 (repr. of 1941 ed.).

Thorough review of early Christian funeral customs, pagan practices which were adopted by the early Christians, and those Hebrew religious practices and ethics which support the Catholic Church's anti-cremation position. Part 1: the concept of death as a long sleep, a summoning by Christ, a voyage to God; Part 2: the rites of death and burial; the laying out and body preparation; the wake; procession; and burial.

194 Russell, Francis. "The Mummy of Red Square." National Review 23:865-66 (Aug. 10, 1971).
    Lenin's death in 1924; preparation of his body; periodic removal of his body from its Red Square tomb; facial features are said to have been largely restored in wax.

195 Sable, Myra. The Positive Role of Grief. Reprinted from the March 1972 issue of Chatelaine Magazine; available from the Memorial Society Association of Canada. (pamphlet)
    Modern funeral practices are greatly to blame for Canadians' fear of facing the reality of death. The worst detriment to recovering from grief is suppressing it, yet Dr. S. J. J. Freeman, chief of service-community psychiatric service at Toronto's Clarke Institute of Psychiatry, points out that funeral directors go to great lengths "to pretend that a death hasn't occurred--by using such expressions as 'loved one,' never corpse or body." By suppressing the natural grief function normal response and recovery is greatly hindered.

196 Sackett, J. B. Ritual of Masonic Service for the Burial of the Dead, and Lodge of Sorrow. Chicago: E. B. Myers, 1870. 120pp.

197 Sarkar, S. S. Ancient Races of Baluchistan, Panjub and Sind. Mystic, CT: Verry, 1964.

198 Scales, William. "The British Funeral Service." Mid-Continent Mortician, March 1960.

199 Schobinger, Juan. "Archaeological Field Studies in the Western Mountain Area of Argentina." Science Invest. 27(10):413-22, 1971.
    Mummified human remains have been discovered in two areas of caves in the western Andean and sub-Andean provinces of Argentina.

200 "Secular Funerals in Britain." American Funeral Director 93(3):28-30 (1970).
    Secular funerals increasing in Great Britain as religious emphasis dies. National Secular Society, established 104 years ago in London, issues guide for arranging non-religious funerals. Includes instructions for consumers to be made apart from the will, when to notify funeral director, services provided by the society, etc.

201 Selbert, Bruce. "Ceremony of the Indian Goodbye. " Mortuary
       Management 60(5):16-18 (1973).
           Elaborate American Indian burial customs, still practiced.
Deceased are returned to their reservations for preparation and buri -
al.   Funeral director's function, preparation and transporting of the
remains.

202 Serner, Arvid. On "Dyss" Burial and Beliefs About the Dead
       During the Stone Age; With Special Regard to South Scandi-
       navia; An Archaeological and Historico-Religious Research.
       Lund, Sweden: Gleerup, 1938.   252pp.

203 Sewall, Samuel. Diary. Boston: Massachusetts Historical
       Society, 1878-82.
           Sections on burial and funeral customs.

204 Sheldon, Roderick D.   Bible Light on Modern Funeral Service
       Customs.   27pp. Available from the NFDA. (pamphlet)
           Reprinted material prepared by minister, author, and
former newspaper publisher.   Passages, followed by explanations,
from the Old and New Testaments as evidence that the Christian
burial service is "a sacred privilege, a solemn memorial, and a
loving expression of an assured expectation. " Expectation of resurrection and a life after death, the author believes, is the basis for
all modern burial customs.

205 Sibun, E. Lloyd. "Funeral Service and Customs in New Zea-
       land. " Reprint of address given at the 38th Annual Meeting
       of the [U. S.] National Selected Morticians, Sept. 27, 1955,
           Mr. Sibun is a funeral director in Auckland, New Zea-
land.

       Silber, Mendel.   Ancient and Modern Modes of Burial.   See
       entry 1370.

206 Simons, George E.   Masonic Funeral Service.   New York:
       Macoy Publishing and Masonic Supply Co. , 1926.

207 Smith, Beverly, Jr. "Farewell Great Lover. " Saturday Even-
       ing Post 235(3):66-69 (Jan. 20, 1962).   Photos.
           Humorous account of Rudolph Valentino's funeral.

208 Smith, Elmer.   The Amish People.   Jericho, NY: Exposition
       Press, 1958.
           Section on funeral customs.

209 Smith, Grafton E.   A Contribution to the Study of Mummifica-
       tion in Egypt, With Special Reference to the Measures Adopted
       During the Time of the XXI Dynasty for Moulding the Form
       of the Body.   Cairo, 1905.   53pp.

210 _____ .   Egyptian Mummies.   London: Allen & Unwin, 1924.
       189pp.

211 _____. The Royal Mummies. Cairo: Institut Français
d'Archéologie Orientale, 1912. 118pp.

212 Sperka, Joshua S. External Life: A Digest of All Jewish
Laws of Mourning; Complete Funeral, Burial, and Unveiling
Services; Kaddish, Yizkor and El Mohle in Hebrew, trans-
lation and transliteration, With a 25 Year Schedule of the
Yahrseit and a 25 Year Caldendar for Yizkor Dates, 2d ed.
New York: Bloch, 1961. 220pp.

Spriggs, A. O. "Embalming and Funerals in Italy." See
entry 559.

213 Steegmuller, Francis. "Burial in Venice." The New Yorker
47(11):99-103 (May 1, 1971).
Igor Stravinsky's funeral, April 15, 1971.

214 Stora, Nils. Burial Customs of the Skott Lapps, tr. by Christopher Grapes. Helsinki: Suomalainen Tiedeakatemia, 1971.
323pp., illus. (in paper).

Stuart, George E. "Who Were the 'Mound Builders'?" See
entry 1381.

215 Summers, Morlais J. "The Influence of American Funeral
Service in the United Kingdom." An Address to the National
Selected Morticians, Sept. 28, 1954.

216 "Sunday Funerals." The Undertaker 1(1):1 (Oct. 1871). Reprinted in Casket & Sunnyside 101(13[centennial issue]):3
(1972).
    The great undertaking debate: whether or not to bury on
Sunday. Grounds for objections included Sunday was "a day set
apart for the worship of God"; permitting burials might lead to other
evils; people would have their "sensibilities blunted, their respect
diminished, and finally, perhaps, commit acts of desecration...."

217 Swift Arrow, B. "Funeral Rites of the Quechan Tribe." Indian Historian 7:22-24 (spring 1974).

218 Taylor, Alma O. "The Funeral Rites of Japan." The Embalmers' Monthly, March 1903.

219 Tegg, William, ed. Last Act, Being the Funeral Rites of
Nations and Individuals.... London: W. Tegg, 1876, 404pp.;
Detroit: Gale, 1973 (repr. of 1876 ed.). 404pp., illus.

220 Tertullian. The Writings of Tertullian, ed. by Alexander
Roberts and James Donaldson. Edinburgh: T & T Clark,
1870.
    See Vol. XV, cap. vi (De Resurrectione) and cap. ix
(De Anima): Christian church in the early period favored burial.

221 Tibbits, James F. "Looking Back Over My Past Life." American Funeral Director 98(8):16-20 (Aug. 1975). Photo.
    Reprint from the Aug. 1909 issue of The Western Undertaker. Author's reminiscences of helping his father as a child, his first case on his own, and anecdotes of his long career as a mortician. Coffins were made to order (to fit the height and width across the shoulders); were "little more than a bare box"; when lined, which was very rare, it was with unbleached muslin. "The ladies at the house [were] in charge of the body."

222 Toors, Frances. A Treasury of Mexican Folkways. Mexico, D. F. , 1947.
    Sections included on Mexican funeral, funeral rites and customs.

223 Toynbee, Jocelyn M. C. Death and Burial in the Roman World, Scullard, H. H., ed. Ithaca, NY: Cornell University Press, 1971. Illus. (Aspects of Greek and Roman Life series.)

    "Traffic Woes Vexed Old-Time Funerals." American Funeral Director. See entry 1610.

224 "Tutankhamun's Golden Trove." National Geographic 625 (Oct. 1963).
    Mourners of Pharaoh Tutankhamun (died 1343 B. C.) spent 70 days mummifying his body to insure its preservation during its journey into eternity. What is left now is skin and bones.

225 Twing, Cornelius L. Knight's Templar Burial Services. New York: Macoy Publishing and Masonic Supply Co. , 1923.

226 "The 2, 000-Year-Old Woman." Time 102(12):55-6 (Sept. 17, 1973). Photo.
    Body of Li Tsang, dead 2100 years, analyzed for cause of death. Body is the best preserved ever discovered. Flesh moist, hair firm in scalp, joints flexible; all organs (with exception of the brain which had collapsed), in excellent condition. Body had been stored inside an airtight coffin filled with a mildly acidic fluid containing mercury compounds. The coffin was placed within six other boxes and packed in five tons of charcoal and clay and buried under 60 feet of earth. See entry 88.

227 Van Rensselaer, Mrs. John King. The Goede Vrouw of Mananha-ta. New York: Scribner's, 1898.
    An account of early Dutch funerals in Colonial America.

228 "Vatican Urged to End Ban on Suicides' Burial." New York Times cxx (41, 312):20 (March 4, 1971).

229 "The Victorian View of Death." American Funeral Director 95(4):32 (1972).

Formal, stereotyped customs of the Victorians; liberal quotes from Morley's book Death, Heaven and the Victorians, (see entry 148).

230 Viski, Károly. Hungarian Peasant Customs. Budapest: Dr. George Vajna & Co., 1932.

231 Voegelin, Erminie. Mortuary Customs of the Shawnee and Other Eastern Tribes. Indiana Historical Society, 1944. 220pp.

232 Vogel, J. O. "On Early Iron Age Funerary Practise in Southern Zamibia." Current Anthropology 13:583-86 (Dec. 1973). Illus.

233 Vulliamy, Colwyn E. Immortal Man; A Study of Funeral Customs, and of Beliefs in Regard to the Nature and Fate of the Soul. London: Methuen, 1926, 215pp., biblio.; Ann Arbor, MI: Finch Press, 1974 (repr. of 1926 ed.).

234 Wagley, Charles. "The Social and Religious Life of a Guatemalan Village." American Anthropologist, Memoirs, vol. 71, part 2, 1949 [monograph].
Description of rural Guatemalan funerals.

235 Wagner, John W. "Undertaking in Mexico." Embalmers' Monthly, Nov. 1900.

236 "Wah Wing Sang Chapel Serves Fabled Chinatown." American Funeral Director 91(11):54-57 (1969).
Interview with New York's leading Chinese funeral director; comparison of Chinese funeral customs with those practiced by descendants in the Western world; detailed description of several customs: providing food and wine for corpse's journey into eternity, funeral procession, memorialization, cemetery rites.

237 Walker, Murray. "Interpersonal Relationships in the Ontario Funeral Industry." Canadian Funeral Service 50(10):25-29 (1972); 51(1):22-24 (1973).
Passivity and hostility are often to blame for unpleasant relations between staff members. The cause is often a lack of advancement opportunity; the solution is providing greater employee motivation by improving salary increment structure, allowing employees the opportunity to increase their technical skills and gain the experience that will enable them to take on greater responsibilities.

238 Wallis, Wilson D. "The Canadian Dakota." New York: American Museum of Natural History, 1947. (Anthropological Papers, vol. 41, part I, p. 1-225.)

239 Warner, W. Lloyd. The Living and the Dead. New Haven, CT: Yale University Press, 1959.

240 Watt, Jill. Canadian Guide to Death and Dying. Vancouver: International Self-Counsel Press, n. d.
     Recommended by the Memorial Society Association of Canada.

     Webb, Charles. "Bermuda Funeral Home. " See entry 1394.

241 Webber, Jay. "Burial Nicaraguan Style. " Casket & Sunnyside 101(8):22-23 (1971).
     History of how Nicaraguans cared for their dead from the Spanish conquest until today. Shipment of bodies from Central America to Spain; steps of body care from the moment of death to burial.

     _____. "Honduran Memorial Park Upsets Traditionalists. " See entry 1395.

242 _____. "In Time of Need. " Mortuary Management 58(9): 10-11 (1971).
     Sr. José Maria Eva, founder of a fraternal death insurance plan in Nicaragua. He and his wife also operate a mortuary and casket manufacturing plant.

243 _____. "Nicaraguan Funeral Directors Cope with Old Customs. " Casket & Sunnyside 101(4):8-9 (1971).
     Present funeral customs in Nicaragua, casket construction, graveside services, funerals, embalming, cost of doctor's preparation of body, lack of cosmetology and cemeteries.

244 _____. "Time for a Short Bier. " Mortuary Management 59(9):14-15 (1972).
     Sketch of funeral customs in Central South America and stories of José M. Eva, leading mortician of Managua.

245 "What a Well-Dressed Mummy Wears. " Science Digest 69:80-81 (April 1971).
     X-ray studies of Cairo Museum mummies show 20% had jewelry hidden in or on their bodies; arthritis; arteriosclerosis; some had their brains still intact.

246 Wheeler, Edward J. Pulpit and Grave. New York: Funk, 1884.

247 Williams, Judy B. "Week Long Festivals Mark Funerals in Taradjaland. " American Funeral Director 93(8):29-30 (1970).
     Central Celebes mountain dwellers' elaborate and lengthly funeral rites.

248 Willison, George. Saints and Strangers. New York, 1945.
     Sections on early American funeral customs.

249 Willoughby, R. Funeral Formalities and Obligations; What to Do When a Death Occurs. London: Universal Publications, 1936. 90pp. (in paper).

250 Willoughby, William C. Soul of the Bantu: A Sympathetic Study of the Magico-Religious Practices and Beliefs of the Bantu Tribes of Africa. Westport, CT: Negro Universities Press, 1971 (repr. of 1928 ed.).

251 Wilson, Arnold, and Levy, Herman. Burial Reform and Funeral Costs. London: Oxford University, 1938. 248pp., tables, biblio., index, appendices.
        Analysis of funeral problems and necessity of reform. Focus on England, with reference to other countries. Historical review of world funeral development; first British reforms; beginnings of the cremation movement necessitated by scarcity of land; analysis of contemporary practice; burial of the poor in 1938; extravagance and the effects of specific customs; cemetery and funeral director costs; laws, organizations, and legislation; recommendations for reforms; arguments for cremation.

252 Wimberly, Lowry C. Death and Burial Lore in the English and Scottish Popular Ballads. Ann Arbor, MI: Finch Press, 1974 (repr. of 1927 ed.).

253 Winlock, Herbert E. Materials Used at the Embalming of King Tut' Ankhaman. New York: Metropolitan Museum of Art, 1941. 18pp.

254 Wolff, Eldon G. "Funeral and Burial Customs of Modern Germany." The Director, July 1950, p. 4.
        Author is curator of history, Milwaukee Public Museum.

255 "Women No Longer Expected to Attend Funerals." American Funeral Director 10(97):90-91 (Oct. 1974).
        Reprint of New York Sun article of Nov. 14, 1889. New York City undertakers say women should not have to attend funerals; Philadelphia directors advise against taking ladies "to the burial grounds.... It subjects them to a great nervous strain." J. R. Knowles asserts "As a rule every large funeral is the cause of the death of at least one person who attends it."

256 Wood, Frank H. E. "Heaven Can Wait--I Hope." The Christian Century 18(9):269-70 (March 4, 1970).
        Pastor of an English-speaking Protestant Church in Latin America buries the husband of a Romanian woman; description of the large metropolitan mortuary, mourning customs; minister drifts off to the wrong funeral procession so when the casket opens and he realizes his mistake, he hastily tries to relocate the proper procession.

257 Wyman, Leland C., Hill, W. W., and Osanal, Iva. "Navajo Eschatology." University of New Mexico Bulletin 4(1):30-31 (1942).

258 Yarrow, Harry C. "A Further Contribution to the Study of the Mortuary Customs of the American Indians." Annual

Report of the Bureau of American Ethnology, 1:87-203 (1879-1880).

259 _____. Introduction to the Study of Mortuary Customs Among the North American Indians. Washington, DC: U.S. Gov. Printing Office, 1880, 114pp.; Ann Arbor, MI: Finch, 1974 (repr. of 1880 ed.).

260 Zimmerman, M. R. "Blood Cells Preserved in a Mummy 2,000 Years Old." Science 180(4083):303-304 (April 20, 1973). Illus., biblio., refs.
    Positive identification and verification of preserved red blood cells found in mummies.

261 Zlotnick, Dov, tr. Tractate Mourning: Regulations Relating to Death, Burial, and Mourning. New Haven, CT: Yale University Press, 1966. (Judaica series, 17.)

B. CONTEMPORARY AMERICAN FUNERAL SERVICE

1. THE FUNERAL DIRECTOR

262 "Alden Whitman--Master of a Neglected Art. " American Fu-
     neral Director 94(5):29-31 (1971).
        New York Times enlivens obit column on the basis of sur-
     vey results. Survey showed many readers turn to the obit section
     before reading the rest of the news. Feature writer Alden Whitman
     interviews famous people and writes their obituaries to be published
     after their deaths.

263 Allen, R. Earl. Funeral Source Book. Grand Rapids, MI:
     Baker Books, 1974. (Paper.) (Preaching Helps series.)

264 Allen, Steve. The Wake. New York: Doubleday, 1972.

265 "Allowance for Funerals of Servicemen Raised. " New York
     Times cxvii (40, 180):34 (Jan. 27, 1968).

266 Bachmann, C. Charles. Ministering to the Grief-Sufferer.
     Englewood Cliffs, NJ: Prentice-Hall, 1964, 144pp. ; Phila-
     delphia: Fortress Press, 1967 (paper); Englewood Cliffs,
     NJ: Prentice-Hall, 1964 (Successful Pastoral Counseling
     series). Unpaged.
        Discusses for priests the meaning of the funeral to the
     survivors and some of the questions and attitudes he will encounter;
     how a pastor and funeral director can cooperate; analysis of the
     friction that currently exists in this area; discussion of current
     parish attitudes and practices concerning how people react, the role
     of the pastor and favored types of funerals, based on questionnaire
     results.

267 Baird, William, and Baird, John E. Funeral Meditations.
     Nashville, TN: Abingdon, 1974.
        Readings for funeral services.

268 Barton, Frederick M. One Thousand Thoughts for Funeral
     Occasions. New York: Harper, 1928. 561pp.
        Large collection of funeral sermons.

269 Bayly, Joseph. The View from a Hearse: A Christian View
     of Death. Elgin, IL: David C. Cook Pub. Co. , 1969.

96pp. (paper).

Chapter 13, "The Funeral Director," and Chapter 14, "Our Death Celebrations," run down the services a funeral director offers, namely, disposing of the human corpse legally and in a manner which makes the memory of it tolerable. Having had three of his sons die, Bayly believes he is uniquely qualified as a funeral director evaluator, and the rating he gives is high. Lists information one must provide director in order for him to do his job--how many expected at the funeral? Do you want the body to be viewed? When? etc. --and services included in the funeral home's basic fee and those which cost extra.

270 Benefits for Railroad Workers and Their Families. Supt. of Doc., U.S. Gov. Printing Office, Washington, DC 20402. Burial benefits for railroad employees and dependents.

271 Benjamin, Michael. "What Is a Funeral Director?" Canadian Funeral Service 47(2):25, 28; 47(3):19-20 (1969).
Young Toronto funeral director states that the complexity of the funeral director's work demands higher education than that now required. Suggests an embalmer be required to have a 12th-grade education and five years' apprenticeship in funeral service to qualify for an embalmer's license. Recommends a six-month correspondence course on specialized topics and a guide to studies leading to the funeral director's license.

272 Bernardin, Joseph B. Burial Services, rev. ed. New York: Morehouse, 1958.
A compilation of funeral services (religious rites), including prayers and hymns.

273 Blackwood, Andrew W. The Funeral: A Source Book for Ministers Grand Rapids, MI: Baker Book House, 1972 (repr. of 1942 ed.). 252pp. (paper).

274 Browning, Everett H., and Raether, Howard C. "Welfare Burial Allowances." The Director 39(2):12-13 (1969).
Results of a survey based on returns from 38 states and Washington, D.C. show that in five states there is no allowance; in one state there is no provision by that state but up to $50 provided by some counties; in 13 states there is a state allowance paid from between $100 and $361; in 19 states counties pay up to $500 and receive some reimbursement from the state; and generally, in those states where county allowances are provided, state supplementation is now allowed.

275 Callaway, Curtis F. Art of Funeral Directing: A Practical Manual on Modern Funeral Directing Methods, Valuable to the Funeral Director, the Assistant, and the Student. Chicago: Undertakers Supply Co., 1928. 240pp., photos. Reprinted in 1944, 688pp.
All aspects of funeral directing; instruction for arranging the funeral itself, as opposed to body preparation, from handling

the first phone call through selling the casket, the different ceremonies, use of flowers, transportation, records, ministers, community problems, sample plans and interior designs for both small
town and large city homes, and a list of paraphernalia. Well illustrated with practical how-to advice. Though dated, much is still
applicable.

276 Chakour, Charles M. Brief Funeral Meditations. Nashville,
    TN: Abingdon, 1971.
        Funeral sermons.

277 "City Welfare Fund to Give Penniless a Private Burial." New
    York Times cxv (39, 647):16 (Aug. 12, 1966).
        New York City to allow $250 for funerals for the poor.

278 Clark, Thomas H. "Report on the Aftermath of the Finley
    Mine Disaster." The Director 41(2):16-17 (1971).

279 "Competitors Helping Each Other." The New England Fu-
    neral Director 1(5):19 (Aug. 1975).
        The Greater Gardner Funeral Director's Association, a
    group of some 17 directors in Winchendon, Gardner, and surround-
    ing localities in Massachusetts, meet on a regular basis to "upgrade
    their profession, solve mutual problems, and provide better service
    to their patrons." They believe themselves unique in New England
    where the standard rule is competition among directors, not mutual
    help. "Victories" through association include working out an autop-
    sies problem with a pathologist, improved relations with local florists,
    learning how to fill out new veterans' benefit forms, keeping up with
    new trends.

280 Compton, W. H. Funeral Sermon Outlines. Grand Rapids,
    MI: Baker Books, 1965. (Paper.) (Dollar Sermon Library.)

281 "The Condolence or Sympathy Visit." The Director 41:2-4
    (Dec. 1971).

282 Conwall, Russell H. One Thousand Thoughts for Funeral Oc-
    casions. Detroit: Gale, 1974 (repr. of 1912 ed.).
        Funeral sermons.

283 Dahl, Edward C. "A Funeral Ministry to the Unchurched."
    Pulpit Digest 32:11-16 (1952).

284 D'Alembert, Jean. Eulogies. New York: Gordon Press, 1974.

285 Daniels, Earl. Funeral Message; Its Preparation and Signifi-
    cance. Nashville, TN: Cokesbury Press, 1937. 108pp.

286 Davis, Elmer. "The Mortician." American Mercury, May
    1927. Repr. in The American Mercury Reader, Spivak,
    Lawrence E., and Angoff, Charles, eds., Philadelphia: Blak-
    iston, 1944, 378pp.

287 Dhonau, Charles O., and Nunnamaker, Albert J. Personalities in Funeral Management: Yourself, Your Problems; An Approach to the Profession from the Mental Side. Cincinnati: Embalming Book Co., 1929. 202pp.

288 [No entry.]

289 Dodson, George M. "Respect Your Profession--Your Community Does." Mortuary Management 59(1):28 (1972).
       Often only after his services are needed does the community express its appreciation for the funeral director. This practice of the community discourages new employees from continuing in the funeral service business.

290 Dressler, L. R. Funeral Hymns, Anthems and Responses. Ann Arbor, MI: Finch Press, 1974.

291 "Effects of Music on the Bereaved." American Funeral Director 95(8):14 (1972).
       Sketch of the therapeutic value of certain types of music on mourners. "Cadence for Sorrow," a booklet, is mentioned as a source for effective pieces.

292 Elzas, Barnett A. Book of Life: Services and Ceremonies Observed at the Death Bed, House of Mourning and Cemetery. New York: Bloch, 1915.

293 Federal Benefits for Veterans and Dependents--VA Fact Sheet IS-1. Supt. of Doc., U.S. Gov. Printing Office, Washington, DC 20402.
       Burial benefits.

       Flanner, Frank B. Cremation and the Funeral Director. See entry 1670.

294 Ford, William Herschel. Simple Sermons for Funeral Services. Grand Rapids, MI: Zondervan, n.d.

295 Francis, C. R. "Funeral Directors Since 1799." The Embalmers Monthly, July 1935.

296 Franz, Anne Hamilton. Funeral Direction and Management. Jacksonville, FL: State Board of Funeral Directors and Embalmers for Florida, 1947. 227pp. Graphs, diagrs., index.
       A simple guide for funeral directing divided into two parts: funeral directing, i.e. the actual preparation and carrying out of the funeral ceremony, and funeral management or the business side. Part I: Ethics, applied psychology, public relations, funeral arrangements for chapel, church, and home, the types of funerals, obituary writing, flowers, pre-arrangement, cremation, and shipping. Part II: site selection, types of ownership and management, personnel, employee relations, apprentices, laws, merchandising, display room decoration and arrangement, advertising, accounting, investing, and service costs.

297 Fulton, Robert L. Death and Identity. New York: Wiley, 1965.
One of the classics, presenting two aspects of the funeral director's work: the profane (disposing of the corpse), and the sacred (filling the living's religious, social, and moral needs).

298 Gassman, McDill. Daddy Was An Undertaker, illustr. by John V. McGraven. New York: Vantage, 1952. 248pp., drawings.
A cheery, adulatory, and Disneyesque biography of Joseph H. McGown, the author's father, and funeral director in Madison County, Ala. Filled with daughter's and his "adventures."

299 Glass, Robert E. "A Team of Tactful Men." The New Republic, April 21, 1947.

300 Glick, Ira O., Weiss, Robert S. and Parkes, C. Murray. The First Year of Bereavement. New York: John Wiley & Sons, 1975.
Funeral directors are among the professionals helpful to the bereaved; American society's ambivalent attitudes towards them; the support they can and do provide; anecdotes; widows' views on funeral directors and open-casket viewing: 52% described it as a negative experience; 30% regretted having looked; 14% were glad.

301 Goldstein, Israel. Mourner's Devotions. Ann Arbor, MI: Finch Press, 1974 (repr. of 1941 ed.).
Funeral sermons.

302 Graham, Rev. Roscoe. Remembered with Love. New York: American Press, 1961. 106pp.
A collection of the author's funeral services and addresses to serve as a model for others. Also includes appropriate poems.

303 Habenstein, Robert W. The American Funeral Director: A Study in the Sociology of Work. Ph.D. dissertation, University of Chicago, Dept. of Sociology, 1954. 408pp., biblio.

304 Hammond, Bart. Address to the Appleton Clergymen's Association NSM Bulletin 58(3):18-20 (March 1975). Photo.
Moving speech by the managing director of Wichmann Funeral Home in Appleton, Wis., urging clergymen (and funeral directors, too) to help the bereaved through understanding and compassion, and offering help when it is needed. How? By touching, loving, being there, showing someone cares, understanding their loss.

   Harmer, Ruth M. "Embalming, Burial, and Cremation." See entry 442.

305 Hart, Scott. "Swing Low, Sweet Chariot." Esquire, May 1947.

   Hasluck, Paul D., ed. Coffin Making and Undertaking. See entry 859.

306 Hayward, William. Obsequiate. New York: Longmans, Green,
     1907.
          Funeral rites and ceremonies.

307 Head, Ralph H. "Funeral Insurance: What Is Its Potential for
     the Future?" Casket & Sunnyside 101(3[centennial issue]):68-
     70 (1972).
          The President of the Pierce National Life Insurance Co.
     foresees "nearly half the funeral bills in America will be paid by
     some form of funeral insurance" by 2071.

308 Hill, T. Arnold. "An Appraisal and Abstract of Available
     Literature on the Occupation of the Undertaker." New York:
     National Occupational Conference, 1936. 8pp., biblio.
          Undertaking described, with reference to contemporary
     funeral service literature. Lists available training, qualities essen-
     tial for success, number of persons employed in funeral service,
     sex and race distribution (in 1910 and between 1920 and 1930), ad-
     vantages and disadvantages, professional organizations, necessary
     preparations for field (qualifications and licensing), remuneration,
     minority group opportunity, etc.

309 Hoffman, Frederick L. Pauper Burials and the Interment of
     the Dead in Large Cities. Newark, NJ: Prudential Press,
     1919. 123pp.

310 Hohenschuh, W. P. Modern Funeral; Its Management, illus.
     by T. Arnold Hill. Chicago: Trade Periodical Co., 1900.
     731pp., appendix.
          Thorough study of undertaking; procedures detailed.

311 "How to Prepare Death Notices." American Funeral Director
     92(1):34-36, 54 (1969).
          How to avoid common mistakes such as getting notices to
     the newspapers late, submitting inaccurate information, etc.; reasons
     for most errors: submitting faulty and inadequate data, not conform-
     ing to newspapers style and format, not observing deadlines, failing
     to inform family you have submitted notice, failing to give instruc-
     tions as regards flowers, donations to charity, etc., incorrect spell-
     ing of names, not verifying information, not taking precaution of us-
     ing phonetic alphabet when giving name spelling over phone.

312 Howard, A. "Logistics of the Funeral." Esquire 70(5):119-
     22, 170-79 (Nov. 1968). Diagr., question list.
          How Robert Kennedy's funeral was organized.

313 Hutchinson, Gerald. "Payees for Lump-Sum Death Payments
     Awarded in 1962." Actuarial Note #5, August, 1963, Dept.
     of Health, Education, and Welfare. Supt. of Doc., U.S.
     Gov. Printing Office, Washington, DC 20402.
          Breaks down Social Security death payments by sex, aver-
     age payment, funeral costs, to whom payment was made (i.e., fu-
     neral home or individual). For 1963 figures, see Long, entry 326.

314 Kates, Charles O. "Commencement Speakers Talk to the
Wrong People" (editorial). The American Funeral Director
98(8):29 (Aug. 1975).
The formula commencement address includes reminders to
the graduates that "they must continue to pursue knowledge and ex-
cellence all their days, " "that upon them rests the future of their
craft, " that "in the years to come they should never stray the slight-
est step away from the path of professional righteousness. " These
ideals should be heard not only by those entering the profession but
those who have been practicing for many years--who may have forgotten their ideals and enthusiasm.

315 Koch, Ron. Goodbye Grandpa. Minneapolis: Augsburg Pub.
House, 1975.
The story of Joey, a boy who at first runs away from
death and then by facing it gains a greater understanding of life.
Last chapter tells of funeral arrangements, visitation, and the funer-
al service through Joey's and his sister's eyes.

316 Kresge, Lee. "Morticians Get Weird Requests. " Northeast
Funeral Director 22(6):7 (1973).
And they carry them out--like the one from a nudist who
wanted to be buried in his birthday suit.

317 Kuehnert, David A. "The U.S. Army Mortuary System in
Vietnam. " The Director 40(4):2-3+ (1970).
Mortuaries on Tan Son Nhut Airbase outside of Saigon and
DaNang Airbase handle up to 750 bodies a month. Seventy Army
personnel and twenty-three civilians make up the staff. Lists procedures followed immediately upon arrival of new corpse: identification, preparation, shipping to the stateside collection points where
it is restored, cosmetized, dressed, and casketed.

318 Kutscher, Austin H. , et al. Acute Grief and the Funeral.
New York: Health Sciences Pub. Corp. , 1974.

319 Lagemann, John Kord. "The Hurt That Heals. " Good Housekeeping, April 1960.

320 Lamers, Dr. William M. , Jr. Death, Grief, Mourning, the
Funeral and the Child. Milwaukee, WI: NFDA, n.d.
(Pamphlet.)

321 Leach, William H. , ed. Cokesbury Funeral Manual. Nashville, TN: Cokesbury, 1932. 224pp.

322 _____ . Improved Funeral Manual. New York: Revell,
1946, 224pp. ; Grand Rapids, MI: Baker Book House, 1956,
224pp.

323 Lee, Robert G. For the Time of Tears: Funeral Sermons.
Grand Rapids, MI: Baker Books, 1971. (Paper.) (Preach-
ing Helps series.)

324 LeVoy, Robert P. "Seven Signs of Success for Funeral Direc-
        tors. " Casket & Sunnyside 100(2):35+ (1970).
        The characteristics that inevitably are part of successful
funeral directors.

325 _____. "Your Telephone Voice 'Tattle-Tale'. " Mortuary
        Management 59(1):22 (1972).
        A director of professional consultants in New York gives
nine speech points for funeral directors to use when counseling or
making funeral arrangements by phone and ways director can evaluate his own telephone voice and in-person performance.

326 Long, Wayne. "Payees for Lump-Sum Death Payments Award-
        ed in 1963. " Actuarial Note #13, Aug. 1964, Dept. of Health,
        Education, and Welfare. Supt. of Doc. , U. S. Gov. Printing
        Office, Washington, DC 20402.
        Breaks down Social Security death payments by sex, aver-
age payment, funeral costs, to whom payment made (funeral home
or individual). For 1962 data, see Hutchinson, entry 313.

327 MacNevin, Robert E. "Why We Do Things the Way We Do
        Now. " Casket & Sunnyside 100(9):8+ (1970).
        Summary of the social revolution impact on funeral direc-
tors.

328 Macoy, Robert. Obituary Rites of Freemasonry. New York:
        Macoy Publishing and Masonic Supply Co. , c. 1910.

329 Meachum, E. , ed. Manual for Funeral Occasions. Cincinnati:
        Standard Pub. Co. , c. 1913. 260pp.

330 Mees, Otto. Outlines for Funeral Sermons and Addresses.
        Grand Rapids, MI: Baker Books, 1974. (Paper.) (Minister's
        Handbook series.)

331 Meyer, F. B. , et al. Funeral Sermons and Outlines. Grand
        Rapids, MI: Baker Books, n. d. (Paper.) (Minister's Hand-
        book series.)

332 Miller, Basil W. Funeral Manual. Dallas: Chandler, c. 1956.
        148pp.

        "More Money to Ease Crowding of Cemeteries. " U. S. News
        and World Report (burial allowances) See entry 1554.

333 Myers, John. Manual of Funeral Procedure. Casper, WY:
        Prairie Pub. , 1956. 81pp.
        Brief rundown of the various church and fraternal order
requirements for funerals.

334 National Catholic Cemetery Conference. Rite of Burial Book.
        Available from the NCCC, Item #615.
        Complete cemetery service with optional readings and

prayers. Vinyl covered, with pages enclosed in clear plastic covers. Authorized by the Bishops' Committee on the Liturgy.

335 _____. Rite of Burial Leaflet. Available from the NCCC, Item #616.
Complete cemetery service with optional readings and prayers, authorized by the Bishops' Committee on the Liturgy.

336 National Funeral Directors Assoc. The Condolence or Sympathy Visit. Milwaukee, WI: NFDA, 1974. (Pamphlet.)

337 _____. National Funeral Directors Association Reference Manual. Milwaukee, WI: NFDA, 1975. 5083pp. (Paper).
Divider indicators provide instant access to five main sections (U.S. Gov., Transportation Laws and Rules, Public and Clergy Relations, Management Aids, and Miscellaneous). Section 1: care of deceased armed forces personnel and burial allowances of civilian employees; information on burial in national cemeteries, Coast Guard burial allowances; National Guard care and disposition; burial benefits, rules, etc. for veterans and a listing of regional offices and centers; provisions under Social Security, railroad retirement; burial allowances to federal employees where death results from injuries; death benefits for local law enforcement officers; summary of 1974 amendments of the Federal Wage and Hour Law and the Fair Labor Standards Act. Section 2: Domestic and foreign transportation rules and regulations; schedule of services available in foreign countries; cost; services available from U.S. State Dept. and its foreign consuls. Section 3: public information and relations, participation in school, church, and civic programs; literature and audio-visual aids available; advertising; educational seminars, and sample ads for local use; similar information relevant to clergy-funeral director relations. Section 4: accounting methods, suggested forms for use in funeral service practice, computation for average cost of operation, depreciation, noninsured health and accident plans, tax deductions for seminar trips, the Federal Truth in Lending Law. Section 5: pre-arranged and financed funerals; legal aspects of disaster; State Board of Committee contract; where to write for birth and death certificates; accredited schools and colleges of mortuary science; funeral service journals; NFDA forms for insurance proceeds assignment, embalming report, autopsy consent, transport authorization, clergyman preference forms and other relevant materials.

338 _____. Should I Go to the Funeral? What Do I Say? Milwaukee, WI: NFDA, n. d. (Pamphlet.)
Discusses what to do, say, not to do or say, and in general how best to console the bereaved during the condolence or sympathy visit.

339 _____. Too Personal to Be Private: A Funeral Director Talks About a Death in a Family. Milwaukee, WI: NFDA, 1971. Illus., 15pp. (Pamphlet).
Reproduced from the 16mm motion picture of the same

title. Short pictorial review with text showing how the family of Tom Wallace, who died unexpectedly, arranges for his funeral with the aid of a funeral home and friends. Woven into the story is the purpose for a funeral and some of the services provided by the funeral home.

340 National Selected Morticians. A Service Book. Chicago: NSM, 1925, 174pp; 1936, 190pp.

341 _____. Social Security Benefits Including Medicare. Chicago: Commerce Clearing House, 1974. 32pp., charts (pamphlet).
    Social Security benefit table and explanations regarding qualification, coverage, insurance, status required, special benefits at age 72, automatic increases in benefits, minimum, delayed retirement, reduced benefits and benefits for disabled persons, divorced wives and widows, and full-time students; lump-sum payments, filing a claim, working after benefits start, veterans and servicemen, self-employed, etc. Under medicare, defines hospital insurance and medical insurance benefits, enrollment, expenses not covered, paying for Medicare, and HMO's (Health Maintenance Organizations).

342 Nevin, W. Scott. Manual for Undertakers. Philadelphia: Manual Pub. Co., 1910. 62pp.

    Oman, John. "The Funeral Director as Grief Counselor." See entry 1212.

    _____. "The Funeral Director as a Human Being." See entry 1213.

    _____. "The Funeral Director as Master of Ceremonies." See entry 1214.

    _____. "How Do You Feel?" See entry 1216.

    _____. "If Only." See entry 1217.

    _____. "Learn to Listen." See entry 1218.

    _____. "The Unmourned." See entry 1219.

343 "Organ Music Should Have a Consoling Radiance." American Funeral Director 92(12):29-30 (1969).
    Virgil Fox advises clean, uplifting sound, major keys, and classical composers for funeral services.

344 Outline Types of Funeral Services and Ceremonies. New York: National Association of Colleges and Mortuary Science, 1961. 93pp., diagrs.
    Brief outlines of the procedures to be followed for Protestant, Roman Catholic, Orthodox Jewish, Conservative and Reformed Jewish, Christian Science, Greek Orthodox, "I Am," Mormon,

Lutheran, and Quaker funerals: fraternal order funerals (Masons, Elks, Grange, Odd Fellows, etc.); American Legion; and military funerals. Diagrams show proper placement for various rites, positioning of pallbearers and guests, and order in the military procession.

345 Pine, Vanderlyn R. Caretaker of the Dead: The American Funeral Director. New York: Irvington Publishers, 1975 (dist. by Halsted Press, div. of Wiley). 219pp., biblio., index, tables.
Case study of the relationship between occupational models and the behavior of people carrying out their work in the organizational setting of the funeral home. Objective: to examine analytically the relationship between the typical conception of funeral directors as "servers" or "bureaucrats" on the basis of an investigation of the everyday behavior of funeral directors. Historical review of caring for the dead from ancient times to the present, home and abroad; specific problems of the funeral director; setting and organization of funeral homes; different behavior patterns of directors in various regions; ways they present themselves outside the funeral home; how directors carry out their work (the first call, making arrangements, selecting casket, visitation, the funeral), nonpublic occupational activities, director and self presentation, duties and activities, various dimensions of directing, and professional-bureaucratic conflict. Author teaches sociology at the State University of New York (New Paltz), is a research analysis consultant and disaster assistance adviser for the NFDA, and was a licensed funeral director for over ten years.

346 _____. "Grief Work and Dirty Work: The Aftermath of an Aircrash." Paper presented at the annual meeting of the Eastern Sociological Society, NY, April 18, 1970; published in Omega 5 (winter 1974).

347 _____, ed. Responding to Disaster. Milwaukee, WI: Bulfin, 1974. 190pp., index, biblio.
Recommended by The American Funeral Director as "a badly needed handbook" for all funeral directors. Funeral directors are an essential member of the groups of people called upon in event of disasters where lives are lost. Fifteen essays by the author and other funeral service authorities on the funeral director's role in a disaster; site protection; legal and medical perspectives; the role of the federal government including planning, the FBI, and assistance; role of the funeral director in four specific examples; the NFDA's plans and preparations for planecrash, and general and natural disasters.

348 Polson, Cyril J., Brittain, R. P., and Marshall, T. K. The Disposal of the Dead. New York: Philosophical Library, 1953, 300pp., biblio.; rev. ed., Springfield, IL: C. C. Thomas, 1962, 356pp., index, tables, biblio.
Comprehensive historical overview of the disposition of the dead--cremation, burial, exhumation, embalming, and funeral

direction: medical and legal requirement and procedures to be followed before disposal; survey of the history and present use of cremation, regulations, and a world-wide survey of its use; burial laws, locations, fees, and the funeral rites of various religions; survey of laws and requirements of exhumation; survey of embalming history and present procedures, with comments on specific problems; funeral direction, the business, coffins, and transportation of the dead.

Porter, William H. , Jr. "Some Sociological Notes on a Century of Change in the Funeral Business." See entry 1007.

349 Potere, William R. , Jr. "A Funeral Procession Dilemma."
The Director 42:2 (July 1972).
Move in Oakland County to abolish funeral processions throughout the state of Michigan. Chronologic review of counter action by funeral directors and sympathizers.

350 "Quality Prospects; Funeral Directors." Flitcraft Courant 71:
32+ (Sept. 1966).

Raether, Howard C. "Successful Funeral Service Practice."
See entry 1227.

351 Rendon, Leandro. "Mortuary Program of the Armed Forces."
Champion Expanding Encyclopedia, July-Aug. 1970.
Benefits, allowances, report forms and other matters relevant to care of the soldier's remains. Emphasis on reimbursements and claims available to funeral directors handling deceased military personnel.

Renourd, Auguste. Undertakers' Manual; A Treatise of Useful and Reliable Information.... See entry 535.

352 Roberts, R. D. "Music for the Christian Funeral." The
Director 41(1):4 (1971).
Select music for the Christian funeral that will inspire hope and faith in the Christian. Using favorite hymns of the deceased adds to grief of the bereaved.

353 Rogers, Frank D. Confessions of an Undertaker. Chicago:
Trade Periodical Co. , c. 1910.

354 _____. Reveries of an Undertaker. Clayton, NY: Thousand
Islands Pub. Co. , 1899. 118pp.

355 Rosen, Elaine L. "How Wives View Their Role in Funeral
Service." Mortuary Management 57(5):34-36 (1970).

356 Saint Gregory Nazianzen and Saint Ambrose. Funeral Orations.
Washington, DC: Catholic University Press, 1974. (Fathers
of the Church series, vol. 22.)

357 Sanderson, Joseph, ed. Pastors' Pocket Manual for Funerals.
Glenfield, CT: Bromfield, 1891.

358 Sargent, Lucius M. Dealings with the Dead; By a Sexton of the Old School. Boston: Dutton & Wentworth, 1856. 2 vols.

359 Sears, Fredrick R. "Army Conducts Seminar in Personal Identification." The Director 39(1):6 (1969).
      Seminar report on body identification of victims of battle or civilian disasters. Anthropologists, medical examiners, and military mortuary officers report various techniques, giving demonstrations in fingerpainting, use of dental charts, x-ray photography. Estimated 42% of the American civil war dead were unidentified, 13. 6% in the Spanish American war, 4% in World War II, 2. 9% in Korea. Practically all Viet Nam war victims were identified.

360 Sheed, Wilfred, and Feltman, Shirley. "The Funeral Business." Jubilee, Nov. 1960.

      Silverman, Phyllis R. The Funeral Director's Wife as Caregiver. See entry 1233.

361 "Small Flags to Be Issued for Veterans' Funerals." New York Times cxii (38, 529):21 (July 21, 1963).
      Veterans Administration reduces flag size from 5 x 9-1/2 to 4 x 7 inches.

362 "Social Security Act Title II Is Changed." Casket & Sunnyside 102(4):8 (1972).
      Details of Social Security payment where there is no spouse and the body of the insured person, believed dead, is not available for interment. See "Social Security Payment When Body Not Available," entry 364.

363 "Social Security and the Funeral Director." Mortuary Management 58(3):18 (1971).
      "Teleservice"--the new reporting and filing service for Social Security benefits. Funeral director or family need no longer file claims personally. Fundamental program outlined and available benefits listed.

364 "Social Security Payment When Body Not Available." The Director 42:4 (March 1972).
      Social Security Act amended by Public Law 92-223 to permit lump sum death payment for burial and memorial service costs for insured person whose body is not available for burial. Applies only where there is not a surviving spouse. See "Social Security Act Title II Is Changed," entry 362.

365 Solomon, David N. "Sociological Perspectives on Occupations." In: Howard Becker, ed., Institutions and the Person (Chicago: Aldine, 1968), p. 8-10.
      Summary of Everett C. Hughes's analysis of the role of the funeral director, the men who do the dirty work of society.

366 Swoyer, Grover E. When Granma Died; Imaginary Conversa-

tions about Conducting the Modern Funeral. New York: Vantage, 1959. 128pp.

"Undertaker Will Offer Drive-In Service." See entry 753.

367 "U.S. Aid for Funerals of G.I.'s Called Too Low." New York Times cxvii(40, 159):8 (Jan. 6, 1968).

368 U.S. Public Health Service. Where to Write for Birth and Death Records, United States and Outlying Areas, P.H.S. Publication 630A-1, rev. Aug. 1964. Washington, DC: U.S. Gov. Printing Office, 1964.

369 Van Wormer, Janet B. Women in Funeral Service. Mimeographed paper, presented at the National Funeral Directors Association, 1970.

370 Venting, R., ed. Funeral Director's Manual; Appropriate Services for the Burial of the Dead. Greenfield, OH: 1906. 110pp.

371 "Veterans Burial Bill Passed." New York Times cxv(39, 476): 21 (April 22, 1966).
    $250 to be allotted for funeral if death is caused by a service-connected disability.

372 Wallis, Charles L., ed. The Funeral Encyclopedia. New York: Harper, 1953; Grand Rapids, MI: Baker Book House, 1973, 327pp., biblio. (paper). (Source Books for Ministers.)

373 Walsh, David. Premature Burial. NY: William Wood, c. 1902.
    Big issue until embalming became prevalent. See also
1607.

374 "What Part Will Women Play in Funeral Service in the Year 1971?" Casket & Sunnyside 101(13[centennial issue]):49ff [3pp.] (1972). Photo.
    In 1925, the editors of The Sunnyside asked women funeral directors and embalmers their prognosis for the year 1971. Their answers ranged from "I don't know" to "women's intuition, soft touch, and attention to detail have served well now (1925) and should 46 years from now."

375 White Chapel Memorial Association. Funeral Customs, Etiquette and Services. Detroit, 1932. 44pp.

376 Wicker, S. "Massachusetts Mortuary Operated by Housewife." Casket & Sunnyside 103(2):14-15+ (1973).
    Haydenville, Mass., woman mortician individualizes each funeral. She attributes her success as a counselor to her years of experience as mother and housewife.

377 Wilder, Harris H., and Wentworth, Bert. Personal Identification; Methods for the Identification of Individuals, Living or

Dead. Boston: Badger, 1918. 374pp.; Chicago: T. G. Cooke, 1932. 383pp.

378 Wilkerson, James P., Jr. "The Importance of the Body." Casket & Sunnyside 102(2):10 (1972).
Basic functions of the funeral director: preparation of the body, filling family's religious and social needs through the funeral, disposition of the corpse. Discussion of embalming, cosmetics, and casketing.

379 Wood, Charles R., ed. Sermon Outlines for Funeral Services. Grand Rapids, MI: Kregel, 1969. (Paper.) (Easy-to-Use Sermon Outline series.)

380 Your Social Security. Free from local Social Security administration offices.
Lists burial benefits.

Zinsser, W. "Time Saver for Busy Mourners." See entry 756.

2. EMBALMING AND RESTORATIVE ART

381 Adair, Maude Adam. The Techniques of Restorative Art. Dubuque, IA: W. C. Brown, 1949. 63pp., illus.

382 Allegro, John M. The Sacred Mushroom and the Cross. New York: Doubleday, 1970.
Section on the origin of embalming and the embalmer. Slimy mucus of the mushroom was thought to impart life and rebirth to the dead in the underworld. Hebrew tale of the 40-day embalming of Joseph.

383 Ball, W. W. Elementary and Practical Treatise on Embalming, with Two Anatomical Charts. Springfield, OH: Hydro-Chloranum Co., 1881. 37pp.
Early treatise on embalming in the United States.

384 _____. Progressive Embalming Science. Springfield, OH: Ball Pub., 1895. 164pp.
Latest embalming techniques practiced in the United States in the late 19th century.

385 Barnard, Howard F. "Restoration and Open Casket Pay Off for Funeral Directors." Casket & Sunnyside 103(4):13+ (1973).
NFDA conference report, the focus of which is Edward C. Johnson's address stressing the importance of restorative art to allow viewing of the deceased. Values and unique practices of the American funeral tradition discussed.

386 Barnes, Carl Lewis. Art and Science of Embalming. Chicago: Trade Periodicals, 1905. 552pp., photos, drawings, index, quiz compends, glossary.

387 _____. Atlas of the Arterial and Venous System; Also a Treatise on Modern Embalming. Poughkeepsie, NY: The Author, 1905. 263pp.

388 Barnes, Thornton B. Quiz Compends. Chicago: Trade Periodical Co., c. 1910.

389 Brodie, D. A., Tate, C. L., and Hooke, K. F. "Aspirin: Intestinal Damage." Science 170:183-84 (1970).
     Chronic aspirin-eater is a potential problem to the embalmer because of deterioration it causes in various tissues.

390 Callaway, Curtis. F. Textbook of Mortuary Practice; The Pathological Conditions of and the Embalming Treatments for over 150 Diseases; Arranged Alphabetically for Easy Reference. Chicago: Undertakers Supply, 1944. 688pp., illus.

391 Champion Expanding Encyclopedia of Mortuary Practice. Springfield, OH: The Champion Co., 1928- .
     Four-page magazine published ten times a year. As of July-August 1975 this series included 1856 pages of practical and useful information for the funeral director and embalmer, without advertising or pushing the Champion Co.'s products. All aspects of funeral science from history (Egyptian embalming practices) to the latest procedural updates. Useful, scholarly articles slanted toward contemporary problems--how to deal with carbon monoxide deaths-- and provide excellent means for funeral director/embalmer to keep up with current trends, practices, and innovations.

392 Clarke, Charles H. Practical Embalming, A Recitation of Actual Experience of the Author and Hundreds of the Most Expert Embalmers of the World. Cincinnati: The Author, 1917. 302pp., illus.

393 Clarke, Joseph Henry. Answers to Questions Contained in Clarke's Quiz Compend for the Students of Clarke's School of Embalming. Cincinnati: J. H. Clarke, 1897. 23pp.

394 _____. Answers to Questions Presented in the Lectures of Clarke's Cincinnati College of Embalming, and to Accompany Fourth and Enlarged Edition of Text Book and Compend. Cincinnati, 1902. 31pp.

395 _____. Clarke's Compend and Text Book on Embalming. Cincinnati, 1902. 136pp.

396 _____. Clarke's New Work on Embalming. South Bend, IN: Western Undertaker, 1894. 196pp.

397   . Clarke's Quiz Compend, 3d ed. Springfield, OH:
         Clarke Chemical Works, 1897. 55pp.

398   . Clarke's Textbook on Embalming ... Includes a
         Chapter on Funeral Etiquette, Code of Ethics, and Such Par-
         liamentary Rules As Are Used in Governing Public Meetings,
         Conventions, etc. Springfield, OH: Clarke Chemical Works,
         1885. 142pp.

399   . Hints on Embalming. Springfield, OH: Clarke
         Chemical Works, 1888. 36pp.

400   . Illustrated and Practical Treatise on Chemical Em-
         balming. Springfield, OH: Clarke Chemical Works, 1881.
         23pp.

401   . Reminiscences of Early Embalming. New York:
         The Sunnyside, 1917. 443pp.
              Excellent reference on the development of American mor-
         tuary science education written by the father of American funeral
         education. A series of letters tracing his career and the develop-
         ment of funeral education. Includes rosters of his students. Valua-
         ble source for post Civil War period.

402   , and Charles O. Dhonau. Answers to Questions Con-
         tained in the Official Text Book on Embalming and Sanitary
         Science. Cincinnati: College of Embalming, nd.

403   , and   . Official Text Book on Embalming and
         Sanitary Science. Cincinnati: College of Embalming, nd.

404 Clarke's Cincinnati College of Embalming. An Epitome of
         Reference for the Students of the Cincinnati School for Em-
         balming. Springfield, OH: H. S. Limbacher, 1883. 39pp.

405 Conference of Embalmers Examining Boards of the United
         States, 1938-1939. Report of the National Conference Board
         and the Advisory Marking Committee ... at the Annual Meet-
         ing Held in New York, N.Y., Oct. 10-11, 1938. N.p., nd.
         38pp.

     Crahan, Emmett J. "Planning the Preparation Room." See
         entry 726.

406 Curry, Gladys P. Textbook on Facial Restoration with a Study
         of the Curry System of Fingerprinting the Dead. Boston:
         Curry Fingerprint Powder Co., 1947. 276pp., photos, index.

407 Deuel, Harry J. Textbook of Chemistry for Students of Em-
         balming, 2d ed. Hollywood, CA: Masters Press, 1935.
         146pp.

     Dhonau, Charles O. Management. See entry 619.

_____. Personalities in Funeral Management. See entry
287.

408 _____, and Nunnamaker, Albert J. Manual of Case Analysis. Cincinnati: Embalming Book Co., 1928. 108pp., illus.
    Every embalming job includes different factors. An analy-
sis of the variables involved, centering on the embalmer, his materials and goals, and the body. The goal is for each embalmer
to be able to attain the desired effect. Not a "how to" book; more
the relating of an approach and philosophical method. Available from
Casket & Sunnyside, 274 Madison Ave., New York, NY   10016.

409 _____, and Prager, G. F. Manual of Restorative Art.
Cincinnati: Embalming Book Co., 1932. 161pp. Illus.

410 Dodge, Asa J. Revised Edition of the Practical Embalmer,
with an Appendix of Four Hundred Questions and Answers on
Anatomy, Embalming, and Sanitary Science. Boston: The
Author, 1908. 257pp.

411 Doery, J. C. G., Hirsh, J., and De Gruchy, C. G. "Aspirin:
Its Effect on Platelet Glycolsis." Science 165:65-66 (1969).
    Embalming problems due to aspirin, perhaps the most
commonly used chemotherapeutic agent.

412 Eckels College of Mortuary Science. Reference Compendium;
A Series of Questions and Answers Pertaining to the Study of
Mortuary Science (Compiled by the Faculty). Philadelphia:
Eckels College of Mortuary Science, 1948. 303pp.

413 Eckels, Howard S. Practical Embalmer; A Practical and Comprehensive Treatise on Embalming. Philadelphia: H. S.
Eckels Co., 1903. 196pp.

414 _____. Sanitary Science. Philadelphia: H. S. Eckels,
1904. 393pp.

415 _____. Sanitary Science; A Reference and Textbook for the
Communicable Diseases, Disinfection and Chemistry for the
Undertaker. Philadelphia: H. S. Eckels, 1918. 483pp.
Illus.

416 _____, and Genung, Charles, eds. Eckels-Genung Method
and Practical Embalmer; A Practical and Comprehensive
Treatise on Embalming. Philadelphia: H. S. Eckels, 1906,
248pp., illus.; 1917, 280pp., illus.

417 Eckels, John H. Modern Mortuary Science, 3d ed. Philadelphia: Westbrook, 1948. 828pp., illus., tables, biblio.,
compend of questions and answers, reference compound,
glossary.
    Mortuary science text; historical and modern funeral cus-
toms; American development of embalming, embalming anatomy,

embalming technique and instruments, preparation, arterial guide, injection, drainage, chemicals, cavity embalming, distention and discoloration; treatment of special cases. Reference compend includes terminology, shipping rules by state, Canada Express rates and miles for shipping.

418   Embalmers' Anatomical Aid and Guide. Chicago: Western, n. d.

419   Embalming Chemical Manufacturers Assoc. Embalming: Ancient Art/Modern Science. Available from the Association (165 Rindge Ave. Extension, Cambridge, MA 02140).
      Explanation of the purposes and benefits of embalming to counter recent arguments against it. Designed for distribution at funeral homes, civic group talks, clubs, schools, churches. Interesting quote from The Jewish Funeral Director 43(1):8 (winter, 1975): ". . . for every member of the community who would ask such a question of you (Is embalming necessary?), there are probably two others who, perhaps having read one of the popular 'exposes' of funeral service, are already sure that the answer is 'no'. "

420   Espy, J. B. Espy's Embalmer, with Nearly Seventy-five Cuts and Instructions Under Each Cut. Springfield, OH: Espy Fluid, c. 1895. 93pp.

421   Fee, Art. "A Whale of a Tale. " Mortuary Management 59(5): 16-18 (1972).
      Whale preserved in 1932 is still in excellent state of preservation. Method of formaldehyde preparation reviewed.

422   Final Report on Literature Search on the Infectious Nature of Dead Bodies. See entry 444.

423   Fitzpatrick. Louis J. "Sources of Gases Formed in Human Remains. " The Dodge Magazine 67(2):9ff [2pp.] (March 1975). Illus. , diagr.
      The numerous sources of gas production are a great source of difficulty to the embalmer; how various forces within the dead cell can cause gas formation involving bacteria and the various causes of such gases.

424   _____. "Timely Technical Tips for the Prep Room: Treating Distentions. " The Dodge Magazine 67(3):18-19 (June 1975). Photo.
      Detailed description of several methods to prevent and treat swellings in the corpse. The causes of distentions are discussed in entry 423.

425   Forestus, Peter. "On the Art of How to Embalm the Dead Human Body. " In: Petrum Offenback, M.D., A New Medical Treatise, Embracing the External and Internal Pathological Ulceration of the Whole Human Body, Frankfort am Main: Zachariane Palthemium, 1605. In the collection of the

National Foundation for Funeral Service Library in Evanston, IL.

426   Francis, Edward. Embalming; Indefinite Preservation of the Body. Washington, DC: U.S. Gov. Printing Office, 1915. 6pp.

427   Frederick, Jerome F. "Ecological Factors in Embalming: Part IV." The De-Ce-Co Magazine 64(5):4-5 (1972).
       Pathogenic yeasts and the environment. Antibiotic treatment has increased the incidence of fungi-and-yeast-caused infection which proliferate after death and are a danger to the embalmer. Outlines disinfection techniques.

428   _____. "Embalming Problems Due to Drug Addiction." The Dodge Magazine 65(1):6-7+ (1973)--cont. in 65(2):6-7+ (1973).
       Drug addiction is a rural and suburban as well as an urban affliction, so it concerns all professional embalmers. Problem arises from prescription as well as illegal drugs. The most common problems in embalming drug addicts discussed, with table illustrating the various drugs and the complications they create. Part 2: the effects of combinations of drugs on the dead body, concentrating on the most common effects, jaundice and low protein in the body.

429   _____. "The Health of the Professional Embalmer." The Dodge Magazine 67(2):4ff [3pp.] (March 1975). Illus., diagr.
       Director of chemical research, the Dodge Chemical Co., and fellow of both American Institute of Chemists and New York Academy of Sciences' fourth article in a series which discusses the methods of disease transmission from the unembalmed body. Article's focus is on "the contact with the various infectious agents (of the unembalmed body)." For information on the resistance of the embalmer to infections refer to previous issues, nos. 65 and 66.

430   _____. "The Health of the Professional Embalmer." The Dodge Magazine 67(3):4ff [3pp.] (June 1975). Photo.
       Fifth in a series of articles, this one concerning how to reduce the risk of infection during the initial contact with the corpse, the most dangerous contact when bacterial counts are highest. "First drainage" of corpse, disinfecting of instruments, surface areas of the preparation room, and the need for unhurried, careful procedures.

431   _____. "Is Embalming Necessary? Article 1." The Dodge Magazine 65(3):4-5 (1973).
       Physiological factors are as important as the psychological and sociologic aspects of embalming. Public health is one example. Facts of bacterial, fungi, and viral pathogens' viability after death outlined; new finding about the effects of grief on body's reaction discussed. Focus of the article: Does embalming reduce the risk of illness to the bereaved whose physical strength is weakened because of emotional state?

432 _____. "Is Embalming Necessary? Article 2." The Dodge
    Magazine 65(4):8-9 (1973).
        Synopsis of the E. C. M. A. -Foster D. Snell Study of the
reduction in microbiological flora within internal organs. A reduction
of 99% is achieved by embalming with commercially available fluids.
Focus of article: The bodies' orifices where immediate contact and
contamination occurs.

433 _____. "The Mathematics of Embalming Chemistry, Part
    II." The De-Ce-Co Magazine 60(6):4-5, 20-21 (1968).
        Modern medical use of chemotherapeutic agents has neces-
sitated constant reformulation of embalming preservative compounds.
No single arterial chemical will overcome abnormalities caused by
these agents. Main systems of the human body involved in drug
therapy: hepatic system (liver), the eliminatory system (kidneys),
and the circulatory system (blood vessels). Refers to data sheets
available which outline adverse effects caused by residual drugs and
their aftereffects in the body.

434 _____. "The Vital Public Health Function of Embalming,
    Part 1." The De-Ce-Co Magazine 61(1):4-5 (1969); Part 2
    61(2):8-21 (1969); Part 3 61(3):6-7, 30 (1969); Part 4 61(4):
    6-7 (1969); Part 5 61(6):4-5+ (1969).
        1: Importance of sanitation in an age when traditional
principles of hygiene are being abandoned in an increasing effort of
our society to cure rather than prevent; is embalming necessary?
2: Survival of bacterial pathogens in unembalmed and putrefying
dead body as a source of contagion to personnel and a public health
threat; documented; references and bibliography. 3: Evidence that
unembalmed human remains constitute a health hazard; rise in path-
ogenic fungal infections; references and bibliography; emphasis on
the antibiotic resistant pathogens. 4: Medical use of cortisone
and related corticosteroids creates favorable environment for growth
of bacteria and fungus in corpse; tables showing published figures
for virus persistence under various conditions. 5: Transmission
of viral particles from unembalmed interred body can be possible
source of infection to healthy living; processes and events whereby
this could happen outlined; documented with references and bibliography.

435 Gale, Frederick C. Mortuary Science. Springfield, IL:
    Charles C. Thomas, 1961. 214pp., illus., index, photos,
    biblio. follows each section.
        Monograph to "familiarize the embalmer, autopsy techni-
cian, anatomy preparator, and those associated with the field of
mortuary science with the basic principles and techniques employed
in embalming, autopsy, examination and anatomical preparations."
Covers Death: its signs, effects on the body, and identification of
unknown bodies; Embalming Technique: historical introduction, embalming sites, preparations, fluids, practices and problems (specific
diseases or causes of death), embalming autopsied cases; Anatomical
Preparations: procurement of cadavers, custodial duties of preparer,
embalming for anatomical study, anatomy museum preparations,
chemical formulas.

436 Gannal, J. M. History of Embalming (and of Preparation in
     Anatomy, Pathology, and Natural History). Paris, 1838.
     Tr. by R. Harlan, M.D., Philadelphia: Judah Dobson, 1940,
     264pp.

437 Gloye, E. E., and Marcus, R. J. "Drug Effect Prediction by
     Computer." Science 169:89-91 (1970).
        Embalmers face numerous complications in preparing re-
     mains of deceased who have been administered various drugs previ-
     ous to death. Of interest to embalmers, therefore, is a recently
     developed computer procedure that predicts the physiological effects
     of specific chemotherapeutic agents and combinations of these agents
     working together.

438 Gordon, W., and Wetzler, Theodore F. "Public Health View
     of Embalming." The Director 39(1):11 (1969).
        Intestine and respiratory tract and skin are inhabited by
     aerobic and anaerobic microorganisms; their possible resistance to
     modern embalming chemicals; modern embalming methods effectively
     prevents transmission of potentially dangerous microbes from the
     dead to the living.

439 Grafe, William T. "1968 Tet Offensive--A Tough Job." Mor-
     tuary Management 56(9):11-20 (1969).
        Problems of refrigeration, embalming, return to the U.S.
     Several case histories, emphasizing problems during war time and
     high volume death periods.

440 Green, F. J. "Biological Stains." Laboratory Management
     7:22-23 (1969).
        Review of how biological stains and dyes attack tissue
     components to produce overall staining effect, including eosin, Azur
     B, and conditions for the proper dyeing of biological tissues.

441 Greenhill, Thomas. Nexpoxndeia; or the Art of Embalming,
     Wherein Is Shown the Right of Burial, the Funeral Ceremonies,
     and the Several Ways of Preserving Dead Bodies in Most Na-
     tions of the World. London: The Author, 1705. 367pp.

442 Harmer, Ruth M. "Embalming, Burial, and Cremation." In:
     [The New] Encyclopaedia Britannica, 15th ed. (Chicago:
     Encyclopaedia Britannica, 1974), p. 736-41.
        The practices of embalming, burial, and cremation and
     the role of burial societies in various civilizations, ancient and
     modern. Short sketch of differing attitudes toward death and ration-
     ales behind burial practices; embalming--its history, ancient methods,
     practices in the Middle Ages and Renaissance, the development of
     modern embalming and modern procedures--the rites for kings, in-
     humation, cave burials, ship burials, exposure to the elements,
     birds and animals, tree burial, cannibalism, second burials, ceme-
     teries, and concern for sanitation; cremation--its history, including
     cremation of military heroes, explanations for curtailing the practice,
     modern cremation; burial societies--their history, religious and sec-
     ular societies, modern societies.

443 Hiller College of Embalming and Necrosurgery. Text-Book.
       Canton, OH: The College, 1919. 330pp.

444 Hinson, M. R. "Final Report on the Literature Search on In-
       fectious Nature of Dead Bodies." Downers Grove, IL: Bib-
       liographic Service, Sept. 1968.
             A literature search for 1963 through 1966, commissioned
by the Embalming Chemical Manufacturers' Association, concluding
that there is no sound scientific basis for the belief that the germ
dies with the host. Infectious organisms spread from the cadaver
by physical contact and by air and infect healthy individuals in contact with unembalmed corpses. Reduction of bacterial flora aided
by injection of compounds as phenols, alcohols, aldehydes, etc.

445 Hirst, Thomas. Quiz Class; A Manual Designed to Coach and
       Prepare Undertakers and Embalmers to Qualify for License
       Before the State Examining Boards. New York: The Casket,
       1921. 73pp.

446 Jackson, Edgar N. "Embalming and the Perfect Effigy."
       The De-Ce-Co Magazine 63(3):4-5+ (1971).
             The centuries-old use of effigy in funeral practice, origi-
nally done for leaders and kings, then for the wealthy middle classes,
and finally for the poor (who only could afford death masks). With
the growth of embalming, effigy-making faded out. The modern
funeral director and embalmer make possible to every man what once
was the prerogative of kings.

447 Johnson, Edward C. "Body Bulk Increases Restoration Prob-
       lem." Casket & Sunnyside 102(9):16 (1972).
             Technical, detailed.

448 _____. "A Brief History of U.S. Military Embalming."
       The Director 41(9):8-9 (1971).
             U.S. war dead have been embalmed and returned home for
110 years--during the Civil War, at the start of the Spanish American War, and during the Korean War. There was very little done
in World Wars I and II.

449 _____. "Displaced Facial or Skull Bones Require Alignment
       before Embalming." Casket & Sunnyside 103(2):10 (1973).
             Detailed description of facial reconstruction of a girl's
head in which every bone had been broken.

450 _____. "Dr. Carl Lewis Barnes Gained Fame as Embalm-
       ing Instructor." Casket & Sunnyside 105(5):6ff [4pp.] (May
       1975). Illus.
             Story of one of the funeral profession's more picturesque
personalities--perhaps America's most famous embalmer instructor.
Also an author, demonstrator, and respected figure in the fields of
education and medicine.

451 _____. "Embalming Stressed at International Meeting."
       Casket & Sunnyside 103(9):22+ (1973).

American experts at the Third Annual Congress of the International Federation of Thanatopractic Associations in Lisbon, Portugal, speak on the funeral and the embalming and restorative arts, and give embalming demonstration. Attempt will be made to establish uniform regulations pertaining to international transport of the dead.

452 _____. A History of the Art and Science of Embalming; A Condensation from a Study Extending Over Three Years. New York: Casket & Sunnyside, 1944. 24pp., biblio.
Detailed description of embalming techniques with extensive bibliography.

453 _____. "How to Make a Restoration without Difficulty When Mandible Is Missing." Casket & Sunnyside 99(4):33, 47 (1969).
Dual problem of restoring lower one-third of the face and emaciation effects. Solution: coathanger and finer wire packed with cotton and fast drying glue.

454 _____. "How to Rebuild When There Is Total Destruction of the Eye." Casket & Sunnyside 99(10):28, 29 (1969).
Detailed description of restoration process, which takes about two hours to complete. Cites case example.

455 _____. "How to Restore Appearance After Thyroid Tumor Removal." Casket & Sunnyside 99(12):27 (1969).
Specific techniques of surgery, materials, etc.

456 _____. "Innovation Is Required in Facial Cancer Cases." Casket & Sunnyside 102(7):10+ (1972).
Detailed description of embalming and restoration of a 53-year-old face cancer victim with step-by-step analysis.

457 _____. Manual of Embalming Treatment. Chicago: The Author, 1947. 62pp., illus.

458 _____. "Restorative Art Requires Psychological Approach." Casket & Sunnyside 105(6):11-14 (June 1975).
The goals in restoring mutilated remains are concealing evidence of the injury and restoring "a recognizable appearance to the features." Psychological techniques which make up for an embalmer's lack of skill: (1) Have a friend or member of the family view the unrestored remains (he will then be aware of the embalmer's task), (2) Promise only that you will do your best to restore recognizable features (do not predict absolute success). (3) Allow time to do an adequate job. (4) Request wrist length sleeves and neck high collars; do not leave it to the family to provide adequate burial clothing. (5) Use a veil over the open portion of the casket to filter the features and discourage touching of the remains.

459 _____. "Restored Remains Presented After Skull and Chest Were Crushed in an Accident." Casket & Sunnyside 103(7):20 (1973).

Train crash victim's mutilated remains are reconstructed on family's request. After seeing the restored body, they expressed relief that their daughter would not be buried in a mutilated condition.

460 _____. "The Value of Restorative Procedures and Viewing." The Director 39(3):8-9 (1969).
Proper restorations are important for viewing as viewing meets the emotional needs of mourners.

461 Johnson, J. D., and Overby, R. "Stabilized Neutral Ortho-tolidine, Colorimetric Method for Chlorine." Analytical Chemistry 41(13):1744-45 (1969).
Embalming.

462 Jones, Barbara M. Design for Death. New York: Bobbs-Merrill, 1967. 304pp., illus.
Comprehensive account of the world's funeral practices. Discusses such subjects as shrouds, coffins, flowers, tombs, etc.

463 Kansas State Board of Embalming. Embalmers Rules, Laws and Regulations 1924. Topeka: The Board, 1924. 48pp.

464 Kerfoot, Edward J. "Formaldehyde Vapor Emission Study in Embalming Rooms." The Director 42:6-7 (March 1972).
Results of studies on toxic properties of formaldehyde and its effects on embalmers; proposal to lower present allowable safe rate of 5 p.p.m. to 2 p.p.m.

Lamers, Dr. William M., Jr. "Gloom at Funerals Replaced by Color." See entry 1185.

465 Landig, R. Victor, and Garton, W. Melvin. Quiz Compend on Mortuary Science. Houston, TX: Landig College of Mortuary Science, 1948. 345pp.

466 Lenard, J. (tr.) "Biological Membranes--Current Approaches." New York Academy of Science 31 (ser. II):872-78 (1969).
Embalming.

467 Lessley, M. Treatise on Embalming. Toledo, OH: Barkdull Printing House, 1884. 156pp.

468 Leverton, Ivor. "The Funeral Director Point of View." Funeral Service Journal, Aug. 15, 1959.

469 Lewis, H. E. Embalmers' Guide: A Practical and Comprehensive Treatise on Embalming, Together with a Complete Description of the Anatomy of the Human Body, Designed to Accompany the Embalmers' Anatomical Aid. Chicago, IL: Western Pub. House, c. 1890. 219pp., photos, appendix.
Early text on embalming. Covers location and raising of arteries, stomach injection, removal of discoloration, cavity em-

balming, procedures for specific causes of death, blood and the circulatory system, organs, the skeleton, the nervous system, muscles and viscera, and the head.

470 Lyman, D. J. "Findings Clarify Nature of Blood Clotting. " Chemical and Engineering News 47 (Jan. 27, 1969). Information important to embalmers.

471 McCully, Charles H. Sanitation and Disinfection with Special Reference to the Communicable Diseases. Chicago: H. S. Fassett, 1906. 184pp.

472 McCurdy, Charles W. Embalming and Embalming Fluids with the Bibliography of Embalming. Wooster, OH: Herald Printing, 1896. 84pp.

473 Mandelkern, J. , and Villarico, S. "Muscular Contraction. " Chemical and Engineering News 46:14-19 (1968).

474 Marhol, M. , and Cheng, K. L. "Simple Ion Exchange Separation of Magnesium from Calcium and Other Metal Ions Using Ethylene-glycol-Bis (2-Aminoethylether) Tetraacetic Acid as a Complexing Agent. " Analytical Chemistry 42:652-55 (1970).

475 Massachusetts Board of Registration in Embalming. Rules and Regulations; Also List of Registered Embalmers. Boston: Office of the Secretary of the Board, 1913. 48pp. (paper).

476 Maugh, T. "Singlet Oxygen: A Unique Microbicidal Agent in Cells. " Science 182:44-45 (1973).

477 Mayer, J. Sheridan. Color and Cosmetics: The Consummation of Restorative Art. New York: Graphic Arts, 1973. 442pp. , biblio. , glossary, diagrs.
Color principles in pigments, vision, and illumination--introduction; visual aspects, colors in illumination; principles of cosmetology--complexion types and materials, corrective shaping, rouging, wax and cosmetics, types of cosmetics; cosmetic implementation--through demonstrations, practice, application of various types of cosmetics, adaption of rouge and application to the lips and cheeks, treatment of discoloration and waxes.

478 _____ . Restorative Art. Philadelphia: Westbrook, 1943, 430pp. , drawings. ; rev. ed. , Bergenfield, NJ: The Author, 1961, 398pp. , biblio. , index. Available from Casket & Sunnyside (274 Madison Ave. , New York, NY 10016).
Bones of the cranium and face; eminences of the head; facial proportions; forms of the head; muscles of expression, the cranium, mastication, the eye, and the nose; muscles of the mouth; triangles of the neck; lines, wrinkles and folds and restoration of wrinkles; hypodermic tissue building; hair restoration; feature modeling.

479 _____. "Techniques Which You May Find Useful in Building Tissues Hypodermically." Casket & Sunnyside 99(5):24-26 (1969).
New means to fill and clean hypodermic syringes; injection tissue builder at temples and other methods; marginal eye socket correction, cheek and submandibular areas, nose and lip injection, hand treatment. Gradual fill recommended; caution against over-filling.

480 Mayer, Robert. "Embalming Techniques When Uremic Condition Exists." Casket & Sunnyside 105(4):24 (April 1975).

481 Mayer, Robert G., Jr. "Restoration Techniques Where Post-Mortem Gas Fills Tissue." Casket & Sunnyside 102(1):12+ (1973).
Summarizes distinguishing characteristics of ante-mortem emphysema and true tissue gas; detailed steps for treatment presented with front view illustration of the face.

482 _____. "A Review of Procedures for Cavity Embalming." Casket & Sunnyside 103(8):18-20 (Aug. 1973).
Ten suggestions for consistent successful embalming detailed, then summarized at the end of the article.

483 _____. "Three Ways to Preserve Facial Tissues if Carotid Arteries Are Occluded or Missing." Casket & Sunnyside 103 (5):16+ (1973).

484 Meade, Gordon M., and Steenken, William, Jr. "Viability of Tubercle Bacilli in Embalmed Human Lung Tissue." American Review of Tuberculosis 59:429-37 (1949).

485 Mendelsohn, Simon. Embalming Fluids; Their History, Their Development and Formulation, from the Standpoint of the Chemical Aspects of the Scientific Art of Preserving Human Remains. Brooklyn, NY: Chemical Pub. Co., 1940. 166pp., illus.

486 _____. "Embalming from the Medieval Period to the Present Time." In: Ciba Symposia. Summit, NJ: Ciba Pharmaceutical Products, Inc., May, 1944.

_____. "The Mortuary Craft of Ancient Egypt." See entry 140.

487 Michel, Gustave H. Scientific Embalmer: A Treatise on Judicial Embalming, Throwing Light on Very Important Questions Which Had So Far Remained Obscure. Cleveland: The Author, 1913, 95pp., illus.; 1922, 188pp.

488 Myers, Eliab. Champion Text-book on Embalming; A Comprehensive Treatise on the Science and Art of Embalming, Giving the Latest and Most Successful Methods of Treatment,

Including Descriptive and Morbid Anatomy, Physiology, Sanitation, Disinfection, etc. Springfield, OH: Champion Chemical Co., 1908. 665pp.

489 _____, and Sullivan, F. S. Champion Text-book on Embalming.... Springfield, OH: Champion Chemical Co., 1897. 336pp.

490 Nakanishi, M., et al. "Phenoxyethanol: Protein Preservative for Taxonomists." Science 163:681-83 (1969).

491 New York Sanitary Co. Perfect Preservation of the Dead, Without Mutilation, By a New and Simple Process. New York: The Company, 1879. 16pp.

492 Nunnamaker, Albert J., and Dhonau, Charles O. Anatomy and Embalming: A Treatise on the Science and Art of Embalming. Cincinnati, OH: Embalming Book Co., 1913. 367pp., illus.

493 _____ and _____. Anatomy, Descriptive and Operative; The General Anatomy of the Human Body As Arranged for the Convenience of Students of Mortuary Science, Revised by Marion Dee Britt [and] Histology: The General Histology of the Human Body as Arranged for the Students of Mortuary Science. Cincinnati: Embalming Book Co., 1935. 313pp.

494 _____ and _____. Dissecting Guide for Embalmers; An Outline of the Gross Structures of the Human Body. Cincinnati: Embalming Book Co., 1931. 214pp., illus.

495 _____ and _____. Hygiene and Sanitary Science; A Practical Guide for Embalmers, and Sanitarians. Cincinnati: Embalming Book Co., 1913. 276pp., illus.

496 One Hundred Embalming Questions Answered. New York: Casket, c. 1934. 63pp.

497 Parker, Joseph R. Origin of Embalming. Boston: New England Institute of Anatomy and Sanitary Science, n. d. 5pp.
    History of embalming and techniques from 4000 B.C. through 1880; the establishment of the first school of embalming. Concentrates on the ancient Egyptians, Coptics, Hebrews, Babylonians, South Americans, and Barbarian tribes.

498 Pawar, V. M., and Ramakrishnan, J. "Investigations of the Nuclear Polyhedrosis of Prodenia Litura Fabricus: II. Effect of Surface Disinfectants, Temperature and Alkalies on the Virus." Indian Journal of Entomology 33(4):428-32 (1971).

499 Pervier, Norville C. Textbook of Chemistry for Embalmers. Minneapolis: Burgess, 1940; 1946, 214pp; 1956, 306pp.

500 Pine, Vanderlyn R. "Comparative Studies of the Anti-Microbial Effects of Selected Antibiotics Against Micro-Organisms of Embalmed and Unembalmed Bodies." The Director 38:15-17 (Sept. 1968).

501 _____. "The Effectiveness of Embalming on Microbes Isolated from the Mouth." The Director 38:12-14 (Jan. 1968).

502 Prager, G. Joseph. Postmortem Restorative Art. Amelia, OH: The Author, 1955. 164pp., biblio., photos.
    Theoretical and practical information combined to give the restorer a full background in facial and body types, their anatomy, and the particular methods of restoring the body to a pre-death appearance; the anatomy of the head; types of heads and characteristics such as nose types, hair, and color; use of cosmetics and other methods of restoration; practical information on dealing with specific problems.

503 "Public Health and Embalming." Northeast Funeral Director 19(2):10+ (1970).
    Documentation of the infectious nature of unembalmed bodies; ten studies cited where public health was endangered; reference to NFDA-sponsored investigation conducted by Dr. Gordon Rose of Wayne State University (Detroit) which confirms the potential infectiousness of unembalmed corpses.

504 Quinn, Seabury. "Who Was the Father of Modern Embalming." American Funeral Director, May 1944, p. 27-30.

505 Rendon, Leandro. "Application of Common Sense." Champion Expanding Encyclopedia, Oct. 1973.
    Common sense on the job is as important, oftentimes, as scientific knowledge. Criteria to be used in checking the thoroughness of the embalming procedure; suggestions for treating eye and neck area swelling and other localized problems.

506 _____. "Cancer Drugs--Methotrexate." Champion Expanding Encyclopedia, May 1972.

507 _____. "Care of Remains of Deceased in the Armed Forces." Champion Expanding Encyclopedia, April 1970.
    The three branches of the military contract for mortuary services with local funeral directors; specifications to be met to satisfy military standards; discussion of current requirements; two classifications of remains: non-viewable and viewable.

508 _____. "Changes in Remains Resulting from the Embalming Process." Champion Expanding Encyclopedia, n.d.
    Because of medication administered before death, normal embalming chemicals and treatments can cause unexpected results. List and discussion of possible post-embalming changes and probable causes.

509 _____. "Early Reminiscences of Funeral Practices." Champion Expanding Encyclopedia, Nov. -Dec. 1970.
Review of some turn-of-the-century conditions when embalming was considered a fad and before modern techniques were invented.

510 _____. "The 'Elderly' Cases." Champion Expanding Encyclopedia, Feb., March 1971.
Second and third parts of a three-part series on problems the embalmer faces in handling cases of the old-age group. Special note of problems caused by arteriosclerosis, capillary fragility, gangrene, complications from pathology of the respiratory system, cancer, diabetes, malnutrition, emaciation, etc; procedures for overcoming these problems.

511 _____. "Embalmers' Techniques and Practices--Survey Results." Champion Expanding Encyclopedia, Jan., Feb. 1970.
Survey of methods and practices; general statistical information; amount of public interest in embalming; amount of fluid concentrate used; injection and drainage techniques; treatment of cavities and disinfections; special features of fluids. Feb. issue continues special features of fluids; restorative procedures.

512 _____. "Embalming--Indefinite Preservation of the Body." Champion Expanding Encyclopedia, June 1969.
Detailed description of methods of thorough preservation, especially of military personnel being transported long distances.

513 _____. "Formaldehyde Study in Preparation Rooms." Champion Expanding Encyclopedia, March 1973.
Study on the amounts of formaldehyde embalmers are exposed to during the embalming process; results outlined. Rendon, a funeral service licensee, who at the time the article was written was doing graduate work in occupational and environmental health, concludes that ample ventilation must be provided and embalming masks worn, and suggests the possible advisibility of wearing respirator masks when working with powdered preparations.

514 _____. "In Use Evaluation of Glutaraldehyde As a Preservative-Disinfectant in Embalming." Champion Expanding Encyclopedia, Sept. 1973.

515 _____. "Laws and Regulations Governing the Composition and Potency of Embalming Fluids in the United States." Champion Expanding Encyclopedia, Jan., Feb. 1969.
Summary of states' requirements concerning embalming preparations. Jan. issue includes states of Alabama through New Hampshire; Feb. issue New Jersey through Wyoming, with a summation and comments on laws and regulations.

516 _____. "A Look at the Past." Champion Expanding Encyclopedia. July -Aug. 1973.

A look at an 1896 manuscript, "Embalming and Embalming Fluids," written by Charles W. McCurdy, which for many years has been an official reference for the U.S. Patent Office.

517 _____. "Major Restorative Art Procedures--Major and Minor Concepts." Champion Expanding Encyclopedia, May 1969.
Synopsis of survey findings among instructors in mortuary science schools and colleges. Probably the first differentiation between major and minor concepts in restoration.

518 _____. "Mechanics of Proper Drainage." Champion Expanding Encyclopedia, Nov. -Dec. 1973.
Proper placement and handling of auxiliary, jugular, and femoral flexible tube plus suggestions to improve drainage from any site chosen.

519 _____. "More Thoughts on Postmortem Restoration." Champion Expanding Encyclopedia, Feb. 1973.
Results of a survey of restorative art instructors, describing "minor" and "major" restorations; thoughts to keep in mind when deciding which, if either, of the procedures should be used.

520 _____. "Mortuary Affairs Program." Champion Expanding Encyclopedia, Jan. , Feb. 1972.
Historical sketch of preparation and disposition of remains in the military; Civil War preparation may have been the impetus that led to popularization of embalming in the U.S.; history of the Graves Registration Service, which began at the close of the Korean War, continued in Feb. issue; the Saigon mortuary; the program to return casualties from South Vietnam to the states; the military's management of funeral service.

521 _____. "Over-Dehydration in Embalming." Champion Expanding Encyclopedia, April 1972.
The common problem of excess loss of moisture from embalmed tissues is caused by: too strong fluids; high drainage promotion solutions; improper injection and drainage methods; over-massaging while applying cosmetics after embalming; exposure of body to dry air without proper protection. Suggestions for overcoming dehydration problems.

522 _____. "Postmortem Bacteriology." Champion Expanding Encyclopedia, Sept. 1970.
NFDA investigation conducted at Wayne State University determines that micro-organisms in unembalmed human remains proliferate in great numbers; type of bacteria found in the lung and brain tissue; need for proper handling of dead bodies; embalming reduces some of the hazards.

523 _____. "Preparation of Remains in Far Off Places." Champion Expanding Encyclopedia, May 1971.
Care of deceased military personnel is a challenge for

the embalmer; data on remains embalmed in overseas mortuaries during the summer of 1970; quantities of embalming preparations used (useful as a guide to purchasing agents); procedures that permitted long distance shipping.

524 _____. "Principles of Restorative Art." Champion Expanding Encyclopedia, part 1, June 1972; part 2, July-Aug. 1972; part 3, Sept. 1972; part 4, Oct. 1972; part 5, Nov. -Dec. 1972.
　　　1: General description of restorative art, procedures, and review of face measurements; 2: restoration of the ear; 3: mouth, with special attention to lips; 4: restoration of the eye--reduction of swelling, eye lashes, upper and lower lid restorations; 5: restoration of the nose.

525 _____. "Principles of Restorative Art." Champion Expanding Encyclopedia, Jan. 1973.
　　　Last (part 6) in a series of articles describing facial feature restoration; restoration of cases involving cancer and burns on the face.

526 _____. "Products for Use on Jaundiced Remains." Champion Expanding Encyclopedia, June 1971.

527 _____. "A Purpose for Embalming Confirmed." Champion Expanding Encyclopedia, June 1973.
　　　NFDA study pointing up the infectious nature of unembalmed bodies spurred subsequent investigations into the effectiveness of embalming chemicals and the embalming operation in ridding the body of contaminating microbes. Review of the study on the use of 2% alkalinized glutaraldehyde solutions which when properly used leave the body safe for funeral service viewing.

528 _____. "A Purpose for Embalming Reviewed." Champion Expanding Encyclopedia, May 1973.
　　　Preservation, sanitation, and restoration are the main reasons for embalming; sanitation, however, is often overlooked as an objective in the modern trend towards leaving the bereaved with a natural last picture of the dead; NFDA reports on the benefits of embalming from the standpoint of public health.

529 _____. "Scheroderma." Champion Expanding Encyclopedia, March 1970.

530 _____. "Short Circulation and Embalming Problems." Champion Expanding Encyclopedia, Oct. 1971.

531 _____. "Some Properties of Chemical Solutions--Effects on Embalming." Champion Expanding Encyclopedia, June 1970.

532 _____. "Tissue Gas--Cause and Treatment." Champion Expanding Encyclopedia, Sept. 1971.

533 _____ . "The Trocar and Its Proper Use." Champion Expanding Encyclopedia, Nov. -Dec. 1971.
Necessity of properly treating thoracic, abdominal, and pelvic cavities to prevent microbial growths which spread to surrounding tissues and eventually seep into the atmosphere. Review of the trocar, its use, guide for proper trocar treatment, diagram, instructions for reaching all important organs.

534 _____ . "Wilson's Disease: A Cause of Greenish Discoloration?" Champion Expanding Encyclopedia, July-Aug. 1971.

535 Renourd, August. Undertakers' Manual; A Treatise of Useful and Reliable Information, Embracing Complete and Detailed Instruction for the Preservation of Bodies; Also the Most Approved Embalming Methods. Rochester, NY: H. A. Nirdlinger, 1878. 230pp.

536 Rose, Gordon W. , Dr. "Study Finds Unembalmed Remains Can Contaminate." The Director 39(11):6 (1969).
Unembalmed bodies can infect those handling them directly or contaminate storage area. Over 25 recognized and potential pathogens have been recovered from human bodies dead of other than infectious diseases. Argues for embalming no matter what the cause of death to avoid possible contamination.

537 _____ , and Bicknell, Alice K. "The In Vitro Effect of Certain Antibiotics on Cultures Isolated from the Unembalmed Body." Antibiotics and Chemotherapy 3:896-98 (Sept. 1953).

538 _____ , and Hockett, R. N. Health and Laboratory Science 8:75 (1971).

539 Sanders, C. Richard. "The Essentials of Professional Cosmetology." The De-Ce-Co Magazine 63(4):4-5+ (1971).
Open casket viewing is psychologically beneficial to mourners. Cosmetic preparation must look natural and pleasing. Suggestions for obtaining information on grooming habits and general appearance of the deceased. Pre-embalming treatments and embalming procedures basic to successful cosmetology job. How to disinfect, wash, cream, and pose features.

540 _____ . "Professional Cosmetology: Cosmetic Surface Preparation Techniques." The De-Ce-Co Magazine 64(1):12-13+ (1972).
Preliminary surface preparation is the basis for the success or failure of cosmetology. Recommended steps, disinfection and cleaning methods, massage and shaving.

541 _____ . "Professional Cosmetology: Cosmetic Treatment of the Eye," parts 1-4. The De-Ce-Co Magazine 64(2):6-7; 64(3):10-11+; 64(4):10-11+ (1972); 65(1):20-21+ (1973).
1: Pre-embalming and cosmetic preparation of eyeballs, lids, lashes, tear-ducts, eyebrows, with suggestions for disinfecting,

pre-embalming, tinting, and application of cosmetics; 2: continuation of part 1, with emphasis on the problems of discoloration, swelling, and wrinkling; 3: correct coloring procedure and final touches, coloring in a way to compensate for angle in casket which casts unnatural light on reclining figure, step by step treatment of eyebrow and eyelashes; 4: the eyes are the major feature in achieving lifelike appearance in the embalmed body. To achieve characteristic expression they must be treated in conjunction with the mouth, lips, nose, and adjacent facial musculature.

542 _____. "Professional Cosmetology: Cosmetic Treatment of Facial Lines and Natural Markings." The Dodge Magazine 67(2):6ff [5pp.] (March 1975). Illus.
        Treatment of facial lines and natural markings important to achieve natural look and proper age appearance of subject; how to avoid a younger or older or death mask appearance, with detailed review of the basic character of facial lines, naso-labial fold, superior labial groove, forehead, "crows feet," upper and lower eyelid wrinkles, sub-orbital pouch, nose, cheek, lip, old age wrinkles, characteristic marks and treatment techniques guide.

543 _____. "Professional Cosmetology," part V. The Dodge Magazine 65(2):10-11+ (1973).
        Cosmetic treatment of the lips and mouth, the anatomical structure being separated in three categories: mucous membrane, upper lip and lower lip. Pre-embalming techniques and methods to restore each feature to its lifelike form.

544 _____. "Professional Cosmetology," part VI. The Dodge Magazine 65(3):10-11+ (1973).
        Methods for countering the effects of disease, age, dehydration of lips. Step-by-step outline of restorative and cosmetic procedure, including cleansing, basic preparatory steps, restructuring of lip contour, and simulation of lip characteristics. Advantages of various waxes for lip restructuring.

545 _____. "Professional Cosmetology," part VII. The Dodge Magazine 65(4):14-15+ (1973).
        Lip coloring techniques with detailed discussion of the procedures to use on the three kinds of lip surfaces: natural, discolored, and the restored or wax lip; types of commonly used lip-tinting cosmetics; characteristics and use of cosmetic brushes; embalming cosmetics as opposed to commercial beauty aids.

546 _____. "Professional Cosmetology: Posing and Cosmetizing the Hands and Arms." The Dodge Magazine 67(3):6ff [5pp.] (June 1975). Photos, drawing.
        Hands and arms, neglected by many embalmers, deserve the same care as the face and neck; pre-embalming treatments, the three basic hand positions, mechanical positioning, cleansing hands and fingernails.

547 Schroyer, William O. Schroyer's Printed, Illustrated Method

for Removing the Blood in the Arteries and Process of Embalming Dead Bodies. Cincinnati, 1904. Illus.

548 Shor, Murray. "Condition of Body Dictates the Proper Embalming Treatment, Not Cause of Death." Casket & Sunnyside 102(11), (November, 1972).
Condition of the body is affected by temperature, length of time since death when embalming procedure begins, clothing, and airborne bacteria, rather than the cause of death.

549 _____. "How to Treat Facial Features to Obtain the Most Lifelike Appearance." Casket & Sunnyside 102(6):16 (1972).
Detailed description of restoration techniques and positioning of features.

550 Slocum, Ray E. "Autopsy Embalming Problems." The De-Ce-Co Magazine 60(6):6-7, 22-24 (1968); 61(1):10 (1969).

551 _____. Embalming Treatments. Boston: Dodge Chemical, c. 1937. 181pp.

552 _____. "The Slocum Compendium: Clinical Observations." The De-Ce-Co Magazine 62(4):4-5+ (1970). Table.
Methods to cope with the effects of drugs on the corpse, including a chart which outlines specific effects of the various chemotherapeutic agents in embalming applications.

553 _____. "The Slocum Compendium: Clinical Observations." De-Ce-Co Magazine 62(5):12-13+ (1970); 63(2):6-7+ (1971); 63(3):12+ (1971); 63(4):26-27 (1971).

554 _____. "The Slocum Compendium: Clinical Observations." The De-Ce-Co Magazine 64(2):10-11+ (1972).
Continuing discussion of arterial injection, with high and pulsating pressure and a controlled flow rate; outline of advantages of this method; possible risk of distention.

555 _____. "The Slocum Compendium: What Constitutes Embalming," parts 1-8. The De-Ce-Co Magazine 61(2):4 (1969); 61(3):4 (1968); 61(4):4 (1969); 61(5):8 (1969); 61(6):8-9 (1969); 62(1):10-11+ (1970); 62(2):22+ (1970); 62(3):10-11+ (1970).

556 Spriggs, A. O. The Art & Science of Embalming. Springfield, OH: Champion Chemical Co., 1949. 619pp., index, compend of questions, diagrs. Available from Casket & Sunnyside (274 Madison Ave., New York, NY 10016).
History of embalming, reasons, origin; death, decomposition; blood vascular system; preparation; injection and drainage; cavity treatment; special cases; use of cosmetics in restoration; bacteria; disease; chemicals; and anatomy.

557 _____. Champion Restorative Art. Springfield, OH: Champion Chemical Co., 1946. 121pp., drawings, compends of ques-

tions, answers. Available from Casket & Sunnyside (274 Madison Ave., New York, NY 10016).
Basic book on restoration for embalmers; procedures for dealing with stains, burns, cancers, feature rebuilding, hair replacement, reducing swelling, and cosmetics.

558 _____. Champion Textbook on Embalming and Anatomy for Embalmers. Springfield, OH: Champion Chemical Co., 1946. 619pp., photos, drawings, compend of questions, answers.
General text; history and origins of embalming, manifestations of death, process of decomposition; blood and the vascular system; preparation of the body for embalming; raising vessels; fluid dilutions to use; method of injection and drainage; cavity treatment; problems of surface tension of fluids; skin discolorations; specific problems caused by various diseases; preparation of children's bodies, autopsied bodies; cosmetology and body restoration; infectious diseases; anatomy.

559 _____. "Embalming and Funerals in Italy." Champion Expanding Encyclopedia of Mortuary Practice, no. 296 (April 1959).

560 "A Statement on the Status of Embalming in Britain." Funeral Service Journal, Aug. 15, 1959.

561 Strub, Clarence G. "Embalming Can Be Forever--Via Plastic Imbedding." Casket & Sunnyside 100(8):8-10 (1970).
Eliminating oxidation, vaporization, and condensation prolongs preservation. Can be "most nearly achieved" by imbedding the embalmed body in clear plastic or synthetic resin.

562 _____. "Embalming Progress Through the Centuries." Casket & Sunnyside 101(13[centennial issue]):24-29 (1972). Photos.
Historical sketch of embalming; where it began; why; its development as related to a country's cultural and scientific achievements. Modern embalming (begun in the 17th century); its development through the 18th and 19th centuries; early embalming in the U.S.; patents from 1864 through 1879, describing materials, mixtures and techniques; late 19th-centry methods; embalming's role in public health and welfare.

563 _____. "Post Mortem Tissue Damage--Its Causes and Prevention." Casket & Sunnyside 100(2):30-31+ (1970).

564 _____. A Quiz Compend of Mortuary Science. St. Louis: Royal Bond, 1946. 203pp. Available from Casket & Sunnyside (274 Madison Ave., New York, NY 10016).
Questions and answers used to prepare for state licensing exams. Anatomy, microbiology, chemistry, pathology, embalming, restorative art, mortuary administration, and mortuary law.

565 _____. "Why Embalm?" Casket & Sunnyside 100(6):12-14 (1970).

Embalming, the author believes, protects the public health and the emotional health of mourners; embalming chemicals, procedure, post burial chemical and non-chemical protection, and imbedding are discussed.

566 _____, and Frederick, L. G.   The Principles and Practices of Embalming, 4th ed.   Dallas: L. G. Frederick, 1967. 712pp., illus., photos., index.   Available from Casket & Sunnyside (274 Madison Ave., New York, NY 10016).
Modern embalming techniques with introduction overview of sanitation, reverence for the dead, dignity, sympathy, efficiency, confidence; aid in detection of crime; personality requirements for embalmer; terminology; duties and responsibilities; historical sketch of ancient, medieval, and modern embalming; the first call; types of death; signs, tests, chronological order of putrefaction; post mortem changes; the preparation room; vascular anatomy; arterial embalming; the variable factors in embalming; embalming agents; chemical composition of arterial fluids; dilution water; arterial solution; pre-embalming analysis; selection and use of vessels for injection and drainage; injection methods; pressure factor; distribution; blood removal; cavity embalming; embalming the normal case; purge, tissue gas, skin slip; distention; discolorations; transient rigidity; dehydration; causes of embalming failure; anticoagulant and coagulant medical therapy; alcoholism, drug addiction, arteriosclerosis, vascular diseases, and asphyxia; the autopsy; blood diseases; burns and scalds; cachexia, carbon monoxide, carbon tetrachloride poisoning; carcinoma and sarcoma; cerebral hemorrhage; cervical injection; communicable diseases; diseases and injuries of the cranium; decomposed subjects; delayed embalming; diabetes and dropsy; drowning; emphysema; fever and food poisoning; frozen and refrigerated bodies; fungus infections; gangrene; gastro-intestinal diseases; heart disease; infant cases; influenza; jaundice; leukemia; lightening and electricity; lymphatic diseases; malaria; uremia; obesity and preservation of fatty tissue; post-disposal preservation; pregnancy; radiation cases; shipping cases; shock; skin diseases; suppuration; syphilis; tuberculosis; ulceration; and other special cases.

567   Sulkin, S. E., and Pike, R. M.   "Survey of Laboratory-Acquired Infections."   American Journal of Public Health 41(7):769.

568   Sullivan, F. A.   Practical Embalming; The Most Approved Methods of Arterial Embalming and Cavity Injection.   Boston: Egyptian Chemical Co., 1887.   104pp.

569   _____.   Sullivan's Catechism.   Boston: Egyptian Chemical Co., 1892.   37pp.

570   Tennessee State Board of Embalmers.   Embalmer's Law. Nashville, TN: The Board, 1914.   42pp.

571   White, Trentwell M., and Sandrof, Ivan.   "The First Embalmer."   The New Yorker, Nov. 7, 1942.
Dr. Thomas Holmes, who claimed to be the father of modern embalming.   In 1863 he invented and patented process of

preserving bodies by electroplating. Lively, informative sketch, although some of the details of Holmes's work and claims are disputed.

> Winlock, Herbert E. Materials Used at the Embalming of King Tut' Ankhaman. See entry 253.

572 Winters, Elwood J. Chemistry and Toxicology for the Embalmer. New York: McAllister School of Embalming, 1939. 216pp., appendix, diagrs.
Text for student embalmers, simply written; inorganic chemistry; organic chemistry; toxicology from simple theory (valence, periodic table) to the practical.

> Wyoming State Board of Embalmers. Embalming Laws of the State of Wyoming. See entry 1093.

3. FUNERAL ECONOMICS AND BUSINESS TECHNIQUES

573 "Accord Is Reached in Funeral Talks." New York Times cxxi (41, 643):58 (Jan. 29, 1972).
Report on the Teamsters Union and New York State Funeral Directors Association contract.

574 "Accounting Method Introduced at Professional Conferences." Casket & Sunnyside 105(4):20ff[4pp.] (April 1975). Photos.
Report of NFDA Professional Conference Series events, highlighting NFDA Research and Analysis Consultant Dr. Vanderlyn Pine's presentation: his new method of recording expenses and quoting prices. His method enables the funeral director to determine costs accurately and quote prices for regular or adaptive services.

575 "Ads to Tell What to Expect from Funeral Director." Advertising Age 36:42 (Feb. 8, 1965). Illus.

576 "America's 100 Richest Negroes." Ebony xvii(7), May 1962. Profits from Negro funerals.

577 Arkin, Joseph. "Insurance Consultants Can Help." Mortuary Management 59(1):32-34 (1972).
Consultants paid by the hour can give funeral directors valuable advice on insurance costs, coverage, and point out areas where they are overinsured.

578 Barnard, Howard P. "Business Survival" [editorial]. Casket & Sunnyside 105(4):10 (April 1975).
Many funeral directors and suppliers need better business methods. Recommended are (1) Dr. Vanderlyn Pine's new method, applicable for both single and multiple unit pricing methods, which

insures accurate estimates and quotes of costs for regular and
adaptive funerals. (2) A simple cost accounting system designed by
the Casket Manufacturers Association.

579 _____. "Industry-wide Cooperation" [editorial]. Casket &
      Sunnyside 105(7):8 (July 1975).
      A plea for competitive and conflicting branches of funeral
service to work out their problems for their mutual good. Their
common problems and common goal--that of serving the public--are
greater than their differences.

580 Barnett, Jim. "Community Events Listed in Mortuary's Adver-
      tising." Casket & Sunnyside 102(11):14+ (1972). Illus.
      Public relations success scheme: New Jersey Funeral
Home allows weekly advertising space in its newspaper to civic,
charity, and public service groups. Ad layout samples.

581 Barron, J. F. "Business and Professional Licensing--Cali-
      fornia, a Representative Example." Stanford Law Review
      18:641 (1965-1966).

582 Beck, John C. "The Casket Industry Begins to Catch Up with
      the Times." Casket & Sunnyside 99(8):22-23, 40 (1969).
      History and forecast for industry by retiring president of
the Casket Manufacturers Association of America. Warns against
over-optimism as industry has always been influenced by current
(and often short-lived) trends. Predicts greater reliance on mass
production and mass marketing methods.

583 Becker, Glenn. "A Funeral Director's Date with 300 High
      School Girls." The Director 42, Sept. 1972.
      Lawton, Ok., funeral director lists questions and areas
of concern of interested group of high school girls. Their estimates
of the average cost of a funeral exceeded the true cost by almost
$1000.

584 Bedford, Jack. "Do As You Are Told." Mortuary Management
      59(5):52-54 (1972).
      Crash course on how to give employees instructions.

585 Berg, William M. "Meet Median Mort." Mortuary Manage-
      ment 56(10):38 (1969).
      Report on the Foran Statistics findings of 1968, pointing
out the national average of revenue and expense of funeral directors.

586 _____. "Meet Nolan Noftl." Mortuary Management 57(2):
      18 (1970).
      Report on the NFDA Survey of Non-Owner Full-Time Li-
censed Employees in Funeral Service: wages, working conditions,
fringe benefits, and employee attitudes covered.

587 _____. "Mortuary Management Interview." Mortuary Man-
      agement 57(12):17-22 (1970).

Interview with Robert L. Waltrip ("Mr. Funeral Director") at Service Corp. International, a multi-unit operation. Policies at SCI, like those of independents, Waltrip says, are geared to serve the public interest.

588 Blackwell, Roger D. "Price Levels in the Funeral Industry." Quarterly Review of Economics and Business 7:75-84 (winter 1967).

589 _____, and Talarzyk, W. Wayne. "Market Segmentation in the Funeral Profession." Mortuary Management 62(1):32ff [5pp.] (1975). Photo.
Both authors are Ohio State University professors and affiliated with Management Horizons, Inc., a Columbus consulting and research firm. Article explains the concepts of marketing, marketing by non-profit organizations, marketing of professional services, the basics of market segmentation ("the process of so designing or featuring a product or service that it will make a particularly strong appeal to some identifiable subpart of a total market"), methods of segmenting markets (geographic, demographic, behavioral), market segmentation applied to funeral firm management, the development of the product offering, facilities, and how market segmentation will help the future of funeral service.

Blair, William M. "Trust Action Charges Coercion to Prevent Funeral Price Ads." See entry 920.

590 Bochra, Thomas A. "What a Funeral Costs." Mortuary Management 56(10):40 (1969).
National prize-winning speech. Breakdown of typical funeral service bill showing costs funeral director incurs.

591 Brennan, William E. "Planning for Profits: A Compensation Method Based Upon Time and Talent, Not Merchandise." The American Funeral Director 98(3):54-58 (1975). Photo, summary charts.
In order to "achieve a renewed sense of self esteem" and to highlight "the key contribution of his profession--service to others at the time of their bereavement," Brennan recommends the funeral director emphasize his skills and the time he devotes to a particular case rather than merchandise. How to draw up a practical method for pricing these intangible services; steps to be taken in drawing a profit plan--the return on investment, constant costs, programmed and direct costs, number and type of funerals, revenue, billing rates. An annual plan for profits for a hypothetical funeral home is outlined.

592 Bryan, H. Cloud. Funeral Director's Guide: Gives at a Glance--Several Prices on Each Casket, with Quality of Trimmings Apportioned Accordingly. Pittsburgh: The Author, 1917. 43pp.

593 "Budget--Budget Who Has the Budget." Mortuary Management 59(3):16 (1972).

Guidelines to help establish a funeral home budget; ways to stay within that budget; emphasis on use of cost analysis as good way to keep costs down.

594 Buell, Gary A. "Immediate Disposition and the Affluent Family." Mortuary Management 62(1):25ff[2pp.] (Jan. 1975). Photo.
    Past president of the Oregon Funeral Directors Association and owner-manager of the Buell Chapel, Springfield, Ore., shows that by "carefully developing a meaningful service, which conforms to our families' needs and personal values, they become aware of the value, and are willing to pay for it." The key to insuring the funeral's marketability is adaptability. It must meet the needs of a new generation with new sets of cultural values, provide for their emotional needs, and help them through the grieving process. Tips on how to do this, what to provide, meaningful ceremonies, informing families that caskets are not mandatory, etc.

595 Buell, Rex. "Funeral Service: 1980." Mortuary Management 56(6):10-11 (1969).
    Forecasts the future look of the funeral industry based on current trends such as corporate ownership of funeral homes, chain operation, greater specialization and requirements for higher education.

596 "Burial Costs Increase." New York Times cxxii(42,015):32 (Feb. 4, 1973).
    Archdiocese of Boston raises funeral fees 12% to 20%.

597 Bustard, William L. "Let the Seller Beware." Casket & Sunnyside 100(2):15+ (1970).
    Executive Secretary of the NSM comments on sale or divestiture, evaluation of real value of organization, how properly to protect interests. Advises directors to consult experts.

598 _____. "Some Comments on Funeral Service Pricing and Quotation Methods." Canadian Funeral Service 50(5):1+; 50(7):5+ (1972).
    Speech by the executive secretary of the NSM at the spring 1972 dinner meeting of the Metro Toronto Funeral Directors Association. Though service oriented, funeral profession should use sound business principles; exposes problems of the "average overhead" theory and fragmented quotation.

599 _____, and Nichols, Charles H. "Successful Funeral Service Practice--Funeral Service Pricing." Mortuary Management 60(5):28 (1973).
    Historical development of the various types of pricing methods commonly used by funeral directors; analysis and pros and cons of using each.

600 Caldwell, Worth W., Jr. "Doing New Things In New Ways." Casket & Sunnyside 101(11):28+ (1971).

President of a Portland, Ore., Funeral Home stresses
need of evaluating practices to determine their worth. Examples:
changing the name mortuary to funeral home; replacing television
advertising with media that would reach local areas which supply
90% of his business; need to provide opportunity for prearrangement
of funerals; psychological value of traditional funerals; need for better public relations for funeral service industry.

601 "Calendars: Effective Advertising Signs." Mortuary Manage-
     ment 58(6):18 (1971).
     Recommends advertising by calendars as they meet select
target audience effectively; describes various styles available.

602 "Canada Reports Rise in Funeral Costs." The American Funer-
     al Director 97(10):32 (Oct. 1974).
     Official Canadian Government survey reports average cost
increase from 1968 to 1972; breakdown of brackets--stillborn, children, adults, indigents, ship-ins; distribution of receipts by costs--
funeral services, vault sales, miscellaneous items, and operating
expenses.

603 Casket Manufacturers Association. Facts and Figures on the
     Burial Casket Industry. Chicago: CMA, n.d. (Pamphlet.)
     Who makes burial caskets, where, how caskets are sold,
how they are made, how many are used annually, dollar volume of
the casket industry, products used in casket making.

604 _____. Your Dues Investment ... What Return Do You Get?
     Evanston, IL: CMA, n.d. (Pamphlet.)
     Full membership dues to casket manufacturers and distrib-
utors who sell caskets to funeral directors are assessed at $1 per
$1000 of gross sales up to $1 million annually and $.50 per $1000
of gross sales over $1 million. Minimum $200 and maximum
$10,000. Associate memberships open to firms which sell caskets
to other than funeral directors and firms that supply the casket industry or funeral directors with textiles, hardware, fluids, etc.
Dues from $200 to $1000 a year. Service provided by CMA include
seminars, meetings, annual convention, information distribution,
business survey reports, marketing and mortality statistics program,
credit information, collection service, freight bill auditing, rate quotations, insurance, safety manual, legal counsel, and public relations
manual.

605 Chern, Cyril. "It's Your Business: Corporation." Mortuary
     Management 60(4):16-22 (1973).
     Advantages and disadvantages of incorporating a funeral
home with mention of Sub-Chapter S corporations, pension plans,
profit sharing, medical and life insurance, and how incorporating
affects them.

606 _____. It's Your Business: Estate Planning." Mortuary
     Management 60(10):32-34 (1973).
     Suggestions for funeral directors when planning their own
estates as well as advising clients who seek help in this area.

607 Church, Norman A. "Advertising Facts--Newspaper Ads That Sell." Mortuary Management 59(2):14-18 (1972).
 Extensive research shows newspaper and phone book Yellow Pages are the best medium to reach prospective audience at the lowest cost. Chart showing why women called particular funeral homes, in order of preference. Women were over thirty, with moderate to strong religious feelings.

608 _____. "Community Research Can Open New Avenues to Volume Increases." Mortuary Management 58(4):22-23 (1971).
 Follow up to earlier Mortuary Management article entitled "How to Find Out What Families Really Think About Your Services with Do's and Don'ts in Making a Survey." See entry 609.

609 _____. "How to Find Out What Families Really Think About Your Services." Mortuary Management 58(2):22-23 (1971).
 Three ways of finding out: eyeball research, share of market research, and community research, the most important in learning what the public thinks about clients and competitors. Six necessary items for survey listed. See entry 608.

610 _____. "Sell Yourself First--Personalized Newspaper Advertising." Mortuary Management 58(8):12 (1971).
 Suggests once a week every week advertising, Tuesday, Wednesday, or Monday, telling about your unique experience, personality, services, etc.

611 _____. "Ten Ways to Build Business Through Advertising." Mortuary Management 56(9, 10, 11), 1969.
 In No. 9 emphasis is on the funeral director's selling himself; advises 5% of gross income should be set aside for advertising. 10: Choosing the right media; advantages and disadvantages of various media; what makes an ad good. 11: Small ads not good; best sizes; best days to advertise; best places to put ad in newspaper (not on the obit page!).

612 _____. "Ten Ways to Build Your Business Through Advertising." Mortuary Management 56(12):12 (1969); 57(1):20 (1970); 57(2):16-17 (1970); 57(3):20-21 (1970); 57(4):26-28 (1970).
 Be sincere--no smart-alecky business; strike balance between sincerity and selling, low-keyed ads; frequent smaller ads more effective than occasional large ones; get high visibility through use of top art and production quality; square mug shots better than head shots; importance of a strong logotype (signature) for the funeral home; effectiveness of direct mailing if not junk mail; prepare good-looking booklets; types of direct mail advisable; 20 public relations and four publicity ideas.

613 _____. "Ten Ways to Build Your Business Through Advertising--Point of Purchase." Mortuary Management 57(5):48-50 (1970).
 Merchandising points regarding casket design and display; sales techniques; importance of clear explanations to purchasers

such as why prices vary. If suggestions are followed, sales should pick up.

614   Clark, Thomas H.   "Mergers, Acquisitions and Multi-Unit Organizations. "   The Director 39(9):14-18 (1969).
    Advantages and disadvantages of mergers; various types of mergers; methods of financing.   Warning against depersonalization of service if service is subordinated to profits.

615   _____, and Raether, Howard C.   "Mergers, Acquisitions and Multi-Unit Organization. "   Mortuary Management 58(4): 24-30 (1971).
    Advantages and disadvantages; when mergers are not beneficial; two main reasons for merging: need for resources that are accessible only to larger forms and where there are problems of management secession or estate.

"Competitors Helping Each Other. "   See entry 280.

616   "A Consumer's Guide to Funerals. "   Northeast Funeral Director 22(9):8 (1973).
    Explanation of several methods of quoting prices: single unit, bi-unit, functional (itemization) methods; NFDA 1971 survey of statistics on funeral prices, directors' investment in facilities and equipment, funeral directors' expenses; discussion of interment versus cremation and monument versus marker; suggestions for families.

617   Crane & Breed Manufacturing Co.   Better Ways for Better Business; A Business Partner in Type Devoted to Fundamental Success Methods and their Application to the Funeral Directing Business.   Cincinnati: Crane & Breed, 1921.   425pp.

618   Curt, Claus A.   "A Way to Answer the Questions of Youth. "   The Director 39(1):15 (1969).
    Summary of funeral director's program presented to visiting youth group: reception, brief history of funeral practices, outline of modern funeral procedures, tour of funeral home including preparation and selection rooms, discussion, religious significance of the funeral, funeral service as a career, question and answer period.

619   Dhonau, Charles O.   Management.   Available from Casket & Sunnyside (274 Madison Ave. , New York, NY 10016).   n. d.

620   Dianis, John E.   "Direct Line: Death Rates. "   Monument Builder News April 1975, p. 35.
    How to use statistics; what they mean to potential sales; how to analyze your community in terms of market potential; how to chart sales and profit for the year.

621   "Difficult Journeys; Service-Based Business Explains Itself Through Service Oriented News on Television. "   Sponsor 20:48-49 (June 13, 1966).

622 Doerschlag, Wolfgang. "Best Investment Reasonable Return."
     Mortuary Management 60(8):14-16 (1973).
     Specifics to assist the funeral director to construct a new
funeral home; how to evaluate a trade area for bringing in business;
the amount of property necessary; how much one should invest in
land, buildings; zoning; building codes; how to raise business areas
property values.

623 Dougherty, Philip H. "Advertising: A Funeral Plan." New
     York Times cxxiii(42, 251):48 (Sept. 28, 1973).
     Halsted & Co. in San Francisco has award-winning ads
according to Esquire.

624 Duvall, William H. "Speak for the Funeral." The Director
     39(6):12 (1969).
     Funeral director tells how he lectures to seminary classes.
Recommends such lectures as a good way to promote better relations
with clergy.

625 Ebeling, R. A. "NFDA Professional Conference." Mortuary
     Management 59(4):12-14 (1972).
     Summary of the activities and speeches given at the sixth
NFDA Professional Conference held March 23-24 in Reno, Nevada.
Speeches by Walczak, Berg and Daugherty, Griffin and Slater, Levoy,
and Executive Director Howard Raether of the NFDA reviewed.

626 Ebner, Jack G. "Private Thoughts on Public Relations."
     Casket & Sunnyside 101(1):25+ (1971).
     The art of getting along with people is more important in
funeral service than in most other professions. Practical approaches
to avoid making bad impressions.

627 Edmands, Michael J. "Dying Business? Young Entrepreneurs
     Have Brought New Vigor to Funeral Parlors, Cemeteries."
     Barron's 49(34):5, 15 (Aug. 25, 1969). See also entry 628.

628 _____. "Undertaker to Entrepreneur; Thanks to Modern
     Management Funeral Parlors Are Thriving." Barron's 51(31):
     11, 15, 17 (Aug. 2, 1971).
     Chains; business analysis.

629 _____. "Young Entrepreneurs Have Brought New Vigor to
     Funeral Parlors." Northeast Funeral Director 18(9):7, 18
     (1969). Also appeared in Barron's (see entry 627).
     Large funeral home companies that have been taken over
by chains or are part of conglomerates; the Oak Ridge Mausoleum
near Chicago, the Rock of Ages Corp. in Barre, Vt., the Funeral
Homes of America, the National Casket Co., and the Boyertown
Burial Casket Co. discussed, among others. Higher mortality partly
the cause of recent upswing in funeral business.

630 Elliott, J. Richard, Jr. "The Funeral Business." Barron's
     Financial Weekly, April 11, 1955.

631 Engel, J. F., and Blackwell, R. D. "Understanding the Con-
     sumer." ESCO Public Relations for F.D.'s 1-9, 2d qtr.,
     1969.
         Aid to funeral directors in improving their marketing;
basic model of consumer patterns, carrying purchaser's decision-
making process through five steps: problem recognition, external
search for alternatives, evaluation, purchase, and post-purchase
evaluation. Funeral director should adapt to changes demanded by
market because he can't alter individuals' predispositions.

632 Fair, Ernest W. "Getting Along with Other Funeral Directors."
     Casket & Sunnyside 100(4):30 (1970).
         Practical advice on giving advice and criticism, association
activities, working out local problems, and complementing colleagues.

633 _____. 'How to Make Decisions and Avoid Ulcers." Casket
     & Sunnyside 100(7):18-20 (1970).
         Recommendations to promote relaxation, avoid confusion;
good all-around advice for the executive.

634 _____. "Is Some Employee Always Mad at You?" Mortuary
     Management 58(5):16+ (1971).
         Seven most frequent complaints and how to handle employee
problems.

635 _____. "Where--Oh--Where?" Mortuary Management 59
     (5):26-28 (1972).
         Why increasing monies are lost by the funeral home opera-
tion although more money is coming in: losses due to reduction in
employee efficiency; fear of raising prices to profitable limit resulting in loss of business; failure to collect debts; supply wastes; buying unnecessary luxury items; poor, outdated bookkeeping; overpay-
ing taxes; other cost problems and suggestions for overcoming them.

636 Farrell, William E. "Legislature Votes 48-Hour Deadline for
     Cemetery Strike." New York Times cxix(40,948):1, 28 (March
     5, 1970).
         New York City Cemetery Strike.

637 "Federal Ambulance Study Spotlights Problem Areas." Ameri-
     can Funeral Director 92(7):27-28; (8):33-34 (1969).
         Analysis of U.S. Dept. of Transportation's National High-
way Safety Bureau report. Shows how funeral homes participate in
America's national highway emergency ambulance service and the
problems involved.

638 "Flint Mortuaries Carry Public Service Advertising." Casket
     & Sunnyside 105(5):38 (May 1975).
         Michigan funeral directors' advertising of interest to others.
Example: "Do people really prefer to be alone in their grief? No.
Being alone makes the pain harder to bear. That's why you should
go to the funeral of relatives and friends and make a condolence or
sympathy visit, too."

639 Foran, Eugene F. Funeral Service Facts and Figures; The
      Findings of a Survey of 1958 Funeral Service Income and Ex-
      pense Data Conducted by Eugene F. Foran for the National
      Funeral Directors Association of the United States, Inc. Mil-
      waukee, WI: NFDA, 1959. 37pp., charts, map.

640 _____. Funeral Service Facts and Figures: The Findings
      of a Survey of 1960 Funeral Service Income and Expense Data
      Conducted by Eugene F. Foran for the National Funeral Di-
      rectors Association of the United States, Inc. Milwaukee,
      WI: NFDA, 1961. 38pp., charts, map.

641 _____. Funeral Service Uniform Accounting Record. Mil-
      waukee, WI: NFDA, n.d.
         Complete reproduction of the Uniform Classification of
      Accounts recommended for funeral service use. Explanation of a
      simple numbering system using three-digit numbers for control
      accounts and one- or two-digit numbers for subsidiary expense de-
      tail. Identifies balance sheet accounts and operating statement ac-
      counts. Section 1: Summaries of Operating Data; forms for State-
      ment of Assets, Liabilities and Net Worth and for Statement of In-
      come, Costs and Expenses; Firm "Income-Pattern" Chart; Depreci-
      ation schedule. Examples of entries for sections 2 (Funeral Service
      Income Analysis and Direct Cost items) and 3 (Funeral Service
      General Journal Record). Additional blank sheets available from
      the NFDA.

642 _____, and Raether, Howard C. "Part V--Funeral Service
      Income and Expense" (from the Raether book, Successful
      Funeral Service Practice). Mortuary Management 59(8):30-32
      (1972). (See entry 702.)
         Cost accounting for those starting their own or purchasing
      a funeral home. Analyzes how cost accounting should be set up based
      on NFDA surveys and consultation with public accountants.

      _____, and _____. "Successful Funeral Service Practice--
      Business Aspects of a Funeral Service Practice." See entry
      1047.

643 _____, and Slater, Robert C. "Part III--Funeral Home
      Practices" (from the Raether book, Successful Funeral Service
      Practice). Mortuary Management 59(5):22-24 (1972). (See
      entry 702.)
         Lists the most effective means of motivating non-owner
      employees: advancement opportunity, wages, interesting work, job
      security, good working conditions, fringe benefits, easy work.

      Franz, Anne Hamilton. Funeral Direction and Management.
      See entry 296.

644 "Funeral Chauffeurs' Union Votes to Strike Next Week." New
      York Times cxviii(40, 542):23 (Jan. 23, 1969).
         New York City chauffeurs' union votes to strike January
1969.

645 "Funeral Cost Question Turning into Ad Hassle; Undertaker
      Groups Hit CBS. " Advertising Age 34:1 (Oct. 28, 1963).

646 "Funeral Directors End Strike. " New York Times (42,328):
      51 (Dec. 14, 1973).
          New York City strike.

647 "Funeral Insurance Firms Fail in Alabama. " American Funeral
      Director 98(5):48 (May 1975).
          30,000 Alabama residents hold $35,000,000 in worthless
burial policies as 11 funeral insurance companies go bankrupt.

648 "Funeral Workers Win a 50.9% Raise. " New York Times cxx
      (41,177):89 (Oct. 20, 1970).
          New York City funeral strike.

649 Griffin, Glenn, and Slater, Robert. "Successful Funeral Serv-
      ice Practice--Chapter 5--Business Aspects of a Funeral
      Service" (from the Raether book, Successful Funeral Service
      Practice). Mortuary Management 60(3):30-31 (1973). Illus. ,
      charts. (See entry 702.)
          Charts, illustrations, and text explaining to the funeral di-
rector how to establish the quartile divisions of a casket selection
room.

650 Hardy, William G. , Jr. "Florida Showcase. " Mortuary Man-
      agement 56(1):8-9 (1969).
          Transcript of unrehearsed television interview with past
NFDA president. Panel of laymen throws questions on costs, caskets,
embalming, memorial societies, price advertising, pre-arrangements,
and need for funerals.

651 Head, Ralph H. "The Obligation to Advise. " Mortuary Manage-
      ment 62(1):24ff [2pp.] (Jan. 1975). Photo.
          The funeral director's obligation is to determine what the
family means if it requests a minimum funeral--cheap, simple, bare
essentials of disposing of the body, private?--and then provide the
appropriate services at a cost the family can afford. Recommends
functional pricing method where the cost of the casket is separated
from the charge for services, facilities, etc. , providing minimum
funerals if the family wants them, and providing impoverished families a decent funeral even if they are unable to pay. Mr. Head is
chairman of the Board of Directors of Pierce National Life Insurance
Co. of California and an active trustee of the NFFS.

652 Hill, J. Gordon. "Accounting for Morticians. " In: J. K. Las-
      ser, ed. , Handbook of Accounting Methods (New York: Van
      Nostrand, 1943), p. 879-889.

653 Hunter, Bud D. 'Hunter of AFS Disclaims Interest in Funeral
      Homes. " Casket & Sunnyside 100(10):24 (1970).
          American Funeral Supply Corp. has taken over International
Order of Golden Rule's services. Author explains it is not associated with funeral chain or competing with funeral directors; owns

"fluid" houses, insurance companies, securities corporations, advertising agencies, casket houses, etc. Predicts industry will expand and become more complex in the 1970's.

654 "In Starting a Business Should You Buy Existing Funeral Home or Build Your Own Facility?" Casket & Sunnyside 102(8):19 (1972).
      Clear analysis of pro's and con's.

655 "Investing in Funeral Home Industry Pays Off." Northeast Funeral Director 19(7):12 (1970).
      Reprinted from the Wall Street Journal. Analysis of three publicly owned funeral home chains--Funeral Homes of America, Service Corp. International, and International Funeral Services, among others. Trend towards merger could raise cost of buying a funeral home.

656 Irvin, Dolores. "Big Funeral Homes vs. Small--How They Do It." Casket & Sunnyside 101(11):12-13 (1971).
      Horis A. Ward's funeral home in Decatur, Ga. Established in 1959, it has grown from 145 services during the year of its creation to 800 in 1970. A staff of 50, including 12 directors and 10 embalmers, handle the work. Design, equipment, functional architectural design, selection rooms, chapel, family rooms, landscaping, and services discussed.

657 Janssen, William. "Expose--The Milwaukee Funeral Service Youth Association--A Practical New Approach to Exposing Youth to Funeral Service." Mortuary Management 59(6):30-31 (1972).
      Youth association sponsored by the Milwaukee County Funeral Directors Association works to correct misconceptions young people have of funeral service and to explore the field of mortuary science--funeral training, public health, law, religion, and other related topics.

658 Kates, Albert R. "We May Soon Find It Harder to Enlist Qualified Recruits." American Funeral Director 94(8):35+ (1971).
      Candidates for funeral service are being drawn off by paramedical programs.

659 Kelly, Lorne. "Help Wanted to Tell Our Story." The Director 41(7):2 (1971).
      The President of the Canadian Funeral Directors Association says that it's the responsibility of funeral directors to inform themselves in order to present the best possible image to the public. They can get out and talk about their problems, but from knowledge, not ignorance.

      Kline, James E. "Phase II--Wage Price Stabilization Campaign." See entry 861.

660 Krieger, Wilber M. A Complete Guide to Funeral Service

Management. Englewood Cliffs, NJ: Prentice-Hall, 1962.
299pp., illus.
Predecessor to the Raether book, Successful Funeral
Service Practice (see entry 702).

661 _____. Successful Funeral Service Management. New York:
Prentice-Hall, 1951. 466pp., index, photos, appendix.
Complete guide for the funeral director beginning with how
to enter the business, necessary characteristics, and managerial
responsibilities by the managing director of NSM and director of
NFFS. How to set up and finance a funeral home, select a location, the necessary investment and working capital. How to secure
and hold business, including advertising, attracting and satisfying
customers. Successful management procedures, the selection room,
inventory control, accounting, records, collections, letters, insurance,
and personnel. Conclusion explores the problem of ethics vis-à-vis
success tactics. State licensing rules listed.

662 Lasser, J. K., ed. Handbook of Accounting Methods. New
York: Van Nostrand, 1943. 1349pp.
Chapter by J. Gordon Hill entitled "Accounting for Morti-
cians.

663 Levin, Kimberly. "Professional Consultation--It's Worth Investigating." Mortuary Management 56(11):36-37 (1969).
Points out where money can be saved and benefits available to each size mortuary. Advocates use of consultants.

664 Locke, Donald C. "Functional Pricing." Canadian Funeral
Service 47(8):23-25; 47(9):23-26; 47(10):23-26 (1969).
Three-part series by the Director of Merchandising Services, International Order of the Golden Rule. Summary of the historical background; developments leading to the necessity of publicizing funeral charges; "the interpretation and annexation of functional pricing" and example of suitable income/expense relationships;
how to determine specific costs; administration and presentation of
functional pricing: recommended wording of price card, preselection
explanation for charges. Functional pricing credit system has improved customer satisfaction and sales over the traditional unit
pricing system, author believes.

665 Loebl, Elizabeth. "How to Train an Assistant." Casket &
Sunnyside 102(1):22-23 (1972).
Seven points director should follow in training his assistant
to understand the job, its needs and problems, and management
principles.

666 Lowes, Earl. "Mortuary Stresses Employee Relations." Casket & Sunnyside 102(9):10+ (1972).
Max Comstock, president of the Comstock Funeral Home
in Peterborough, Ont., points out the importance of good employ-
ment and personnel management practices. To get employee's loy-
alty and ultimate performance, recommends offering competitive

wages and fringe benefits, hiring only carefully screened applicants, thoroughly training new personnel and providing advancement and salary raise opportunities.

667 "Lucrative Investments. " New York Times cxxi(41, 560): sect. III, p. 3 (Nov. 7, 1971).
Corporate ownership of funeral homes.

668 Matthews, William F. "Positive Public Relations. " Casket & Sunnyside 101(5):12-18 (1971).
Good public relations needed to counteract bad publicity of the 1960's. Includes "A Resume of the Values of the Funeral" and "A Program for Every Funeral Service Manager. "

669 Meola, Louis F. "Carelessness and Poor Tax Advice Can Put You In Jail, But You Don't Have to Be a Millionaire to Save on Taxes. " Casket & Sunnyside 99(5):16-18, 48, 50, 83 (1969).
Case study of a funeral director who went to prison for tax evasion. Common pitfalls, most of them due to carelessness, and how to avoid them; tips on how to save money. One way: establish a foundation.

670 _____. "An Easy Way to Prepare Your Own Tax Returns. " American Funeral Director 96(2):24-28 (1973). Charts.
Certified Public Accountant gives short-cuts to prepare tax forms for the funeral director who does not maintain complete books but does keep a check book and a funeral register. Sample charts help clarify procedure. Author recommends operations which handle more than 100 funerals per year hire a certified public accountant.

671 _____. "How to Prepare Your Form 1040. " American Funeral Director 93(2):30-32 (1970).
Nationally known public accountant in the funeral service field recommends ways for filling out Schedule C--the business section. Detailed steps outlined, work sheets, charts and when it is more economical to call in a CPA or tax expert rather than preparing your own forms.

672 _____. "IRS Agents May Force You to Shift from Cash Basis. " American Funeral Director 93(6):29-30 (1970).
Landmark case where Treasury Dept. may insist that funeral homes change to an accrual basis. Analysis of an appeal (by Wilkinson-Beane, Inc. , mortuary in Laconia, NH) of a tax court decision which upheld a deficiency assessment against it. U. S. Court of Appeals said the mortuary should have used the accrual method. Detailed explanation of the two methods of accounting.

673 _____. "Itemization May Increase Your Total Profit Margin. " American Funeral Director 96(8):22-24 (1973).
Itemization regulations can be a boon to funeral directors. Analysis of various state laws. Charts and references available upon request from the author.

674 _____ . "Now's the Time to Review Your Income Tax Status." American Funeral Director 95(11):26-27 (1972).
Detailed discussion of legal ways to reduce income tax paid by funeral directors.

675 _____ . "Out-of-Pocket Payments." American Funeral Director 96(9):28-31 (1973).
List and explanation of ways funeral directors can keep records of cash expenditures in order to save time, money, and both at tax time. The author is a certified public accountant specializing in funeral home accounting procedures. Funeral merchandizing forms available from author on request.

676 _____ . "Should You Incorporate?" American Funeral Director 93(11):29-30 (1970).
Certified Public Accountant gives benefits of incorporating: pension programs similar to other corporate business; ability to participate in sick pay plan, group term insurance; ability to bypass corporate tax and death benefit exclusion provisions.

677 "Merchants of Death." Forbes Magazine 106:59 (Nov. 15, 1970). Photos.
Analysis of the large companies that are acquiring chains of funeral homes--reasons for corporate interest in funeral industry; cost figures of operating successful mortuaries (one of the deterents to corporate interest); advantages held by individual owners when negotiating with chain owners.

678 Miller, Miriam McD. "A Taxpayer's Briefing." Mortuary Management 57(2):14 (1970); 57(10):24+ (1970).
Variety of tax cases involving funeral directors. Brief summary of current IRS procedures and practices related to the 1969 tax reform act. Attention to the special withholding tables, computation of taxes by IRS for individuals, and related items concerning deductions.

679 Mulholland, John F. "Borthwick's in Honolulu." Mortuary Management 60(1):20 (1973).
William Borthwick's successful funeral home operations described, his influence in the mortuary profession; detail of cemeteries in Hawaii.

680 "Multi-Unit Operations: Advantages of Branches Shown by Kraeer Florida Mortuaries." American Funeral Director 92(5):30-32 (1969).
Nationally prominent Florida funeral director cites the advantages of opening branches to funeral home and community: easy accessibility to people who are served; lessening traffic problems; increased efficiency by switching personnel to branches with heaviest work load; cut down idle time; improved use of equipment, especially vehicles; central purchasing to take advantage of discounts; attracting better personnel with better salaries, advancement potential, benefits; shared experiences and exchange of ideas promote better methods.

681 National Funeral Directors Assoc.   Code of Professional
     Practices for Funeral Directors.   Milwaukee, WI: NFDA.
     4pp.
         Suggested practices to serve as guides for the funeral
director in dealing with customers; guides for dealing with the clergy;
and guides for intra- and inter-professional relationships.

682 _____.   1969 NFDA Personnel Survey.

683 "New Black Shop Offers Mass Media Ad Buy for Morticians. "
     Advertising Age 43(12):66 (March 20, 1972).   Photo.
         Wright, Edelen Advertising develops nation-wide campaign
for black funeral homes.

684 "New Small Business Exemption Affects Funeral Service. "
     The Director 42:cover (May 1972).
         Funeral homes and mortuaries can meet the small business
exemption under Nixon's phase II if they meet certain specifications,
which are listed and explained.

685 "NFDA and NSM Appear Before Senate Subcommittee on Labor
     re Proposed Amendments to the Federal Minimum Wage Law. "
     The Director 41(10):2-3 (1971).

686 Nichols, Charles H.   "An Analysis of Pricing Methods. " Mor-
     tuary Management 60(8):22-23 (1973).
         Continuation of Raether's book, Successful Funeral Service
Practice (see entry 702).   Analysis of the functional pricing method
and outline of objectives of pricing programs from the view of the
director as well as the public's needs.

687 _____.   "Funeral Service Pricing. " Mortuary Management
     60(9):25-26 (1973); 60(11):40 (1973).   Charts.
         The graduated recovery approach, which allows the direc-
tor to distribute overhead costs over a period of time through the
monthly number of funerals.   Details how to figure costs, realize
profits, and set prices.   Charts illustrate how to distribute the overhead.   Second article focuses on proper pricing methods for child
and infant funerals and merchandise pricing for the incomplete funeral.   Proper use of correct forms is discussed.

688 _____.   "How Can Funeral Directors Here Apply a Fair
     Method of Costing for Their Client and Themselves ?" Casket
     & Sunnyside 101(6):6-8 (1971).
         Among subjects discussed: ship-in and ship-out, caskets
and other merchandise, welfare and below cost cases, procedures
for establishing costs for adult services for salaries, automobile
expense, facilities, selling and administrative expenses.

689 Nicholson, L. E.   "How the Other Fellow Does It--The Valen-
     tine-Owned Mortuary Is a Home with a Heart. " Casket &
     Sunnyside 102(5):15+ (1972).   Illus.
         Award winning funeral home in Pasadena, Cal. , the Woods-
Valentine Funeral Home.   Description of setting and facilities, with

photographs and floor plan. Handles about 250 services a year.
Guides to its success: newspaper and bus advertising, small items
put in churches and clubs to keep firm's name in the public eye.

690 Ninker, Robert. "Funeral Economics Tomorrow." <u>Mortuary</u>
<u>Management</u> 60(9):14-16 (1973).
Attempt to answer the puzzler with increased recognition
of the therapeutic benefits of the funeral, why are Americans turning
more to immediate disposal methods or body donation? Costs of
funerals appear a major factor, and the author, the executive secretary of the IFDA, advises directors to seek ways to lower them.

691 Nobile, Philip. "Maverick Morticians Tell How They Keep
the Price Down." <u>Northeast Funeral Director</u> 22(1):4 (1973).
Two maverick directors of Economy Creations, Inc., a
funeral service in Staten Island, NY, answer author's questions
such as what is your average bill? Answer: a modest $265, casket
included.

692 "Nothing Seems to Revive This Stock." <u>New York Times</u>
cxxiii(42, 568): sect. III, p. 39 (Aug. 11, 1974).
Service Corp. International.

693 Pace, Eric. "Undertakers Draft Ethics Codes to Give Notice
of Funeral Costs." <u>New York Times</u> cxiv(39, 283):1, 30
(Aug. 13, 1965).
National Funeral Directors Association and National Selected Morticians announce codes of ethics.

694 Parker, Leo T. "How to Avoid Liability Losses." <u>Casket &</u>
<u>Sunnyside</u> 100(7):22-23+ (1970).

695 Pastore, Matthew M. "How to Compute Goodwill Value of Your
Business." <u>Casket & Sunnyside</u> 103(1):10+ (1973).
Certified public accountant gives methods of computing
goodwill value of operation for estate tax or selling purposes.
Methods are based on profits and include average gross profit
method, net profit capitalization method, and average selling price
per call method. Relevant IRS regulations included.

696 Pierce, W. H. "Convention Exhibits: Challenge and Opportunity." <u>Mortuary Management</u> 62(1):34 (Jan. 1975). Photo.
Chairman of the board of Pierce Chemicals/Mortician's
Supply in Dallas proposes joint convention planning committees of
funeral directors and suppliers. The goal: better cooperation and
"stronger and more valuable convention exhibits."

697 Pine, Vanderlyn R. "Measurement Procedures for Estimating
Goodwill." <u>American Funeral Director</u> 94(1):28-31; 94(2):28-
34 (1971).
Critical assessment of four measurement procedures for
estimating goodwill: (1) gross operating income percentage procedure
(uses average gross operating income for a set time and makes

goodwill equal to a standard part of this); (2) average gross profit procedure (utilizes average yearly gross profit for same number of years and puts goodwill at that amount); (3) the multiple net profit procedure (figures the average adjusted net profit multiplied by five to set the amount of goodwill); and (4) the annual adult funeral and standard service procedure (average number of total adult funerals per annum multiplied by annual average adult service). Another procedure combining the first four described.

698 _____. A Statistical Abstract of Funeral Service Facts and Figures of the United States. Milwaukee, WI: NFDA, 1974. 63pp., charts.
    Management statistics compiled from a 1973 study of sample funeral homes sponsored by the NFDA. Purpose: to provide its members with a basis of comparison with their own organizations, not a pricing pattern. Detailed income and expense data including general information on forms of ownership, collection procedures, personnel, motor equipment and investment; sources of income; funeral service operating income for the entire U.S. and separate regions; average funeral service operating expense (similarly broken down into regions); funeral service margins; a summary of findings; ranges in prices of funerals (broken down sectionally); funeral service operating income (broken down into non-veterans, all veterans, non-eligible and all eligible, and veterans of specific wars); funeral service operating income (broken down by sex).

    Pollitt, John V., president of the CMA, guest editorial. See entry 1222.

699 "Precasters Acquire New Ideas As to Methods and Products for Improving Plant Design and Safeguarding Against Labor Difficulties." Casket & Sunnyside 105(5):56-65 (May 1975). Illus.
    New precast concrete materials and products; hints on plant design and layout; ways to improve labor relations and employee communications.

    "Price Ads Beget Baiting, Funeral Men Tell Senate." Advertising Age. See entry 1009.

    "Price Advertising Opposed By U.S. Funeral Directors." New York Times. See entry 1010.

    "A Professional Approach to Funeral Service Advertising." Canadian Funeral Director. See entry 180.

700 "Public Finds NFDA Brochures Readable and Informative." The Director 42:2-3 (June 1972).
    Readership analysis of questionnaire responses with detailed discussion of public's reaction to each brochure.

    "Public Opinion Survey Favored Funeral Home Ambulance Service." American Funeral Director. See entry 893.

701 "Public Service Boost Key to Funeral TV Ads." Advertising
Age 46(5):61 (Feb. 3, 1975).
A. J. Desmond & Sons, Troy, Mich., sponsors TV ads
which boost worthwhile local institutions such as Boy Scouts and
Junior Achievement. Terry Desmond, vice-president, says the object of this service is to make the funeral home's name familiar
to the public.

Quinn, Seabury. "The Case of the Discriminatory Regulation."
See entry 1075.

_____. "The Case of the Funeral Discount Offer." See
entry 1076.

702 Raether, Howard C., ed. Successful Funeral Service Practice.
Englewood Cliffs, NJ: Prentice-Hall, 1971. Index, charts,
biblio. (Available from NFDA.)
Selections by Raether, executive secretary of the NFDA
since 1948 and editor of The Director, and other well known funeral
service experts, designed to help funeral directors manage more
successfully. Trends, conditions and determining factors in funeral
service; the whole-man-total-funeral concept versus the owner-mana-
ger-technician concept; licensing, education, and recruiting; funeral
home personnel practices, with specific recommendations; review
and comparison of funeral service income and expense patterns;
business aspects such as account classification, computation data of
operational costs, collection methods, insurance; the federal truth
and lending law--where it applies, required disclosures, discount
provisions, etc., examples of the provisions applicability to funeral
homes; casket selection room evaluation; overview of funeral service
pricing; pricing methods analysis and review of past and present
methods--itemization, standard unit pricing, straight multiple, application of ratios to a predetermined price, markup plus a recovery
and profit factor, average overhead concept, merchandise and service
markup, service charge of bi-unit method, functional pricing, and
other means followed by tests by which director can decide which one
to use; sample forms for director's use; step-by-step stages of funeral service process; public information programs; clergy relations;
legal considerations; prearranging and prefinancing funerals; mergers, acquisitions and multi-unit organizations; funeral home design,
decoration, and lighting; contemporary analysis of the funeral and
the funeral director.

703 _____, and Foran, Eugene. "Part IV--Funeral Service Income and Expense" (from the Raether book, Successful Funeral Service Practice). Mortuary Management 59(9):16-18
(1972). (See entry 702.)
Detailed discussion of factors that make up the system of
industry expenses, service income items, and ways to establish price
and figuring averages.

704 Rappaport, Alfred. An Analysis of Funeral Service Pricing
and Quotation Methods. n.d. Available from NFDA, with

supplement, "Procedures and Pitfalls"--an earlier paper related to same subject. 39pp. (paper).
Evaluation of the various funeral service pricing and quotation approaches. Specified goals determine the method to be used,
as there is no one "best way." The economics of funeral service;
essential characteristics of regulated industries; fundamental guidelines for pricing; cost accounting and funeral service pricing; comparison of itemized and unit quotation methods. Supplement was
originally presented at the annual meeting of the National Selected
Morticians, Oct. 15, 1969. It covers recent trends and their impact on funeral service; the choice industry has between taking a
leadership role in a changing society and being led by the pressures
imposed by that society; accounting systems as a tool that aids in
making decisions once certain social goals have been decided; proposed approach to developing information relevant to basic business
decisions that is consistent with socially responsible behavior.

"RCMP Warns: Your Funeral Home Files Could Be Aiding a
Criminal." Canadian Funeral Director. See entry 185.

705 Ricci, Ritchey. "Funerals Need Skilled Directors." Northeast
Funeral Director 22(2):4 (1973).
Funeral directors' activities, services; pricing methods for
funeral service, including full itemization, the unit, bi-unit, and
functional pricing methods. Despite changing trends, basically the
director's objectives have remained: caring for the body, providing
services to the bereaved, and dignifying man.

706 Riordan, Michael. "Prank Calls Disturb Funeral Homes."
Northeast Funeral Director 21(11):24 (1972).
How to combat or expose prank false alarm death calls.

707 Rosser, M. L. "Mortuary's History Parallels Chicago's."
Casket & Sunnyside 102(9):20+ (1972).
The 109-year history of the Williams-Kampp Funeral Home
in Chicago, which handles almost 400 cases a year; present problems
(lack of cemetery space; escalating operating costs; lack of public
interest in bereaved family members).

708 Schultz, Whitt N. "If You Can't Change Facts Try Bending
Your Attitudes." Mortuary Management 59(10) (1972).
Employees must have good attitude if the business is to
succeed. Pessimists should be dismissed and replaced with people
with flexible, positive outlooks.

"Senators Inquire Into Funeral Ads." See entry 1019.

709 "The Sex Ad Controversy." American Funeral Director 95(6):
26 (1972).
NFDA President Amos Dunn's open letter responding to
previous American Funeral Director editorials. These editorials
criticized the effectiveness of the advertising programs authorized
by the Board of Governors of the NFDA. Dunn's letter justifies

the program in reaching and influencing the public regarding the
values of funerals.

710 Silverman, Stephen. "Better Protection at Reduced Rates. "
      Mortuary Management 57(1):22 (1970).
          Tips to save dollars. See Leo T. Parker, "How to Avoid
Liability Losses, " entry 696.

711 Smith, Rita. "Funeral Costs Depend on Desires of the Living. "
      Northeast Funeral Director 21(3):13+ (1972).
          Interviews with Buffalo, N. Y. , funeral directors and at-
torney for the Erie-Niagra Funeral Directors Association. Customs
and trends, with author's conclusion that the cost of the funeral can
be great or small, depending on the survivor's wishes.

712 Stetson, Damon. "Workers Strike Funeral Homes. " New York
      Times cxiv(38, 968):39 (Oct. 2, 1964).
          New York City funeral home employees strike.

713 Stevens, Robert D. "Will a Union Organize Your Work Force?"
      Casket & Sunnyside 101(8):8-11 (1971).
          Suggested methods to negotiate during early stages of
unionization of funeral service employees, handle grievances; value
of putting all offers in writing.

714 "Strike of Funeral Homes Continues as Talks Recess. " New
      York Times cxx(41, 170):29 (Oct. 13, 1970).
          New York City strike.

     Summers, Peter. "Big Funeral Homes vs. Small. ... " See
      entry 751.

715 "3D Group Supports Undertakers' Code. " New York Times
      cxiv(39, 284):20 (Aug. 14, 1965).
          National Funeral Directors and Morticians (Black group)
wishes to associate itself with NFDA/NSM code.

716 "Timing--A Must for Funeral Advertising. " Mortuary Manage-
      ment 60(10):12-13 (1973).
          How, when, and where to advertise.

717 "Union Ends Strike at Funeral Homes. " New York Times cxiv
      (38, 976):10 (Oct. 10, 1964).
          New York City funeral home workers accept Metropolitan
Funeral Directors offer.

     "U. S. Gains Clearance on Funeral Price Ads. " See entry
      1244.

     Walker, Murray. "Interpersonal Relationships in the Ontario
      Funeral Industry. " See entry 237.
          Solution to personnel problems.

718 "Ways Surveyed to Obtain and Keep Young People. " Casket &
      Sunnyside 103:16 (Aug. 1973).
      Summary of the results of a survey conducted by Dr.
Charles Nichols, director of the National Foundation of Funeral Service. Effective recruiting techniques and suggestions for keeping young
people in the service. Copies of the summary available from the
NFDA.

719 "What's Your Cost per Year to Display a Casket?" The Jew-
      ish Funeral Director 43(1):28ff[2pp.] (winter 1974).
      NFDA determines that to display a casket (just making
space in the selection room, not the price of the casket or inventory) costs $291.78. Formula for arriving at this cost: "multiply
your building occupancy cost per square feet allotted to each casket"
(include all annual costs of occupying a building--taxes, depreciation, electricity, heat, water, insurance, salaries and payroll taxes,
supplies, maintenance, repair, decoration). To figure cost per
square foot, divide the annual occupancy cost by the occupancy
space; to compute the average space allotment per casket, divide
the square footage of the selection room by the number of caskets
displayed.

720 Wilton, Richard. "Vitality in Advertising. " The Director
      XLV(5):6-7 (May 1975).
      Owner/manager of Peoria, Ill., mortuary's two-year
radio advertising campaign; resulting requests to talk to teacher,
student, nurses, clergy, civic and church groups; examples of especially successful wordings of ads. For further information, contact author (Wilton Mortuary, 2101 North Knoxville, Peoria, IL
61603; 309-688-2454).

721 Wright, Sewell Peaslee. Ethical Advertising for Funeral Di-
      rectors. Chicago: Trade Periodical Co., 1924. 154pp.,
      illus.

4. FUNERAL HOMES

722 Alfonsi, William E. "Fifteen Costly Mistakes to Avoid in
      Funeral Home Remodeling. " Casket & Sunnyside 101(9):12-
      21 (1971).
      Advises hiring professional designers; proper heating and
cooling equipment to reduce future maintenance problems; tips on
best new products and materials, furnishing, traffic patterns, private areas for clients, professional accouterments, etc.

723 "America's Oldest Funeral Establishment. " Casket & Sunny-
      side 101(13[centennial issue]):52-59 (1972). Photos, drawings.
      The history of Kirk & Nice, which has been serving the
residents of Germantown, Pa., and surrounding areas for 200 years.
Its history is a microscopic history of American funeral service.

723a "Automotive Mourning; Drive-In Funeral Home." Time 91(14)
        61-62 (April 5, 1968).
        Atlanta mortician Hirschel Thornton installs five picture
windows for viewing of body from car.

724   "Buckmiller's New Building: Neighbors Saw the Sketch ... and
        Liked What They Saw." The American Funeral Director 98
        (8):26-28.
        Buckmiller Brothers Funeral Home's Prospect, Conn.
branch. Contemporary, residential-looking design. Construction
and some decorative details.

725   "Chippenham Chapel: The New Bliley Mortuary Near Richmond,
        Va." The American Funeral Director 98(3):48-53 (March
        1975). Photos, floor plan.
        Detailed site and construction description of the Joseph W.
Bliley Co.'s James River, Va., branch mortuary, with personality
profiles on its officers.

726   Crahan, Emmett J. "Planning the Preparation Room." The
        Dodge Magazine. Series of articles published in 1973, 1974,
        and 1975 issues by a contributing editor-specialist in prepa-
        ration room planning.
        As embalming is such an important part of funeral prac-
tice, preparation room must be adequately supplied and enough money must be budgeted for its operation and maintenance. Goal in
remodeling or construction is efficiency. Lists tips to save man-
hours and irritation and increase efficiency; proper equipment and
materials that will do the job and meet local and state sanitary,
electrical, building, and plumbing regulations; requirements of state
boards of embalming and state boards of health; specifications of
the Occupational Safety and Health Act.

727   "A Design that Reflects Simplicity and Warmth." American
        Funeral Director 98(4):31-35 (April 1975). Photos, floor
        plan.
        Photo-essay of the new contemporary one-story Martin-
Bails Funeral Home in Emmetsburg, Iowa.

        Doerschlag, Wolfgang. "Best Investment Reasonable Return."
        See entry 622.

728   _____. "Funeral Home Design--Here Comes the Specialist."
        Mortuary Management 58(12):16-18 (1971).
        Graduate architect from Ohio State University and vice-
president of Funeral Home Industries, Inc., of Columbus tells advantages of using a specialist to design your funeral home; discusses
legal and design fees and zoning.

729   _____. "Funeral Home Design: The Public Areas." Amer-
        ican Funeral Director 96(7):40-42 (1973).
        Funeral home planning service and president-architect
author details do's and don't's for funeral home's public areas--

parking lot, entrance, lobby and reception, selection and "slumber" (body reposal) rooms, restrooms, lounge, etc.

730   Gerhart, Leighton G.   "Indiana Mortuary Is Rebuilt After De-
        struction by Tornado. "   Casket & Sunnyside 105(4):12-18
        (April 1975).   Photos.
              Details of the rebuilt Thornburg Funeral Home in Parker,
Ind.   During reconstruction, competitors, churches, and lodges provided space for the Thornburg's to continue working.   Goodwill
"over the years," says funeral home spokesman, "can come back a
hundredfold. "

731   "Glen Oak's New Mortuary. "   American Funeral Director 98
        (4):24-26 (April 1975).   Photos, floor plan.
              The new Hursen Funeral Home, the first to be built on
cemetery property in the Chicago area.

732   "Hazard. "   Mortuary Management 59(3):30-31 (1972).
              U.S. Bureau of Standards suggestions outlined in a way to
provide valuable information to funeral directors who wish to avoid
job hazards in the daily operation of the funeral home.

733   Hogan, Barbara.   "How the Other Fellow Does It--Old Funeral
        Home Reflects Modern Thinking. "   Casket & Sunnyside 102
        (5):12+ (1972).   Illus.
              Facilities of the new Mayer Funeral Home in Austin,
Minn. , with blueprints and photographs.   Furniture, decoration, and
fixtures all integrated to create an atmosphere of eternal life rather
than death.   Modifications in service such as playing modern music
to meet modern trends.

734   "Humphrey Design Features a Dramatic Roof Profile. "   Ameri-
        can Funeral Director 98(6):26-28 (June 1975).   Photos, floor
        plan.
              Dramatic design of the new Humphrey Funeral Home in
Russellville, Arkansas.   Interior features described in detail.

        Irvin, Dolores.   "Big Funeral Homes vs. Small--How They Do
        It. "   See entry 656.

735   Kelly, Thomas E.   "Light Up Your Landscape. "   American
        Funeral Director 95(11):33-34 (1972).
              Parking lots and landscaping become important as funeral
services move to the suburbs.   Guidelines to proper landscaping and
lighting techniques for various situations.

736   Ketcham, Howard.   "Color--Its Use in the Funeral Home. "
        Casket & Sunnyside 100(7):14-17 (1970).
              Helpful hints for proper use to boost sales and goodwill,
using knowledge of changing attitudes toward color tones, awareness
of combinations, etc.

737   Leonard, Walter and Leonard, Phyllis.   "Arizona Mortuary

Designed for Simplicity of Operation." Casket & Sunnyside 103(7):12+ (1973). Illus., floor plans.

Practical design to reduce number of personnel needed through management techniques, reduce maintenance and allow emphasis on personal service. Photographs and floor plans describe lighting techniques, decoration, and furniture selections.

738 Lindquist, Martin G. Plans for Funeral Homes; Elevations, Floor Plans, Salesroom Layouts and Analytical Discussions. Cincinnati: C. J. Krehbiel, 1931. 40pp. (paper).

MacConnell, Stephen T. "Funeral Home Zoning in Residential Areas: A Discussion of a Recent Maryland Case in Which the Funeral Home Prevailed." See entry 1059.

739 Math, Howard. "Choosing Proper Settings for Your Funeral Home." Casket & Sunnyside 100(1):36-37 (1970). Arrangements of caskets.

740 National Funeral Directors Assoc. Handbook of Occupational Safety and Health Standards [loose-leaf binding]. 1975. Available from the NFDA.

A guide for funeral directors to determining liabilities and responsibilities as established by the Federal Occupational Safety and Health Act, to complying with federal standards, and to providing a working environment where injuries and illnesses will be reduced. Federal record-keeping requirements; occupational safety and health standards regarding walking and working surfaces, housekeeping, egress, boilers and elevators, accident signs, color coding, fire protection, electrical supplies, sanitation, medical and first aid, personal protective equipment and apparel, safety rules, training, storage, guarding equipment, tools, cleaning with compressed air, lock out procedures; safety and standards to be observed with regard to use of formaldehyde, including storage, handling, ventilation, protective apparel; regulations concerning employer and employee duties, enforcement, imminent danger, citations, penalties, inspection priorities, sources of standards, trade secrets, administration of the law, variances. Appendices: directory of offices with addresses and telephone numbers for states and territories, information sources, specifications for railings, toe boards and covers, fire extinguishers, standby systems, storage systems, national electrical code, toilet and washing facilities, eye and face protector guide, flammable and combustible liquid containers, approved materials for mechanical power transmission apparatus, and standard materials and dimensions.

_____. Occupational Safety and Health Act Handbook. See entry 1064.

741 "The New Cook-Walden Funeral Home." American Funeral Director 98(5):28-30 (May 1975). Drawing, photos, floor plan.

New Austin, Texas, 24,000 sq. ft. funeral home, "designed for optimum control" in the traditional style.

742 Nichols, Charles H. "Selection Room Lighting." Casket &
    Sunnyside 100(1):24+ (1970).
        Advice from the director of the NFDA based on results of
a survey on funeral home lighting. Considerations pro and con of
various types of commonly used lighting.

    Nicholson, L. E. "How the Other Fellow Does It--the Valen-
    tine-Owned Mortuary Is a Home with a Heart." See entry
    689.

743 Paul, Eugene. "Design Plus Color Psychology = Profits."
    Mortuary Management 57(3):18-19 (1970).
        Good color scheme can give proper atmosphere, enlarge
rooms, tie them together, mark distinctive areas to lend identification and recognition. Advice on combinations, shades, tones, and
specialized lighting.

744 Peterson, William A. "Modular Design--We Design 'Sdrawk-
    cab'." Mortuary Management 59(1):18-19 (1972).
        "Sdrawkcab is backwards spelled backward and is the idea
behind modular design. Construction is completed in stages as
money is available and increased business demands larger facilities,
but at each stage the uncompleted edifice looks "complete."

745 _____. "Thinking of Redesigning? Go Professional." Cas-
    ket & Sunnyside 100(1):30+ (1970).
        Professional consultants point out faults which can be elim-
inated with prior planning and evaluation of funeral home needs.

    "Precasters Acquire New Ideas As to Methods and Products:
    NPCA Convention Agenda Includes Suggestions for Improving
    Plant Design and Safeguarding Against Labor Difficulties."
    See entry 699.

746 "Robert Murphy Opens New Mortuary in Alexandria, Va."
    Casket & Sunnyside 105(7):10ff(5pp.) (July 1975). Photos,
    floor plans.
        Detailed description of all features of the centrally-located
colonial structure, including heating and air conditioning systems,
rheostat-controlled recessed lighting techniques, furnishings, decorative motifs, special equipment.

747 Schroeder, George C., Jr. "Designing for a Funeral Home:
    And Let There Be Light." Mortuary Management 58(10):34-
    39 (1971).
        Reprint of article in Illuminating Engineering 65(4), April
1970. The value of properly lighting the funeral home; the different
types of lighting appropriate for various purposes.

748 Sigal, Pincus J. "The Importance of Home in Funeral Home
    Design." Mortuary Management 56(5):24-25 (1969).
        Home-like atmosphere is most appealing to the majority
of funeral home visitors; relation of exterior design to community

and surrounding buildings; hazards of too commercial or churchy look.

749 _____. "To Remodel Now or Later--That Is the Question. "
Casket & Sunnyside 100(1):8+ (1970).
The answer is, now! Escalating costs will continue.
Analysis of cost factors concerning construction, borrowing.

750 Smalheiser, Irwin. "Factors to be Considered in Choosing
Best Possible Site for Your New Funeral Home. " Casket
& Sunnyside 99(1):24-26, 58, 59 (1969).
Study based on surveys in 200 cities showing the most
successful techniques in chosing a new mortuary setting. It must
not be too close to a present facility; must attract new customers;
in an area where sufficient numbers of family live who are likely
to contact your firm; the design should be appropriate to the volume
potential; and the site should have maximum physical exposure.

751 Summers, Peter. "Big Funeral Homes vs. Small--How They
Do It. " Casket & Sunnyside 101(11):14-15 (1971). Illus.
The Dunham-Timmons Funeral Home in Fedonia, Kan.
(pop. 3500), handles about 65 cases a year, all with a staff of four
(the two owners and their wives). Owners are extremely active in
community affairs.

752 "This Undertaking Is Entering Its Second Century. " Casket &
Sunnyside 101(13[centennial issue]):62-63 (1972). Photos.
The story of the Hunter Edmundson-Striffler Co. of McKees-
port, Pa. , from its founding 106 years ago to the present day.

753 "Undertaker Will Offer Drive-In Service. " New York Times
cxvii(40, 227):33 (March 14, 1968).
Hirschel Thornton Funeral Home in Atlanta.

754 "Viewing the Remains; Atlanta's Drive-In Mortuary. " Nation
207(8):261-62 (Sept. 23, 1968).
Atlanta mortician Hirschel Thornton installs five picture
windows to allow viewing from car.

Wall, Jerry. "Forest Lawn Cemetery Erects New Mortuary
in Beaumont. " See entry 1618.

755 Wirtzfield, Roy. "Free Enterprise. " Mortuary Management
60(4):12-15 (1973).
Directors can avoid somber effects by replacing dark colors and heavy drapes with light, cheerful materials; business office
and arrangement rooms on separate floor from visitation rooms and
those where services are held.

756 Zinsser, W. "Time Saver for Busy Mourners. " Life 64(19):
22 (May 10, 1968).
Irreverent review of Hirschel Thornton's drive-in funeral
home in Atlanta.

5. FUNERAL SERVICE EDUCATION

Barnes, Carl Lewis. Art and Science of Embalming. See entry 386.

Barnes, Thorton B. Quiz Compends. See entry 388.

757 Belleau, Wilfred E. Funeral Service as a Career. Milwaukee: Park Pub. House, 1956. 26pp., appendix, biblio., footnotes.
An analysis of funeral service for guidance personnel, students and veterans describing funeral service, its history, importance, the nature of the work; colleges: their entrance requirements, training curriculum, costs; qualifications for the field, necessary licensing, how to enter the field, working conditions, remuneration, opportunities, advantages, disadvantages and women's role in funeral service. Appendices list associations, publications, and licensing requirements by state.

Benjamin, Michael. "What Is a Funeral Director?" See entry 271.

758 Berg, David W., and Daugherty, George C. Perspectives on Death. Baltimore: Waverly Press, 1974. 69pp., biblio.
Designed as teacher's aid in presenting AV material listed in Part IV, Audio-Visual Material (in several places). See student activity booklet, entry 768.

759 _____. "Teaching About Death." Today's Education 62:46-47 (1973).
"Perspectives on Death" course. Curriculum includes instruction on the funeral director and field trips to funeral home and cemetery.

760 Berg, William M. "Conference Solves Accreditation Dilemma." Mortuary Management 57(11):34-35 (1970).
Summary of meeting of the 67th Annual Convention of the Conference of Funeral Service Examining Board, New Orleans, Oct. 23-24, 1970, where the Commission of Schools as adjunct of the American Board of Funeral Service Education was created to establish and rule on all accrediting procedures. An Institute on Curricula was also created.

Callaway, Curtis F. Art of Funeral Directing.... See entry 275.

_____. Textbook of Mortuary Practice.... See entry 390.

Clarke, Joseph Henry. Answers to Questions Contained in Clarke's Quiz Compend.... See entry 393.

_____. Answers to Questions Presented in the Lectures of Clarke's Cincinnati College of Embalming.... See entry 394.

_____. Clarke's Compend and Textbook on Embalming. See entry 395.

_____. Clarke's New Work on Embalming. See entry 396.

_____. Clarke's Quiz Compend, 3d ed. See entry 397.

_____. Clarke's Textbook on Embalming.... See entry 398.

_____, and Dhonau, Charles O. Answers to Questions Contained in the Official Text Book on Embalming and Sanitary Science. See entry 402.

_____ and _____. Official Text Book on Embalming and Sanitary Science. See entry 403.

Clarke's Cincinnati College of Embalming. An Epitome of Reference for the Students of the Cincinnati School for Embalming. See entry 404.

761 Commission on Mortuary Education. Future of Funeral Service Education; The Report of the Commission. Milwaukee, WI: National Funeral Directors Association, 1957. 112pp., spiral bound, index.
      Report of the NFDA commission created in April 1956 to survey the field. Background survey of the social and economic aspects of the industry and its place in society past, present, and hopes for the future; the nature of American funeral directing; comparison of the "mass mortuary" with the local funeral home; the problems of funeral service such as recruiting, licensing, and the occupational dilemma of embalmers; professional image; how to cultivate professionalism and thus rise above funeral service as a vocation; rejection of the idea of merchandising in favor of providing service; types of licensing; problem areas of funeral service education; sixty specific recommendations for funeral education, licensing, school communication, and the role of NFDA in education; the results of a funeral service field questionnaire, mortuary student questionnaire, and a listing of state requirements. See entries 773, 774, 781, 783.

762 Corley, Elizabeth Adam. Tell Me About Death, Tell Me About Funerals. Santa Clara, CA: Grammatical Sciences, 1973. 35pp.
      For children.

763 Crane, Elliott, H. Prof. E. H. Crane's Manual of Instructions to Undertakers. Kalamazoo, MI: Crane and Allen, 1886. 142pp.

764 "Curricular Improvement Stressed by Conference." American Funeral Director 94(12):38 (1971).
      Conference of Funeral Service Examining Boards' activities

during the year; impact of its work relating to education, exams, and licensing.

Curry, Gladys P. Textbook on Facial Restoration. . . . See entry 406.

765 Curry, Tom. "What Is the Future of Funeral Service Education?" Casket & Sunnyside 102(1):16+ (1972).
Suggests changes in outlook and practices to prepare students realistically. Changes include scientific techniques, public relations techniques, skill in handling clients; increased instruction in sociology, psychology, and community politics to be accompanied by instruction in the advanced mortuary administrative and management techniques and technical skills in preparing the body; continuing education through special programs, seminars, and keeping up with the latest news, etc., through reading field journals and publications.

766 Cvach, Jerome J. "On the Positive Side." The Director 43: 6-7 (June 1973).
Young funeral director has a column "About Funerals" in community newspaper not only for his own satisfaction but to further the ideals of funeral service.

767 Daugherty, George, and Berg, David. The Individual, Society, and Death. Available from Educational Perspectives Assoc. (Box 213, Dekalb, IL 60115). n.d. 193pp. (paper).
Anthology of readings, fiction, non-fiction, and poetry, on funeral practice, costs and other aspects of death.

768 _____. The Student Activity Book. Available from Educational Perspectives Assoc (Box 213, Dekalb, IL 60115). 54pp. (paper). (Perspectives on Death series.)
Designed for classroom use; various activities to involve children with death; to be used in conjunction with The Teacher's Resource Book, entry 769. See Part IV, Audio-Visual Material, in the present work.

769 _____. The Teacher's Resource Book. Available from Educational Perspectives Assoc. (Box 213, Dekalb, IL 60115). (Paper). (Perspectives on Death series.)
Teacher's guide for teaching the six-week course on death using the Perspectives on Death unit. Daily lesson plans, suggestions, bibliography and vocabulary listing. To be used in conjunction with The Student Activity Book, entry 768. See Part IV, Audio-Visual Material, in the present work.

Deuel, Harry J. Textbook of Chemistry for Students of Embalming. See entry 487.

770 Ebeling, R. A. "Education." Mortuary Management 59(4):8 (1972).
Calls for more specialized vocational training and extended

education for those already involved in funeral service. Problems funeral directors have in getting adequately trained personnel discussed.

> Eckels, Howard S. Sanitary Science; A Reference and Textbook for the Communicable Diseases, Disinfections and Chemistry for the Undertaker. See entry 415.

> Eckels College of Mortuary Science. Reference Compendium; A Series of Questions and Answers Pertaining to the Study of Mortuary Science. See entry 412.

771 "Education: A Single-Edged Necessity" [editorial]. The New England Funeral Director 1(5):3 (Aug. 1975).
   Advocates attending seminars "geared toward preparing funeral directors to meet the challenges and changes of today and tomorrow." The director cannot buy the new adaptive funerals at the supermarket or purchase bereavement pills, but the profession can "broaden its virtues as a needed public service rather than suppress its faults by attacking its detractors and ignoring a public which is searching for new values in old traditions."

772 "Explain Details of Proposed Pennsylvania Mortuary School." American Funeral Director 98(7):16-17 (July 1975).
   The planned mortuary education program, to begin Sept. 1976, will be a one-year pre-mortuary program followed by a two years' program of integrated studies. It will be given at the Northampton County Area Community College in northeastern Pa.

773 Ford, William Herschel. "The Future of Funeral Service Education." Mortuary Management 55(12):4-5 (1968).
   History and development of those organizations working for advancement of funeral service education. Procedures and services of the American Board of Funeral Service Education, problem areas, and how funeral directors and Board can help solve them. Other articles: entries 761, 774, 781, 783.

774 Franklin, C. M. "The Future of Funeral Service Education." Mortuary Management 56(1):12-13 (1969).
   The past ten years in funeral service education: setbacks, causes, and five basic factors on which funeral service education should be based. For other articles on the subject see entries 761, 773, 781, 783.

775 "Funeral Director: An Unlikely Career Choice?" Northeast Funeral Director 22(9):11 (1973).
   Why pick the funeral service for a career? Counsel for the Massachusetts Funeral Directors Association and Joyce Lain Kennedy in a "Career Corner" column list reasons.

> "Funeral Service Poll ... Funeral Directors Favor Higher Educational Requirements." See entry 955.

776 "Government Recognizes School Accreditation." Casket & Sunnyside 102(6):26 (1972).
U.S. Office of Education recognizes the ABFSE as the accrediting agency for funeral service colleges.

777 Grafe, William T. "My Three Years in the Army's Mortuary Affairs Program." Mortuary Management 56(5):14-18 (1969).
Army's Memorial Activities academic course of mortuary affairs, identification, map reading, temporary cemetery operation, and return. The handling of corpses in the DaNang Mortuary in Vietnam. Processing, identification, storage, embalming, and return to the States.

778 Haney, Lynn. "How to Succeed in Undertaking: Go to School." New York Times cxxi(41,560): sect. III, p. 3 (Nov. 7, 1971). Photo.
Funeral Service education. A tour through the American Academy's McAllister Institute in New York. Students' curriculum discussed.

779 Hansen, F. Lloyd. Funeral Service as a Profession (booklet). Milwaukee, WI: NFDA, 1952.

780 Hardy, William G. "The Funeral in a Changing World." The Director 40(3):12-13 (1970).
Funeral service is being affected by sociological, psychological, and religious changes that affect all aspects of our society. Funeral has lost its community focus and its meaning, when if it were done properly, it could be extremely helpful to the bereaved. Suggests directors attend seminars and keep up with new knowledge of the profession so they can adequately serve the public.

781 Heilmann, Karl O. "The Future of Funeral Service Education." Mortuary Management 56(3):22 (1969). See also entries 773, 774, 761, 783.

Hiller College of Embalming and Necrosurgery. Text-book. See entry 443.

Hirst, Thomas. Quick Class; A Manual Designed to Coach and Prepare Undertakers and Embalmers to Qualify for License Before the State Examining Boards. See entry 445.

782 "Jacobs Lauds Work of Continuing Educational Program." Northeast Funeral Director 20(2):6+ (1971).
Text of a speech by the chairman of the Joint Commission on Funeral Standards of the Union of Orthodox Jewish Congregations of America and the Rabbinical Council of America to the Jewish Funeral Directors Continuing Education Program in New York. Historical review of joint work of the Commission and the Jewish Funeral Directors Association; survey of problems remaining; the positive accomplishments such as the agreement on the ACCORD,

the adoption of the "Nine Point Program, " and work on the local level. Discussion of the Flatbush Vaad plan.

>Janssen, William. "Expose--The Milwaukee Funeral Service Youth Assoc.... A Practical New Approach to Exposing Youth to Funeral Service." See entry 657.

>Kates, Charles O. "Commencement Speakers Talk to the Wrong People." See entry 314.

783 Keenan, Paul R. "The Future of Funeral Service Education." Mortuary Management 56(2):14-15 (1969). See also entries 761, 773, 774, 781.

784 Kennedy, Joyce Lain. "There's Good Pay in Mortician Field." Northeast Funeral Director 21(1):10 (1972).
Difference between funeral directors and the embalmers' functions; demand; earnings; preparation; schooling requirements of each. Refers for further information to the NFDA's career booklet.

785 Landig, R. Victor. Basic Principles of Funeral Service. Houston: Scardin Printing Co., 1956. 282pp., photos, drawings, diagrs.
Introduction book for the student covering the procedures of funeral arrangement and administration of the funeral home; business law; the rudiments of sanitary science; glossary of terms and questions for review.

>_____, and Garton, W. Melvin. Quiz Compend on Mortuary Science. See entry 465.

>Lewis, H. E. Embalmer's Guide: A Practical and Comprehensive Treatise on Embalming.... See entry 469.

786 Lohman, Keith D. "The Student Mortician: A Study of Occupational Socialization." Colorado Journal of Educational Research 9(4):45-50.
Information on funeral service school gathered from classroom observation, interviews, and questionnaires: 30% of students are sons of funeral directors; there's been a decline of class attendance and increased problems, and a lowering interest in the subject. Interpretation is limited to the scope of this study and no conclusions are drawn. Urges more, similar studies. Extensive bibliography on the development of professionalism and occupational identification.

787 Lowery, Martin J. "National Recognition of Accreditation: A Giant Step Forward for Funeral Service Education." The Director 42:6-7 (May 1972).
The Commission of Schools of the American Board of Funeral Service Education is officially recognized as the accrediting body for funeral service education. The effects of this on the funeral industry described, such as assistance and objectivity of people

outside the industry and the possibility of getting student loans from the National Defense Fund.

788   Margolis, Otto, et al.   Thanatology Course Outlines--Funeral Service. With editorial assistance of Lillian G. Kutscher. New York: MSS Information Corp. , 1975.

789   Martin, Edward A.   Psychology of Funeral Service, 5th ed. Grand Junction, CO: Sentinel Printers, 1970.   288pp. , biblio. , index, glossary.   Available from Casket & Sunnyside (274 Madison Ave. , New York, NY 10016).
        A basic psychology reference as it applies to the funeral director: personality traits, emotional stability; physiology of the nervous system and glands; learning and memory; emotion and the adjustment to mental conflict; grief and sentiment as they relate specifically to the role of the funeral director and how he should deal with them; definition and description of various religious beliefs and the psychological basis and effects of religious concepts; the psychology of good public relations; practical considerations for the funeral such as music, good restoration; summary of the nature of funeral service and how the student can put psychology into action.

790   Matthews, William F.   "The Relevance of Funeral Service Psychology: A Viewpoint. "   The Director 42:7-8 (Dec. 1973).
        Psychology should be included in funeral service education and licensing requirements to insure the funeral service's future, fill social responsibility, and to give personnel greater satisfaction in their work.

791   _____, Waring, Sumner J. Jr. , and Zarnke, Norman J. "Future of the Funeral?"   Casket & Sunnyside 101(2):12 (1972).
        Future will call for improved communications, counseling, inservice training, and knowledge of psychology; a need for continuing education; tougher educational and licensing standards; jobs of greater responsibility require more education.

792   "Mercer College Offers Program. "   American Funeral Director 98(7):18 (July 1975).
        Mercer County (NJ) Community College's mortuary science program, to begin Sept. 1976, is designed to help offset the present shortage of licensed funeral directors in the state.   It is the first such program in NJ to meet all state educational licensing requirements.   The American Academy's McAllister Institute (NYC) official casts gloomier outlook for student placement--says jobs are getting scarcer and starting one's own business is near impossible.

793   Mortuary Operation As a Career.   Chicago: Institute for Research Devoted to Vocation Research, n. d.   24pp.

        Myers, Eliab.   Champion Text-book on Embalming. ... See entry 488.

_____, and Sullivan, F. S. Champion Text-book on Embalming. . . . See entry 489.

794 National Funeral Directors Assoc. Funeral Service--A Heritage, A Challenge, A Future (NFDA Vocational Guidance booklet). n. d. Available from the NFDA.

795 _____. Funeral Service--Meeting Needs, Serving People (NFDA Vocational Guidance booklet). n. d. Available from the NFDA.

796 _____. Pharmaceutical, Anatomical and Chemical Lexicon; The National Funeral Directors' Official Textbook. Chicago: Donohue and Henneberry, 1886. 575pp., biblio.

797 _____. State License Laws Pertaining to Funeral Directors and Embalmers. 1966. Available from NFDA.

798 Nicholas, Charles H. Mortuary Operations As a Career. Evanston, IL: National Foundation of Funeral Service Press, 1974. 52pp.
        Vocational monograph by the director of the National Foundation of Funeral Service. History of the vocation, its importance, impressions of young practitioners; typical funeral home, facilities, equipment; types of jobs available, typical duties; a typical funeral service and the multiplicity of tasks involved. Attractive features and disadvantages of the vocation; qualifications necessary for the career, including academic course prerequisites and apprenticeships. Average salaries and wages, median weekly duty hours, benefits, etc., job opportunities, how to get the first job, jobs related to funeral service, opportunities for women. Organizations, trade journals, suggested reading. List of Funeral Service State Examining Boards' State Board Rosters; Funeral Director's and Embalmer's Licensing Rules and Regulations; accredited mortuary schools as listed by the American Board of Funeral Service Education, Inc., and endorsed by the Conference of Funeral Service Examining Boards.

799 _____. Recruiting and Retaining Young People in Funeral Service Careers: A Study of Opinion. Evanston, IL: National Foundation of Funeral Service Press, 1973. 74pp. Appendices.
        A study of the means to be used to recruit and retain new funeral directors based on the answers to 500 questionnaires sent to funeral directors, students and drop-outs of funeral schools, and high school and college students facing career choices. Part 1: responses of funeral service personnel and students; 2: opinions of unaffiliated youth; 3: conclusions and recommendations. The study measures the acceptance and rejection rate of specific proposals made in the questionnaire (e. g., 86% favored visitation at funeral homes for youth groups and classes as a good recruitment practice). Appendices: profile of the responding group, the acceptance percentages for suggested recruitment practices, and the acceptance percentages for the suggested retention practices.

Nunnamaker, Albert J., and Dhonau, Charles O. Anatomy and Embalming: A Treatise on the Science and Art of Embalming. See entry 492.

_____ and _____. Anatomy, Descriptive and Operative.... See entry 493.

Pervier, Norville C. Textbook of Chemistry for Embalmers. See entry 499.

Quinn, Seabury. A Syllabus of Mortuary Jurisprudence.... See entry 1077.

800 Quist, Walter P. "One Man's View of Funeral Service Education." Mortuary Management 57(2):12 (1970).
Advocates consultants to answer questions on the danger of contamination of disease from dead bodies to living, effectiveness of non-licensed employees; funeral director should decide which of his duties are most important and the greatest service to society.

801 Rudman, Jack. Civil Service Examination Passbook: Mortuary Caretaker. Plainview, NY: National Learning, c. 1974. (Paper.)

Spriggs, A. O. The Art & Science of Embalming. See entry 556.

802 Stadt, Ronald and Hertz, Donald. "Growing Need for Teachers in Funeral Service Education." The Director 42:2-3 (May 1972).
Industry lacks qualified instructors; suggests prospective mortuary science instructors with B.A.'s be urged to get their M.S. degrees.

803 Strub, Clarence G. "Education for Funeral Service." Casket & Sunnyside 102(4):20 (1972).
Premortuary college education, professional education, internship, and continuing education; funeral service education should offer more than a cram course for the state board exams; differences between community and private colleges and apprenticeships.

804 _____. "Funeral Education I: Thinkers or Tinkers?" Casket & Sunnyside 99(7):20-21, 37; 99(9); 99(10); and 99(12) (1969).

_____. A Quiz Compend of Mortuary Science. See entry 564.

805 _____. "Third Eye Enucleation Course at Iowa Has Record Enrollment." Casket & Sunnyside 100(3):10-11+ (1970).
Potential role of the funeral director in health care discussed.

806 Thorsell, W. K. "A Rationale for Licensure in Funeral Service." The Director 40(10):7-9 (1970).
       History of funeral service is the basis for modern laws governing the industry; social changes in the U. S. and proposed changes in licensure; regulations should be enforced to protect the public health and other interests.

807 "Turning the Clock Back 25 Years." American Funeral Director 98(8):10-11 (March 1975).
       For the history buff: controversy over mortuary education a quarter century ago; state board regulations and their "make-or-break licensing examinations"; promise of curriculum reform.

       Winters, Elwood J. Chemistry and Toxicology for the Embalmer. See entry 572.

6. DOCTOR AND CLERGY RELATIONS

808 Allen, R. Earl. "A Pastor's View of Funerals." The Director 41(7):10-11 (1971).
       Therapeutic and theological worth of funerals; helps mourners to accept facts; gives them hope of everlasting life. Service should include mention of heaven.

       _____. Funeral Service Book. See entry 263.

809 Anderson, Walter H. A Treatise on the Law of Sheriffs, Coroners and Constables, with Forms. Buffalo, NY: Dennis & Co., 1947.

       Bachmann, C. Charles. Ministering to the Grief-Sufferer. See entry 266.

810 Barish, Marvin I. "The Law of Testamentary Disposition--A Legal Barrier to Medical Advance." Temple Law Quarterly 30:40 (1956).

       Blackwood, Andrew W. The Funeral: A Source Book for Ministers. See entry 273.

811 The Catholic Burial Rite. Collegeville, MN: The Liturgical Press, 1971. 65pp. (paper). Available from the NFDA.
       Liturgy of the Catholic burial rite and mass of requiem, according to officially approved English texts, 1971, and song supplement. Rite at the Church entrance; mass for the dead; final commendation when celebrated at the grave; alternative scripture readings from the Old and New Testaments; responsorial psalms; alleluias verses; and gospels.

812 "Changing Way of Death." Time 93(15):60 (April 11, 1969). Illus.

Churches simplify funerals, especially Catholics with the
"white funeral, " where emphasis is placed on the resurrection.
Death is a happy event with the deceased going to heaven.

813 Christensen, James L. The Complete Funeral. Westwood,
      NJ: Fleming H. Revell Co. , 1967. 159pp. , notes, poetry
      index, subject index, index of aids for specific circumstances.
          Pastor of Central Christian Church, Enid, Ok. , and grad-
uate of the Seminary at Phillips University gives suggestions for the
ministry: how to help the bereaved make funeral arrangements with
morticians; plan for the burial; funeral service and interment; make
the service meaningful in terms of the deceased's life; and help the
bereaved to recover. Specific items to be arranged include where
the service will be held, when, will there be music, cremation,
place of interment, memorial meditation, biblical meditations, suggestions for funeral music, funeral service and interment materials.

814 _____ . Funeral Services. Old Tappan, NJ: Revell, 1959.

815 "Christian Service for the Dead. " America 120(7):183-84
      (Feb. 15, 1969).
          Editorial urges more emphasis on resurrection and less
morbidity in Catholic funerals.

816 "Cleric Defends Modern Funeral. " New York Times cxiii
      (38,617):71 (Oct. 17, 1963).
          The Rev. Edgar N. Jackson assails Mitford book at New
York Metropolitan Funeral Directors meeting.

817 DeLong, A. Hamilton. Pastor's Ideal Funeral Book. Cincin-
      nati: Jennings and Graham, 1910.

818 Duffield, George, and Duffield, Samuel W. Burial of the Dead;
      Pastor's Handbook for Funeral Services and Consolation of
      the Afflicted. New York: Funk, 1882 and 1918.

     Duvall, William H. "Speak for the Funeral. " See entry 624.

819 Failla, Silvio J. "What Funeral Directors Should Know About
      Funerals Used to Interpret New Catholic Funeral Rite. " The
      Director 41(8):11 (1971).
          The executive secretary of the New Jersey Funeral Direc-
tors Assoc. advises how to handle the philosophy and language presented in the filmstrip, "Death of a Christian, " a Federation of
Diocesan Liturgical Commissions' project dealing with the new mandatory Catholic Church liturgy. Suggests using the NFDA film "Of
Life and Death" and the Ave Maria Press production "Through Life
to Death" cassette. All states, cities, communities, and parishes
should speak of the values of the funeral.

820 Feagle, John R. "The Autopsy Problem ... A Pathologist's
      View. " American Funeral Director 95(5):28-30 (1972).
          A diplomat of the American Board of Pathology on proce-
dures and reasons for post-mortem exams and the need for clear

mutual understanding of the work of pathologists, physicians, and
funeral directors.

821　Forman, J.　"Relationship of Autopsy Surgeon and Embalmer.
　　　(Preliminary Report)." Ohio State Medical Journal 30:167
　　　(March 1934).
　　　　　　Ohio Embalmers Assoc. recognizes benefits to be derived
by cooperating with pathologists, coroners, and other physicians
who do autopsies; the embalmers' and cosmetologists' work would
be much simpler were the vascular tree of corpses kept intact and
the body's exterior left unmutilated.

822　Fulton, Robert L.　"The Clergyman and the Funeral Director:
　　　A Study in Role Conflict." Social Forces 37:317-23 (April
　　　1961).
　　　　　　An analysis of this survey of clerical attitudes toward
undertaking and undertakers is found in the May 1961 issue.

823　　　　　　. A Compilation of Studies of Attitudes Toward Death,
　　　Funerals and Funeral Directors--Participated in by the Clergy,
　　　the Public (Including Critical Segments Thereof) and Funeral
　　　Directors.　Minneapolis:　Privately printed, 1971.　Available
　　　from the NFDA.
　　　　　　See analysis of this survey of clerical attitudes toward
undertaking and undertakers in the May 1961 issue of Social Forces.

824　Harmon, Nolan B.　Pastor's Ideal Funeral Manual.　Nashville,
　　　TN:　Abingdon-Cokesbury, 1942.　224pp.

825　Helwig, F. C.　"Autopsy from Standpoint of the Undertaker."
　　　Hospitals 12:73-77 (June 1938).
　　　　　　Physician notes that carelessness of physicians greatly
hampers or prohibits the funeral directors' carrying out their work
successfully.　Suggests that the pathologist consider the directors
as friends who often secure permission for necropsy exams when
the pathologist cannot.　Young pathologists might watch how embalmers work to understand their problems; meetings with pathologists and funeral directors to remove suspicions and misunderstandings; promote better relations.

826　Hutton, Samuel W.　Minister's Funeral Manual.　Grand Rapids,
　　　MI:　Baker Books, 1968.

827　Knowlton, W. W.　"Autopsies--Funeral Directors--and More
　　　Autopsies." Hospitals 10:60-65 (Jan. 1965).
　　　　　　Recommendation for cooperation between hospital authorities and funeral directors regarding autopsies; an expanded role of
the funeral director from purveyor of pine boxes to modern-day
embalmer and comforter to the bereaved; ideas to promote cooperation; postmortem procedure to minimize mutilation of body.

828　Krauskopf.　"The Law of Dead Bodies, Impeding Medical
　　　Progress." Ohio State Law Journal 19:455 (1958).

829 Lowndes, Jack P. "How Can the Minister and the Mortician Work Together for the Benefit of the Bereaved?" Casket & Sunnyside 101(8):16-18 (1971).

830 Mahoney, David M., J. C. D. "Bishop Writes on Prayer for the Dead." The Catholic Cemetery 15(7):13-14 (1975) [repr. from The Catholic Advance, Nov. 7, 1974].
       The Bishop of Wichita argues for body burial, as the soul "will not exist for eternity without the body," and against cremation and other "pagan customs ... which grew out of pagan belief that the body no longer mattered." Liturgy should be a dignified recognition of death and must not detract from its reality. Honest grief should be encouraged and the promise of resurrection should give hope.

       Mees, Otto. Outlines for Funeral Sermons and Addresses. See entry 330.

       Meyer, F. B., et al. Funeral Sermons and Outlines. See entry 331.

831 Moritz, A. R. "Repair of Body After Autopsy." Hospitals 12:78-81 (June 1938).
       Undertakers' reluctance to accept autopsies is frequently the fault of pathologists who make the undertakers' task of restoration needlessly hard. Care should be taken to insure the embalmer's work is not significantly increased as a result of the autopsy. Suggests postmortem procedure, placing a glass cannula in the large arteries to ease the injection of embalming fluids.

       National Funeral Directors Association. Code of Professional Practices for Funeral Directors. See entry 681.

832 "New Catholic Funeral Rites Are Described and Distributed." Casket & Sunnyside 102(2):28 (1972).
       Explanation of the difference between the rosary and scripture services.

       Saint Gregory Nazianzen and St. Ambrose. Funeral Orations. See entry 356.

       Sanderson, Joseph, ed. Pastors' Pocket Manual for Funerals. See entry 357.

833 Seymour, Robert G. Pastor's Companion for Weddings and Funerals. Philadelphia: A. J. Rowland, 1898. 42pp.

834 Smith, Donald B. "The Clergyman's Key Role." Mortuary Management 62(1):17ff[2pp.] (Jan. 1975). Photos.
       Donald Smith of Smith Market Research Services, on the basis of a five-year study and interviews of 1340 opinion-molders (including 600 clergymen), concludes there is a great need for closer personal relationships between the clergy and funeral directors. Suggests ways to do it.

835 Stenn, Frederick. "The Achievement of the Committee on
    Necropsies of the Institute of Medicine of Chicago." Pro-
    ceedings of the Institute of Medicine of Chicago, 26:244-51
    (July 1967). Biblio.
        Review of the Institute's significant contributions; its educa-
tional program to inform the public, undertaking profession, hospital
administrators, physicians and pathologists in order to foster greater
acceptance of autopsies; early misunderstandings between physicians
and morticians; solutions; extensive bibliography with comments.

7. ASSOCIATIONS, DIRECTORIES, PERSONALITIES

836 American Blue Book of Funeral Directors, 1975, 22d ed.   New
    York: Kates-Boylston Publications (1501 Broadway, 10036).
        A major commercial directory of more than 22,000 funeral
directors. Arranged both alphabetically and geographically, it covers
directors in the United States and abroad.

    Bellush, Bernard. He Walked Alone: A Biography of John
    Gilbert Winant. See entry 10.

837 Berg, William. "The Impossible Dream Fulfilled." Mortuary
    Management 56(3):10-14 (1969).
        History of the National Foundation of Funeral Service, in-
cluding portrait of its founder, W. M. Krieger, and co-founder,
George N. Olinger, and interview with present director Dr. Charles
H. Nichols, noting goals and accomplishments of the organization.

838 _____. "Interview with Paul G. Hamilton." Mortuary
    Management 57(11):21-28 (1970).
        Hamilton, a licensed funeral director, is founder and pres-
ident of International Funeral Service (IFS). Incorporated in 1966,
IFS made its first acquisition the following year and by 1970 owned
62 mortuaries. Emphasizes the advantage of corporate control:
funeral homes can draw young people into the business by offering
better fringe benefits, salaries, etc. while retaining separate identity.

839 _____. "National Convention Review." Mortuary Manage-
    ment 57(11):13-19 (1970).
        Review of activities at the NFDA's 89th convention at New
Orleans, Oct. 25-29, 1970, president-elect Frederick R. Sears, and
summary of speeches, committee reports, and resolutions.

840 Bustard, William L. "Bustard of NSM Links Conglomerates to
    Golden Rule." Casket & Sunnyside 100(10):22 (1970).
        Relationships among the American Funeral Supply Corp.,
Service Corp. International of Houston (SCI), Financial Corp. International, The Order of the Golden Rule, the International Order of
the Golden Rule, and Funeral Management Services, Inc.

841 Casket Magazine. Casket Manufacturers; This List Includes Those Who, in Addition to Manufacturing, Also Do a Jobbing Business. New York: Casket, 1934.

"Directory of Domestic and Foreign Airlines." See entry 901.

842 Directory of Memorial Associations. 1975. Available from the Continental Assoc. of Funeral and Memorial Societies, Inc. [free].
Directory of members of memorial and funeral societies.

843 Eckels's Undertakers' Directory, Reference Book and Shipping Guide of the United States and British America, Together with State Board of Health Rules and Special Laws and Ordinances Governing the Transportation of Dead Human Bodies. Philadelphia: H. S. Eckels & Co., 1905. 666pp.

844 Fulton, Robert. A Bibliography on Death, Grief, and Bereavement, 1845-1973, 3d ed., rev. Available from the Center for Death Education and Research.

845 McClelland, E. H. The Literature of Mortuary Science; A Survey with a List of Books and a Tentative List of Periodicals and Other Serials [mimeographed]. National Assoc. of Colleges of Mortuary Science, 1949. 92pp.

846 Margolis, Otto, ed. Funeral Service Abstracts, 1969-1974. Westport, CT: National Assoc. of Colleges of Mortuary Science and the Embalming Chemical Manufacturers Assoc. After 1975 will be re-named Thanatology Abstracts and will be published by Allan R. Liss, New York.

847 Melby, Lynn L. "Allied Memorial Council Gets It All Together." Mortuary Management 62(1):18ff[2-1/2pp.] (Jan. 1975).
The executive director spells out the services of the AMC, a non-profit organization founded in 1963 to calm "the panic within funeral service of the early sixties." The AMC produces and distributes a motion picture, slide presentation, a book and other tools to help funeral directors and allied members in their public relations efforts; provides means of resolving legal conflicts within the funeral profession before they are in bill form in Congress; works with trade groups promoting cooperation on local levels.

848 Middle States Undertakers' Directory; A Complete List of the Undertakers in the States of Illinois, Indiana, Michigan, Ohio, Pennsylvania, Wisconsin, and the City of St. Louis; the Public Cemeteries; and an Alphabetical Directory of Manufacturing, Wholesale, and Supply Houses. Springfield, MA: W. B. McCourtie, 1907.

849 Miller, R. H., and DeBow, R. R., eds. National Green Book of Funeral Directors and Embalmers and Florists. Chicago: National Green Book, 1956. 115pp.

850   National Funeral Directors Assoc.   The 1972-1973 Directory.
       Available from the NFDA.
            Membership roster of the NFDA.   Lists 14,059 members
of the Association's affiliated state associations.

851   National Selected Morticians.   The Code of Good Funeral Prac-
       tice.   Evanston, IL: NSM.   11pp. (pamphlet).
            The National Selected Morticians is an international organ-
ization of independent funeral directors dedicated to creating high
standards of funeral service and providing its members with knowledge, experience and skills to better help the communities and
families they serve.   Among the standards of service this code book
affirms; provide the public with information about funerals, the
services and responsibilities of directors, and the costs; make arrangements before they are needed; offer a wide range of price
categories; quote conspicuously and in writing charges for funeral
services and give reasonable adjustments in costs when less than
the full offering is desired; make no additional charges without prior
approval of the purchaser; make no misleading or false representations to the public; maintain well qualified staff and complete, suitable equipment; and respond to the needs of the poor.

852   Townshend, John.   A Catalogue of Books Relating to the Dis-
       posal of the Bodies and Perpetuating the Memories of the
       Dead.   New York: privately printed, 1887.   74pp.
            Unannotated bibliography, arranged in two parts, one by
author, the other by subject.

853   Undertakers' Directory; A Complete List of the Undertakers in
       the States of Connecticut, Maine, Massachusetts, New Hamp-
       shire, New Jersey, New York, Rhode Island, and Vermont;
       the Public Crematories in these States; and an Alphabetical
       Directory of Manufacturing, Wholesale and Supply Houses....
       Springfield, MA: W. B. McCourtie, 1907.

                    8.   ALLIED INDUSTRIES

                          Caskets

854   "'Back to Nature' Caskets Largely a Phony Issue. "   CMA Sales
       Letter 2(4):2 (May 15, 1975).
            Comment on an article that appeared in a syndicated column
in April 1975 in the Washington Star-News and picked up in news-
papers throughout the country.   The back to nature pine box (to be
used as a bar now, coffin later), advertised at $95 in kit form and
$160 assembled, is a rip-off compared to the "good quality non-
sealer metal caskets, high quality cloth covered caskets, and even
fully finished minimum hardwoods" manufactured by the casket industry.   See also entry 856.

Beck, John C. "The Casket Industry Begins to Catch Up with the Times." See entry 582.

Casket Magazine. Casket Manufacturers.... See entry 841.

855 "Casket Company and Funeral Home Sued for Alleged 'Defective' Casket." CMA News Letter, Aug. 1975, p. 1.
$500,000 lawsuit filed in Puerto Rico, the first such case filed in a Puerto Rican court, alleging a casket failed to prevent decomposition of the remains despite a written guaranty. The manufacturer countered that there is no way that any casket can protect a body indefinitely from decay and that decomposition is also caused by conditions other than penetration of exterior elements. The body after three weeks' burial is said to have been in an advanced state of decay.

Casket Manufacturers Assoc. Facts and Figures on the Burial Casket Industry. See entry 603.

_____. Your Dues Investment ... What Return Do You Get. See entry 604.

856 "CMA Views Rip-Off on 'The Plain Box'." Casket & Sunnyside 105(7):20 (July 1975).
The Casket Manufacturers of America responds to the Washington Star-News article on the trend back to nature and the double-use coffin. CMA alleges the pine box advertised is triple the price CMA members ask for the same product. See also entry 854.

856a "Cradle to Grave." Newsweek 82(23):122 (Dec. 3, 1975).
Rocky Mountain Casket Corp., Whitefish, Mont., sells old-fashioned pine coffins to use as wine rack, hope chest, bar, coffee table--whatever, until it's time to serve its ultimate purpose. Standard 3/4-inch knotty pine model sells for $160; manager Sharon Morrison says requests come in from all over the nation but their popularity does not extend to the general funeral industry.

857 Crowley, Gary L. "If God Meant Us to Have Fiberglass Caskets He Would Have Planted Fiberglass Trees." Mortuary Management 62(1):37 (Jan. 1975).
Reasons why fiberglass is a good material for caskets: it is lightweight; does not rust, corode, or oxidize; is unaffected by air, liquids, acid or alkaline materials, or gases.

858 The Evolution of the Modern Casket (ms. photostat). Collection of the NFDA, Milwaukee, WI.

859 Hasluck, Paul D., ed. Coffin Making and Undertaking. New York: Funk & Wagnalls, n.d. [ca. 1928]; New York: Cassell, n.d. Illus.

860 Herrick, George S. "The Facts About Casket Textiles."

Reprint contained in a brochure entitled Casket Manufacturing, n.d. Avail. from Casket & Sunnyside.

861 Kline, James E. "Phase II--Wage Price Stabilization Campaign." Casket & Sunnyside 102(1):8+ (1972).
The executive secretary of the Casket Manufacturers of America analyses Nixon's Phase II wage stabilization campaign: price categories, salary and pay increases; appeal procedures; government published regulations.

Lamers, Dr. William M., Jr. "Gloom at Funerals Replaced by Color." See entry 1185.

862 LaVigne, Richard H. "People First." Northeast Funeral Director 21(3):8 (1972).
The executive vice president of the National Casket Co. forecasts a shift toward conservatism on the part of middleclass youth. Funeral directors must sell (and therefore casket manufacturers must produce) what people want. Effective market studies will say what. Motives of the funeral industry, however, must not lack basic integrity so that public trust will replace present public suspicion.

863 "Life-styles: Lively Idea at Rocky Mountain Casket." Sales Management 110(4):4 (Feb. 19, 1973). Photos.
Simple coffins.

McCracken, Joseph L. "A View of the Present and Future of the Funeral." See entry 1187.

864 "Man's Best Friend. R.I.P." Christian Century 87(43):1303 (Oct. 28, 1970). Photo.
Folder from the Hoegh Pet Casket Co. stimulates thoughts on man and his relationship to animals and their relationship with the ecosphere.

865 National Hardwood Magazine, May 1962.
Detailed description of modern manufacture of Jewish coffins.

"Onyame Will Give Them a Better Place in Heaven." American Funeral Director. See entry 163.

Pace, Eric. "Undertakers Draft Ethics Codes to Give Notice of Funeral Costs." See entry 693.

Peabody, D. W. "... and Dust to Dust." See entry 1071.

866 Pitt, William. "Fiberglass--A Big Surprise." Mortuary Management 62(1):36ff[3pp.] (Jan. 1975). Photo.
Funeral directors and casket manufacturers have ignored fiberglass in the past. CMA's survey on "American Attitudes Toward Death and Funerals" pointed up that public opinon "places fiberglass

caskets in much higher potential demand than current market sales." Reasons fiberglass is desirable in casket manufacture; how to display them to advantage.

867 "Preliminary Report Finds 'No Recognized Hazard' in Casket Materials Containing Polyvinyl Chloride." CMA Management Letter, Aug. 25, 1975, p. 1.
Author states, however, that there is a "possible adverse effect from smokestack emissions [from] the combining of chlorine from the polyvinyl chloride with hydrogen in the atmosphere to form hydrochloric acid...." Other kinds of plastics are recognizably unsuitable for cremation because they do not burn easily and emit smoke and fly ash into the air.

868 Renourd, Charles A. The Casket's New Anatomical Plates Drawn with Special Reference to the Requirements of Embalmers. New York, 1921. 67pp., illus.

869 "A Success Story Built on Unhappy Products." Financial World 141(14):24 (April 3, 1974). Photo.
Hillenbrand Industries reviewed. Owns Batesville Casket Co., the world's largest. Analysis of Batesville Casket.

Tibbits, James F. "Looking Back Over My Past Life." American Funeral Director. See entry 221.

870 Versagi, F. "Casket-maker." Air Conditioning, Heating and Refrigeration News 99:5 (July 29, 1963).

871 Ward, Tom. "Which Way the Wind? Casket & Sunnyside 100 (2):20-22 (1970). Illus.
Illustrated article by the style and promotion director of a casket company. New developments in casket design.

872 _____. "Why Does One Casket Outsell Another?" Casket & Sunnyside 100(9):16+ (1970).
Fadism. Current demand is for brighter colors, single tones, stainless steel shells and straight tailoring of insides. To meet changing trends and preferences, directors must be flexible in picking casket selections and also in the arrangement of their selection rooms.

873 "Warns Against Cremating Caskets of Polystyrene." Casket & Sunnyside 105(6):4 (June 1975).
While polystyrene caskets are recommended by Monsanto Polymers and Petrochemicals Co. for burials "because they combine the best features of both wooden and metal caskets while eliminating various problems" of each, for cremation they are unsuitable. Current crematoriums were built to burn wood caskets and "generally do not have adequate air and fuel mixing facilities necessary for complete combustion of polystyrene caskets." Concentrations of hydrocarbons build up in the chamber pockets, can cause explosions, and emit heavy black smoke into the air.

(8 cont.) <u>Hearses and Ambulances</u>

874   Adler, Nancy J.   "Kennedy's Cycle Corps Supplied Not by
        Police But by Mortuary. "   <u>New York Times</u> cxvii(40, 300):54
        (May 26, 1968).
              California Mortuary Service maintains necessary parapha-
nalia for local funeral directors.   Candidate Robert Kennedy rented
their motorcycle escorts for his campaign parade.

875   "Ambulance Drivers Under Wages Law. "   <u>New York Times</u>
        cxv(39, 613):27 (July 9, 1966).
              Minimum wage dispute.

876   "Auto Funeral Car Carried 29. "   <u>The American Funeral Direc-
        tor</u> 10(97):63 (Oct. 1974).   Illus.
              Short article on the S. W. Mather Casket Co. 's funeral car
made in 1910.

877   "Brooklyn Funeral Uses a Horse-Drawn Hearse. "   <u>New York
        Times</u> cxxi(41, 604):19 (Dec. 21, 1971).
              Woman wants the same horse-drawn hearse to carry her
body as carried her husband and father.

878   "Concerning the Evolution of Styles in Hearses. "   <u>Sunnyside</u>
        March 15, 1913, p. 14-15.

        "Federal Ambulance Study Spotlights Problem Areas. "   See
        entry 637.

879   "Fuel Economy Emphasized in 1975 Funeral Cars. "   <u>The Amer-
        ican Funeral Director</u> 10(97):66-76 (Oct. 1974).   Illus.
              Description and photographs of the newest professional
vehicles.   Points out new features and style variations of various
makes.

880   "Hand-Drawn Hearse Found in England. "   <u>The American Funer-
        al Director</u> 10(97):109 (Oct. 1974).
              The Parish Council of Allonby, Cumberland, will preserve
this "real find" for posterity.   It has four wood wheels, iron tires,
open and topped by a fancy canopy.

881   Herchner, Henry C.   "Ways of Conducting an Automobile Fu-
        neral. "   <u>American Funeral Director</u> 96(10):88-90 (1973).
              Reprint of an 1917 article on the transitional stage when
both horse and automobile were used to transport bodies.

882   Latham, Paul R.   "Evolution of the Casket Auto. "   <u>Mortuary
        Management</u> 56(10):28 (1969).
              Short history of motorized funeral vehicles.

883   McCall, Walter M. P.   "Classic Era of the Carved Funeral
        Coach. "   <u>American Funeral Director</u> 95(10):86+ (1972).
        Illus.

McCall, a well-known automobile history buff, discusses
the evolution of the funeral hearse, its style, and ornamentation
during the 1930's.

884 _____. "The Evolution of the Contemporary Funeral Car."
Canadian Funeral Service 50(8):7+ (1972). Illus.
Development of the funeral car from the first motorized
hearses produced in the early 1900's to the Superior "Crown Limited" introduced in 1970, the ornate carved panel type, and the sharp-
lined limousine and landau styles. See entry 886.

885 _____. "The Funeral Car Industry in Canada." The American Funeral Director 10(97):77-81 (Oct. 1974). Illus.
Illustrated historical sketch of the most noteworthy of
Canada's funeral car manufacturers including the Mitchell Hearse
(incorporated in 1884 as the O. J. Mitchell Co.), Dominion Man-
facturers Ltd., and other pioneers such as Smith Bros. Motor Body
Works and A. B. Greer & Son Co.; the manufacturing process;
building from scratch or conversion of luxury cars into funeral
coaches. Profile of John J. C. Little, famous customer designer
and last of the "all Canadian funeral car designers." Funeral transportation in Canada today is largely U.S. provided. According to
McCall, "Outside of one or two local conversion builders, there are
no funeral car manufacturers in business in Canada today" while up
to the 1950's Canada "had a small but flourishing funeral car industry."

886 _____. "The Funeral Coach Industry in Canada." Canadian
Funeral Service 50(10):7+ (1972).
Follow-up to article on "The Evolution of the Contemporary
Funeral Car," Sept. 1972 (entry 884). Most auto equipment in Canada is presently American manufactured. Fascinating anecdotes and
recall of earlier times when Canada boasted many of its own coach
manufacturers.

887 _____. "James Cunningham, Son & Co." American Funeral Director 96(10):69-72, 73 (1973).
Follows the funeral hearse and coach firm's growth through
135 successful years from a one-man show to a national corporation.

888 McPherson, Thomas A. American Funeral Cars and Ambulances
Since 1900. Glen Ellyn, IL: Crestline, 1973. 350pp., photos.
Organized chronologically with a brief synopsis for each
year. Hundreds of captioned hearse and ambulance photographs; the
only such reference available.

889 _____. "Post-War Era Witnessed Vast Demand for Funeral
Vehicles," parts 1 and 2. Casket & Sunnyside 105(6):7-10;
105(7):16-18 (1975).
Pictorial essays of funeral vehicles from 1945 through 1952
and in 1954 the end of Henney and the Packard professional vehicle
line; the purchase by Wayne Works of Richmond, Ind., of the Meteor
plant; the Eureka's switch from wood to steel-framed body; the trend-

setting "Beau Monde Floral Coach" by the Superior design studio;
Meteor's rival "Crestwood" in 1955 and the last of the revolutionar-
ies--the S & S "Park Place" which had a convertible roof that when
raised made the car look like the old landaus.

890 _____. "What Happened to the Funeral Hearse?" Casket
 & Sunnyside 101(13[centennial issue]):30-33 (1972). Photo.
 Photo-essay of funeral hearses from the earliest horse-
drawn decorated vehicles of the 1880's to the large motor hearses
(1920's), the early electric casket wagons, the first landaus in the
1930's, limousines of the post World War II era, the dramatic styl-
ing change of 1959 with the "Crown Royale Landaulet" from Superior,
and the combination limousine and landau "Paramount," introduced
in 1963 by Miller-Meteor.

891 Martin, Edward A. "Hearse and Funeral Cars." Unpublished
 manuscript, 1947, Archives of the NFDA, Milwaukee, WI.

892 Perlmutter, Emanuel. "Funeral Drivers Begin Walkout. New
 York Times cxv(39,453):73 (Jan. 30, 1966).
 New York City strike.

893 "Public Opinion Survey Favored Funeral Home Ambulance Service." American Funeral Director 92(3):46-50 (1969).
 Funeral home conducts a public opinion pole to see preferred type of ambulance service with Danville, Va., residents.
Incentive to participate in poll was a $50 U.S. Savings Bond to
the winner of a random draw from those responding to the questionnaire. City voted 89.7% in favor of the funeral home ambulance service.

894 Snyder, Keith. "Miller Meteor History." Mortuary Management 60(11):41-45 (1973). Illus.
 The Miller Meteor Carriage and Hearse Co. from its creation in 1853 to the present day. Pictures showing evolution of the
American hearse, vintage models.

895 "State Mediation Board to Enter Hearse Drivers' Strike Today."
 New York Times cxv(39,454):29 (Jan. 31, 1966).
 New York City strike.

(8 cont.) Air Transit

896 "Airlines Give Continually Greater Mortuary Service." Casket
 & Sunnyside 103(3):18+ (1973).
 List of improved and expanded services such as special
loading equipment, speed reservations by use of computers, compact
casket covers, etc.

897 Baer, Dr. Berthold A. "The World's First Flying Hearse."
 Casket & Sunnyside 101(13[centennial issue]):44-46 (1971).
 Photos, drawings.

Reprint of The Sunnyside's Oct. 21, 1921, article by the owner of the world's first flying hearse--at the time the largest passenger carrying craft. Details of construction and interior features.

898 "Computer Nets Expedite Transit Case Shipments." American Funeral Director 95(3):38-53 (1972).
Advantages in using computerized systems in arranging shipment of human remains air cargo; eight major airlines explain their services; mailing addresses of 17 airlines that provide transit case services to funeral directors.

899 Covington, W. P. "Air Shipping Human Remains." Mortuary Management 56(5):20-22 (1969).
Profile history of air shipment, with emphasis on jet transport; problems and what the funeral director can do to help; rate structure; the best way to prepare corpse for air shipment.

900 _____. "What to Do When Shipping or Receiving Human Remains." Casket & Sunnyside 100(3):22-24 (1970).
Description of procedures and problems of shipping and receiving by commercial air transport.

901 "Directory of Domestic and Foreign Airlines." Casket & Sunnyside 103(3):26+ (1973).
Eleven-page index and directory with information on foreign and domestic airlines which ship human remains.

902 "Growth in Oversea Travel Reflected in Survey Data." American Funeral Director 96(3):36-42, 47 (1973).
Detailed outline of nine major airlines' services and percentages of funeral directors using air transport facilities to and from foreign countries.

903 Hathaway, William S. Jr. "When to Use an Air Hearse." Casket & Sunnyside 100(3):18-19+ (1970).
Points out advantages and recommends using specialized air hearse companies instead of scheduled air lines for distances of 100-600 miles. Costs given.

904 "Rules Drafted for Flying Uncasketed Remains." Casket & Sunnyside 105(5):23 (May 1975).
Regulations proposed for discussion at the regular meeting of the Flying Funeral Directors of America include proper embalming; secure wrapping and support; private unloading; horizontal position for transit.

905 "Shipment by Air Hearse is Direct, Economical." American Funeral Director 96(3):48-50+ (1973).
Funeral directors cite advantages of air hearse transport. Page 87 of this issue lists air hearse/ambulance services available.

906 "Shipment Services by Air." Casket & Sunnyside 102(3):11-34 (1972).

America's first air funerals; airlines describe their facilities and special service features for funeral directors.

907 "Standardized Procedures Simplify Air Shipments. " American Funeral Director 98(3):32-40 (March 1975). Photos.
Airline rules regarding material and design of caskets, identification papers; proper securing of remains within the casket; factors directors should consider in preparing the corpse for shipment such as cargo compartment temperature, lack of levelers at freight dock platforms; arrangements the director and airline should make before shipment; facilities and services provided by the leading airlines.

908 "Two Unsolved Problems in Air-Shipment--Containerization and Damage Claims. " Casket & Sunnyside 100(3):30+ (1970).
Report to the NFDA convention in Portland, Ore.

909 "Versatile Air Hearses Meet a Vital Need. " American Funeral Director 98(3):32-40 (March 1975). Photos.
Scheduled airlines provide adequate transportation of human remains between large cities; air hearses are gaining popularity for shipping to out of the way spots; eliminates transfers; saves time and money. Most widely used craft is the Piper Cherokee, followed by other Piper, Beechcraft, Cessna and other manufacturers' aircraft.

(8 cont.) Flowers

910 Funeral Flowers; Album of Designs. Chicago: Florists' Pub. Co. , 1934. 95pp. , illus.

911 Society of American Florists. The Logic of Funeral Flowers. Available from AMC. 10pp. (pamphlet).
The value of flowers as suitable expressions of sympathy. The Allied Memorial Council advises that pamphlet be distributed to clergy.

912 Williams, Marc. Flowers-by-Wire: The Story of the Florists' Telegraph Delivery Association. Detroit: Mercury House, 1960.

C. ANALYSIS, ALTERNATIVE PROPOSALS, AND THE
   FUTURE OF FUNERAL SERVICE

        1. INVESTIGATIONS, ANALYSES,
           STATISTICS AND CRITICISM

   Allen, R. Earl. "A Pastor's View of Funerals. " See entry
     808.

913 "Anonymous Chicago Group Attacks Mitford Book. " Publishers
     Weekly 184:44-45 (Nov. 18, 1963).
          Attack on Jessica Mitford's The American Way of Death
(entry 993).

914 "Archbishop Scores Burial 'Escapism'. " New York Times
     cxvi(39, 712):62 (Oct. 16, 1966).
          The Most Rev. John J. Krol labels U. S. funerals extrava-
gant, escapist, and commercial.

915 Ayres, B. Drummond, Jr. "Poor Southerner's Way of Death:
     Paying Pennies a Week to Depart in Style. " New York Times
     cxxiv(42, 791):47 (March 2, 1975).
          Combine of 11 Alabama funeral insurance companies goes
broke, affecting thousands of poor people who paid small weekly
premiums for a decent funeral.   Modern Home (the bankrupt company) policies are to be honored by Vulcan Life.   Poor Southerners'
funeral beliefs and customs are detailed.

916 Bailey, Warren S. "A Funeral Service Investigation. " Mortu-
     ary Management 58(1):24-25 (1971).
          Report on funeral practices in California by an agent in the
Trust and Trade Practice Div. of the California State Attorney General's office.   Detailed review of pricing methods and mortuary cost
accounting.

917 Baker, Russell. "Undertakings. " New York Times cxxiv
     (42, 722): sect. VI, p. 6 (Jan. 12, 1975).
          Body snatching with a new twist.   Satirical look at how
kinless bodies are claimed by undertaker agents who collect part
of state burial allowances allocated for the poor.

918 "Bible Termed Bar to Burial Abuses. " New York Times
     cxiii(38, 884):14 (April 10, 1964).

Senate Antitrust and Monopoly Subcommittee hears Canon Howard Johnson who believes people are not prepared to cope with deaths and are therefore susceptible to unscrupulous morticians. Johnson emphasizes, however, most funeral directors are honest. Sen. Hart says no group has the right to eliminate price competition; urges curtailment of the Federal Trade Commission investigation hearings.

919 Bigart, Homer. "Funeral Customs Raising Protests." New York Times cxii(38, 573):35, 44 (Sept. 3, 1963).
        Clergy back simpler ceremonies. Wilber Krieger of NSM, Charles Nichols of NSM, New York State Funeral Directors Assoc. counsel George Goodstein, and Herbert Herrlich of Frank E. Campbell, a large New York Funeral Home, offer comments on Jessica Mitford's The American Way of Death (entry 993). Canon Howard Johnson of St. John the Devine relates his experiences with parishioners who are unprepared for death and therefore prey to unscrupulous morticians. The Rev. Thomas K. Thompson comments on funerals and possible reforms.

920 Blair, William M. "Trust Action Charges Coercion to Prevent Funeral-Price Ads." New York Times cxvii(40, 117):1, 30 (Nov. 25, 1967).
        NFDA is charged in anti-trust violation for forbidding members to advertise.

921 Bowman, Leroy. American Funeral: A Study in Guilt, Extravagance, and Sublimity. Washington, DC: Public Affairs Press, 1959, 181pp., index; New York: Paperback Library, 1964; Westport, CT: Greenwood Press, 1973, 181pp.
        The definitive study of American funeral practices, which helped to open discussion on the to-then untalked about topic. Threefold purpose: (1) "Aquaint reader with the basis of changes of commercial exploitation directed at undertakers." (2) "ascertain what particular circumstances influence the methods he uses," and (3) "uncover the social and psychological factors that underlie conspicuous display" (of bodies). Part 1, State Setting and Performance, deals with peoples' attitudes towards (and avoidance of) death, analyzes response and roles when death strikes a family, and examines group behavior at funerals. Part 2 casts a critical eye at the funeral business, analyzing various "scenes" between the funeral director and customer: how the funeral director sells; interactions between director and customer, director and clergy, social agencies, physicians; competition between director and clergy; director's role in the community, striving for professional status; the commercial factors which influence the funeral business. Part 3 measures the influences of social change on funeral business; charts the rise of cities and suburbs, conglomerate ownership, co-ops and memorial societies, secularization of society, and body donations, and their effects on funeral directing. Recommendations for de-materializing the funeral and making it more meaningful.

922 Brantner, John P. "I Speak for the Funeral." The Director 42:11-13 (May 1972).

Clinical psychologist says survivors need the funeral and why and how funeral directors by acting as educators can help replace fear and revulsion of death with an understanding of how it is integrated with life.

923   Brown, Charles M. "Reducing the High Cost of Dying." The Christian Century, Oct. 21, 1926.

924   Caley, Harold F. Funeral Transactions and Consumer Protection. Unpublished paper, Osgood Hall Law School, 1968.

925   "Californians Note More Unconventional Funerals." The American Funeral Director 10(97):82-83 (Oct. 1974).
            Do-it-yourself "alternative services" are still few in comparison to the number of traditional ones, but their 8 to 10% increase in the last eight years is considered significant. The trend is seen in young and old alike, both wanting to personalize and give meaning to funeral services. The San Francisco Chronicle is quoted as reporting that the trend away from limousines and elaborate rites toward memorial societies and pre-arrangements is confined to eggheads; the middle class still wants tradition.

            "Casket Company and Funeral Home Sued for Alleged 'Defective' Casket. See entry 855.

926   Casket Manufacturers of America. American Attitudes Toward Death and Funerals. 46pp. Available from the CMA and any member supplier.
            Landmark study for the industry; has evoked much comment, thinking, and restructuring. Findings include public's over-estimation of funeral costs; public attitude towards funeral service; percentage of the population favoring burial over cremation and immediate disposal; price quotation methods public prefer; relative importance of various casket features; attitudes towards clergymen at funerals; humanist funerals; music; flowers; pre-arrangement; memorial societies; and extended payment plans. Concludes that the majority of Americans still favor the traditional funeral but want to know what they are paying for. See also entry 1003.

927   Charlton, Linda. "F.T.C. Asks Rules to Curb Funeral Home Practices." New York Times Aug. 29, 1975, p. 1.
            The Federal Trade Commission suggest regulations that would bar many present funeral industry practices such as embalming corpses without family's permission; requiring embalming before cremation; misrepresenting the need for embalming. Suggests funeral directors be required to display the least expensive caskets with the more expensive; to give accurate pricing by phone and provide detailed, dated price list for caskets; to prominently display casket prices and have available itemized price lists for all funeral services and merchandise saying the customer is required to choose only the items he wishes and will be billed only for those he selects. Federal laws should pre-empt state laws forbidding funeral homes to advertise. "Bait and switch" practices to be prohibited. J. Thomas Rosch, director of the F.T.C.'s Bureau of Consumer

Protection, is quoted as saying the F. T. C. investigation turned up evidence of "a compelling need for consumer protection. "

928 "Checking the Burial Bills. " Business Week no. 1819 (July 11, 1964), p. 36.
   Review of government investigations of the funeral industry in Washington, DC, Wisconsin, and New York; Senate hearings; and NFDA-NSM controversy over professionalism and advertising.

929 Cockrell, Eustace. "O Death, Where Is Thy Sting?" Fortnight, June 1955.
   Includes unflattering portrait of Hubert Eaton and Forest Lawn.

930 Coriolis [pseud. of Robert Forrest]. Death--Here Is Thy Sting. New York: Collier, 1963; Toronto, McClelland, 1967, 139p.

931 "Cost of Being Buried; Justice Department's Antitrust Suit. " America 117:703-704 (Dec. 9, 1967).
   Editorial comment on Justice Dept. 's suit against NFDA's position on advertising. Also comments on the good of the funeral director.

932 Davidson, Bill. "The High Cost of Dying. " Collier's, May 19, 1951.

933 Death in America. Expanded re-issue of a 1974 issue of American Quarterly. Available in paper or hardback from American Quarterly (Box 1, Logan Hall, University of Pennsylvania, Philadelphia 19174).
   Articles and essays on death and dying.

934 Dowd, Quincy Lamartine. Funeral Management and Costs; A World Survey of Burial and Cremation. Chicago: University of Chicago Press, 1921. 295pp. , biblio.
   Social scientific study of the funeral with information on modern cremation movement; description of being at a cremation. Contrasts U. S. customs unfavorably with those of many European countries.

935 Dugan, George. "Lavish Funerals Scored by Jews. " New York Times cxv(39, 431):13 (Jan. 8, 1966).
   Moses Feuerstein, president of the Union of Orthodox Jewish Congregations, attacks modern, commercial funerals.

936 Dyer, Arthur. "British Ideas of American Methods. " American Funeral Director 96(6):42-44 (1973).
   British undertaker in the early 1900's describes the American funeral.

937 Erteszek, Victoria. "The Marketing of a Mortuary ... as Seen from the Outside. " Mortuary Management 57(4):20-21, (1970).

College term paper with general recommendations for public service advertising, advertising cooperatives for small firms, values of pre-need selling.

938 Farber, M. A. "City Studying Allegations of Kickbacks by Morticians." New York Times cxxii(42, 189):54 (July 28, 1973).
New York City investigates kickbacks to medical examiners' employees for body referral. Metropolitan Funeral Service named.

939 _____. "U. S. and City Investigating Fraudulent Burial Scheme." New York Times cxxiii(42, 380):1, 34 (Feb. 4, 1974).
New York funeral fraud and body-snatching scheme laid to funeral homes that have agents pose as kin of kinless people and then have the state pay them for a welfare burial.

940 Federal Trade Commission. Funeral Industry Practices: Trade Regulation Proceeding. 16 CFR Part 453. Washington, DC: Federal Trade Commission. Reprinted from the Federal Register, Aug. 29, 1975 (40 F. R. 39901).
Regulations designed to curb deceptive funeral practice, protect consumers, and stimulate competition within the funeral industry, to be implemented by mid-1976. Definitions of funeral terms such as funeral services, industry member, crematory, etc.; listing of exploitative practices (embalming without permission, taking custody of a deceased person without authorization, refusing release to a family member, etc., requiring casket for immediate cremation, overcharging for services done by third parties; misrepresentations of laws in connection with sales and services; public health necessities, and religious customs; list of acts FTC defines as deceptive (failure to display three least expensive caskets, failure to inform customers of alternate casket colors, interfering with customer's selection, disparaging customer's choice of inexpensive merchandise; failure to disclose price information over the telephone, present customers with price list of caskets, services, and other merchandise, and display prices for caskets and vaults prominently, provide on request prices for transportation, embalming, use of facilities for viewing, funeral service, casket, hearse, limousine, services, vaults; failure to deduct charges for services or items customer does not select. Funeral homes are to be required to retain documents for three years after date of distribution to customers. Statement of reason for the proposed rule includes the customer's vulnerability to unfair practices because emotional state at time of grief; the history of some funeral director's practices which "exploit" customer's disadvantaged position or "which interfere with personal selection of merchandise and services"; the fact that "many customers have been injured by misrepresentations" concerning the alleged necessity to embalm, have a casket, purchase a burial vault. The FTC found that the unavailability of prices restricts competition and that some industry action "inhibits" economical funeral offerings, pre-need arrangements, immediate disposition services, or memorial societies.

941 "FFDA Statistical Survey Shows Few Ratio Changes." American Funeral Director 98(7):22-23 (July 1975).
    Federated Funeral Directors of America's 1974 Statistical
Supplement based on approximately 115, 000 adult funerals in 1974.
Statistics given include "trends in the last 20 years, expense breakdown, average 1974 operating expenses, distribution of sales by
price groups, and average by state"; new statistics chart showing the
average investments in inventories; specifications on the average net
price of adult funerals, cash advance, operation costs, average casket cost; average net expense of funeral, profit before federal taxes,
percentage of gross profit to average sale; average sales expense
per funeral, promotion expense, supply costs, business service expenses, and salaries.

942 "Findings" of the Professional Census Conducted by Dr. Vanderlyn R. Pine, NFDA Management Analyst. Available from the
National Funeral Directors Assoc. 30pp.
    Results of census conducted in 1971 to provide a scientific
sampling base for future studies of the NFDA. Questions were asked
confidentially of NFDA member organizations; 60. 4% responded. Data
published include total NFDA members in each state and region; mean
age of directors and years active in the profession; numbers licensed
as funeral director, embalmer, or both; years of formal education completed; kind of professional training received; size of market area;
number of complete adult funerals conducted during 1970-71; mean and
median number of funerals; association of member firms with allied
services such as ambulance, monument, or cemetery; percentage of
funerals conducted for Protestants, Catholics, Jewish, or other religious groups; proportion of funerals which included public viewing
with a public service and public committal service, the less-than-
total funeral broken down into funerals that include no viewing and
a private funeral, a graveside service only, immediate disposition
with a memorial service, immediate disposition without any service;
whether the director serves a specific ethnic group.

943 Folta, Jeannette R. "Attitudes Toward the Contemporary Funeral." The Director 42:6-9 (July 1972).
    Analysis of attitudes based on responses of students and
other persons who attended a workshop sponsored by the NFDA and
the Vermont State Nurses Assoc. Opinions classified under categories include Services expected from the funeral home; Decisions
expected or desired from the funeral home vs. Decisions to be made
by the person making arrangements; Type of service desired; Reasonable cost of funerals; Type of information desired in funeral home
advertising.

944 Forrest, Robert (under pseud., Corioles). Death, Here Is
Thy Sting. See entry 930.

945 "FTC Hints at Controls." The New England Funeral Director
1(5):7 (Aug. 1975).
    Federal Trade Commission justified $164, 718 budget re-
quest to complete its investigation of the funeral industry on grounds

consumers spend about $2 billion a year for funeral services. Corrective measures FTC may recommend include setting industry standards in the form of Trade Regulations Rules, Industry Guides, or model State legislative proposals; publishing the investigative report; consumer education materials giving essential data about funeral arrangements; a consumer education guide for arranging funerals and descriptions of alternatives to traditional customs; "regularizing the availability of comparative price data" on funeral costs at specified mortuaries.

946 "FTC Sees Lack of Price Competition & Price Information As Major Problems." Mortuary Management 62(1):54ff[3pp.] (Jan. 1974).
      Evaluation of the Federal Trade Commission spokesman's speech at the 1974 CMA convention. Gurmankin states the basic purpose of the FTC's investigation "is to identify unfair or deceptive practices or unfair methods of competition which contravene the laws enforced by the Commission, and to formulate recommendations for correcting the problems encountered." He specifically notes that on the retail level, directors' lack of competitive pricing has resulted in "over-capacity, preserved inefficiency, and high prices." Highlights of speech quoted. Single copies of the entire speech available from the CMA.

947 "FTC Staff Report Shows Wide Variations in Prices Charge by District of Columbia Funeral Homes." Federal Trade Commission News, released Feb. 28, 1974. For copy, write Legal and Public Records Div., Federal Trade Commission, Washington, DC 20580.
      This report is the first major attempt by the federal government to collect and publish basic information on funeral prices. Findings include: the least costly funerals ranged from $210 to $900 and cremations $80; the average cost for a complete funeral in 1973 was $1137, excluding cemetery costs, burial vaults, and other expenses that upped the price to $1886; cost variations quoted by funeral directors depended on the casket used, not the services provides; funeral buyers in Washington have a hard time learning of the least expensive service and merchandise available from funeral homes.

948 "FTC to Combat Deceptive Funeral Home Practices." NRTA News Bulletin, Oct. 1975, p. 1, 4.
      Federal Trade Commission proposes regulations designed to curb deceptive funeral practice, protect consumers, and stimulate competition within the industry. Regulations, to be implemented by mid-1976, received wide support from NRTA-AARP and other national consumer-oriented organizations. Proposal follows a two-year investigation, which FTC official says exposed practices by some of the 22, 500 U.S. funeral homes that did "economic and emotional" injury to clients. Association executive director Bernard E. Nash concurred, saying "The proposals were long overdue," and citing "a history of misrepresentation and non-disclosure of vital information" by some funeral directors. Service Corporation

International, the largest funeral home chain in the U.S. censured
for overcharging for obit notices, flowers, and cremations furnished
by third parties, and ordered to refund charges since Jan. 1971.

949 Fulton, Robert. Death, Funerals, Funeral Directors. Avail-
     able from the NFDA. 52pp., graphs.
          The first reports of the findings of a 1959 study, compiled
and interpreted by a professor of sociology at the University of
Minnesota, undertaken in the light of the increase in criticism by
some members of the funeral profession; it contains information to
provide a basis for rectifying the relationship between church and
funeral industry. A second report is included on the findings of a
1962 study on the attitudes of people toward death, grief, and the
funeral. A third report is an analysis of the funeral and the funeral
director based on a 1967 study on the overview of the funeral, the
funeral director, the American public's attitudes toward death. And
lastly, the most important findings from a second survey on the contemporary American funeral, (1970) is included.

950 _____. "The Sacred and the Secular: Attitudes of the
     American Public Towards Death, Funerals and Funeral Di-
     rectors. In: Fulton, Death and Identity (New York: Wiley,
     1965).

951 "Funeral Costs Rise Slowly." American Funeral Director 10
     (97):108 (Oct. 1974).
          Ten-line item which quotes recently released statistics
from the Bureau of Labor: living costs since 1967 have increased
48.3% and the costs of funerals, 35.4% between July 31, 1973, and
and July 31, 1974, living costs went up 11.8% and funerals, 7.1%.

952 "Funeral Director Suspended." New York Times cxxiii(42, 5777):
     39 (Aug. 20, 1974.
          Albert E. Seay, Riverhead, L.I., fined $3500 and has
license suspended five years for violations.

953 "Funeral Fee Is $600." New York Times cxxii(42,449):17
     (April 14, 1974).
          Correction of Times article April 7 entitled "Wide Range
of Funeral Prices Found Here in Consumer Study" (entry 961).

954 "Funeral Home Business Will Be Studied by F.T.C." New
     York Times cxxiii(42, 274):50 (Oct. 21, 1973).

955 "Funeral Service Poll--Funeral Directors Favor Higher Educa-
     tional Requirements." Mortuary Management 57(5):20-23
     (1970).

956 "Funeral Statistics Surveyed by NFDA." Casket & Sunnyside
     103(2):21+ (1973).
          NFDA releases "Statistical Abstract of Funeral Service
Facts and Figures of the U.S." Regional and national level data
on funeral prices and costs; number conducted per mortuary;

number of employees--licensed and unlicensed; fringe benefit plans; wages, salaries; and investments.

957 "Funerals, Pharmacies, Land Frauds Investigated." Congressional Quarterly Almanac 1964, vol. 20. Washington, DC: Congressional Quarterly Service, 1965, p. 100-1001.
Report of the Senate Antitrust and Monopoly Subcommittee Hearings on the funeral industry. Lists witnesses and condenses testimony.

958 Gebhart, John C. Funeral Costs; What They Average; Are They Too High?; Can They Be Reduced? New York: G. P. Putnam's Sons, 1928; Ann Arbor, MI: Finch Press, n. d. 319pp., diagrs., photos, index, appendices.
A report of the findings of the Advisory Committee on Burial Survey formed in 1926. Comprehensive analysis, covering the social origin of burial customs; funeral management in the U.S., its transformation from undertaking to funeral directing; cemeteries; cremation; monuments; the economics of each; costs of funerals analyzed with charts and tables to visualize the comparisons of average costs, child expenses, veterans, paupers, widows, Negroes; experiences of family welfare societies with extravagant funeral expenditures, by dependent families; "What is a reasonable bill?" Description of various state practices and government allowances; funeral management abroad, customs, costs for European nations; the economics of the burial industry--economics of suppliers, growth of the funeral service business; Committee's conclusions and recommendations (far less thorough than the analyses). Appendices: state training requirements; average costs for industrial policy holders by state and selected cities and average costs for children in the states; number and amount of charges for specific items for "insufficient asset" group; and summary of reports from family welfare societies on extravagance in expenditures and exploitation by undertakers. The classic study of funeral extravagance.

959 _____. Reasons for Present-Day Funeral Costs; A Summary of Facts Developed by the Advisory Committee on Burial Survey in the Course of an Impartial Study of the Burial Industry. New York: Metropolitan Life Insurance, 1927. 39pp., illus., charts.

960 Gilman, Richard. "The Loved One Is in the Slumber Room, Laid Out in Style." New York Times cxii(38, 564): sect. VII, p. 4 (Aug. 25, 1963).
Review of Jessica Mitford's The American Way of Death (entry 993).

Glick, Ira O., Weiss, Robert S. and Parkes, C. Murray. The First Year of Bereavement. See entry 300.

961 Gold, Gerald. "Wide Range of Funeral Prices Found Here in Consumer Study." New York Times cxxiii(42, 442):38 (April 7, 1974). Price list.

New York City funerals range from $400 to $1200 for requested "inexpensive funeral. " Two-thirds of funeral homes discourage or refuse to give price quotes over the telephone. Cremation costs ranged from $235 to $687 for direct cremation through a funeral home. Cemetery graves range from $255 to $660. See also "Funeral Fee is $600, " entry 953.

962 Goodstein, George. "'Scientific Neglect, '" Northeast Funeral Director 21(8):4-5 (1972).
Counsel of the New York State Funeral Directors Assoc. suggests at its 1972 annual meeting that directors take a good look at new ideas and developing trends in the industry before discarding them. Examples: unrestricted pre-arrangements and burial insurance; quick disposal; mortuaries operated by religious corporations or cemeteries; short funerals sponsored by memorial societies; flexible or fragmentized funeral; graduated recovery pricing; public funeral corporations which are becoming increasingly involved in mortuaries, cemeteries, and insurance; casket companies' funeral finance plans; fringe benefit programs sponsored by unions that provide total or partial coverage of funeral expenses.

963 Gordon, Mitchell. Furor Over Funerals. " Wall Street Journal April 21, 1965, p. 1.

964 Gould, Jack. "TV: The Funeral Rite. " New York Times cxiii(38, 624):67 (Oct. 24, 1963).
Review of television show "The Great American Funeral. "

965 "Grieving Widow vs. the Funeral Director. " Northeast Funeral Director 20(4):6 (1971).
Reprint of March 4, 1971, news item in the Boston Globe; case story of a physician's widow's difficulties in carrying out her husband's wishes for a simple funeral. Proposed legislation requiring two public members on the state board which presently comprises five funeral directors. Help might come from the Memorial Society, which suggests that members arrange inexpensive funerals and burials in advance of death.

966 Harbison, Janet. "New Patterns for American Funerals. " Presbyterian Life Aug. 1, 1964, p. 8ff.

967 Harmer, Ruth Mulvey. "Funerals That Make Sense. " Modern Maturity 17(3):59-61 (June-July 1974).
The funeral industry has nurtured the idea that you can take it with you and survivors' guilt can be eased by a luxurious funeral. Result: the funeral is often the most expensive American purchase after house, car, and college. Middle-income people and the poor are equally victimized. Brief sketch of the industry's development from when funerals were community ceremonies and undertaking a sideline, to the Civil War and the development of embalming when it became big business. 1939 backlash against economic exploitation and anti-religious overtones taken on by funerals. The development of memorial societies, their functions, and activities of a selected few throughout the U. S.

968 _____. The High Cost of Dying. New York: Collier Books, 1963. 256pp., index (paper). (Orig. ed. publ. by Crowell-Collier now out of print). (Paperback eds. available from Continental Assoc. 59 E. Van Buren St., Chicago 60605).
This and Jessica Mitford's The American Way of Death (entry 993) opened the flood of criticism against the funeral industry and brought about the subsequent self-analysis and reform of that industry. Focuses on the economic aspects of American burial, tracing evolution of funeral rites from earliest times; chronicles rise of the American funeral industry, the increase of the undertaker's social status, along with the cost of his services and decline of his ethical standards. Describes the undertakers' practices, principles, costs of his services, cemetery charges, state laws, permanent and endowed care, purchasing of lots, markers, and full description of nonprofit burial societies that aim to restore dignity of the funeral service while keeping down its cost.

969 _____. "The High Cost of Dying." The Progressive, March 1961.

970 Hastings, R. J. "Are Funerals Dying Out?" Christianity Today 13:13-14+ (Nov. 22, 1968).

971 Havemann, Ernest. "Are Funerals Barbaric?" McCalls, May 1956.

972 Head, Ralph. "The Reality of Death--What Happens When It Is Ignored?" Casket & Sunnyside 101(6):20-24 (1971).
Value of the funeral as observed from the humanistic, societal, emotional, and theological phases. Comparison of the memorial service and private funerals as opposed to traditional ones.

973 "The High Cost of Dying." Economist, Sept. 6, 1962.

974 High, George D. "Changing Standards in a Changing Society." The Director 39(5):9 (1969).
Hard look by society at traditional funerals and the need for funeral directors to eliminate those parts of the service the public wishes dropped.

975 Hopton, Frederick C. Ethical Funeral. Glenshaw, Pa.: The Author, 1946. 137pp.

976 "How America Spends Its Money." Ladies Home Journal, Dec. 1961.
Funeral costs.

977 "How Not to Read a Book." New York Times cxiii(38, 620): sect. IV, p. 10 (Oct. 20, 1963).
Times editorial on Congressman James B. Utt's attack on Jessica Mitford. See Oct. 18th issue of the Times for Utt's allegation that Mitford was a communist (see entry 980).

978 "Inquiries Increase Regarding Funeral Costs." The Jewish

Funeral Director 43(1):24ff[2pp.] (winter 1975) [repr. from The Director, Dec. 1974].

Average price of American adult funerals in 1972 (not including welfare funerals or interment receptacle, burial clothing, cemetery plot, crematory costs, monument, marker, clergy honorarium, flowers, obituaries, etc.) was $1097; in 1973, $1117. According to the Bureau of Labor Statistics, between 1967 and Sept. 30, 1974, the average cost of living increased 51.9% compared to an adult funeral cost increase of 36.5%. Author stresses the importance of pointing out the value of funeral service now that such emphasis is placed on its cost.

979 "Inquiry Pressed on Funeral Costs." New York Times cxiv (39,110):46 (Feb. 21, 1965).

New York State Attorney General Lefkowitz's office investigates funeral directors. May seek wider controls over the industry.

980 "Jessica Mitford Called Pro-Red." New York Times cxiii (38,618):63 (Oct. 18, 1963).

Congressman James B. Utt (R-Calif.), in Congressional Record, labels Mitford as "pro-communist, anti-American." Cites past association. "Beneath comment," responds Mitford. See entry 977.

981 Jones, Annette Bousquet. "The Dear Departed." Northeast Funeral Director 20(9):4 (1971).

Begins with tongue-in-cheek comparison of splendid habitat of the "dear departed" with is simple life when he was alive. Ends with a list of nine funeral instructions. The first: "Coffin to be the cheapest available."

982 Karolkiewicz, Henry V. "Funeral Directing and the Public." Northeast Funeral Director 22(6):4 (1973).

Practicing funeral director endorses Massachusetts Legislature for its action in voting down proposed legislation which the author says claimed to cut down funeral costs but in effect would not. Supports argument with statistics that compare funeral cost increases with increases in other fields.

983 Kaye, Nancy. "Fighting Fancy Funerals." Medical Economics, Jan. 29, 1962.

984 "'Kildare' TV Producers Defend Funeral Episode." New York Times cxiii(38,700):43 (Jan. 8, 1964).

Norman Felton, executive producer of "Dr. Kildare," answers funeral industry's objections to Kildare episode dealing with unscrupulous funeral directors. Felton is quoted saying "There are men in every profession who do a disservice to that profession. This was a story depicting that type of individual."

985 Kinsolving, Lester. "Morticians and Marble Orchards." Northeast Funeral Director 21(10):10 (1972).

Criticism of funeral directors, their poor relationships

with the clergy, pointing out the scandals exposed in The American
Way of Death and The High Cost of Dying. Refers to California's
bill promising major reforms by requiring that each service and
costs be itemized before signing of a contract and prohibiting crematories from requiring that corpses be casketed.

986   Magrisso, Abe, and Rubin, Donald. "Death's High Toll."
       AFL-CIO Industrial Union Digest, fall 1961.

987   and   . "The High Cost of Dying." National
       Maritime Union Pilot, March 23, 1961.

988   Mahoney, Joan. "Lectures on Death, Funerals Aid Greater
       Boston Families." Northeast Funeral Director 21(1):4 (1972).
            Home economist with the Middlesex County Extension Serv-
    ice of Concord, Mass., conducts lecture and question-and-answer
    periods on "The High Cost of Dying--Fact or Fallacy?" Local funer-
    al director responds to questions.

989   Manaugh, Francis A. Thirty Thousand Adventures; An Informal
       Disclosure of Observations and Experiences in Research in the
       Funeral Industry. Laguna Beach, CA: The Author, 1934.
       329pp.

990   "Many Burial Ads Dupe Public, Senators Are Told." New York
       Times cxiii(38, 883):13 (July 9, 1964).
            Senate Antitrust and Monopoly Subcommittee hears Bruce
    Hotchkiss, president of the NFDA, Harry Gilligan, past president of
    the NFDA, and Thomas Clark, general counsel of the NFDA dispute
    propriety and worth of advertising funeral costs.

991   Martin, Edward A. "The Enemy Within." Casket & Sunnyside
       100(2):17+ (1970).
            Former NFDA president points up problems created by di-
    rectors who weaken the profession by their own poorly thought out
    actions. They must be controlled by efforts of other members or
    by enforcement of public regulations by law.

992   Mencken, H. L. The American Language, 4th ed. New York,
       1936.
            Sharp comments on morticians.

993   Mitford, Jessica. The American Way of Death. New York:
       Simon and Schuster, 1963, 333pp., index, biblio; New York:
       Fawcett World, 1973.
            Watershed study that opened the floodgates of criticism of
    the funeral industry. Discussion of the psychological strategies used
    by funeral directors, public relations techniques, euphemistic language
    to diffuse the reality of death, merchandising techniques, legal intri-
    cacies, the waste of embalming, allied industries, cremation, what
    the public really wants, comparison of simple, dignified and inexpen-
    sive European funerals. Appendices: how to organize a memorial
    society; eyebanks; body donations. Over 100,000 copies sold in
    hardback.

994 _____ . "Prisons and Funerals." New York Times cxxii
     (42, 228), Sept. 5, 1973.
          Comparison of funeral and prison costs (too high for both);
both are big industries built on suffering, hypocrisy, greed, and
public gullibility.

995 "More on Dr. Elisabeth Kubler-Ross." The Director LV(4):10
     (April 1975).
          Quotes the Minnesota Daily item on Dr. Kubler-Ross as
switching from her previous negative feeling toward funeral directors
to a more positive one. The change was effected by a recent meeting with 35 directors who she believed were "taking a unique approach to their work." She did say, however, that "she would rather
have people tell patients before they die that they are loved and skip
the schmaltzy eulogies later."

996 Morgan, Al. "The Bier Barons." Playboy, June 1960; also
     repr. in Sociological Symposium I:28-35 (1969).
          Lampoon of funeral service practice in Hollywood, especial-
ly of Forest Lawn Cemetery and its founder, Dr. Hubert Eaton.

997 Murray, Don. "What Should a Funeral Cost?" Coronet, Oct.
     1961.

998 Myers, Ruth Marie. "Mortician's Daughter Polls Fellow Class-
     mates." Casket & Sunnyside 105(5):12ff[4pp.] (May 1975).
          In a concise paper written for an Adams State College
class, the author states, "It is about time that the public came to
appreciate the value of the funeral director-embalmer.... With
time, the ignorance toward the funeral profession, built upon super-
stitions of past generations, must give way to enlightenment...."
She conducted a survey concerning funeral practice on a random
selection of 71 students to find out their views on death and "to
affirm or contradict my belief as to the public being prejudiced towards persons involved in funeral practice." Discusses the reality
of being a director--the 3:00 a.m. phone call; and necessity of
embalming, training, and for the public to recognize the value of
the profession.

999 National Funeral Directors Assoc. But I Never Made Funeral
     Arrangements Before! Milwaukee, WI: NFDA (pamphlet). n.d.
          Topics sketched include the funeral, the visitation or
wake, having the body present and viewed, the service and committal,
and whether children should attend the funeral.

1000 _____ . Findings of the Professional Census. Available
     from the NFDA.

1001-1002 [No entry.]

1003 "New Study on Consumer Attitudes Toward Death and Funerals
     Now Available to Cemeterians." The Cemeterian, Nov.
     1974, p. 20-21.

Review of the CMA's recently released book, American Attitudes Toward Death and Funerals (entry 926), prepared by a CMA research team to show trends in funerals and related activities.

Ninker, Robert. "Funeral Economics Tomorrow." See entry 690.

1004 Pine, Vanderlyn R. Funeral Service Facts and Figures. Milwaukee, WI: NFDA, 1973. 38pp.

_____. A Statistical Abstract of Funeral Service Facts and Figures of the United States. See entry 698.

1005 _____, and Phillips, Derek L. "The Cost of Dying: A Sociological Analysis of Funeral Expenditure." Social Problems 17(3):405-17 (1970).
Funeral cost information on 351 adult funerals in small towns in the northeastern U.S. illustrating the correlation between soci-economic status and money spent for funerals. Findings: $800 or more is spent by over 18% of the low status group and about 56% of the middle status group; women spend more than men at every level; more is spent among elderly; more spent on spouses than on other relatives; expenditures are higher with unexpected deaths.

1006 Plumb, J. H. "De Mortuis." Horizon 9(2):40-41 (spring 1967). Photos, drawing.
The death of Hubert Eaton and the thought of Forest Lawn prompts the author to note other "absurdities" of burial: pet cemeteries, cryonics, mummies, and medieval tomb sculptures.

1007 Porter, William H. Jr. "Some Sociological Notes on a Century of Change in the Funeral Business;' Sociological Symposium I:36-46 (1968).
Changes in funeral business during the last 100 years: technological development of goods and services; occupational status; public image of the funeral director; organizational patterns, arterial embalming (the most significant technological change, permitting extension of the period between death and interment that has made the funeral home the focal point of the funeral); burial insurance; grief psychology as a significant concept; educational development; and improved relations with the clergy.

1008 Prescott, Orville. "The High Cost of Dying." New York Times cxii(38,567):31 (Aug. 28, 1963).
Review of Jessica Mitford's The American Way of Death (entry 993).

1009 "Price Ads Beget Baiting, Funeral Men Tell Senate." Advertising Age 35:6 (July 13, 1964).

1010 "Price Advertising Opposed By U.S. Funeral Directors." New York Times cxiv(38,979):28 (Oct. 13, 1964).
NFDA poll shows 19 to 1 opposed.

Raether, Howard C. "The Place of the Funeral: The Role of the Funeral Director in Contemporary America. " See entry 1225.

_____. "The Role of the Funeral Director. " See entry 1226.

1011 Rapaport, Henry N. "Dignity in Death" United Synagogue Review, winter 1964, p. 9, 23. Photo.
    In convention speech to the United Synagogue, chairman criticizes cosmetology, open caskets, music, and flowers as out of place in the Jewish funeral; grief therapy should come from the Torah, not from a funeral director; congregations should educate their members against the practice of embalming, cremation, and using indestructible caskets and encourage a return to traditional funeral practice which is dignified and unostentatious.

1012 "Rep. Utt Skeptical on C. B. S. Motives. " New York Times cxiii(38, 619): 53 (Oct. 1963).
    Rep. Utt refuses to appear on "Great American Funeral"
show.

1013 Resen, Elaine L. "The Public's Need to Know--A Personal Survey. " Mortuary Management 57(10):26+ (1970).
    On basis of her own survey, author believes that the public needs to know more about the funeral service industry; public is put off by and suspicious of some directors' secretiveness on pricing, services, etc.

1014 Robb, Christina. "What Price Death?" Northeast Funeral Director 21(5):6-8 (1972).
    U.S. and Massachusetts statistics based on interviews with the legal counsel and past president of the Mass. FDA, the president of the Memorial Society of New England, the marketing chief of the National Casket Co. , and Jessica Mitford. Review of the functions of the Mass. Board of Registration in embalming and funeral directing. Concludes that funeral costs in New England are approximately the same as for the nation as a whole, services and use of goods make up over 75% of the total cost of a funeral, and complaints come mostly from customers, rarely from officials.

1015 Roth, Jack. "Shakedown Plot Is Charged to 3. " New York Times cxiv(39, 163):39 (April 15, 1965).
    An assistant attorney general, an investigator from the Attorney General's office, and a lawyer are accused of attempting to extort $2000 from Andrew Terregrossa of the Terragrossa Funeral Home.

1016 Rugaber, Walter. "F. T. C. Finds Wide Cost Spread in District of Columbia Funerals. " New York Times cxxiii(42, 405):26 (March 1, 1974).
    F. T. C. charges that a "feeble competition environment" exists among D. C. funeral homes. Prices vary for the same service. Findings available from F. T. C. Legal and Public Records Div. , Washington, DC 20580.

Sable, Myra. The Positive Role of Grief. See entry 195.

1017 Salamone, Jerome. "The Status of Funerals and Funeral
       Directors. " American Funeral Director 90:69-74 (Oct. 1967).

1018 Samson, Harry G. The Mystery of Death; or, The Social
       Significance of Mortuary Beliefs and Customs; Being an Ad-
       dress at the Seventh Annual Meeting of National Selected Mor-
       ticians, Oct. 5, 1924. Des Moines, IO, 1924. 20pp.

1019 "Senators Inquire into Funeral Ads. " New York Times cxiii
       (38, 882):17 (July 8, 1964).
            Senate Anti-Trust and Monopoly Subcommittee opens
   hearings; hears Wilber Krieger of NSM; Nicholas Daphne, a San Francisco mortician; and Edmund Oberton, suspended from the NFDA for
   publicizing prices.

1020 "A Shift in Attitudes on Funerals Noted. " New York Times
       cxvii(40, 089):25 (Oct. 28, 1967).
            NFDA survey finds there is a nation-wide drift towards
   less expensive, non-religious funerals.

1021 "Sigma Mu Sigma Questionnaire Results Available. " Northeast
       Funeral Director 18(6):15-16 (1969).
            Summary of replies to questionnaire opinion poll on con-
   torversial subjects, conducted by an honor society at the New England
   Institute of Anatomy, Sanitary Science and Embalming. Poll sent to
   members of the Institute's Alumni Society residing in New England.
   Questions on enforcement of state board regulations, dual licenses,
   post-graduate education, mortuary college entrance requirements,
   fair wages, billing procedures.

1022 "Some Comparative Statistics on the Cost of Living and Dying."
       The Director XLV(5):4 (May 1975).
            U.S. Bureau of Labor Statistics reports that between
   1967 and March 31, 1975, the cost of adult funerals has risen 41. 8%
   compared to the average cost of services, which have risen 57. 8%,
   doctors' fees, 65%, and hospital services, 127. 8%. During 1974
   the cost of adult funerals rose 7% and the overall cost of living,
   12%.

1023 A Special Correspondent. "The High Cost of Dying. " Econo-
       mist, Sept. 16, 1962.

1024 "The Sting. " Newsweek, April 15, 1974, p. 88.
            Views from both the funeral industry's critics and its
   representatives. Critics: prices rose in the decade preceding April
   1973 by 32. 1%; directors in the Chicago area quote a base price for
   embalming, coffin, and funeral service at over $1300 with an addi-
   tional $700-odd for burial plot. Labor costs account for 29% of a
   funeral director's overhead. The industry counters: expenses could
   be sizably cut if people would use their living rooms for embalming
   and viewing; funeral directors can't take advantage of sorrowing
   families since they depend heavily on repeat business; licensing

boards are getting tougher; cremations are gaining popularity; funeral societies are spreading. Newest trends: high-rise mausoleums and drive-in viewing services, air conditioned carpeted mourning rooms.

1025 Strub, Clarence G. "Holy Waste or Unholy Haste?" Casket & Sunnyside 100(12):11-13 (1970).
    Funeral practice contributes to the American death-defying, death-denying syndrome.

1026 "Survey of Attitudes Shows Both Good & Bad." Mortuary Management 62(1):22ff[3pp.] (Jan. 1975). Photos.
    More comment on the CMA's study of American Attitudes Toward Death and Funerals (entry 926). Author finds the attitudes of the public encouraging (the youth especially), considering the recent bad publicity; warns the public's misconceptions about profits, prices, preference for simpler funerals, however, are reason for concern and appropriate action; key to solving the director's problems may be services--"personal services, human concern, and sympathetic helpfulness are far more important to people than facilities or merchandise--or even low price."

1027 Throckmorton, Burton H., Jr. "Do Christians Believe in Death?" Christian Century 86(21):708-10 (May 21, 1969), with discussion, 86(30):998 (July 23, 1969).
    Funerals; people's reactions to death.

1028 Trussell, C. P. "Funeral Inquiry Opening Tuesday." New York Times cxiii(38, 879):22 (July 5, 1964).
    Senate Antitrust and Monopoly Subcommittee, chaired by Sen. Hart, to inquire about pricing, selling, and advertising practices.

1029 Tunley, Roul. "Can You Afford to Die?" Saturday Evening Post 234(24):24, 80, 82 (June 17, 1961). Photos.
    Jessica Mitford is among those in the San Francisco area who is fighting the high cost of funerals. Neil Brown of the San Francisco Funeral Directors Association defends "our high standard of dying." Thorough analysis of both sides of the issue.

1030 Turner, Fred B. "The Procession: A Part of the Contemporary Funeral." The Director 41:14-15 (Nov. 1971).
    Letter to Florida newspaper speculating what it would be like if funeral processions were ended--a move favored in some states.

1031 U.S. Congress. Senate. Committee on the Judiciary. Subcommittee on Antitrust and Monopoly. Antitrust Aspects of the Funeral Industry (pursuant to S. Res. 262) on July 7-9, 1964. 326pp., tables, appendices.
    Witnesses, in order of appearance: Wilber Krieger, managing director of NSM, offers statement overview of industry and NSM and its code of ethics (16pp.); questioning (22pp.). Edmund Overton, Overton Funeral Home, Janesville, Wis., testifies about

Wisconsin FDA's and NFDA's anti-advertising policy; describes background and his firm's suspension from WFDA and NFDA for advertising prices (15pp.). Nicholas Daphne, San Francisco mortician
who has worked with a cooperative funeral society and was, therefore,
excluded from the S.F. FDA and harassed by them (14pp.). Howard
Raether, Bruce Hotchkiss, Glenn Griffin, Harry Gilligan, and Thomas
Clark, NFDA, discuss the NFDA's role in the funeral industry, answer previous statements, discuss advertising, pre-need arrangements, etc. (86pp.). William W. Chambers, Washington, D.C.
funeral director, discusses the restraint imposed by state boards;
says advertising will lower prices (8pp.). Howard Johnson, Canon
of St. John the Divine, New York City, discusses clergy's views,
condemns lack of knowledge and discussion of death, describes
modern American funeral ritual (12pp). Harry Haskel, Director of
Death Benefits, Dept. of International Ladies' Garment Workers
Union, tells of his dealings with funeral directors; his average bill
from directors in 1963 was $924 (15pp.). Tables of funeral and
casket costs; further testimony by Wilber Krieger relative to costs
(13pp.). Appendices: FTC Trade Practice Rules; NSM Code of
Ethics; various court decisions; Overton, Wis., FDA correspondence;
NFDA Constitution and By-Laws; "The American Funeral," by Thomas
Glidden, past president of NFDA, reprint from Pastoral Psychology,
June 1963; hearing exhibits; Better Business Bureau's brochure on
pre-arranging; "Pke Istam Sanctam Unctionem" by Msgr. Francis
McElligott, reprint from Extension, Dec. 1963; "The Occasion of
Death and Burial--A Religious Ceremony," by Rev. Robert F. Allen,
reprint from Catholic Cemetery, May 1964; Subcommittee correspon-
dence and publicity; National Labor Relations Board hearing of the
Isa Kaufman Chapel, Inc., and Michigan Mortuary Employees Assoc.;
NLRB hearing of Riverside Memorial Chapel and International Broth-
erhood of Teamsters, etc.; written correspondence with recommendations from interested parties; income tax chart of the NFDA; National Recovery Administration (NRA) code for funeral directors.

1032   .   .   . Special Committee on Aging.
        Preneed Burial Service, Hearing, May 19, 1964. Washington,
        DC: U.S. Gov. Printing Office, 1964. 28pp.
        Hearings of May 19, 1964: statements by Richard N.
Carpeter, of New Mexico Attorney General's office, and W. Dan
Bell, Rocky Mountain Better Business Bureau; written statements by
Howard C. Raether, NFDA, and Allan Bachman, National Better
Business Bureau. Topic: mail-order, pre-need burial insurance,
focusing on several firms engaged in fraudulent or quasi-fraudulent
practices. Raether explains the NFDA's policy; W. M. Krieger explains NSM's position. The Better Business Bureau submits its
pamphlet on pre-need insurance.

1033 Walter, F. R. "A Thought: 'High Cost of Dying'." The
        Director 42(7):10 (1972).
        A clergyman's defense of funerals and funeral directors
in response to an article in an eastern newspaper on non-profit
burial societies and economic funerals. Believes the director is
as entitled to his profit as businessmen in other professions.

1034 Weber, Max. The Protestant Ethic and the Spirit of Capi-
talism, tr. by Talcott Parsons. NY: Scribners, 1930.
292p.
Analysis of the relationship between commerce and religion, including funerals.

1035 "What Was the Most Important Contribution That Was Made to
Funeral Service in the Past 100 Years?" Casket & Sunnyside 101(13[centennial issue]):8ff.[4pp.] (1972). photos.
Leaders of the profession give answers: provisions for
viewing in funeral homes as private residences became smaller and
impractical environments for displaying body; improved embalming
techniques; conducting services in funeral homes rather than homes
or churches; motorized funeral vehicles. Predictions for the future,
based on recognized changes to "socio-economic stimuli," include
mergers, greater involvement in post-funeral operations (grief counseling), other pricing methods, different approaches to selling in
order to preserve profits while simultaneously serving the public.

Wilson, Sir Arnold and Levy, Herman. Burial Reform and
Funeral Costs. See entry 251.

2. MORTUARY LAW, COURT DECISIONS,
PROPOSALS FOR REFORM

Barish, Marvin I. "The Law of Testamentary Disposition ...
A Legal Barrier to Medical Advance." See entry 810.

1036 Bernard, Hugh Yancey. Law of Death and Disposal of the
Dead. Dobbs Ferry, NY: Oceana, 1966. 113pp., index,
biblio., appendix, table of cases.
Case studies pointing up the legal principles of burial
(the re-interment of Quanah Parker) and the foundation for modern
American burial law (the Samual Ruggles Report); the funeral industry, transportation regulations concerning embalming, funeral
directors, the codes of ethics of the NFDA and the NSM; pricing
and trade practices; liability of funeral directors; body donations by
survivors and pre-arranged by the dying; vital statistics and legal
documents; pre-need funerals; coroners and medical examiners;
statutory regulation of cemeteries and other matters concerning
cemeteries; cremation, crematories, columbaria, monuments, and
markers.

1037 California. State Board of Funeral Directors and Embalmers.
Laws, Rules, and Regulations. Oakland: California State
Board of Embalmers, 1916, 47pp. (paper); Sacramento, CA:
State Printing Office, 1933, 15pp.

Castel, J. G. "Some Legal Aspects of Human Organ Transplantation in Canada." See entry 1752.

1038 "City Morgue Aids Barred from Work for Funeral Homes."
      New York Times cxxiii(42, 426):35 (March 22, 1974).
            To curtail unethical practices by some funeral homes, city
morgue aids are prohibited to do work for them.

1039 Clark, Thomas H. "Court Upholds Substantial Funeral Bill."
      The Director 41(3):10 (1971).
            Virginia Supreme Court holds total bill of $6300 (about
2% of the deceased's estate) is not a disproportionate share of the
value of the estate to spend on the funeral and that it duly reflected
his station in life.

1040 _____. "Primary Duties of Executive Employee Clarified
      for Federal Wage and Hour Law." The Director 41(3):10
      (1971).

1041 _____, and Raether, Howard C. "Forms to Be Used in
      Compliance with the Federal Truth in Lending Laws." The
      Director 39(9):7-9 (1969).
            Description of law and recommendation of the single unit,
bi-unit, and multi-unit pricing methods and applicable funeral agreement forms.

1042 _____, and _____. "Funeral Service Affected by Price
      and Wage Freeze." The Director 41(9):3-4 (1971).
            Effect of Richard Nixon's Phases I and II on the funeral
industry.

      "Concerning the Ultimate Question." See entry 1753.

1043 "Connecticut Passes Disclosure Law." The New England
      Funeral Director 1(5):11 (Aug. 1975).
            Connecticut is the first New England state to require dis-
closure of all funeral costs. Failure to comply can result in revocation or suspension of the funeral director's license. The law decrees
that customers must be given a written statement showing "(1) the
price of the service that the person or persons have selected and what
is included therein; (2) the price of each of the supplemental items of
service and/or merchandise requested; (3) the amount involved for
each of the items for which the firm will advance monies as an accommodation to the family; (4) the method of payment."

1044 "Connecticut Requires Mandatory Disclosure." American Fu-
      neral Director 98(6):49 (June 1975).
            The Connecticut Legislature's Regulation Review, which
enacts laws while the State Assembly is not meeting, approved the
mandatory disclosure rule proposed by the State Board of Examiners
of Embalmers and Funeral Home Directors. Directors must state in
writing: the cost of services and what they include; cost of additional services and merchandise requested; cost of all items for which
the funeral home has advanced money; method of payment; guarantee
that the funeral home will charge only what it pays out for services
it has done, such as grave opening. Impetus for rules' adoption

came from the Federal Trade Commission. Failure to comply can result in license suspension or revocation.

1045 Dews, Richard P. Mortuary Law. Nashville, TN: The Author, 1946. 241pp.

Federal Trade Commission. Funeral Industry Practices: Trade Regulation Proceeding. 16 CFR Part 453. See entry 940.

1046 Fellows, Alfred. Law of Burial and Generally of the Disposal of the Dead. See entry 67.

1047 Foran, Eugene, and Raether, Howard. "Successful Funeral Service Practice--Business Aspects of a Funeral Service Practice." Mortuary Management 60(1):30-32 (1973).
From Raether's book on funeral service practice. Explanation of the Truth in Lending Law and its application to funeral home operations. Detailed discussion of where the regulation applies and where it doesn't.

1048 Fowler, Elizabeth M. "Personal Finance: Paying Funeral Bills." New York Times cxxiii(42, 558):35, 43 (Aug. 1, 1974).
Riverside Memorial Chapel v. Edward Albert.

1049 "The Funeral Director's Liability for Mental Anguish." Hastings Law Journal 15:464 (1964); digest in Law Review Digest 14:102 (1964).

1050 Harris, Thomas I. "Regulation 'Z'." Mortuary Management 59(8):14-15 (1972).
Recount of the duty of the funeral home to comply with the Federal Regulation Truth in Lending Law and a discussion of various specifications of this law.

1051 Hogan. "Indecent Treatment of a Corpse." Arkansas Law Review 4:480 (1950).

"Human Tissue Act...." See entry 1760.

1052 Jabine, William. "The Law Says...." Mortuary Management 58(1):28-29 (1971).
What constitutes a reasonable funeral expense? Supreme Court of Appeals reverses a lower court's order concerning estate executors' refusal to pay the full amount of an expensive funeral-- Scott Funeral Home, Inc. v. First National Bank of Danville, Va., 176 S.E. 2d 335.

1053 _____. "The Law Says...." Mortuary Management 59(8): 22-24 (1972).
Florida Court of Appeals sustains the appeal by the Florida Board of Embalmers and Funeral Directors requesting that

a state resident not be allowed to act as a funeral director without proper licensing.

1054 _____. "The Law Says...." Mortuary Management 62(8): 19-20 (July/Aug. 1975).
　　　　Highlights of District Court of Appeals of Florida, Second District, decision. Court upheld the State Board of Funeral Directors and Embalmers' contention that a corporation none of whose employees is licensed as a funeral director violates State statutues by storing dead bodies before cremation.

1055 Jackson, Percival E. The Law of Cadavers and of Burial and Burial Places, 2nd ed. Englewood Cliffs, NJ: Prentice Hall, 1950. 734pp.

　　　Kansas State Board of Embalming. Embalmers Rules, Laws and Regulations 1924. See entry 463.

1056 Kilburn, Robert L. "The Man from OSHA." Mortuary Management 60(3):8-12 (1973).
　　　　Every funeral home is bound by the provisions of the Federal Occupational Safety and Health Act, regardless of its size. List of government publications; detailed information on OSHA.

　　　Krauskopf. "The Law of Dead Bodies, Impeding Medical Progress." See entry 828.

1057 Kuzenski. "Property in Dead Bodies." 9 Marquette Law Review 17 (1924).

1058 "List of Services Is Now Mandatory in State of California Prior to Contract." Casket & Cemetery 102(2):8 (1972).
　　　　1971 California law requires that a family before entering into a contract with a funeral home be given a list of services and merchandise charges and that casket prices be conspicuously displayed. Discussion of merchandising requirements relevant to cremation.

1059 MacConnell, Stephen T. "Funeral Home Zoning in Residential Areas: A Discussion of a Recent Maryland Case in Which the Funeral Home Prevailed." The Director XLV(5):2-3 (May 1975). Illus.
　　　　NFDA's general counsel believes that the Maryland Court of Special Appeals' Dec. 1974 decision to uphold the rights of a funeral home to build on land zoned residential may reverse that state's courts and legislators' tendency to deny such applications. Generally grounds for denial are that residential land for a funeral home would be "detrimental to the general health and welfare of the nearby residential community." Description of land, the funeral director applicants' positions, the protestors' arguments and responses to the specific objections (increased traffic, psychological effects, and effect on property values and commercial expansion). Warns that "in this case the applicant was requesting a special exception for his use, which exception had already been classified as

permissible by the country legislature. The burden of proof which must be carried by the applicant ... would vary in situations where zoning change or a variance from an existing zoning law is requested." See Louis E. Anderson, et al. v. Eugene Sawyer, et al. (Court of Special Appeals of Maryland, Dec. 16, 1974).

Massachusetts Board of Registration in Embalming. Rules and Regulations, also List of Registered Embalmers. See entry 475.

Meyers, David W. The Human Body and the Law. See entry 1764.

_____. "Organ Transplantation and the Law." See entry 1765.

1060 Morse, H. Newcomb. "Licensing Grant Implies a Right to Inspect." American Funeral Director 94(8):20+ (1971).
      District Court upheld the right of reasonable inspection by state and federal governments.

1061 Morse, H. Newcomb. "Seller Not Responsible for Fluid Accidents." American Funeral Director 94(4) (1971).
      The funeral director is the one responsible. --335 Mich 197, 55 N W 2d 795.

1062 "Morticians Must List Price." New York Times cxviii (40, 500):21 (Dec. 21, 1968).
      New York State Court of Appeals' decision demanding that funeral directors list price of merchandise and services.

1063 National Funeral Directors Assoc. The Law and the Right to Grieve. Available from the NFDA.

1064 _____. Occupational Safety and Health Act Handbook. Available from the NFDA.
      Violators of federal laws are subject to jail and/or fines up to $10, 000. Funeral directors now are more vulnerable to job safety complaints since recent laws facilitate means for workers to lodge complaints. Laws spelled out.

National Selected Morticians. Social Security Benefits Including Medicare. See entry 341.

1065 Neilson, William A. W., and Watkins, C. Gaylord. Proposals for Legislative Reforms Aiding the Consumer of Funeral Industry Products and Services. Burnsville, NC: The Celo Press, 1973. 152pp. (paper). Available from CAFMS and MSAC.
      Neilson-Watkins Report commissioned by the Memorial Society of Canada and the Continental Association of Funeral and Memorial Societies in the U. S. Comprehensive study of U. S. and Canadian legislation dealing with funeral arrangements. Topics

include anatomical donations and specific recommendations for legislative reform. Three draft laws detailed: (1) establishing the legal right of self disposition; (2) a deceptive trade practices and consumer protection act for the funeral service industry; and (3) a model funeral service industry act which combats industry self-government and promotes the public's interest. Authors are specialists in consumer law.

1066 "Note: Economic Due Process and Occupational Licensing in California." Hastings Law Journal 15:364 (1964).

1067 "Note: A Model Professional and Occupational Licensing Act." Harvard Journal Legislation, 5:67 (1967).

Olender, Jack H. "Donation of Dead Bodies & Parts Thereof for Medical Use." See entry 1767.

1068 Packel, Israel. "Spare Parts for the Human Engine." Pennsylvania Bar Association Quarterly 37:71 (1965).

1069 Parker, L. T. "How Funeral Directors Can Avoid Legal Pitfalls." Casket & Sunnyside 99(11):11-12 (1969).
Legal complexities and requirements regarding beneficiary insurance and liabilities; laws governing cemeteries and burial plots; problems funeral directors should watch for.

1070 Pastore, Matthew. "Itemization Is a Revival of Century Old Practice." Casket & Sunnyside 102(6):8 (1972).
Itemization of sample 100-year-old funeral bills in New York, Colorado, and California; discussion of New Jersey's proposed itemization law and the impracticability of multi-unit pricing.

1071 Peabody, D. W. "... and Dust to Dust." New York Times cxxiv(42,944):25 (Feb. 3, 1975).
Crucial ecological problem: modern burial equipment does not allow natural elements of the body to recycle into the ecosystem.

1072 Perley, Sidney. Mortuary Law. Boston: G. B. Reed, 1896. 220pp.

1073 "A President May Order State Funeral for Anyone." New York Times cxviii(40,610):31 (April 1, 1969).
President has the power to order state funerals.

1074 "Price Index to Include the Cost of Dying, Too." New York Times cxiii(38,636):17 (Nov. 5, 1963).
Funeral costs are added to Consumer Price Index; effort to keep track of funeral costs.

1075 Quinn, Seabury. "The Case of the Discriminatory Regulation." The Dodge Magazine 67(2):19ff(3pp.) (March 1975). Illus.

Lively narrative pointing up the legal principles involved in Needham et al. vs. Proffitt, 220 Inc. 265, 41 NE 2d, 606, decided by the Supreme Court of Indiana 12 May 1942. When the fictional funeral director advertises in local newspaper and is enjoined against such action, the Court concludes that it can see no rationale for disallowing newspaper advertising when radio advertising is allowed. The regulation of the State Board of Embalmers under which revocation of the director's license was sought, the Court ruled "clearly discrimatory, and void."

1076 _____. "The Case of the Funeral Discount Offer." The Dodge Magazine 67(3):23ff(2pp.) (June 1975). Photo.
Fictionalized story illustrating the legal principles involved in Boyd vs. Gason et al. 298 Pac 2d, 301; 179 Kan 753, decided by the Supreme Court of Kansas, 9 June 1956.

1077 _____. A Syllabus of Mortuary Jurisprudence ... for Use by Students of the Renouard Training School for Embalmers, New York City, and the Williams Institute of Embalming, Kansas City, Kansas. Kansas City, KA: C. Williams, 1933. 128pp.

1078 Robinson, Layhmond. "New Tax Dates Voted in Albany." New York Times cxiii(38,769):27 (March 17, 1964).
New York State Senate also passes Lefkowitz funeral itemization bill.

1079 _____. "Rockefeller Signs School Aid Bill." New York Times cxiii(38,797):41 (April 14, 1964).
Rockefeller signs into law Lefkowitz's funeral reform bill requiring funeral bill itemization in New York State.

1080 Ruggles, Samuel B. Law of Burial; Report to the Supreme Court of the State of New York, in 1856. Albany, NY: Weed, Parsons, 1858. 44pp.

1081 "Rules Governing Transportation of Dead Bodies, Adopted by the National Board of Health." In Proceedings, NFDA, 1897.

1082 Schanberg, Sydney H. "Funeral Abuses Attacked in Bill." New York Times cxiii(38,750):1,28 (Feb. 27, 1964).
New York State bill proposed by Attorney General Lefkowitz requires that funeral bills be itemized.

1083 "Six Funeral Homes in Area Are Fined for Bill Violations." New York Times cxx(41,258):12 (Jan. 9, 1971).
Funeral homes penalized for preparing false bills and other consumer protection violations.

Stason, E. Blyth, et al. "The Uniform Anatomical Gift Act." See entry 1770.

1084 "State Adopts Tighter Rules to Regulate Funeral Homes."

New York Times cxxiii(42,405):26 (March 1, 1974).
New York requires funeral homes to list business phone
numbers in order to curb "fly-by-night" establishments.

1085 "State to Require Morticians to Itemize Fees in Advance."
New York Times cxxii(42,113):81 (May 13, 1973).
New Jersey to require funeral homes to itemize services
and merchandize charges on contract before clients sign.

1086 Street, Arthur L. H. American Funeral Law; A Manual of
Law Affecting Funeral Directors and Embalmers. Chicago:
Grade Periodicals, 1924. 200pp.

1087 _____. Street's Mortuary Jurisprudence; A Treatise on the
Legal Rights and Liabilities Involved in the Operation of
Funeral Establishments. New York: Kates-Boylston Pub-
lications, 1948. 229pp.

1088 Stueve, Thomas F. H. Mortuary Law. Cincinnati, OH:
Cincinnati College of Mortuary Science, 1966. 102pp.
Propositions and principles of mortuary law delineated
through leading English and American cases; introduction and definition of mortuary law and its sources (general, statutes, cases, and
common law); legal aspects of dead bodies, their disposal; rights
and duties of survivors to dispose of the dead; rights of the party
undertaking disposal with respect to embalming, autopsies, photographs, etc.; rights and duties of the mortician concerning custody
of the body, funeral contracts, custody of effects, preparation,
direction of the funeral, and permits; definition of funeral director's
bill of charges; liability for funeral expense of the estate, dependents,
volunteer, executor, or the state; the law of disinterment; and laws
concerning mortuaries and cemeteries (general regulations, zoning,
types of cemeteries, public or private, the right to bury in a cemetery, sale of lots, use of markers and monuments; visitation; and
criminal offenses arising from vandalism. Specific cases are cited
throughout; review questions are included.

Tennessee State Board of Embalmers. Embalmers' Law.
See entry 570.

1089 Tomasson, Robert E. "Package Funeral Barred by Court."
New York Times cxvii(40,138):30 (Dec. 16, 1967).
Court rules that prices for merchandise and services
must be itemized by New York State funeral directors.

1090 Wagner, Johannes, ed. Reforming the Rites of Death. Paramus, NJ: Paulist-Newman, 1974. 180pp. (Concilium
series, vol. 32.)

Watkins, E. S. Law of Burials and Burial Grounds. See
entry 1393.

1091 Weinmann, George H. Survey of the Law Concerning Dead

Human Bodies. Washington, DC: National Research Council, 1929. 199pp.

1092 "Wisconsin Fines Funeral Homes." New York Times cxvii (40, 122):31 (Nov. 30, 1967).
NFDA and Wisconsin affiliates found guilty in state antitrust case because of ad policy.

1093 Wyoming State Board of Embalmers. Embalming Laws of the State of Wyoming. Cheyenne, WY: State Board of Embalming, 1913. 16pp.

3. MEMORIAL SOCIETIES AND CONSUMER EDUCATION

1094 Allied Memorial Council. Understanding for the Future. Seattle: Allied Memorial Council, n. d.
What to consider when pre-planning: wills and personal records; government and other benefits; costs of funeral home services; cemetery costs including grave and liner, crypt or niche, endowment care, burial service and memorialization; services provided by the clergy, florists, monument firms, and attorneys; the importance of the funeral as an outlet for grief, a show of support from friends and family, and a help for the bereaved in accepting death.

1095 American Funeral Directors Service. The Key to Understanding. St. Louis: Associated Funeral Directors Service, 1966. 20pp. (booklet).
Family guide to information on funerals and modern funeral service, including pre-arrangements, what to do in case of violent or accidental death, costs and arrangements of funerals, veterans' and Social Security benefits, death or burial away from home, embalming, various mortuary services available such as shampooing, hair trimming, manicure, dressing the body, providing funeral coach, etc.

1096 American Lutheran Church. Appointed Once to Die. Available from the NFDA (paper).
The Commission on Research and Social Action makes observations, comments, and suggestions to families of the American Lutheran Church on what to do when death comes: notify pastor, enlist his counsel in making burial arrangements, engage a funeral home to conduct burial and complete legal papers and publish obituary notices; notify employers, the executor of the will, insurance companies, banks, attorney, governmental offices, social security administration, retirement board or pension groups. Describes how music, casket opening and closing, flower arrangements, etc. can be conducted so they conform to proper church practice.

1097 Arvio, Raymond Paavo. The Cost of Dying and What You Can

Do About It. New York: Harper and Row, 1974. 159pp.,
index.
Queens College professor and active advocate for funeral
reform details how to pare the cost of the standard $3000 funeral
(in Rockland County, N.Y.) to $230 plus $75 crematory charges for
immediate cremation; $220 plus cemetery expenses for immediate
burial; $405 plus $75 crematory costs for cremation with viewing
and attendance; $460 and cemetery expenses with viewing and at-
tendance; and $75 for delivery to a medical school. Detailed de-
scription of memorial societies, consumer owned and operated funeral
facilities--the best means of providing quality funerals at minimal
cost; how to get help in starting a co-op, its operation, etc. Arvio
has helped found memorial societies throughout New York state and
invites interested persons to contact him at Route 45, Pamona, NY
10970.

1098 Association of Better Business Bureaus, Inc. Facts Every
Family Should Know About Funerals and Interments. New
York, 1953.
Dated, but information still useful.

"Benefits for Railroad Workers...." See entry 270.

1099 Consumer Information Bureau, Inc. What Every Woman Should
Know. Available from the NSM. 17pp. (pamphlet).
Brief sketch of NSM and its significance to the public;
what to do in the event of a death in the family; who to contact;
funeral customs and traditions; full list of funeral director's services; funeral merchandise--kinds of caskets available etc.; cost of
funeral services; benefits such as Social Security and Railroad Retirement, Veterans' Administration, Union or Employer Pension
Funds, insurance, fraternal orders, Workmen's Compensation to
which widow may be entitled; burial away from home; transportation
home if death occurs away; payment of funeral service expenses.

"A Consumer's Guide to Funerals." See entry 616.

1100 Continental Association of Funeral and Memorial Societies,
Inc. Funeral & Memorial Societies. Burnsville, NC: Celo
Press, 1973. Available from CAFMS.
Concise pamphlet answers questions about memorial societies: what they are, who controls them, membership, how pre-
planning helps at time of death, how planning saves money and how
much, how to join, transfering membership, the three alternatives
for body disposal (earth burial, cremation, and bequeathal to medical or organ banks), and where and when embalming is mandatory.
List of U.S. member societies.

1101 _____. Handbook for Memorial Societies. N.p., n.d.
Available from CAFMS.
Instructions for organizing and operating a memorial
society; how to gain local support; relations with funeral directors,
churches, labor unions, and other groups; mailings; literature;

publicity; sample by-laws; meetings; financial policy and federal tax
exemptions; alternative services to offer--earth burial, cremation,
funeral and memorial services, medical bequests; geographic areas
best served; when to publicize; how to gain cooperation of funeral
directors; how to prepare incorporation papers.

1102 _____. How to Organize a Memorial-Funeral Society.
N. p., n. d. Available from CAFMS.
Step-by-step instructions for organizing a memorial society, including what literature exists on the subject, what groups to
contact for endorsements, in what media to advertise first public
meeting, what motions to introduce at this meeting, and what operational procedures to adopt once the group is organized.

1103 _____. The Memorial Society. Burnsville, NC: Celo
Press, 1963. Available from CAFMS.
The function of the memorial society; need for advance
planning; cremation; memorial services and meetings; bequests of
bodies to medical research; eye banks; reciprocal services of memorial societies.

1104 _____. Putting My House in Order. N. p., n. d. Available from CAFMS.
Two-page form to record information such as burial
wishes, insurance policy, and other information for family in case
of death.

1105 Council of Better Business Bureaus, Inc. "Comparing Costs
Can Cut Funeral Expense." "Tips for Consumers" newspaper column available from the Consumer Information Department of the Council of Better Business Bureaus, Inc.,
1150 17th St., N. W., Washington, DC 20036. Released
March 15, 1975.
In light of the findings of the Federal Trade Commission's
study--i. e. that there are a variety of choices available to the pub-
lic--the Better Business Bureau gives tips on how to shop for comparative prices and other matters to be considered by the person
making funeral arrangements. Many banks offer free service to
help survivors collect proper death and pension benefits through
Special Organizational Services which emphasize pre-mortem financial planning. For information write Special Organizational Services,
P. O. Box 202, Athens, TX 75751.

1106 Daly, Margaret. "Death in the Family: How to Be Financially Ready." Better Homes & Gardens 51(7):22,28 (July
1973).
Things to prepare for in case of death: instructions for
funeral, wills; how to plan funeral and estimate costs; cremation
as alternative; how funeral costs are paid, i. e. by Social Security
or Veterans' Administration benefits, etc.

1107 Deachman, Tom. How to Beat the High Cost of Dying (pamphlet). Reprinted from Weekend Magazine, May 1, 1971,

with figures up-dated to include statistics available May 1,
1974. Available from the Memorial Society Association of
Canada.
    One of the best ways to keep down funeral costs is to
join a memorial society. Rundown of funeral cost statistics; gross
profits (regional); reasons for difference in costs in the different
provinces. Because of memorial society activities, the average
funeral cost in British Columbia is $125 compared to the national
average of $700. Profile of the memorial society: membership,
services, cost ($5 usually for single, $10 for family life membership), goals (simple funerals without embalming or cosmetology).
Many psychologists believe making up the dead to look like the living prevents the bereaved from facing the reality of death. Attitudes
of the conventional funeral industry towards memorial societies; the
industry's attempt to introduce legislation like the U.S.'s giving
members control of licensing and setting standards. The Society
defeated it, fearful the industry would make embalming and cosmetology mandatory. The 1970 takeover of 23 funeral homes across
Canada by Service Corporation International (SCI) of Houston, Texas
and International Funeral Services (IFS) of Des Moines, Iowa.

1108 "Death Without Debt." Everybody's Money. Autumn, 1974.
         p. 24-26.
    All about memorial societies--organizations dedicated to
preplanning funerals in order to keep them simple, dignified, and
economical. Planning through a memorial society can slice up to
50% off typical cremation costs. (The Bay Area Funeral Society
in California charges $225 for immediate cremation, including funer-
al director services, compared to the usual fee of $350 to $400.)
Membership for a family ranges from $5 to $20. Disposition options available include immediate burial without embalming, cremation after embalming, cremation after a simple service, immediate
cremation without embalming, and bequeathal and organ donation.

1109 Diamond, Dorothy. How to Meet a Family Crisis. Good
         Reading Communications, Inc., P.O. Box 450, Stamford,
         CT 06904, 1971. Available from the National Funeral Di-
         rectors Association. 15pp. (paper).
    Pamphlet urging individuals and families in need to con-
sult credentialed professionals rather than quacks and fortune tellers.
What to do in the event of a death in the family; who to notify; services provided by a funeral director such as ordering flowers, notify-
ing relatives and friends, over and above the basic arrangements for
burial, cremation, transportation of body, embalming, etc.

Directory of Memorial Associations. See entry 842.

1110 Ewing, Gretchen. "Funerals Can Be Simple." Northeast
         Funeral Director 20(1):10 (1973).
    Brief look at the function of memorial societies--their
goals and services. Views are predominantly those of two officers
of the Lehigh Valley Memorial Society, Inc., in Pennsylvania.

Federal Benefits for Veterans and Dependents. See entry
293.

1111 Flanagan, William, ed. "Personal Business: Making the Ultimate Decision. " Business Week no. 2372 (March 17, 1975).
Details funeral pre-planning, instructions one should leave;
suggests simple funeral and use of a memorial society. Quotes one
society's prices.

1112 Fordahl, Edna K. Planning and Paying for Funerals. St.
Paul, MN: Agricultural Extension Service, University of
Minnesota, 1969. 33pp. HM-72ca.

1113 Fowler, Elizabeth M. "Personal Finance: Awareness of
Basic Funeral Facts May Save Survivors Needless Costs. "
New York Times cxviii(40, 668):55, 57 (May 29, 1969).
Funeral costs and the consumer's need for foreknowledge
of costs, services, and merchandise available.

1114 "Funeral Societies--How They Help. " Changing Times 27(5):
21-23 (May 1973). Drawing.
An overview of memorial societies, especially those be-
longing to the Continental Association of Funeral and Memorial Societies. What they do, their differences, and how to avoid phony
societies.

1115 Good Reading Rack Service, Inc. How to Meet a Family
Crisis. Available from the NFDA.

1116 Goodwillie, Walter S. The Last Rites; or, Buried by His Own
Friends. A Plan in Detail, for the Organization of Burial
Associations, of Burial Associations, Lodges, or Societies.
Boston: The Author, 1891. 9pp.

1117 Grollman, Earl A. , ed. Concerning Death: A Practical
Guide for the Living. Boston: Beacon Press, 1974. 365pp. ,
index, (paper). Also available from the NFDA.
Twenty articles by various authors on the preparation for
death and the practical dealing with its aftermath, including Ross's
"The Law and Death" (wills, how estates are taxed, the adminis-
trator's responsibilities); Lyons's "Insurance and Death" (selection
of a reputable company and competent agent); alternatives to insurance and Social Security, Civil Service, veterans' and/or servicemen's benefits; "The Coroner and Death"; "The Funeral and the
Funeral Director"; "How to Select a Cemetery" (kinds of cemeteries,
what one should ask before selecting a particular one, how price is
determined, the need for vaults or concrete liners, and removing a
body from one cemetery to another; Winters on how to choose a
memorial dealer, the cost of a memorial, judging quality, what type
of symbols, inscriptions, etc., are appropriate; Irion on cremation,
explaining the process, who to call, costs, advantage and disadvantages; and a chapter on organ donation and transplantation, the legal
implications and if it eliminates the funeral.

1118 Hill, David S. "How to Plan Your Own Funeral." Reader's
      Digest p. 61-68, Oct. 1975. Condensed from The Kiwanis
      Magazine, Sept. 1975.
            One of the better, concise how-to-plan-it-yourself articles.
One, decide on traditional body-present service or the alternative
memorial service where the remains are not present. Two, burial
(interment underground or above ground entombment in a mausoleum)
or cremation. Cremains can be put in an urn and stored in a columbarium or scattered. Body bequests for science or transplants.
Death benefits. Costs for funeral services, cemeteries and memorialization. Memorial societies--their function, services, and costs.
Funeral and burial pre-payments--how to do it and when it's advisable.

1119 Kates, Charles. "When Is a Profit Not a Profit?" [editorial].
      American Funeral Director 98(6):31-32 (June 1975).
            Commentary on the news report about the Lutheran Burial
Association of Chicago, a memorial society, which offers a religious
(as opposed to a commercial) funeral for $1000--$400 for the director; $150 to the Church; $50 to the pastor; the remainder for the
memorial society for "casket, administrative costs, and for chari-
table purposes." Kates believes the customer is "getting a funeral
service worth about $600 and paying $1000 for it."

1120 Knauer, Virginia H. "The Not-Talked-About-Much Consumer
      Expense." Northeast Funeral Director 20(12):12-13 (1972).
            The cost of a funeral can rank third in a family's big-
cost expenditures after a house and car. It can be reduced by pre-
arrangements, government benefits, comparison shopping for caskets
and services, cremation, avoiding contracts which hold survivors to
post-disposal costs, donation of body to medicine, joining memorial
societies and co-operative burial associations. List of publications
on federal survivor's benefit programs.

1121 Lamont, Corliss. A Humanist Funeral Service. Boston,
      1947; New York: Horizon Press, 1954.

1122 Maisel, Albert Q. "Facts You Should Know About Funerals."
      Pleasantville, NY: Reader's Digest Assoc., Inc., 1966.
      Reprint from the Sept. 1966 issue. For copies write Re-
      print Editor, Reader's Digest, Pleasantville 10570.
            Balanced look at funeral service; points out that some of
its severest critics agree the minority of dishonest directors have
tarnished the image of the honest majority. Critics uniformly warn
the public, however, that the funeral business, like any other, will
sell its most expensive services and merchandise wherever possible.
The buyer should beware and shop around. Topics covered: economics of the trade, where to seek advice on funeral directors, what
is the "first call," types of funerals available, what to look out for
such as hidden extras, types of coffins, cremation versus burial,
and memorial societies. Final advice is to walk out on a dishonest
director who is trying to gyp you as there are many honest ones
ready to serve.

1123 Margolis, Sidney. Funeral Costs and Death Benfits. New
York: Public Affairs Pamphlets, n.d. (Public Affairs
Pamphlet no. 404.)

1124 "Memorial Societies: A Plan for Simple, Inexpensive Funerals." Good Housekeeping, Aug. 1962.

1125 Memorial Society Association of Canada. Church Comment on
Funerals (pamphlet). Available from the Association.
      Quoted comments from the Anglican Church of Canada,
the Baptist Church, the Presbyterian Church of Canada, the Religious
Society of Friends (Quakers), the United Church of Canada, and the
Roman Catholic Church. All agree that dignified simplicity of funerals is in keeping with the original dictates of the Christian church
and that the ostentatious expense of modern funerals is in direct opposition to the Christian concept of death and immortality; money
spent on flowers, funerals, and memorialization is often better spent
on family necessities; the casket should be closed before the funeral
service.

1126 Morgan, Ernest. A Manual of Death Education and Simple
Burial, 7th ed. Burnsville, NC: The Celo Press, 1975.
64pp., index, biblio. (paper). Available from CAFMS or
the Memorial Society Association of Canada.
      As the number of editions implies, one of the best stand-
ard references in the trade. Part 2: how to have a simple burial;
cremation as an alternative to earth burial; list of financial resources
available at death--social security, union and fraternal benefits, insurance and employee benefits, veterans benefits; various funeral
prepayment plans available through life insurance, mutual aid, and
credit union plans; and how to plan a simple funeral if there is no
memorial society nearby. Part 3: memorial societies--volunteer
groups who have formed in order to obtain simple, economic body
disposal through advanced planning; directory of societies with addresses, founding date, membership number, fee, and minimum cost
of cremation for each society. Part 4: donating the body to medical research; list of foundations and medical schools which need
donations of specific organs (eyes, ear bones, kidneys, glands, etc.)
as well as whole bodies, with addresses; list of medical schools
throughout Canada, the U.S. and territories, including addresses,
phone numbers (day and nights and holidays), degree of need, and
radius within which transportation is provided free.

1127 Murray, Alice. "High Price of Dying Is Eased by L.I.
Group." New York Times cxxiii(42,358):102 (Jan. 13, 1974).
      The Memorial Society of Long Island offers advice on
simple funerals. Funeral directors at first ignore the Society, but
now cooperate and are getting referrals. Pre-arrangement; the New
York Funeral Director Association's reaction to memorial societies.

1128 Myers, James Jr. Cooperative Funeral Associations. Chicago: Cooperative League of the U.S.A., 1946. 39pp.,
illus.

Background information on funeral costs; cooperatives'
activities in trying to cut down costs.

1129 National Funeral Directors Association. The Pre-arranging
and Pre-financing of Funerals. Milwaukee, WI: NFDA,
n. d. (Pamphlet.)
Emphasizes that while pre-arrangements are often tentative, they are nonetheless extremely helpful to survivors--financial-
ly, emotionally, and simply logistically. Chart of basic data on
state pre-need trust laws.

_____. Should I Go to the Funeral. See entry 338.

1130 _____. Some Thoughts to Consider When Arranging a
Funeral. Available from NFDA (pamphlet). n. d.

1131 _____. Some Questions and Answers About Your Child
and Death. Available from NFDA. n. d.

1132 _____. Someone You Love Has Died--Some Thoughts and
Suggestions About Funerals. Available from NFDA (brochure). n. d.
Visitation, service, committal, and discussion of whether
children should attend. Guide for a family. Reprinted in The Director 40(12):6-8 (1970).

_____. Too Personal to Be Private.... See entry 339.

1133 _____. What About Funeral Costs. Available from NFDA
(pamphlet). n. d.

1134 _____. What Do You Really Know About Funeral Costs?
Milwaukee, WI: NFDA, 1974. 6pp. (pamphlet).
Average costs for funeral services, interment receptacle,
interment and cremation, monuments. Definition of the various
methods of quoting prices for funeral service and the categories of
charges that make up the cost of a funeral: professional services
of the director and his staff, charges for disposition of the body,
memorialization, and miscellaneous expenses such as out-of-town
transportation, clergyman's honorarium, etc.

1135 _____. When a Death Occurs: Needs--Concerns ... Decisions. Milwaukee, WI: NFDA, 1974. Illus. (pamphlet).
Highlights of basic needs arising when death occurs such
as choosing a funeral director, the funeral, final disposition, alter-
nates to the funeral, costs, organ and body donations, pre-need, etc.

1136 National Selected Morticians. A Helpful Guide to Funeral
Planning. Evanston, IL: Consumer Information Bureau,
Inc., subsidiary of NSM, 1975. 24pp., illus. (pamphlet).
Choices available in selecting a funeral service, pre-
planning funeral services, the funeral, clergy, services provided by
the funeral director, funeral artifacts, costs, payment considerations,

social security and veterans administration benefits, disposition alternatives, alternative ways to express sympathy (flowers, charity donations), anatomical gifts, and the code of good funeral practice by which members of NSM operate.

1137 _____. Pre-Planning the Funeral: Why? Who? How? Evanston, IL: NSM. 7pp. (pamphlet). n. d.
        Common mistakes made when people preplan their own funerals, how to avoid these, and the code of the NSM. Two forms to be filled out to inform those who will plan funerals, including space for important personal data and burial instructions.

        _____. Social Security Benefits.... See entry 341.

1138 Neale, Robert E. The Art of Dying. New York: Harper & Row, 1973.
        Alternatives to traditional services and means of disposition.

1139 Nora, Fred. "Memorial Associations." In: Cooperative League of the U.S.A., 1962.

1140 "Of and by the People." Mortuary Management 62(8):8 (July-Aug. 1975).
        Report of the Sacramento Consumer Protection Bureau's distribution of pamphlet entitled "The Last Consumer Problem: A Funeral," which lists legal requirements for a funeral and comparative costs of local funeral homes' services and products. Mortuary Management asks directors, "Why must someone elso do this important function in your place?"

1141 Osborne, Ernest. When You Lose a Loved One. New York: Public Affairs Committee, 1958. 28pp., biblio., drawings (pamphlet).
        The funeral, its function; practical considerations to be made about costs; the consolations of religion; the stages of grief; the role of mourning; how children cope with death and how adults can help them. Helpful guide for laymen on death and funerals, especially the psychological aspects.

1142 Pope, Leroy. "Funeral Costs Spawn New Business." Northeast Funeral Director 22(4): (1973).
        The "New Business" comprises approximately 130 memorial societies. California boasts 100,000 membership. The NFDA, however, maintains that since 1963 the average funeral cost increase is lower than the general index of goods and commodities. The executive director and the president of the New York State Funeral Directors Assoc. give their ideas on present trends of cost, direct burials, cremation, and related subjects.

1143 Rowley, Kathleen A. "Burial Fees--From Budget to Spendthrift." Northeastern Funeral Director 21(4):14+ (1972).

New Jersey area options for disposing of the dead: donation to science; cremation; burial in cemetery plot; interment in a
mausoleum; cryogenic preservation; cost of each; veteran benefits.

1144 Sher, Byron D. "Funeral Prearrangement: Mitigating the
       Undertaker's Bargaining Advantage. " Stanford Law Review
       15:415 (1962-63).

1145 "Toronto Memorial Society Holds Annual Meeting. " Canadian
       Funeral Director 3(6):5-9 (June 1975).
           Quotes from the Society's spring newsletter, section en-
titled "Inflation and the Funeral Business. " To get funeral directors
to sign contracts with the Society, contracts must include price
escalation clause; unit and functional pricing methods must be de-
fined, as well as "extras"; the article also considers the rise in un-
orthodox funerals (cremation, donation of body to science, donations
to charities instead of flowers) and the funeral service establishment's attempts to regain the initiative taken by memorial societies
in lowering costs, alternative funeral services, etc.

1146 "Twenty Thousand Funerals a Year. " American Funeral Di-
       rector 93(4):33-34 (1970).
           Cooperative societies handle almost half the funerals in
Scotland. The Scottish Cooperative Wholesale Society has 36 "depots"
or branches, a casket factory, a monument shop where monuments
are designed, cut, and inscribed. Employs between 500 and 600
people, office personnel, funeral directors, drivers, masons, joiners,
etc.

       "Veterans Burial Bill Passed. " See entry 371.

1147 Voorhis, Jerry. The Cooperatives Look Ahead. The Public
       Affairs Committee, 1952.
           Cooperative activities in cutting funeral costs.

       Watt, Jill. Canadian Guide to Death and Dying. See entry
       240.

1148 "What You Should Know About Funeral and Burial Costs. "
       Good Housekeeping 174:180 (Feb. 1972).
           Results of survey on funeral expenses for 1969. Average
cost of funeral director's services was $926; 18. 7% were less than
$200; 6. 2% were between $200 and $499; 22. 8% between $500 and
$799; 26. 2% from $800 to $999; 14. 2% from $1000 to $1199; 8. 5%
from $1200 to $1499; 2. 7% from $1500 to $1999; . 7% over $2000.
Funeral directors' services include embalming, transportation, casket, arranging of visitation hours and funeral; consultation with the
bereaved and clergy; filling out legal forms. Optional expenses:
limousines, flower car, special burial clothes; cemetery plot,
markers, memorials, death notices, cremation, urns and other items
are not included.

Your Social Security. See entry 380.

4. THE FUNERAL PROFESSION RESPONDS

1149 "Attitudes Toward Funerals Changing." Northeast Funeral
Director 22(4):23 (1973).
There's an increasing tendency to talk more freely about
burial and one of the subjects raised is whether to have funerals.
Both sides of the argument are presented. Based on an article,
"How to Escape Your Own Funeral," originally published in the
Christian Herald.

1150 Bates, Bill. "Is Anybody Listening?" Mortuary Management
62(8):11-12 (July/Aug. 1975).
Funeral directors' denying they are faultless is counter-
productive, yet they must fight the "nothing-can-be-done-about-criti-
cism-syndrome" by (1) learning to be a death educator, (2) acquiring
skills to help grievers recover, and (3) learning to identify grievers'
special needs in order to make the funeral therapeutic. Spells out
how to help individuals through the stages of grief, how the director
should respond to each manifestation of grief, etc.

1151 Blackwell, Roger D., and Talarzyk, Wayne W. American
Attitudes Toward Death and Funerals. Evanston, IL: CMA,
1974. 48pp.
CMA-sponsored study report designed to tell funeral directors and suppliers the trends in American consumer thinking on
funerals, preferred methods of final disposition, what the public
estimated the average cost of the funeral to be, methods of pricing
the public prefers, and other information that will help directors
and suppliers better evaluate their markets and develop future market strategies accordingly. (See entry 1178.)

1152 Bucknam, Ceil. "Funeral Termed Valuable Therapy." Northeast Funeral Director 21(5):10 (1972).
The Rev. Paul E. Irion addresses New Hampshire Funeral
Directors Assoc. seminar. Leads discussion on the responsibilities
of funeral directors in meeting the needs of the bereaved and on
comforting mourners.

1153 "Burial Business Hears Voices." Business Week no. 1784:
80, 83-84 (Nov. 9, 1963).
Thorough assessment of the profession's response to
Mitford's The American Way of Death (entry 993) and its economic
impact. Investment and income of funeral directors and number of
people in funeral service and related industries.

1154 Bustard, William L. "Funeral Customs Defended." New
York Times cxiii(38,598):18 (Sept. 28, 1963).
President of NSM in a letter to the Times criticizes
Homer Bigart's article of Sept. 3. Defends industry.

1155 Calhoun, Jay R. "The Funeral Director Needs to Direct."
      Mortuary Management 62(8):13 (July/Aug. 1975). Photo.
          Critics find that the main problem with the funeral in-
dustry is its services are "routine, meaningless, or irrelevant to
a growing share of the public." Not surprisingly an increasing
number of people are turning to direct disposal methods. The solution is up to the funeral director. He must guide the family in
planning a meaningful, personalized event to mark the end of a loved
one's life and to express their grief.

1156 Casket & Sunnyside. Legal Decisions for Funeral Directors.
      New York: Casket, 1933. 47pp.

1157 "A Comparison of NFDA Statistics and Those of the United
      States Government." The Director XLV(5):4ff(2pp.) (May
      1975).
          Commerce Department's funeral service and crematory
statistics, based on a national census of funeral homes, are compared to the NFDA's, based on Eugene F. Foran and Dr. Vanderlyn
R. Pine's studies.

1158 "Counselor" [editorial]. Mortuary Management 62(8):10 (July/
      Aug. 1975).
          Counseling service is the profession's only hope for con-
tinuing the business of funeral directing. The charge that funeral
directors are not qualified to counsel is unfounded because no one,
no matter how well trained, is qualified to deal "with a population
near 205 million, where no two are alike either physically, emotionally, or spiritually." The only qualifications are professional dedi-
cation, "humanization," and confidence.

1159 "Dr. Joyce Brothers and Children Going to Funerals." The
      Director XLV(4):9 (April 1975).
          Advises children be allowed to attend funerals because
rituals observing major changes in our lives help us to adjust to
these changes, especially to death. Time to mourn is necessary for
children to "work through their feelings of grief and loss. Funerals
often help to relieve anxiety for it provides an accepted outlet for
the mourner's grief."

1160 Douthitt, James E., and Drum, Kenneth L. "The Changing
      Role of the Funeral." The Director 42(9):6-7 (1972).
          Emphasis of modern funerals--on the living rather than
the dead--should be therapeutic and cathartic.

1161 Ebeling, R. A. "Era of Accountability." Mortuary Manage-
      ment 59(2):8 (1972).
          Funeral directors and members of funeral industry must
demonstrate the values to be gained from providing total funeral
service.

1162 _____. "Some Syndicated Writers Pollute the Public Mind."
      Mortuary Management 58(12):8 (1971).

How the funeral director can rebut articles critical of the funeral industry.

"Education: A Single-Edged Necessity." See entry 771.

1163   Fitzgerald, Edward R. "Immediate Disposition--Fancy or Fact?" Mortuary Management 62(1):11ff[4pp.] (Jan. 1975). Photos.
President of the NFDA's vies towards direct cremation with a warning for the funeral director that "to simply provide what he is first requested to provide is sometimes an expedient surrender of his responsibilities." Must explain first the value of viewing the dead body, "the meaning of procession and ceremonious disposition." In the end, however, the director should give the arrangers of the funeral what they wish--nicely. "We don't let the emotions of management come into play to the point we regard these people as second class clients." If economy is a great importance, the director should offer his services "whether he gets paid or not." Much of the industry's bad press due to misconceptions aggravated by some directors' unwillingness to discuss costs openly. Determination of price is a matter of economics; how prices are quoted a matter of clearly communicating to the consumer "in terms [he] can understand and accept." Bulk of article on finding a common sense approach to pricing, communicating to the public that most of the cost of a funeral covers "professional services and facilities--not merchandise," and reasons and ways to avoid government imposed pricing techniques.

1164   Friskel, Joseph. "Look to the Past to Plan Future Business." Casket & Sunnyside 103(4):22 (1973).
Fundamental values and needs remain despite apparent changes in society. The funeral, therefore, will continue to have an important place in that society, filling a basic human need that will never change.

1165   Fruehling, James A. "Toward Professionalizing the Future of Funeral Service." NSM Bulletin, LVIII(3):3-5 (March 1975).
NSM's Education Consultant discusses how the funeral industry can effectively meet changes; the two recent events indicating a need for change: the Federal Trade Commission's June 1974 paper urging the enactment of mandatory itemization of funeral costs and WTTW's (Chicago's Public Broadcasting System) review of the alleged abuses within the industry and shoddy marketing tactics of funeral directors. With the federal government and media demanding changes, funeral service must evaluate itself, determine the significance of outside criticism to better insure its future. Discusses the funeral director, his problems, is he a professional or a businessman, i.e. concerned primarily with service or sales; professionalizing funeral service; the role professional organizations can play in "anticipating and facilitating future developments" by reviewing and updating education, research, ethics, self-evaluation; potential implications of supplanting merchandising as the conceptual foundation for funeral service with a professional service model.

1166 "Funeral Official Answers Attacks." New York Times cxii (38, 583):31 (Sept. 13, 1964).
Cornelius M. Franklin, president of the NFDA, defends profession at the New Jersey State Funeral Directors Assoc. Convention. Calls Jessica Mitford's book "a negative diatribe."

Glick, Ira O., et al. The First Year of Bereavement. See entry 300.

1167 Green, Orin. "Changing Minnesota Attitudes Concerning Funeral Service." Casket & Sunnyside 101(9):8-10 (1971).
Funeral directors should take the lead in meeting public's tendencies to disregard irrelevant traditions and rites. Changing attitudes should be studied by both publicly owned operations and independent family homes.

1168 Greer, John C. "Tips to Help You Build a Better Public Image." Casket & Sunnyside 103(7):18+ (1973).
Funeral director's image is directly related to the director and his staff's deportment and actions. This can be improved by being active in the community, showing interest in public concerns and members of the local community, and joining churches, service clubs, or civic groups.

Hammond, Bart. "Address to the Appleton Clergymen's Association." See entry 304.

1169 Head, Ralph. You Can Cry at My Funeral. Evanston, IL: NSM. 3pp. (pamphlet). n.d.
Reasons for having a funeral including its being an affirmation of the Christian belief in an afterlife; lets the bereaved see others share his grief; helps one face the reality of death; affords respect of the body worthy of the value one placed in it during life. Implied is a profound disapproval of sea-burial or scattering of cremated ashes. The cost the author figures as 20¢ a week for every week he lives.

Horn, F. "Cryonics: Challenge to the Funeral Industry." See entry 1734.

1170 "Howard C. Raether Answers Some Questions About Funeral Service." Casket & Sunnyside 101(12):11 (1971).
Among questions answered: should caskets be required when body is to be cremated? Can present funeral service practice compete with the short funeral services? What is the advisability of a son continuing in his father's small mortuary operation?

1171 Irion, Paul E. The Funeral--An Experience of Value. Milwaukee, WI: National Funeral Directors Assoc., (1957). 15 pp. (paper.)
Text of the professor of pastoral theology's (Lancaster Theological Seminary, Lancaster, Pa.) address, Oct. 24, 1956, given at the 75th annual convention of the National Funeral Directors

Association, held in Milwaukee. Analysis of the value of some contemporary funeral practices--what is done, and why it is done. Emphasizes the funeral is to meet clients' needs, not merely a ceremonial rite. Needs vary through the centuries: primitive rites appeased the spirit of the dead and prevented its return by destroying the corpse and its belongings by fire; Old Testament Hebrew rites dramatized the loss brought about by death; modern day American funerals show the bereaved community and family support, offer a means for them to actualize their loss, to express sorrow. Funeral's greatest values: gives mourners something meaningful to do; helps them face reality; sets climate for mourning and the fellowship of friends and relations; and lends dignity to man.

1172 _____. The Funeral and the Mourners: Pastoral Care of the Bereaved. Nashville, TN: Abingdon-Cokesbury, 1954. 186pp., biblio., index.
　　　Suggestions, based on psychological studies of grief, on how the funeral can supply human needs, work positively, and offer important therapy in recovering from grief. Analyzes for the priest the psychology of bereavement, lessons to be learned, the various symptoms and stages of grief, the function of the funeral, the elements of the service, funeral practices. Evaluates the funeral service; pastoral care as a context for the funeral; the funeral and its implications for the church and the ministry.

1173 _____. The Funeral: Vestige or Value? Nashville, TN: Abingdon Press, 1966. 240pp. Available from the NFDA (paper).
　　　Serious analysis of contemporary funerary practices and their value. Among topics discussed: what the funeral can do to conserve significant values, descriptive picture of a funeral, modern man and the funeral, analysis of contemporary critiques of the funeral. Christian meanings in the funeral, new designs and response to emerging trends--cremation, memorial services. Guide for group discussions.

1174 _____. A Manual and Guide for Those Who Conduct a Humanist Funeral Service. Baltimore: Waverly Press, 1971. 52pp. (paper). Available from the NFDA.
　　　Designed for funeral directors or anyone who leads a funeral service. Common needs of the bereaved and guides for the funeral conductor; a standard pattern for organizing a funeral, keeping in mind the needs of the bereaved; a representative service for general use; special resources for use at children's funerals, or where death was untimely or a suicide. Rationales for suggested patterns and representational service, plus use of "resources"--quotes from poems of Bryant, Whitman, Wordsworth, etc.

　　　Jackson, Edgar N. The Christian Funeral: Its Meaning, Its Purpose, and Its Practice. See entry 104 and also Jackson's The Significance of the Christian Funeral, entry 105.

1175 _____. For the Living. New York: Channel, 1964. 95pp. (paper).

1176 _____. Understanding Grief. Nashville, TN: Abingdon
          Press, 1957.

1177 Kates, Charles O. "Did This Survey Prove Anything?"
          American Funeral Director 94(6):29 (1971).
          Critique of Psychology Today article on how Americans
view funerals.

1178 _____. "A Survey that Proves the Gloom-Mongers Wrong."
          American Funeral Director 97(10):32 (Oct. 1974).
          Comment on the CMA's well publicized study (see entry
1151) demonstrating that Americans "not only show an overwhelm-
ing preference for the traditional funeral but, judging by the present
attitudes of the under-25 group, they will continue to do so for many
years to come." Cremation, immediate disposal, and memorials
will continue to increase but for the foreseeable future will remain
minority practices. Funeral service, however, must adapt to changing needs and public demand, offer smaller and more private services and the option of "humanistic services." Most Americans over-
estimate the cost and profits of funeral directors. The industry must
correct this misconception by establishing better communication with
the public.

1179 _____. "What Are Your Intentions, Mr. President?" [edi-
          torial]. American Funeral Director 98(7):27-28 (July 1975).
          Exhortation to newly-elected president of the state associ-
ations to lead: "funeral directors today need leadership more than
ever," advises Mr. Kates, "and, judging by what so many have
said to us, they are not universally satisfied with the performance
of their association officers. Strength of purpose, independence of
thought, firmness under pressure--these are the qualities they seek
in their leaders..." and "a willingness to try out new ideas, grasp
new opportunities, face the challenges of the future, not hide from
them."

1180 _____. "What's Right? What's Wrong?" [editorial].
          American Funeral Director 98(4):29-30 (April 1975).
          Editor cites cases of funeral director conduct which
violates "a tenet of good form or taste or etiquette or common
sense, rather than a major ethical imperative." He asks what
constitutes appropriate behavior and recommends standards be met
"indirectly through the subtle pressures of tradition, convention,
early training, and respect for the good opinion of colleagues." He
suggests anonymously written officially sanctioned commentaries as
a means of airing and pointing out faults or weaknesses within the
industry.

1181 Kelly, Thomas E. "Services for the Bereaved: Cochran's
          Staff Chaplain." American Funeral Director 96(3):56C-56D
          (1973).
          Wichita, Kan., funeral home hires an ordained minister
full time to act as chaplain and officiant at funeral services when
requested by the deceased's family. Most of his work is post-funeral counseling.

1182 Kidd, J. L. "An Ecumenical Funeral Service for the 'New' Church." The Director 39:3 (1969).

1183 Kutscher, Austin, et al. Acute Grief and the Funeral. See entry 318.

Lagemann, John Kord. "The Hurt That Heals." See entry 319.

1184 Lamers, Dr. William M. Jr. "Funerals Are Good for People --M.D's Included." Medical Economics, June 23, 1969, p. 46.
Only the traditional funeral service can provide the type of setting in which survivors can resolve their grief. Memorial service lacks basic elements such as timing (it takes place after feelings are the most intense); bereaved aren't actively involved with events which would remind them a death has actually taken place; absence of the body tends to add to the illusion there's not been a death. The various functions that are a part of the traditional funeral take time, enforce the reality of death.

1185 _____. "Gloom at Funerals Replaced by Color." Casket & Sunnyside 102(7):18+ (1972).
The use of new embalming chemicals and techniques permits brightening of flesh tones to give a more natural appearance. New casket designs, woods, metals, and colorful fabrics help lift the gloom out of the funeral. Directors' dress changed, funeral home decor brightened, and stylish limousines have replaced the more somber carriages and hearses.

LaVigne, Richard H. "People First." See entry 862.

1186 Litzinger, John C. Know Your Mortician: An Inside View of the Funeral Profession. New York: Exposition, 1963. 50pp.
In response to the many stones cast at the modern mortician, a brief summary of the mortuary profession beginning with a history of undertaking and embalming, a discussion of funeral costs and profits (which are not exhorbitant), free ambulance service, mourners, funeral directors' serving the public; what individuals can do to prepare for death.

1187 McCracken, Joseph L. "A View of the Present and Future of the Funeral." The Director 41(3):5 (1971).
Former president of the NFDA urges vault manufacturers and their representatives to meet individual needs and desires of the public and impress this obligation on the funeral director. Youth want a simpler service, casket, and vault. The burial merchandise market will fall off, author warns, if the demand for the funeral diminishes.

1188 McDougall, Marvin. "A Student Examines the Values of Funeral Service." Canadian Funeral Director 3(7):8-11 (July-Aug. 1975).

Prize-winning essay of Funeral Service Education student at Humber College, Toronto, covering the history of funeral service, what is funeral service, and the value of funeral service.

Mahoney, David M., J.C.D. "Bishop Writes on Prayer for the Dead." See entry 830.

1189 Margolis, Otto S. "Funeral Service ... A Challenge and a Responsibility." Northeast Funeral Director 22(11):8+ (1973).

1190 _____. Grief and the Meaning of the Funeral. New York: MSS Information Corp., 1975.

1191 Martin, Edward A. "Public Judges You by What You Do and Say." Casket & Sunnyside 100(12):16 (1970).
Importance of service to families from the standpoint of public relations. Suggests offering freedom of casket and service selection, vocational guidance, honest quotation of facts and figures, and carrying out survivor's rather than the deceased's wishes as means of pleasing customers.

1192 _____. "Traditional Service Is Comforting to Survivors." Casket & Sunnyside 102(9):22+ (1972).
It is the duty of the funeral director to communicate to all people and groups the value of the funeral. He should counter criticism with factual information and by not depriving survivors of their right to plan a funeral service. For them, it is comforting and meets basic needs for the majority of bereaved families.

1193 Matthews, William F. "Funeral--Funeral Director the Future." Mortuary Management 58(12):12-15+ (1971).
Address presented at the NFDA annual convention in Kansas City, Mo., challenging funeral directors to realize their potential to become one of the foremost caretaking professions in the U.S. Research and publications that link funeral service to psychological, sociological, and theological values have given the funeral industry the opportunity. Argues that higher educational requirements are needed for funeral service professionals.

_____. "Positive Public Relations." See entry 668.

1194 Melby, Lynn L. Dead Is a Four Letter Word. Seattle, WA: Dabney Pub., 1975. 119pp., biblio. (paper). Available from the Allied Memorial Council.
The executive director of the Allied Memorial Council gives the positive side of the funeral interment industry: funeralization, preplanning, death education, the funeral director, memorialization, cremation, the ways people deny death, cryogenic preservation, the use of euphemism in the language of death, and a broad view of the funeral process's goals and values.

1195 Meyers, Richard. "A Death in the Family. Mortuary Management 62(8):21 (July/Aug. 1975). Illus.

Author's reminiscence on the slow painful years preceding his 87-year-old grandmother's death and the sense of "relief and peace" that came over him seeing her cosmetized and beautifully dressed in the funeral home viewing room. "Her appearance reminded me of earlier years with pleasant memories and enjoyable times...." Reminds directors that "We are not conducting 'just another funeral service,' but the funeral service of a very special person."

1196 Michael, Lorilee. "New Philosophy Initiated at Funeral Chapel." Northeast Funeral Director 20(9):10+ (1971).
Bill Bates, manager of Milwaukee's Bates Southgate Chapel, believes funeral directors should direct their efforts first toward meeting the bereaved's emotional needs. Services without the use of caskets and without the body present.

1197 Mitford, Jessica. "Have the Undertakers Reformed?" The Atlantic 215(6):69-73 (1965). Drawing.
Mitford's comments on the changes wrought upon her and the funeral industry by her 1963 book, The American Way of Death (entry 993). Industry response and public relations efforts; funeral costs dropped due to consumer initiative, funeral and memorial societies increased, and body donations rose sharply. Comments on Senate Anti-Trust and Monopoly Subcommittee hearings.

1198 "More on WTTW 'Since the American Way of Death'." The Director XLV(4):10 (April 1975).
Quotes the FDSA of Greater Chicago bulletin's report that the actual viewing audience of the documentary "Since the American Way of Death" was far short of the producers' expectations.

1199 Morrison, Reg T. "The Privilege of Grief." National Cremation Magazine, Jan.-Feb.-March 1975, p. 5-6. Photo.
President of Tucson Memorial Parks and the CAA argues for the "proper funeral" as an opportunity for persons to act out their grief, too powerful and deep to express in words or otherwise. "Ritualized behavior ... vents powerful feelings so that the bereaved can get on more readily with the important tasks of living." People who are prohibited from venting feelings often become neurotic or lose their effective capacity. Attacks new trend in English law which tends to place disposition with the person who will die, often denying the next of kin a means for acting out his grief in a salutary way. Committing the body of a loved person, for instance, to fire, if one is afraid of fire, can be emotionally shattering. Advises cemeterians to give survivors whatever they want to best help them to overcome their grief.

1200 "Mortician Groups Fight Critics--and Each Other." Business Week no. 1877:34 (Aug. 21, 1965).
The NFDA-NSM code of ethics battle and general problems of the post-Mitford industry.

Murray, Alice. "High Price of Dying Is Eased by L.I. Group." See entry 1127.

1201 National Foundation of Funeral Service. <u>Facts About Funeral</u>
      <u>Service Every Family Should Know.</u> Evanston, IL: NFFS,
      n. d. 19pp. (brochure).
            Sketch of funeral service including services provided by
      funeral directors, the psychological values in funeral customs, ethi-
      cal funeral directors' willingness to complete free-arrangements,
      provide choice of service (earth burial, mausoleum entombment,
      cremation, or body bequeathal for medical research), and offer a
      wide range of prices; financial aspects of funeral service; embalm-
      ing (required in some states if corpse is to be transported by com-
      mon carrier, if burial is delayed several days, or if death was
      caused by certain infectious diseases); optional items beyond require-
      ments proved by the funeral director.

1202 National Funeral Directors Assoc. <u>The American Funeral--</u>
      <u>Caring for the Dead--Serving the Living--Giving Dignity to</u>
      <u>Man.</u> Available from the NFDA (pamphlet). n. d.

1203   . <u>The Funeral Facing Death as an Experience of</u>
      <u>Life.</u> n. d. Available from the NFDA. 39pp. , illus.
      (booklet).
            Concise look at immediate post-death activities: the
      funeral and alternatives to the funeral. Illustrations of typical
      American caskets and burial vaults; discussion of the funeral,
      visitation or wake, committal, the funeral home's staff, facilities,
      merchandise, final disposition, costs of services and merchandise
      provided by the funeral director, costs of final disposition and me-
      morialization, alternatives to the funeral with the body present, col-
      leges of funeral service or mortuary science education, language to
      be used in the post-Evelyn Waugh era, the future of funeral service
      in the United States.

1204   . <u>Should the Body Be Present at the Funeral?</u> Mil-
      waukee, WI: NFDA, n. d. Illus. (pamphlet).
            Body present versus immediate disposition of the body
      followed by a memorial service. Argument for having the body pres-
      ent; the value of body viewing; organ and body donations.

1205   . <u>The Significance of the Christian Funeral.</u> n. d.
      Available from the NFDA (booklet).

                . <u>Too Personal to Be Private: A Funeral Director</u>
      <u>Talks About a Death in a Family.</u> See entry 339.

                . <u>When a Death Occurs: Needs--Concerns ... De-</u>
      cisions. See entry 1135.

1206   . <u>Why Do We Have Funerals, Anyway?</u> Milwaukee,
      WI: NFDA, n. d. (Pamphlet.)
            Topics covered include having the body present, viewing,
      public versus private funerals, calling hours (visitation, wake, shiv-
      ah), flowers and memorials, the attendance of children at the funer-
      al, and the funeral as a valuable experience.

1207 _____. With the Body Present. Milwaukee, WI: NFDA, n.d. (Pamphlet.)

National Selected Morticians. The Code of Good Funeral Practice. See entry 851.

_____. You Can Cry at My Funeral. See Head, Ralph, entry 1169.

1208 "NFDA Holds Arizona Seminar." Mortuary Management 58(2): 28-30 (1971).
Funeral directors' reactions to the NFDA's educational program at the Camelback Inn, Scottsdale, Ariz., Jan. 4-7, 1971, on two types of funerals; the contemporary religious funeral and the humanist funeral. The Rev. Paul Irion, author and professor of pastoral theology at the Theological Seminary of the United Church of Christ, Lancaster, Pa., points out the need for alternative types of funeral rites.

1209 "NFDA Professional Conferences Focus on the Future of the Funeral." Casket & Sunnyside 102(4):38 (1972).
Subjects of conferences include: funeral directors' need to share the funeral experience with bereaved families; necessity of offering clients a choice of merchandise and services; need for directors to adapt to social changes and public's demands.

1210 Nichols, Jane, and Nichols, Roy. "The Unsatisfied: Where Do They Get Their Ideas? Attitudes? Where Do They Come From? Why Do They Ask for Something Different?" Mortuary Management 62(1):26ff[6pp.] (Jan. 1975). Photos.
The reasons people opt for abbreviated funeral services include: a desire to avoid confronting the body and thereby death, to avoid appearing "weak," to avoid inconvenience, to be different, to reduce costs. It is the director's responsibility to ferret out the reasons behind a request for short services and "based on the needs of the client he is serving (as opposed to his own needs/values/wishes) find reasonable, meaningful alternatives and solutions." Important to provide the service most appropriate to the survivor's emotional and financial needs. Analysis of funeral service profession: "We are not without fault"; tendency towards crassness, serving profits instead of people; perpetuation of untruths ("bodies must be embalmed," "you must buy a casket," "use a vault," sales gimmickry such as "seven-step exterior finishing," "permaseal," "watertight integrity" of caskets).

Ninker, Robert. "Funeral Economics Tomorrow." See entry 690.

Nobile, Philip. "Maverick Morticians Tell How They Keep the Price Down." See entry 691.

1211 "Notes on People" [i.e., on Raoul Pinette, president of the NFDA]. New York Times cxxiii(42,269):39 (Oct. 16, 1973).

Cost of living up 41. 3% between 1963 and 1973, compared with the cost rise for funerals of 32. 1%.

"Of and by the People. " See entry 1140.

1212 Oman, John. "The Funeral Director as a Human Being. " The De-Ce-Co Magazine 65(5):26-27 (1972).
To counteract the aversion many people feel towards him as a constant reminder of death, funeral director must let himself be known as a human being. Suggestions for ways director can involve himself in the community and relate positively to the public.

1213 _____ . "The Funeral Director as Grief Counselor. " The De-Ce-Co Magazine 64(2):4-5+ (1972); 64(3):8-9+ (1972).
Part 1: Funeral director can gain increased stature in community by voluntarily assuming a grief counseling role, even after the funeral service. Detailed description of steps he can take to establish himself as one who continues to help the bereaved. 2: To become a good grief counselor, director must learn to empathize with others' feelings, attitudes. Description and examples of "psychodrama" method of learning the art of comforting and understanding.

1214 _____ . "The Funeral Director as Master of Ceremonies. " The De-Ce-Co Magazine 64(4):4-5+ (1972).
Problems that arise when a funeral director acts without thought or patience towards the bereaved family or friends. Ways he and his personnel can avoid such problems, emphasizing the importance of paying attention to details, confirming arrangements, and appreciating the emotional state of the family in mourning.

1215 _____ . "Funeral Service in the Year 2000. " Mid-Continent Mortician 44:9, 18 (1968).
Funerals are becoming secularized because of the public's disenchantment with the ecclesiastical establishment. Predictions for 2000: as real estate costs rise, cremation will become universal; more night-time services so as not to interrupt business work day; elimination of funeral processions to prevent traffic problems. Economic situation for 2000 also discussed.

1216 _____ . "How Do You Feel?" The Dodge Magazine 65(2): 19+ (1975).
Funeral director must become adept at interviewing in order to meet the needs of the bereaved. Suggestion how to become a better grief counselor, with outline of the most obvious do's and don't's in the interview.

1217 _____ . "If Only. " The Dodge Magazine 65(3):9+ (1973).
Various ways guilt manifests itself in the bereaved and ways the funeral director can become adept at recognizing and dealing with them and thus alleviating the bereaved's grief.

1218 _____ . "Learn to Listen. " American Funeral Director 95(10):96 (1972).

Listening is essential in counseling. Oman, a Methodist minister and university psychology professor gives ten steps a funeral director should follow in developing understanding of his clients.

1219 _____. "The Unmourned." The Dodge Magazine 64(4):11+ (1973).
How the funeral director can put death into proper perspective and thus alleviate the grief of the bereaved.

1220 _____. "What Price Death?" The Dodge Magazine 65(1): 12-13+ (1973).
To stem recent criticism of the industry, the funeral director must analyze what chaff can be weeded out--what is mere show and what is necessary. How to unemotionally advise clients in choiçe of services, caskets.

Pace, Eric. "Undertakers Draft Ethics Codes to Give Notice of Funeral Costs." See entry 693.

1221 Parkinson, C. "Schoedinger Spells Service." Casket & Sunnyside 102(2):18 (1972).
The Schoedinger Funeral Home in Columbus, Ohio, its past and future, the importance of education to fight criticism, disposal cases, advertising, expenses, and the value of being service oriented.

1222 Pollitt, John V. [Guest editorial.] Mortuary Management 62 (1)4 (Jan. 1975). Photo.
By the president of the CMA. Inflation, FTC investigations, and recent CMA survey on public attitudes toward death and the funeral demand that for the funeral director's own good he present to the buying public itemized costs (functional pricing methods). People still want funerals but because of inflation they need less expensive options. Author's advice to directors: "tighten up your operation, reduce your expenses, reduce expenses not producing profit."

Pope, Leroy. "Funeral Costs Spawn New Business. See entry 1142.

1223 Raether, Howard C. "The Funeral Director's Association." Casket & Sunnyside 101(13[centennial issue]):79-82 (1972).
The executive secretary of the NFDA sees in the next 100 years of funeral service an improvement in language (away from euphemism to realistic images); fewer total funerals but a continuing need for funerals as "an experience of value"; more deaths away from home; more humanist or secular funerals, folk-type services with guitar music; greater dissemination of knowledge on the subjects of grief, death, bereavement. Directors' obligations will be "to reelect strength, act carefully and wisely and to continue to grow in the public interest for the good of all who are members of the funeral profession."

1224 _____. "Letters to Authors of Articles in National Publications." The Director 41(8):12-13 (1971).
        Letters to Sylvia Porter (after her column on funeral
costs) and to Ralph Ginzburg of Moneysworth, pointing out that the
values of a funeral service must be considered as well as costs.

1225 _____. "The Place of the Funeral: The Role of the Funeral Director in Contemporary America." Omega 2:136-
49 (1971). Refs.
        Contemporary ways of dying which deny the survivor the
opportunity to experience the loss of death, to say good-bye; the
contemporary funeral; the trends affecting it; reasons for changes in
funeral customs (based on the change in American families' life
styles); identification of these changes: (1) from predominance of the
religious to that of the secular, (2) from large to small groups,
(3) from stable to mobile, (4) from adult-centered to child-centered,
(5) from a communal idealogy to a democratic, (6) from integrated
to individualized groups, and (7) from a neighborhood surrounded
family to isolated families in urban environments. Reasons funeral
practices and funeral directors get the brunt of public criticism;
present practices which should be continued and why (such as visitation or wake, viewing of the body, graveside committal, public funeral); the funeral as a religious service; child attendance at the funeral;
alternate forms of the funeral and funeral establishments (cooperatives, labor union funeral homes, and memorial societies); the future
of the funeral and the funeral director.

1226 _____. "The Role of the Funeral Director." Omega 2(3):
136-49 (1971).
        The executive director of the NFDA on the role of the
funeral director in contemporary American culture. Analysis of
customs such as body viewing, visitation periods, avoiding attendance
at graveside. Alternate forms of the funeral. Future of funeral.
Funeral director's role.

1227 _____. "Successful Funeral Service Practice." Mortuary
Management 59(3):11-13 (1972).
        Introduction and first chapter, of Raether's book of the
same title, consider the need for funeral directors and an evaluation of the community's needs for funeral homes and their personnel's services.

1228 _____. "The Times Are Changing--So Must Funeral Trade."
n.d. Available from the NFDA.
        Society's shifting attitudes towards funerals and interment;
the need for funeral director association officers and members to
keep up with the trends (quick disposal of remains and funeral services without the body present).

1229 _____. "What Will NFDA Mean 10 Years Hence?" Casket
& Sunnyside 100(12):26 (1970).
        Lump-sum and veterans' benefits, ecology and cemeteries,
dead bodies as public property, study of 1980 demography, death and
distribution of income by ages.

1230 "The 'Right' Funeral." American Funeral Director 95(2):30+
(1972).
Report of lectures given at the eighth funeral service
seminar sponsored by the NFDA. Subjects: counseling bereaved,
funeral directors' communication abilities, need of directors to make
their services consistent with family's requirements.

1231 Rose, M. Dudley. "The Funeral Has a Future." Mortuary
Management 59(6):10-14 (1972).
Despite change in type of funeral service in the modern
age, there is a continuing need for funeral rituals. Several arguments in support of this thesis.

Sable, Myra. The Positive Role of Grief. See entry 195.

1232 Schanberg, Sydney. "Undertaker Laments Funeral Gibes."
New York Times cxiii(38, 799):39 (April 16, 1964).
Review of Frank E. Fairchild's speech to New York
Rotarians on some of the social problems of being a funeral direc-
tor. Fairchild is owner of Fairchild Sons, Inc., Funeral Home.

1233 "Secular Funerals in Britain." See entry 200.

1234 Silverman, Phyllis R. "How You Can Help the Newly Bereaved." American Funeral Director, May 1970, p. 43-93.

1235 _____. "Services for the Widowed During the Period of
Bereavement." In: Silverman, Phyllis R., Social Work
Practice (New York: Columbia University Press, 1966).

1236 _____. "Services to the Widowed: First Steps in a Program of Preventive Intervention." Community Mental Health
Journal 3:37-44 (1969).

1237 _____. The Widow-to-Widow Program. Mental Hygiene.
Reprint available from NFDA (booklet).

1238 Slater, Robert. "The Funeral--Beginning at the Beginning."
Canadian Funeral Director 3(7):20-21 (July-Aug. 1975).
Professor at the Dept. of Mortuary Science, University
of Minnesota, funeral director, and clergy relations consultant to
the NFDA explains that we have lost "our classroom for death,
which was the old-style, multi-generational family." The funeral
director cannot restore the classroom but can provide reality--con-
vince the family a death has occurred; a concept of memory; the
means for the family to express its grief; a means of support for
the bereaved; and funerals adaptive to the needs of the bereaved.

1239 _____, ed. Funeral Service Meeting Needs ... Serving
People. Milwaukee, WI: NFDA, 1974. 19pp., illus.,
biog. (brochure).
Sketches of various aspects of funeral service: history
contemporary practice; educational requirements; goals and available

services; director's responsibilities; employee salaries; owner's income; career opportunities for women.

"The Sting. " See entry 1024.

1240 Strugnell, Cecile, and Silverman, Phyllis R. "The Funeral Director's Wife as Caregiver. " Omega 2:174-78 (1971). Reprint available from the NFDA (pamphlet).
 Role funeral director's wife can play in helping bereaved families her husband serves. Comparison of Waugh and Mitford's view of the "merchants of death" with Fulton's of the man who does the unenviable, thankless task of disposing of society's dead. Proper burial is necessary, authors believe, to meet religious, moral, and social needs of the bereaved. Findings of questionnaire to members of the NFDA's wives; kinds of help that can be offered (applying for pensions, referral to appropriate community resources for counseling); financial benefit of recruiting wives.

1241 Tari, William A. "Expanded Counseling Program Urged for Funeral Service. " Casket & Sunnyside 103(9):15+ (1973).
 More and more funeral directors are incorporating counseling as part of their offered services. Three categories: pre-need, at-need, and post-need.

1242 "Training in Adaptive Funeral Is Provided. " Casket & Sunnyside 105(7):4-5 (July 1975).
 M. K. Bates and Associates teach employees, on location in the funeral home, the "arranging and promotion of the 'adaptive' funeral. " Bates was formerly the director of the Life Centered Division and director of research and development for Uniservice Corp. He has worked with university psychologists and gerontologists in developing patterns for new types of funerals.

1243 "Undertakers Ask for Time on T. V. to Answer 'Kildare'. " New York Times cxiii(38, 699):67 (Jan. 7, 1964).
 Los Angeles County Funeral Directors Assoc. counter what they believe was a misleading impression of funeral directors given on "The Exploiters" episode of "Dr. Kildare. "

1244 "U. S. Gains Clearance on Funeral Price Ads. " New York Times cxvii(40, 353):20 (July 18, 1968).
 NFDA agrees to allow its members to advertise funeral merchandise and service costs.

1245 Wagner, W. "What a Funeral Can Do When Death Strikes Suddenly. " The Director p. 40, (June 1970).

1246 Ward, Tom. "What Do We Do with the Spotlight?" Casket & Sunnyside 102(7):12+ (1972).
 With the funeral service under severe public scrutiny, the best thing funeral directors can do is to demonstrate and speak of its benefits; conduct educational programs for the public; talk frankly about products, service, goals, etc., at all appropriate

moments (seminars, conventions, regional association meetings); industry must develop public relations techniques to educate the community as to the benefits of funerals to the bereaved and the services offered by the funeral director.

1247 Waring, Sumner James Jr. "The Future of the Funeral--of the Funeral Director." Northeast Funeral Director 21(1): 12-13 (1972).
    Suggestions for insuring the future success of the profession: greater attention to Americans under 35; combining funeral operations at the local and regional levels; stricter educational and licensing requirements; constant awareness of clients' needs; support and use of the NFDA; individual contribution to the profession.

1248 Werness, John L. "We Can Overcome." The Director 39(6): 1 (1969).
    President of the NFDA reviews forces working in society to simplify the funeral. Lists values achieved by traditional funeral.

1249 Wheatley, Edward W. "Sales and Marketing of Funeral Service in 2071." Casket & Sunnyside 101(13[centennial issue]): 65-67 (1972).
    University of Miami associate professor of marketing recommends that the funeral industry "think about, initiate, and implement change." Funeral industry over the next 100 years will be influenced by present life styles, trends to "be modern," the corresponding passing of tradition, changing sex roles, urbanization, advance in technologies, broad-based dissemination of knowledge, trend away from religious to the secular, concentration of power in government and corporations, and greater specialization.

II. INTERMENT AND OTHER MEANS OF DISPOSITION

A. CEMETERIES AND MEMORIAL PARKS

1. HISTORICAL, FOREIGN, ETHNIC, AND REGIONAL

1250 Adams, William H. Famous Caves & Catacombs. Plainview,
      NY: Books for Libraries, 1974 (repr. of 1886 ed.; Essay
      Index Reprint series).

1251 Allegheny Cemetery, Pittsburgh. Allegheny Cemetery; His-
      torical Account of Incidents and Events Connected with Its
      Establishment, Charter and Supplemental Acts of Legisla-
      tion, Reports of 1848 and 1857, Proceedings of the Corpora-
      tors, June 21, 1873, Rules, Regulations, etc. List of
      Officers...; Remarks on the Ornamentation and Arrangement
      of Cemeteries, Funeral Oration of William McCandless, Esq.
      on Commodore Barney and Lieut. Parker. Pittsburgh:
      Bakewell & Marthens, 1873. 166pp.

1252 _____. Allegheny Cemetery, Pittsburgh, Pennsylvania,
      1844-1934. Pittsburgh, 1934. 21pp.

1253 _____. Allegheny Cemetery, Pittsburgh, Pennsylvania; Its
      Origin and Early History, Also a Report of Its Condition,
      Progress, and Business During the Last Ten Years, June 1,
      1900 to May 31, 1910. Pittsburgh, 1910. 117pp.

1254 Allen, Francis D. Documents and Facts Showing the Fatal
      Effects of Interments in Populous Cities. New York: F.
      D. Allen, 1822. 24pp.

1255 Andrews, Frank. Burials in the Old Stone Fort Cemetery at
      Schoharie, New York; Copied from the Gravestones, June
      Nineteen Hundred and Sixteen. Vineland, NJ: Privately
      Printed, 1917. 32pp.

1255a Aronson, Harvey. "Hurrying By a Testament to L. I. Past."
      New York Times cxxi(41, 644): Sect. 1A, p. 6, (Jan. 30,
      1972).
            Historical cemetery, Town of Huntington discovered on
      Long Island.

1256 Ashbee, Paul. Earthen Long Barrows in Britain. Buffalo, NY: University of Toronto Press, 1970.
The burial mounds of the prehistoric inhabitants of Great Britain.

1257 "Athens, Short of Graves, Plans to Build Catacombs." New York Times cxvi(39, 859):26 (March 12, 1967).
Underground cemeteries planned as partial solution to Athens's grave shortage.

1258 Atticus [pseud.]. Hints on the Subject of Interments within the City of Philadephia. Philadelphia: W. Brown, 1838. 22pp.

1259 Austin, Edwin. Burial Grounds and Cemeteries; A Practical Guide to Their Administration by Local Authorities; With Forms Showing a Simple Way of Keeping the Necessary Books and Records; Model Scale of Fees and Regulations; and Statistics of the Chief Municipal Cemeteries in the British Isles. London: Butterworth, 1907. 60pp.

1260 Baker, Thomas. The Interments Act: 1879. Public Health Amendment: the Cemeteries Clauses Act, 1847, and Compendious Abstracts of Other Incorporated Statutes. London: Knight & Co., 1879. 156pp.

1261 _____. The Laws Relating to Burials, with Notes, Forms and Practical Instructions. London: W. Maxwell, 1857. 249pp.

1262 Barrett, Samuel A. Ancient Aztalan. Westport, CT: Greenwood Press, 1974. (repr. of 1933 ed.).
Earthworks.

1262a "Bermuda Cemeteries Show the Real Island." American Funeral Director 98(4):19-20 (April 1975).
Description and history of St. Anne's churchyard, one of the oldest cemeteries in the New World. Today, most Bermudians are buried eight to a tomb below ground.

1263 Bishop, John George. Strolls in the Brighton Extramural Cemetery Series 1 and 2. Brighton, England: Fleet, 1864-1867. 110pp.

1264 Blegen, Carl W., et al. The North Cemetery. Athens, Greece: American School of Classical Studies at Athens, 1964 (distr. by Institute for Advanced Study, Princeton, NJ). (Corinth series, vol. 13.)

1265 Bowen, H. C. Ancient Fields. New York: British Book Center, 1974. (repr. of 1963 ed.).
Earthworks.

1266 Bruckner, Karl. Golden Pharaoh. New York: Pantheon,
1959. Illus.
Egyptian tombs.

1267 Burial Questions Further Examined, from a Layman's Point
of View. Is There a Grievance? London: W. J. Johnson,
1880. 19pp.

1268 Busnell, David I. Native Cemeteries and Forms of Burial
East of the Mississippi. Washington, DC: U.S. Gov. Printing Office, 1920. 160pp.

1269 "Byblos." American Funeral Director 96(2):39-40 (1973).
Illus.
One of the oldest, maybe the oldest continuously inhabited
town north of Beirut in coastal Lebanon. Necropoli have been un-
earthed which date back to Phoenician and Neolithic periods.

1270 Cemetery; A Brief Appeal to the Feelings of Society in Behalf
of Extramural Burial. London: William Pickering, 1848.
33pp.

1271 "The Cemetery at Tanggok." American Funeral Director 93
(2):42-46 (1970).
Land for the United Nations Memorial Cemetery honoring
men who fought in Korea was donated by the Republic of Korea in
1951. Facilities include a 100-seat chapel, memorabilia hall, display and rest rooms, administration building, and a memorial gate-
way.

1272 Chadwick, Edwin Sir. Report ... on the Results of a Special
Inquiry into the Practice of Interment in Towns. London,
1843; Philadelphia: C. Sherman, 1845. 41pp.

1273 "Chinese in Taiwan Observe 'The Tomb-Sweeping Festival'."
American Funeral Director 95(5):18 (1972).
Festival of Ching Ming: a way of providing perpetual
care of cemeteries. Every spring, families pay honor to their ancestors by offering prayers to the spirits and restoring and beautify-
ing family burial sites.

1274 Church of England. Central Council for the Care of Churches.
Care of Churchyards. London: Church Assembly, 1930.
40pp.

1275 Claflin, W. H. Stalling's Island Mound, Columbia County,
Georgia. Millwood, NY: Kraus Reprint [orig. pub. 1931].
(Paper.)

1276 Cleaveland, Nehemiah. Greenwood Cemetery: A History.
New York: Gordon Pr., 1974. See also entries 1290,
1299, 1300, 1301, 1302, 1303.

1277 Cleveland, Ray L. Ancient South Arabian Necropolis: Objects from the Second Campaign 1951 in the Timnac Cemetery. Baltimore: Johns Hopkins University Press, 1965. Illus.

1278 Cobb, Augustus G. Earth Burial and Cremation. New York: Putnam, 1892. 173pp., illus.

1279 Coffin, John G. Remarks on the Dangers and Duties of Sepulture; or, For the Living. Boston: Phelps and Farnham, 1823. 74pp.

1280 Collison, George. Cemetery Interment; Containing a Concise History of the Modes of Interment Practised by the Ancients; Descriptions of Pere la Chaise, the Eastern Cemeteries and those of America, the English Metropolitan and Provincial Cemeteries. London: Longman, Orme, Brown, Green, and Longmans, 1840. 420pp.

1281 Corwin, John H. Burial Law, with a Note on the Law of Burial Grounds, Burials, etc. New York: G. W. Dillingham, 1889. 39pp.

1282 Cotton, William D. Sketch of Mound Cemetery, Marietta, Ohio, 3d ed. Marietta, OH: The Author, 1925. 51pp.

1283 Dahlinger, Charles W. A Place of Great Historic Interest. Pittsburgh's First Burying-Ground. Pittsburgh, 1919. 32pp.

1284 Davies, Maurice R. R. Law of Burial, Cremation, and Exhumation, 3d ed. London: Shaw & Sons, 1971, 244pp.; Ann Arbor, MI: Finch Press, 1974. Index, biblio., footnotes, appendices, tables of cases and statutes.
Comprehensive analysis of British legal principles, provisions, and cases of law of body disposal and disinterment. Three parts: (1) burial law. (2) cremation laws; (3) exhumation and disused burial ground law; statutes and provisions in bold type to aid reader. Proceeds through the various laws, summarizing and grouping them chronologically. Summaries of the law useful to layman as is "translation" of legalese to everyday prose. Important case decisions noted.

1285 Dennis, George. Cities and Cemeteries of Etruria. London: Murray, 1883. 2 vols.

1286 Dougherty, Philip H. "The Benisch Family: An Institution in Itself." New York Times cxxi(41,672): sect. 1A, p. 16, Feb. 27, 1972.
Henry Benisch and Mount Hope Cemetery, New York City.

Edwards, I. E. S. The Treasures of Tutankhamun. See entry 62.

Ellis, Hilda R. Road to Hel: A Study of the Conception of Dead in Old Norse Literature. See entry 63.

1287 Elzas, Barnett A. Jewish Cemeteries. New York: The
Author, 1910. 7 vols.

1288 _____. Old Jewish Cemeteries at Charleston, S.C.; A
Transcript of the Inscriptions on Their Tombstones, 1792-
1903. Charleston, SC: The Author, 1903. 112pp.

1289 "Family Prays Above the Churchfloor Graves." The American
Funeral Director 98(8):14 (Aug. 1975).
Short review of Basque burials. Until 1787 villagers were
buried under the floor of the Church. Currently, the head woman
of a family prays on a tumba, a spot on the Church floor beneath
which generations of her or her husband's family are entombed.

1290 Ferretti, Fred. "Green-Wood: 'A Haven of Posthumous
Americana'." New York Times cxx(41,399):47, 55 (May 30,
1971). Photos.
Green-Wood Cemetery in Brooklyn, N.Y. See also
entries 1276, 1299, 1300, 1301, 1302, 1303.

1291 Florin, Lambert. Boot Hill: Historical Graves of the Old
West. Seattle: Superior, 1966. 192pp.

1292 Folsom, Franklin. "Mysterious Mounds at Poverty Point."
Science Digest 69(2):46-48 (Feb. 1971).
Indian burial mounds at Poverty Point, La.

1293 Forest Hills Cemetery, Boston. Forest Hills Cemetery.
Boston, n.d. 36pp.

1294 Fox, Cyril. Life and Death in the Bronze Age: An Archaeol-
ogist's Field Work. Fernhill, 1959 (dist. by Humanities
Press, Atlantic Highland, NJ).
Mounds.

1295 Goodwin, Michael. "Technicality Stalls Landmark Plan."
New York Times cxxiii(42,526):88 (June 30, 1974).
New York City Landmark Commissions wants to make
Moore Jackson Cemetery a city landmark.

1296 Gordus, A. A. "First Century A.D. Culture in Ohio: Hopewell Indian Burial Grounds." Chemistry 41(5):10 (May 1968).
Illus.

1297 Granqvist, Hilma N. Muslim Death and Burial. Copenhagen:
Munksgaard, 1965. 287pp.

1298 "Gravediggers Strike in Peru." New York Times cxiv(38,973):
18 (Oct. 7, 1964).

1299 Greenwood Cemetery, Brooklyn. Exposition of the Plan and
Objects of the Greenwood Cemetery. New York: Narine,
1839. 31pp.

Brooklyn, N.Y., cemetery. See also entries 1276, 1290, 1300, 1301, 1302, 1303.

1300 _____. Green-wood Cemetery; Its Rules, Regulations, etc. New York: Houel, Macoy & Van Buren, 1845. 31, 37 pp. See also entries 1276, 1290, 1299, 1301, 1302, 1303.

1301 _____. A Report of the Receipts and Expenditures of Greenwood Cemetery from 1839 to 1861. New York: J. Russell, n.d. 94pp. See also entries 1276, 1290, 1299, 1300, 1302, 1303.

1302 _____. Rules and Regulations of the Greenwood Cemetery with a Catalogue of the Proprietors and Mr. Cleaveland's Descriptive Notices. New York: Pudney & Russell, 1851. 31, 64, 46pp. See also entries 1276, 1290, 1299, 1300, 1301, 1303.

1303 _____. _____. ...Supplemental Catalogue of Proprietors to May 12, 1873. Brooklyn, N.Y.: Eagle Print, 1873. 112pp. See entry 1302.

1304 Grinsell, Leslie V. The Ancient Burial-Mounds of England. Westport, CT: Greenwood Press, 1975 (repr. of 2d ed., rev., pub. 1953 by Methuen, London, with a new introd.). Biblio.

Haestier, Richard E. Dead Men Tell Tales: A Survey of Exhumations.... See entry 87.

Hanigan, Maureen W. "The Rising Grave." See entry 1848.

1305 Hedges, Florence B. B. Story of the Catacombs. Cincinnati: Jennings & Graham, 1909. 148pp.

1306 Henshall, Audrey S. Chambered Tombs of Scotland. Chicago: Aldine, 1963 (vol. 1), 1972 (vol. 2). Illus.

1307 Hills, Thomas. Three Ancient Cemeteries in New Hampshire. Boston: M. B. Fairbanks, 1910. 64pp.

1308 Holmes, Mrs. Basil. London Burial Grounds; Notes on Their History from the Earliest Times to the Present Day. London: Unwin, 1896. 339pp.

1309 Homewood Cemetery, Pittsburgh. Rules, Regulations, and General Information; Revised and Approved July 8, 1912. Pittsburgh, PA, 1912.

1310 Hooton, E. A. Indian Village Site and Cemetery Near Madisonville, Ohio. Millwood, NY: Kraus Reprint [orig. pub. 1920]. (Paper.)

1311 "The Horses of Arlington. " American Funeral Director 94
      (8):24+ (1971).
      Brief history of ceremonies at Arlington National Ceme-
tery and description of some of the famous horses in the caisson
platoon.

      Hotz, R. "Cosmic Spirit; Final Resting Place of Three Soviet
      Spacemen. " See entry 1851.

1312 "How the Vikings Buried Their Dead. " Life 54:54 (Sept. 15,
      1967).
      Eskimos discover a Viking burial ground while digging a
foundation for a new school. It is believed that the Vikings had
strict regulations governing burial procedures.

1313 Hurst, Sidney C. Silent Cities; An Illustrated Guide to the
      War Cemeteries and Memorials to the Missing in France and
      Flanders, 1914-1918. New York: Dutton, 1929. 407pp.,
      31 maps, 959 illus.

1314 Jackson, Samuel Macaulay. The New Schaff-Herzog Encyclo-
      pedia of Religious Knowledge. New York: Funk & Wagnalls
      Co. , 1908. Vol. 2, pp. 307-309.
      Good description of sepulture.

1315 Jett, Dora C. Minor Sketches of Major Folk and Where They
      Sleep; The Old Masonic Burying Ground, Fredericksburg, Va.
      Richmond, VA: Old Dominion Press, 1928. 128pp.

1316 Johnson, Elden. The Arvilla Complex (Minnesota Prehistoric
      Archaeology Ser.) St. Paul, MN: Minnesota Historical
      Society, 1973. Illus. (paper).

1317 Kaganoff, Benzion C. "From Machpelah ... to Beth She'arim."
      American Cemetery 46(9):32-33 (1973).
      History of the Jewish people's burial customs, beginning
with the time of Abraham when burial was commonly in rock vaults.
Burying the dead in the earth began when the Jews left Palestine for
Babylonia. In the third century Beth She'arim, an underground
necropolis, became the center of Jewish burial. The methods of
burial there are described in detail.

1318 Kates, Brian C. "The Crypts of the Capuchins. " American
      Funeral Director 94(9):22 (1971).
      Unique burial place of Capuchin friars, princes and
princesses, nieces and nephews of several Roman Catholic popes.
On the walls and ceilings of each crypt the skeletons are weirdly
arranged. Crypts are located on the second floor of the Capuchin
Church of Santa Maria della Concezione near the Vatican in Rome
and have become a tourist attraction.

1319 "Kazanluk: On Looking into a Thracian Tomb. " UNESCO
      Courier 21:35 (June 1968). Illus.

1320 Kerin, Charles A. Privation of Christian Burial; An Historical Synopsis and Commentary. Washington, D.C.: Catholic University of America, 1941, 279pp.; Ann Arbor, MI: Finch, 1974.

1321 King, Blanche B. Under Your Feet: The Story of the American Mound Builder. Plainview, NY: Books for Libraries, 1974 (facsim. repr. of 1939 ed.).

1322 King, S. G. Douglass. "High on a Rafter Rests Henry Trigg." American Funeral Director 94(11):43-44 (1971).
    Eighteenth-century Englishman directed his coffined body be placed on a rafter beneath the roof of one of the outbuildings on his estate to prevent grave robbers from pilfering his grave and exhuming his remains.

1323 Kip, William I. (Bishop). Catacombs of Rome as Illustrating the Church of the First Three Centuries. New York: Redfield, 1854. 212pp.

    Kler, Joseph. "Sickness, Death, and Burial Among the Mongols of the Ordon Desert." See entry 115.

1324 Kotker, Norman. "Encounter: 'Heaven Smiles, But Even Here the Smile Fades'." New York Times cxxiv(42,764): sect. X, p. 9 (Feb. 23, 1975). Drawing.
    Bermuda cemeteries.

    Kurtz, Donna C. and Boardman, John. Greek Burial Customs. See entry 116.

1325 Lapham, Increase A. The Antiquities of Wisconsin as Surveyed & Described.... New York: AMS Press. (repr. of 1855 ed.).

1326 "Let Sleeping Bones Lie." The Christian Century 88(40):1157 (Oct. 6, 1971).
    Condemns the digging up and display of Indian graves. They are as sacrosanct as Whites' graves and should not be converted into tourist attractions.

1327 Lindley, Kenneth A. Of Graves and Epitaphs. London: Hutchinson, 1965. 176pp., illus.

1328 Lloyd, Seton. Mounds of the Near East. Chicago: Aldine, 1963.

    Long, C. R. "Wooden Chest from the Third Shaft Grave." See entry 127.

1329 Loudon, John C. On the Laying Out, Planting and Managing of Cemeteries, and On the Improvement of Churchyards. London: Longman, Brown, Green, and Longman, 1843. 120pp.

1330 Ludbrook, Albert M. Romance of the Roman Catacombs, and
      other Addresses. Melbourne: Austral Printing and Publish-
      ing, 1936. 122pp.

      Macdonald, A. J. Monuments, Grave Stones, Burying Grounds,
      Cemeteries, Temples, etc. See entry 1874.

1331 Mackall, Louis. Oak-hill Cemetery; or, A Treatise on the
      Fatal Effects Resulting from the Location of Cemeteries in
      the Immediate Vicinity of Towns. Washington, D. C.:
      Polkinghorn, 1850. 24pp.

1332 McMillan, R. Bruce. "Early Canid Burial from the Western
      Ozark Highlands." Science 167(3922):1246-47 (Feb. 27,
      1970). Photo.
          One of the earliest known instances of pet burial (c. 5500
      B. C.) found in Rogers Shelter, Arkansas. Many Indians in South-
      eastern U. S. followed same practice later. In 1966 in Benton County,
      MD, dog bones were found in a basin-shaped pit grave with rock
      covering, dated by radiocarbon techniques at 5540 B. C. Later dog
      graves were lined in shell.

1333 McWhirter. "Taj Mahal: Its Beauty Veils a Mogul's Ruthless
      Whim. " Life 63:44-63 (Nov. 3, 1967). Photos.
          Photo essay of the world's most extravagant tomb together
      with a brief history.

      Madden, Richard R. Shrines and Sepulchres of the Old and
      New World ... Including Notices of the Funeral Customs of
      the Principal Nations, Ancient and Modern. See entry 133.

1334 Marble, C. C. Addresses of the Dead; Date of Birth, Burial
      and Location of Burial of Prominent and Celebrated People.
      New York: G. W. Dillingham, 1887.

1335 Maruchhi, Orazio. Evidence of the Catacombs for the Doc-
      trines and Organization of the Primitive Church. London:
      Sheed & Ward, 1929. 113pp.

1336 Masters, L. J. "Chambered Tombs of Scotland" (review ar-
      ticle). Antiquity 48:34-39 (March 1974). Biblio.

1337 Mathews, Cornelius. Behemoth: A Legend of the Mound-
      Builders. New York: Somerset Pub. , 1974 (repr. of 1845
      ed.).

1338 Mayes, Herbert R. "Say It in Stone. " Saturday Review 54:
      14-15 (Sept. 4, 1971).
          Highgate Cemetery in London where such luminaries as
      Karl Marx, Herbert Spencer, George Eliot and members of Charles
      Dickens's family are buried.

1339 Mines, John F. Walks in Our Churchyard; Old New York;
      Trinity Parish. New York: Peck, 1896. 181pp.

Morley, John. Death, Heaven and the Victorians. See entry 148.

1340 Mount Auburn Cemetery, Boston. Acts of Incorporation and By-Laws of the Proprietors of the Cemetery of Mount Auburn. Boston: Rand, Avery, 1872. 60pp.

1341 _____. A Catalogue of Proprietors in the Cemetery of Mount Auburn. Boston: J. Munroe, 1855. 108pp.

1342 _____. Catalogue of the Lots in Mount Auburn Cemetery ... the Charter, By-laws, etc. Boston: Rand & Avery, 1857. 159pp.

1343 Myron, Robert. Shadow of the Hawk: Saga of the Mound Builders. New York: Putnam, 1965. Illus. (for children grade 7 and up).

1344 Nelson, Soren, and Nelson, L. G. A History of Church Street Graveyard, Mobile, Alabama. Mobile, AL: Mobile Preservation Assoc., 1963.

1345 Northcote, J. Spence, and Brownlow, W. R. Roma Sotterranes, or Some of the Roman Catacombs. London: Longmans, Green, Reader, Dyer, 1869.

1346 Oliphant, George H. H. Metropolitan Interments Act. London: Longman, Brown, Green and Longmans, 1850. 100pp.

1347 Pace, Eric. "A Boom in Tomb-Building Brings Good Cheer to Cairo's City of the Dead. " New York Times cxviii(40,440): 29 (Oct. 13, 1968).

Parkinson, Sarah W. Memories of Carlisle's Old Graveyard; Containing a List of the Inscriptions on All the Stones in the Enclosure in 1898 and Describing a Walk Through a Part of the Graveyard. See entry 1891.

1348 Pascalis-Ouvière, Felix. An Exposition of the Dangers of Interment in Cities. New York: W. B. Gilley, 1823. 167pp.

1349 Peabody, Charles. Exploration of Mounds, Coahoma County, Mississippi, 1904. Millwood, NY: Kraus Reprint, c. 1974. (Paper.)

1350 Perch Lake Mounds, with Notes on Other New York Mounds and Some Accounts of Indian Trails. New York: AMS Press. (repr. of 1905 ed.).

1351 Perkins, Frank H. Handbook of Old Burial Hill, Plymouth, Massachusetts. Plymouth, MA: Pilgrim Bookstore, 1902.

1352 Piattoli, Scipione. Essay on the Danger of Interments in

Cities (trans. from the French). New York: W. Grattan, 1824. 82pp.

1353 Pleasants, Henry. History of the Old Eagle School, Tredyffrin, in Chester County, Pennsylvania, With Alphabetical Lists of Interments in the Graveyard and of German Settlers in Chester County. Philadelphia: Winston, 1909. 180pp.

1354 Prentis, Edward. Ye Antient Buriall Place of New London, Connecticut. New London, CT: Day, 1899. 40pp.

Pullins, Jerald L. "Cemeteries--Their Future & Their Past." See entry 1586.

1355 "Raising the Dead." Time 98:72 (Nov. 29, 1972).
    Rio de Janeiro's fast growing population and limited land space has inspired plans for skyscraper cemetery. Conventional plots cost $5000; tombs in Brazilian architect Silva E. Souza's 39-story mausoleum go for $1800 with tenancy guaranteed in perpetuity. The poor and needy get in on special dispensation. Eight-story garage, two churches, 21 chapels and a rooftop heliport for receiving bodies included.

1356 Rauch, John H. Intramural Interments in Populous Cities, and Their Influence Upon Health and Epidemics. Chicago: Tribune Co., 1866. 68pp.

1357 "Rector Puts Curse on Vandals; It Seems, for a While, to Work." New York Times cxiii(38, 699):35 (Jan. 7, 1964).
    West Sussex, England rector "curses" cemetery vandals. Damage quickly repaired, by police.

1358 Reisner, George A. History of the Giza Necropolis. Incl. vol. 2, The Tomb of Hetep-Neres, the Mother of Cheops, rev. ed. Cambridge, MA: Harvard University Press, 1955. Illus.

1359 _____. A Provincial Cemetery of the Pyramid Age Naga-Edder, pt. 3. Los Angeles: University of California Press, 1932. (U. C. Publ. in Egyptian Archaeology, vol. 6.)

1360 Robinson, William. Cremation and Urn-burial; or, The Cemeteries of the Future. London: Cassell, 1889. 198pp.

1361 _____. God's Acre Beautiful; or, The Cemeteries of the Future. London: John Murray, 1883. 128pp.

1362 Ronan, John. "Resurrection in Illinois." Saturday Review 55(48):52-55 (1972).
    Indian burial mounds discovered in Illinois in 1900; 45 years later the State purchased property and erected a museum. Over 1000 skeletons have been unearthed; some date back to the 10th century.

1363 Ross, Ernest L. Historical Cemetery Records of Bradly County, Tennessee. Cleveland, TN: The Author, 1973. 2 vols., 408pp., 302pp.

1364 Rowe, Chandler W. Effigy Mound Culture of Wisconsin. Westport, CT: Greenwood, 1974 (repr. of 1956 ed.).

1365 Rudenko, Sergei I. Frozen Tombs of Siberia: The Pazyryk Burials of Iron-Age Horsemen, ed. and trans by Thompson, M. W. Los Angeles: University of California Press, 1970. Illus.

1366 Scheele, William E. Mound Builders. Mountain View, CA: World Publishers, 1960. (For children, grades 5-8.)

1367 Schmidt, Erich F. Alishar Huyuk, Seasons of 1928-1929, pts. 1 and 2. Chicago: University of Chicago Press, 1933. (Researches in Anatolia, vols. 4 and 5.) Mounds.

1368 _____. Anatolia Through the Ages: Discoveries at the Alishar Mounds, 1927-29. Chicago: University of Chicago Press, 1931. Illus. (paper).

1369 Sears, William H. Excavations at Kolomoki: Final Report. Athens: University of Georgia Press, 1956. (Paper.)

1370 Silber, Mendel. Ancient and Modern Modes of Burial. Albuquerque, NM: The Author, 1911. 15pp.

1371 Silverberg, Robert. "And the Mound-Builders Vanished from the Earth." American Heritage 20(4):60-63, 90-95 (June 1969). Photos, drawings.
Analysis of modern treatment of the Hopewell and Temple Indian mounds; speculation about what happened to their builders.

1372 _____. The Mound Builders. New York: Ballantine, 1974. (Mockingbird Books.) (Paper.)

1373 _____. Mound Builders. Greenwich, CT: New York Graphic Society, 1970. Illus. (for children, grades 9 up).

1374 _____. Mound Builders of Ancient America: The Archaeology of a Myth. Greenwich, CT: New York Graphic Society, 1968. Illus.

1375 Simmons, William S. Cautantowwit's House: An Indian Burial Ground on the Island of Conanicut in Narragansett Bay. Providence, RI: Brown University Press, 1970. Illus.

1376 Simpson, James, and White, Alvin D. History of the Cross Creek, Pa., Graveyard and Cemetery. Parsons, WV: McClain, 1969.

1377 Small, J. P. "Aeneas and Turnus on Late Etruscan Funerary Urns." American Journal of Archeology 78:49-54 (Jan. 1974).

1378 Spiegel, Irving. "Jews Protest Move to Exhume Nazi Camp Graves." New York Times cxviii(40, 573):3 (Feb. 23, 1969).
Government authorities propose to exhume Jewish bodies from Bergen Belsen. Jews protest.

1379 Squier, Ephraim G., and Davis, E. H. Ancient Monuments of the Mississippi Valley. New York: AMS Press, c. 1974 (repr. of 1848 ed.). Illus.
Mounds.

1380 Stone, Elizabeth. God's Acre; or, Historical Notices Relating to Churchyards. London: John W. Parker, 1858. 406pp.

1381 Stuart, George E. "Who Were the 'Mound Builders'?" National Geographic 142(6):782-801 (Dec. 1972). Map.
Pages 792-94: the first culture of the Burial Mound Period (which existed from 1000 to 300 B.C.), namely, the Adena, named for the great mound on the Adena estate near Chillicothe, OH; the Adena's obsession with honoring their dead; elaborate, carefully wrought articles buried with deceased; enormous mounds, some over 70 feet; elaborate rites for the Adena elite who were interred in log-lined tombs or burned to ash in clay crematory basins.

1382 Sypher, A. H. "Not All the Yanks Can Go Home." Nations Business 54(10):31-32 (Oct. 1966). Photo.
American cemetery at Normandy.

1383 Thomas, Cyrus. Work in Mound Exploration of the Bureau of Ethnology. St. Claire Shores, MI: Scholarly Press, c. 1974 (repr. of 1887 ed.).

1384 "Tombs for Owners to Join Pets Are Offered in Tokyo;" New York Times cxxi(41, 842):18 (Aug. 15, 1972).
Owners can be buried with pets at Tama Dog & Cat Memorial Park, Tokyo.

1385 Tuck, James A. "Archaic Indian Cemetery in Newfoundland." Scientific American 222:112-21 (June 1970). Photos, maps, drawings.
Thorough analysis of northwestern Newfoundland burial ground at Port Au Choix, over 4000 years old. Burial techniques, analysis of artifacts buried with bodies.

1386 "2 Concerns Sued for $34. 5 Million." New York Times cxiv (39, 058):26 (Dec. 21, 1964).
Irving Trust and T. J. Stevenson sued by Cementerio Jardin Monumental de Maracaibo, S. A., over Venezuelan cemetery development.

1387 Von Der Olsten, Hans H. Alishar Huyuk, Season of 1930-32,
pt. 2. Chicago: University of Chicago Press, 1937. (Research in Anatolia, vol. 8.) Pt. 3, 1937 vol. 9).
Mounds.

1388 _____. Discoveries in Anatolia, 1930-31. Chicago: University of Chicago Press, 1933. Illus (paper).

1389 _____, and Schmidt, Erich F. Alishar Huyuk, Season of
1927, pt. 2. Chicago: University of Chicago Press, 1932.
(Researches in Anatolia, vol. 3.)

1390 Wales, William. Rockland Cemetery; Illustrated Suggestions
and Associations Connected with It and a Brief Statement of
the Superior Advantages Presented to Those Who Desire
Beautiful Resting Places for Their Dead. New York: A.
F. D. Randolph, 1881. 157pp.

1391 Walker, George A. Gatherings from Graveyards with a History of the Modes of Interment. London: Longman, 1839.
258pp.

1392 Ware, Sir Fabian A. G. Immortal Heritage; An Account of
the Work and Policy of the Imperial War Graves Commission During Twenty Years, 1917-1937. New York: Macmillan, 1937. 81pp.

1393 Watkins, E. S. Law of Burials and Burial Grounds. Bristol,
England: White Swan Press, 1948, 126pp.; Ann Arbor, MI:
Finch, 1974.

1394 Webb, Charles. "Bermuda Funeral Home." Casket & Sunnyside 101(12):16 (1971).
Thorough discussion of practices of Bermuda funeral
home, including details of disinterment (allowed no earlier than one
year after interment); six caskets are tiered into one grave.

1395 Webber, Jay. "Honduran Memorial Park Upsets Traditionalists." Mortuary Management 57(1):12 (1970).
Jardin de Paz Suyata (Garden of Peace) Memorial Park
is not the traditional time-tested (for 450 years) high-walled park
containing marble and granite sculptures. Tradition rules the rest
of Honduras's funeral industry, however. Few embalmers practice
in any part of South America; physicians embalm in some countries;
viewing is in homes; interment usually 24 hours after death; bodies
are carried to cemeteries on the shoulders of male friends; few
hearses; women do not attend burial ceremonies. Cost of grave
opening and closing approximately $175.

1396 Weidenmann, Jacob. Modern Cemeteries; An Essay Upon the
Improvements and Proper Management of Rural Cemeteries.
Chicago: Monumental News, 1888. 165pp.

1397 Weigall, Arthur. Tutankhamen and Other Essays. Port
      Washington, NY: Kennikat, 1971 (repr. of 1924 ed.).
      Tombs.

1398 Wente, E. F. "Prince's Tomb in the Valley of the Kings."
      Journal of Near Eastern Studies 32:223-34 (Jan.-April 1973).
      Illus.

1399 White, Alvin D., and Caldwell, James A. History of the
      Mount Prospect Graveyard and Cemetery. Parsons, WV:
      McClain, 1972.

1400 Wickes, Stephen. Sepulture; Its History, Methods and Sanitary
      Requisites. Philadelphia: P. Blakiston Son & Co., 1884.
      156pp.

1401 Wilford, Lloyd A. Burial Mounds of the Red River Headwa-
      ters. St. Paul, MN: Minnesota Historical Society, 1970.
      (Prehistoric Archaeology series.) (Paper.)

1402 Willoughby, C. C. Turner Group of Earthworks, Hamilton
      Co., Ohio. Millwood, NY: Kraus (repr. of 1922 ed.).

1403 Woods, George A. "'Was It a Long Trip Home to This Val-
      ley?'" New York Times cxx(41,182): sect. X, p. 15 (Oct.
      5, 1970). Drawing.
      Visit to an old New England cemetery.

2. CONTEMPORARY AMERICAN

1404 Adler, Sydney. Cemeteries: Legal and Business Problems.
      Practicing Law Institute, 1972. 160pp.
      By the chairman of the institute.

1405 American Cemetery Assoc. The Cemetery. Columbus, OH:
      American Cemetery Assoc., 1975. 2pp.
         The increase in pre-need purchase of cemetery space;
      how pre-purchase helps families; criteria for selecting a proper
      cemetery; review of the different means of disposition--traditional
      cemeteries, memorial parks, mausoleums, and columbaria; serv-
      ices available from a good cemetery.

1406 _____. International Cemetery Directory. Columbus, OH:
      American Cemetery Assoc., 1974. 271pp.
         A clear, comprehensive, uniform directory of cemeteries;
      listings arranged by nation, state or province, and city, the United
      States cemeteries first. Within each city, cemeteries are alphabet-
      ically arranged by name of cemetery; zip codes are included, and
      where available, telephone numbers and area codes; affiliated groups,
      national, regional, state, and metropolitan cemetery associations,

allied associations and trade press; order form for directory copies inserted.

1407 American Cemetery Association Convention Proceedings. Annual; available from the American Cemetery Assoc.

1408 American Cemetery Association Membership Register and Proceedings. Available from the American Cemetery Assoc.
Lists ACA members, cemeteries, addresses, services, and products sold.

1409 American Monument Assoc., Inc. How to Plan the Monument Cemetery of Tomorrow Today. Orlean, NY: American Monument Assoc., 1958. 54pp., illus., graphs.
Instructional book describing the preliminary steps to organizing a cemetery; features; factors in modern cemetery design, including the entrance, administration building, roads, curbing, service buildings, chapels, plantings; record keeping; future growth; veterans' section; war memorial; cenotaphs; lawns; water supply; color; sample contour studies, topographic surveys to obtain maximum number of salable lots, minimum road lengths, pleasing contours of land, lot sizes, management, selling, mausoleums, sample designs of actual cemeteries with details of corner treatments, fraternal sections, companion lots, and specifications for memorial work such as agreement by quarriers, monument builders; permits required; soliciting; prohibited materials; approval of design by cemetery; monument sizes; workmanship; and list of suggested cemetery rules and regulations.

1410 _____. Planning Now for Tomorrow. Available from the Assoc. 14pp., illus., diagr.
The advantages of preplanning for a family monument; the two general types of cemeteries: (1) the traditional community monument cemetery where 90% of American families have purchased lots and (2) the non-monument cemetery; tips on selecting a cemetery, avoiding promoters, and selecting a plot; recommends members of the Monument Institute of America as qualified to advise proper size and execute design of memorial; information one should provide family about cemetery plot; blank form for interment instructions; plot diagram and sample plot diagrams as guides for designing one's own.

1411 "Arlington to Be Closed to Tourists' Vehicles." American Funeral Director 93(9):38 (1970).
Vehicles barred from Arlington National Cemetery with the exception of special tourist buses, next of kin, funeral processions, officials of the cemetery or those who have official business there.

1412 "Armed Forces Interment Allowance Increased." The Director 41(7):1 (1971).
Allowance increased $625 when remains are consigned to funeral home for subsequent burial in a civilian cemetery; $375 for

same procedure but for burial in a government cemetery; and $75
in cases where the next of kin requests consignment directly to a
government cemetery.

1413 "Ashes to Ashes, Dust to High Rise Mausoleum." Engineer-
    ing News-Record 186:16 (Feb. 11, 1971). 1/3p.
        Nashville, Tenn., 20-story, 68,000-acre complex. Mon-
ey-maker and land-saver.

1414 Auerbach, Herschel. 'How a Graduate Student Improved Our
    Cemetery." American Cemetery 46(3):30 (1973).
        Former president of the Illinois Cemetery Association and
executive vice-president of Shalom Memorial Park in Palatine, Ill.,
tells how a part-time employed graduate student streamlined procedures, systems, and operational methods, saving the cemetery many
times what it paid out in salary.

1415 Barnes, Irston R. "Why Not Save Present Suburban and Urban
    Open Spaces?" The Cemeterian (special ecology ed.), Nov.
    1971, pp. 61-62.
        Counters arguments that cemeteries should be closed in
the cities and that future burials be relegated to less valuable rural
areas. Cemeteries have historical significance and are valuable
environmentally and psychologically as open space. Some, like
Mount Auburn Cemetery in Cambridge, Mass., provide sanctuary to
migratory birds.

1416 Bart, Peter. "California's Forest Lawn Adds Big Painting to
    Tourist Lures." New York Times cxiv(39,301):67 (Aug. 31,
    1975).
        The unveiling of "The Resurrection" and discussion of
Forest Lawn in general and its art policies.

1417 _____. "Founder of Forest Lawn Is Entombed." New York
    Times cxvi(39,693):31 (Sept. 27, 1966.
        The entombment of Dr. Hubert L. Eaton, the founder of
Forest Lawn Cemetery.

1418 Basile, Dominick S. "Boy Scouts Clean Up 17th Century Ceme-
    tery." New York Times cxxiii(42,491):96 (May 26, 1974).

1419 _____. "Cemetery Becoming a Dump." New York Times
    cxxiii(42,379):87 (Feb. 3, 1974).
        Historic 314-year-old cemetery in Queens let go to ruin.

1420 Belfrage, Cedric. "Be Happy--Go Cemetery." American
    Mercury. July 1951.

1421 Biondi, Nicholas A. "Ecology and the Cemetery." The Ceme-
    terian (special ecology edition), Nov. 1971, pp. 22-23.
        No solutions but raises probing questions about the future
of cemeteries as population and the interest in ecology grows: will
burial be permitted in rural cemeteries nearby homes whose water is

supplied by wells? Will cemeteries be required to buy surrounding land as a buffer? Will above-ground vaults replace inground interments? Will the church be forced to endorse cremation "as a normal means of disposal?"

1422 "Black G. I. Buried in White Cemetery." New York Times cxix(41, 126):14 (Aug. 30, 1970).
     Hillcrest Memorial Garden Cemetery in Ft. Pierce, Fla., first refuses, then allows burial of Spec 4 Pondexteur E. Williams.

1423 "Black Soldier's Burial Is Held Up in Florida." New York Times cxix(41, 120):38 (Aug. 24, 1970).
     Spec 4 Pondexteur E. Williams's burial is barred in Hillcrest Memorial Gardens in Ft. Pierce. See also entry 1556.

1424 Blandford, M. J. "In Consecrated Ground." Critic 32:52-53 (March 1974).

1425 B'nai B'rith Messenger, Jan. 13, 1961.
     Discussion of Forest Lawn's ownership of Mount Sinai Memorial Park controversy.

1426 Bradford, Charles A. Heart Burial. London: George Allen and Unwin, 1933. 256pp.

1427 Brennan, Raymond. California Cemetery Law. Los Angeles: Interment Assoc. of California, 1934. 153pp.
     Rules and regulations governing California cemeteries.

1428 _____, and Brennan, Lois W. Law Governing Cemetery Rules and Regulations; National in Scope; An Analysis of the Power of Interment Organizations to Enact Rules and Regulations; Continuing Model Rules and Regulations, Case Annotations, Practical Comments, Model Forms. Los Angeles: Interment Assoc. of California, xiii, 237pp. (1935). Revised xxiii, 265pp. (1951).

1429 "A Brief History of Concrete Burial Vaults in America." Casket & Sunnyside 101(13[centennial issue]):38-41 (1972). Photos.
     History of the concrete vault business beginning about 1903, problems under which builders worked, shipping difficulties, steps in the manufacturing process, and a short profile on the National Concrete Burial Vault Association.

1430 Browne, Thomas, Sir. Hydriotaphia; or, Urn Burial, ed. by Frank C. Huntley. Bound with The Garden of Cyrus. Northbrook, IL: AHM Pub., 1966. (Crofts Classics series.)

1431 _____. Urne-Buriall, and the Garden of Cyrus, ed by John Carter. New York: Cambridge University Press, 1974.

1432 Bruce, Bob L. "Answer to Criticism Is Positive Use."
The Cemeterian (special ecology edition), Nov. 1971, p. 26.
New York State Assoc. of Cemeteries president discusses
problems and solutions to two major problems: (1) the use of limited space by cemeteries and (2) rising property and income taxes.
In answer to allegation that cemeteries waste on the dead space
needed by the living, he demonstrates that cemeteries benefit the
living by relieving acres of concrete with trees and grass. Suggests
cemeterians encourage the public to use their grounds for appropriate
activities--botany studies, parks, fishing, and consider alternate
means of disposition, such as cremation and mausoleums, to conserve land. Urges planning now for fifty years ahead.

1433 _____. "Cemeteries Must Adapt to Ecology." Casket &
Sunnyside 102(11):50+ (1972).
To avoid continued pressure to redesignate "unproductive"
use of their space, cemeteries must open up to the public--not for
them to picnic or "rabble rouse," but to watch birds, meditate,
study nature. Cemeterians must also maintain plantings, restore
dilapidated structures, and replant where necessary.

1434 Calkins, Scott. "Funeral Director Holds Key to More Vaults
Sales." Casket & Sunnyside 100(12):20-21 (1970).
The percentage of vaults used in relation to recorded
deaths; use of concrete vaults versus metal outside enclosures; why
families buy vaults; who sells them.

1435 Calvary Cemetery, Brooklyn. The Visitor's Guide to Calvary
Cemetery, With Map and Illustrations. New York: J. J.
Foster, 1876. Illus., map.

1436 Carpenter, Edwin H. Cemeteries in the City of Los Angeles.
Los Angeles: Dawsons, 1974.

1437 "Catholics Oppose Suggestion on Making Cemetery a Park."
New York Times cxviii(40, 739):30 (Aug. 8, 1969).
Holy Cross Cemetery in Brooklyn, N.Y.

1438 "Cemeteries." American Funeral Director 95(8):23 (1972).
The Preservation Society, a group of citizens in the Boston area, attempts to restore and maintain neglected historic cemeteries where many early patriots are buried.

1439 "Cemeteries for Pets Increasing in Number." American Fu-
neral Director 96(3):16+ (1973).
Statistics released by the National Association of Pet
Cemeteries show pet cemeteries up over 50% from 1971 to 1973.
Association has 48 member cemeteries; price for interment ranges
from $25 to over $2000. Average is between $80 and $120.

1440 "Cemeteries Now Offer Living New Place to Relax in Peace."
Northeast Funeral Director 22(2):8 (1973).
New and growing practice in U.S. to open cemeteries to

public for bicycling, jogging, fishing, meditation and study in developed areas. In non-developed areas some cemeterians allow sports. Opposing spokesmen's views aired.

1441 "Cemeteries Work on 15,000 Burials." New York Times cxix (40,954):53 (March 11, 1970).
The New York City strike.

1442 "Cemetery Associations Release Data on Space Availability Study." Northeast Funeral Director 21(6):10 (1972).
Highlights from the statement made to the Committee on Veterans' Affairs of the House of Representatives on behalf of two national and regional cemetery associations. Presently there is cemetery space for U.S. needs for the next 140 to 160 years; the average cost of burial plots and interment; the industry's efforts to clean up any alleged poor practices.

1443 "Cemetery Fund Ended." New York Times cxxiii(42,534):27 (July 8, 1974).
United Nations ends support of the Korean War Cemetery in South Korea.

1444 Cemetery Handbook; A Manual of Useful Information on Cemetery Development and Management. Madison, WI: Park and Cemetery, n.d. 520pp.

1445 "The Cemetery Lot: Rights and Restriction." University of Pennsylvania Law Review 109:378 (1961). Student note, signed "R.S."

1446 "Cemetery Owners Ending Racial Bias in Flint, Michigan." New York Times cxvi(39,764):38 (Dec. 7, 1966).

1447 "Cemetery Owners Reply in Kind to New Jersey's Undertakers." New York Times cxv(39,653):71 (Aug. 18, 1966).
N.J. cemetery owners accuse funeral directors of preying on survivors' grief.

1448 "Cemetery Policy Scored by Judge." New York Times cxxii (41,962): 111 (Dec. 13, 1972).
Flower Hill Cemetery, N.J. has been removing hazardous tombstones (i.e., ones that might fall and injure workers) without owners' permission. Judge orders a stop to this.

1449 "Cemetery Relocation Is Balked by Cost and Law." New York Times cxix(40,811): sect. VIII p. 8 (Oct. 19, 1969).

1450 "Cemetery Strike Near Settlement." New York Times cxvi (39,812):14 (Jan. 24, 1967).
New York City strikers reach tentative accord. See entries 1453, 1454.

1451 "Cemetery Strike Spurs Guard Pleas." New York Times cxxi

(41, 527):20 (Oct. 5, 1971).
San Francisco cemetery strike. Some urge the National Guard be called to bury the dead. See entry 1452.

1452 "Cemetery Workers Obtain Agreement in California Strike. "
New York Times cxxi(41, 528):22 (Oct. 6, 1971).
San Francisco cemetery strike ended. See entry 1451.

1453 "Cemetery Workers Reach Agreement in Pact Dispute. " New
York Times cxvi(39, 790):17 (Jan. 2, 1967).
New York City cemetery workers strike ends. See entries
1450, 1454.

1454 "Cemetery Workers Will Strike Today. " New York Times
cxvi(39, 791):44 (Jan. 3, 1967).
New York City cemetery workers strike for higher wages.
See entries 1450, 1453.

1455 "Cemetery Workers Ratify Pact with $10. 50 Raise. " New
York Times cxiii(38, 699):66 (Jan. 7, 1964).
New York City cemetery workers union contract.

1456 Chowins, Christopher. "Cemetery Planting. " Horticulture
47(2):26-27, 55 (Feb. 1969). Photos.
Considerations and suggested species for grave plantings.

1457 "Church to Broaden Burial Integration. " New York Times
cxiii(38, 798):42 (April 15, 1964).
St. Paul's Rock Creek Church in Washington, D. C. agrees
to bury Negroes in its Rock Creek Cemetery.

1458 "Citizens Digging of Graves Gets Publicity. " The Director
XLV(4):10 (April 1975).
Chesterfield, Ill. : trendy reversion to the old custom of
friends and relatives doing the digging and filling in of graves. The
purpose is not to allay cost but to express "sympathy to the family. "

1459 "Clark Grave Vault Push Aims to Build Funeral Men's Image."
Advertising Age 36:38 (Nov. 15, 1965).

1460 Clark, Thomas H. "Court Restricts Sale of Markers by
Cemetery. " The Director 41(3):10 (1971).
A N. J. Superior Court rules that a sales agency with
exclusive rights to sell graves and plots in a particular cemetery
has an unfair advantage in selling grave markers for that cemetery.

1461 "Continuous Concrete Cells: Crypts for 11, 400. " Engineering
News-Record 188(21):13 (May 25, 1972).
Holy Cross Cemetery in Colma, Cal., installs three
acres of reinforced concrete tandem crypts. The 7. 7 x 2. 7 x 5. 7
deep crypts eliminate much digging and maintenance.

1462 Corwin, John H. Beauty for Ashes; Brooklyn Trust Co., et al. vs. Greenwood Cemetery, Impleaded, etc., with a Note on Sepulchral Law. New York: The Author, 1915. 28pp. (paper).

1463 "Court Backs Negro on Bias in Burial." New York Times cxv (39, 680): 23 (Sept. 14, 1966).
J. J. Merrill Spencer vs. Flint Memorial Park, Flint, Mich.

1464 "Court Bars Sale of Burial Places." New York Times cxxi (41, 705):33 (March 31, 1972).
Court rules that family lot owned for over 100 years can not be divided.

1465 "Court Tells Florida Cemetery to Bury Black G. I." New York Times cxix(41, 124):1, 10 (Aug. 28, 1970).
Hillcrest Memorial Gardens in Ft. Pierce, Fla., is told to admit Black G. I.

Cremation Association of America. Answers to Questions Most Often Asked About Cremation. See entry 1651.

1466 Cummings, Judith. "Vandalism Is on the Increase in City's Cemeteries." New York Times cxxiii(42, 332):45 (Dec. 18, 1972). Photo.

1467 Darnton, John. "Pinelawn Is a Prosperous City of the Dead." New York Times cxx(41, 301):90 (Feb. 21, 1971).
Pinelawn, N. Y. (Long Island), the home of eight cemeteries.

1468 "Des Moines Eases Rule on Graves." New York Times cxxii (41, 899):45 (Oct. 11, 1972).
Special markers allowed for infants' graves.

1469 "Detroit Cemetery Strike." New York Times cxix(40, 967):33 (March 24, 1970).

1470 Dickinson, Ernest. "Cemeteries 'Go Public'." New York Times cxxiii(42, 372): sect. VIII, p. 10 (Jan. 27, 1974).
Cemeteries used by the public for parks, hiking, etc.

1471 "A Dilemma of a Cemetery Park." New York Times cxvi (40, 023):47 (Aug. 23, 1967). Photos.
St. Ann's Church in Bronx, N. Y.

1472 Dincauze, D. Cremation Cemeteries in Eastern Massachusetts. Salem, MA: Peabody Museum, 1968. 103pp., illus., maps (paper).

1473 "Diversification in the Concrete Burial Vault Industry." Casket & Sunnyside 102(8):43 (1972).
Vault manufacturer explains two types of diversification:

horizontal, where new products unrelated to burial vaults are added to your line, and vertical, where your line is simply enlarged.

Dougherty, Philip H. "The Benisch Family: An Institution in Itself." See entry 1286.

1474 Drewes, Donald W. Cemetery Land Planning. Pittsburgh: Matthews Memorial Bronze, 1964. 91pp., plans.
Landscape architect plans cemetery properties; site choosing, planning land data collection; types of plans; site studies: road construction and traffic control; road design and drainage construction; proper grading for drainage; garden plans with discussion of layout, planting, placement of feature memorial. Brief coverage of the construction program, enlargement, reclamation of land and the rehabilitation of old cemeteries. Concentration is on land.

1475 Eaton, Hubert. The Comemoral. Los Angeles: Academy Press, 1954.

1476 "Ecumenism in the Cemetery" (editorial paragraphs). The Christian Century 86:1411-12 (Nov. 5, 1969).
Many Catholic cemeteries refuse burial to non-Catholics, thus splitting families in death.

Edmands, Michael J. "Dying Business? Young Entrepreneurs Have Brought New Vigor to Funeral Parlors, Cemeteries." See entry 627.

_____. "Young Entrepreneurs Have Brought New Vigor to Funeral Parlors." See entry 629.

1477 Edwards, Tom. "Will They Recycle Our Cemeteries?" Northeast Funeral Director 20(10):14 (1971).
Why not strip-mine cemeteries for iron ore? Ethical question of what to do with the body remains. Suggests as metals in the post-environment age become scarce, enlightened society might "find important environmental reasons for freeing cemeteries of their caskets."

1478 Eliasberg, K. "Does the Knollwood Decision Auger an End to Cemetery Bootstrap Deals?" Journal of Taxation 27(3):224-30 (Oct. 1967).

1479 "Enquiry on U.S. Cemeteries Urged by Four from Jersey." New York Times cxv(39,628):46 (July 24, 1966).
Four New Jersey Congressmen want Congress to look into federal cemeteries.

1480 The Environment: Is There a Place For Us? Re-issue of the Special Ecology Edition of The Cemeterian, Nov. 1971. Available from the ACA. 64pp., illus.
Updated issue of the original. Articles on cemeterians, the "original ecologists"; basic facts cemeterians need to know about

ecology; how greenery within cities reduces heat and pollution; reprint from the July 1970 issue of The Catholic Cemetery on "Ecology and the Cemetery"; expanded use of cemetery land as gardens, limited recreation areas; pollution and the cemetery; maintenance of grounds through composting. Foreward-thinking, excellent publication.

1481 The First Fifty Years Were the Hardest: A Brief History of the Concrete Burial Vault Business. Columbus, OH: National Concrete Burial Vault Assoc., 1953.
      Attributed to Page Hereford.

1482 "First International Conference in Amsterdam Highly Successful." The Cemeterian 39(4):1-9 (May 1974). Photos.
      The first international plenary session of cemetery officials held April 19-26, 1975 in Amsterdam under the sponsorship of the American Cemetery Assoc.

1483 Fosburgh, Lacey. "St. Mark's Building Playground in Its Cemetery, the City's Oldest." New York Times cxix (40,924):1,44 (Feb. 9, 1970). Photo.
      St. Mark's Church in New York City is building a playground in its cemetery.

1484 Fowler, Elizabeth M. "Personal Finance: Family Planning for Cemetery Plot Provides Assurance in Time of Need." New York Times cxviii(40,658):67, 75 (May 19, 1969). Chart.
      Costs, types of plots, different kinds of cemeteries.

1485 _____. "Planning Burial Can Save Relatives Stress Later." Northeast Funeral Director 18(7):14 (1969).
      Steps to cut down funeral costs and avoid problems: buy cemetery plot in advance of need; rural area prices lower than urban cemeteries; keep deed to plot in accessible place; avoid weekend burials; consult cemetery personnel on costs and gravesites.

1486 Franklin, Ben A. "Episcopalians In Capital Clash on Negro Burial in Church Plot." New York Times cxiii(38,787):12 (April 4, 1964).
      St. Paul's Rock Creek Church, Washington, D.C., refuses burial for Miss Viola Wilson in their Rock Creek Cemetery. See also entry 1457.

1487 Fraser, C. Gerald. "City Witness Calls for Housing in Central Park and Cemeteries." New York Times cxvii(40,058): 51 (Sept. 28, 1967).
      Harold Ostroff asks that housing be constructed on ground now occupied by cemeteries.

1488 "Free Burial Offered G.I. s." New York Times cxvi(39,708): 25 (Oct. 12, 1966).
      Valhalla Cemetery, St. Louis.

1489   "Free Burial Plots in Private Cemeteries Could Cost Vets
        More Than Expected." Northeast Funeral Director 21(1):
        7 (1972).
            Veteran should beware of "free burial plots for veterans"
schemes.

1490   "'Free Grave" Programs Condemned at Hearing." American
        Funeral Director 95(5):18 (1972).
            Activities of the Ethics Committee of the National Assoc.
of Cemeteries summarized; its response to the Senate Veterans Affairs Committee charge that they have adopted misleading practices.

1491   French, S. "Cemetery as Cultural Institution: the Establish-
        ment of Mount Auburn and the Rural Cemetery Movement."
        American Quarterly 26:37-59 (March 1974).

1492   Garceau, Carroll. "The Physical Plant and the Physical
        Plan." The Catholic Cemetery 15(7):6ff(8pp.) (March 1975).
        Photo.
            Speech delivered at the National Catholic Cemetery Con-
ference by the director of technical services, Catholic cemeteries,
Archdiocese of Chicago. Topics included: cemetery design, contours, landscaping, building planning and placement, utility planning.
Summary of Chicago's operations and problems, Nahir's goals--con-
tinued orderly expansion, conservation of land, updating and renovat-
ing present cemeteries, and general improvement of operation and
maintenance. The Archdiocese of Chicago needs approximately 15
to 20 acres a year of developed burial property.

        "Glen Oak's New Mortuary." American Funeral Director.
        See entry 731.

1493   Glueck, Grace. "Artists Find 'In' Place on L.I." New York
        Times cxviii(40,423):49 (Sept. 26, 1968). Photos.
            Artists want to be buried in the Green River Cemetery,
The Springs, N.Y. (Long Island).

        Gold, Gerald. "Wide Range of Funeral Prices Found Here in
        Consumer Study." See entry 961.

        Goodwin, Michael. "Technicality Stalls Landmark Plan."
        See entry 1295.

1494   Gordon, J.J. Cemetery Management. Chicago: Cemetery
        Beautiful, 1915. 204pp., illus.

1495   Graham, Fred. "Blacks Get Equal Rights Even in Death."
        New York Times cxix(41,126): sect IV, p.14 (Aug. 30 1970).
            Spec 4 Pondexteur Williams is refused burial in the Hill-
crest Memorial Gardens cemetery in Ft. Pierce, Fla. Family sues
and the cemetery is forced to permit the burial. See also entries
1422 and 1556.

1496 "Grave Situation. " Christian Century 87(34):1027 (Aug. 26, 1970).
Comments on humorous cemetery names and unusual obituary requests.

1497 "Grave Squeeze. " Newsweek 72(12):94 (Sept. 16, 1968).   Photo.
World-wide cemetery land shortage and the solutions being implemented: high-rise mausoleums and cremation.   Situation in Japan, Rio, Sicily, West Berlin, Britain and the U.S. mentioned.

1498 "Gravediggers Strike on Coast. " New York Times cxiv(39,084): 8 (Jan. 26, 1965).
Stockton, California strike.

1499 "Gravediggers Vote to End Their Strike. " New York Times cxvi(39,814):18 (Jan. 26, 1967).
New York City strike. See entries 1532, 1540, 1600, 1601.

Grollman, Dr. Earl A. , ed. Concerning Death: A Practical Guide for the Living. See entry 1117.

1500 Hall, T. H. , III, and Beaton, W. R. "Partial Taking of a Cemetery with a Contingent Liability. " Appraisal Journal 35:107-15 (Jan. 1967).
Real estate appraisal of cemetery land.

1501 Halsted, Donald. "How Much High Risk-High Yield Investment Can a Cemetery Make ?" The Cemeterian 39(4):27-29 (May 1974).
Investment tips by the Investment Counsel for the Woodlawn Cemetery, Bronx, N.Y.   Topics covered include differing state laws governing investments, dividing "defensive" securities (high quality bonds) and "aggressive" (high-grade common stocks and convertible bonds and preferred stocks), how to protect against inflation.

1502 Haney, Roy. "Pollution and the Cemetery. " The Cemeterian (special ecology edition), Nov. 1971, p. 49-50.
How the cemeterian can combat pollution as well as the ecologist: compost rather than burn leaves, mulch instead of burning brush, keep gasoline and diesel engines finely tuned to reduce exhaust fumes, reduce spraying, "build" soil, cover unused areas with vegetation, minimize use of commercial fertilizers, conserve water, plant creatively to cut down noise pollution.

1503 Hare & Hare (architects). Modern Park Cemetery. New York: Civic Press, 1916.

1504 Hemphill, Paul. "Room at the Top. " New York Times Magazine section, Dec. 9, 1973, p. 125.
H. Raymond Ligon's Woodlawn Cross Mausoleum and Funeral Home near downtown Nashville, Tenn.   Rationale for this $12 million 20-story mausoleum and cold storage for 129,000 bodies is the increasing cost and decreasing availability of land.   Mausoleum

covers seven acres and will bury the same number as 192 acres of cemetery plots. Burial costs average $2500 for coffin, hearse, police escort, flowers, viewing, grave charges, etc. Crypt charges average $2000 for which survivors have visiting privileges in carpeted, air-conditioned, muzak, cushy sofa comfort.

1505 "High Rise, Automated Kyoto Tombs." Mortuary Management 56(9):22-24 (1969). Illus.
    Ten-story Japanese Buddhist Shrine with 17,300 automatic compartments costing $2800 to $9500. Pictorial feature.

1506 "High-Rise Cemetery Is Planned for Rio." New York Times cxxi(42,658):10 (Feb. 13, 1972).
    Twenty-nine-story Rio Mausoleum will include special drainage system to carry decomposition gas and liquids.

1507 "High Rise Mausoleum." Casket & Sunnyside 101(11):21 (1971).
    Associated Press reports details of the 20-story, high-rise mausoleum being built in Nashville, Tenn. H. Raymond Ligon, the funeral director, offers a one-stop service to meet funeral and memorialization needs. Night funerals for a busy populace's convenience. Plans two units providing crypts for 128,500 caskets on a 14-acre site. Earth interment would require almost 10 times as much land.

1508 "High-rise Mausoleum Cuts Costs of Interment." Engineering News-Record 188(7):13 (Feb. 17, 1972). Photo.
    Thirty-nine story mausoleum in Rio de Janeiro with built-in odor and liquid disposal system.

    Hoffman, Frederick L. Pauper Burials and the Interment of the Dead in Large Cities. See entry 309.

1509 Houghton, Albert A. Concrete Monuments, Mausoleums and Burial Vaults. New York: Henley, 1910. 65pp.

1510 "Hubert Eaton, Flamboyant Head of Forest Lawn, Is Dead at 85." New York Times cxvi(39,688):74 (Sept. 22, 1966).
    Personality portrait and obit of Herbert Eaton, founder of Forest Lawn Cemetery, Los Angeles.

1511 Hughes, Cary. "New Underground Mausoleum to Provide Total of 3100 Crypts." Casket & Sunnyside 103(5):42+ (1973).
    Memphis Memorial Park realizes land is running out for interment use. Solution: one of the first underground mausoleums in America. Details of promotion and pre-need sales program publicity.

1512 Hunter, Marjorie. "Vietnam Swayed Cemetery Policy." New York Times cxvi(39,842):7 (Feb. 23, 1967).
    Number of war dead forced expansion of military cemeteries.

1513 "Inquiry on Prices Due on Cemeteries." New York Times cxix(40, 937):70 (Feb. 22, 1970).
New York State attorney general's office runs inquiry on state's cemeteries' pricing methods and costs.

1514 Interment Assoc. of America. Modern Concepts of Cemetery Responsibility and Service. Minneapolis, MN: Interment Assoc. of America and Interment Exchange of America, 1957. 15pp.

1515 Interment Assoc. of California. Manual of Standard Crematory-Columbarium Practices, rev. ed., 1941. Available from the Cremation Assoc. of America.
Recommended policies and procedures of management and operation.

1516 Interments in National Cemeteries. Pamphlet available from the U.S. Army Memorial Affairs Agency (A) Dept. of the Army, Temporary Bldg., 2nd and T Sts., S.W., Washington, DC 20315.

1517 International Cemetery Directory. Available from the American Cemetery Assoc.
Lists cemeteries, executives, and directories.

1518 Jabine, William. "The Law Says...." Mortuary Management 57(2):24 (1970).
Florida Supreme Court rules that the operation of a cemetery is an inalienable right if it is carried on without damage to public health, welfare, or morals and that the Court cannot deny an application on the grounds of "no need."

1519 _____. "The Law Says...." Mortuary Management 58(3): 20 (1971).
Appellate Division of the New Jersey Supreme Court extends Court's 1959 ruling that a cemetery association may not sell grave markers to mean that cemetery agents may not engage in such activity, even when no profit is realized.

1520 Jackson, Edgar N. "Be Thankful for Cemeteries." The De-Ce-Co Magazine 63(4):7+ (1971).
Cemeteries fill ecological, social and personal needs. All three discussed.

Jackson, Percival E. The Law of Cadavers and of Burial and Burial Places. See entry 1055.

Jackson, Samuel Macaulay. The New Schaff-Herzog Encyclopedia of Religious Knowledge. See entry 1314.

1521 Jacobs, Paul. "The Most Cheerful Graveyard in the World." The Reporter, Sept. 18, 1958.

1522 "Japan Is Turning to 'Locker-Tombs'. " New York Times cxx
      (41, 196):11 (Nov. 8, 1970).
         To save land, Japanese are storing urns (for cremated
remains) in multi-story buildings.

1523 "Jews Win Ruling on Burial Here. " New York Times cxix
      (40, 899):59 (Jan. 15, 1970).
         Court rules in New York City strike, Jews allowed to
bury dead despite gravediggers' objections.

1524 Kimbel, Steve. "Some Who Lie in Arlington Were Not War-
      time Heroes. " American Funeral Director 94(1):40-42
      (1971).
         Non-military heroes buried at Arlington National Ceme-
tery include Abner Doubleday, the inventor of baseball; Admiral
Richard E. Byrd, Polar explorer; George Westinghouse, inventor
of the airbrake; Robert Todd Lincoln, Pierre L'Enfant, and Ignace
Jan Paderewski. William Howard Taft and John F. Kennedy are
the only presidents buried there.

1525 Klupar, G. J. Modern Cemetery Management. Hillside, IL:
      Catholic Cemeteries of the Archdiocese of Chicago, 1962.
      418pp. , photos, diagrs. , plans, charts.
         A comprehensive reference for cemetery administrators
emphasizing principles and providing practical examples: organization (goals, needs, organization of people, and public relations);
personnel administration (employee standards and relations, policies,
training, internal communication, union relations, and safety); cemetery development: (use of a consultant, expansion preparation and
plans, building the cemetery); sales and service (definition of goods
and services, administering a counseling program, service representatives, providing family needs (more than one plot, decorations,
pricing and income care); cemetery operations and maintenance
(supervisory functions, work force organization, scheduling and planning, cutting costs, interment procedures, chapels, flowers, cemetery and building maintenance, turf, mausoleum, landscape and
equipment, grass cutting, grave planting, evaluating operations);
regulations governing cemeteries (religious regulations, civil law,
governmental regulation, maintenance funds and "perpetual care, "
lot ownership, disinterment and burial, vacation of cemeteries,
exemptions, internal regulation, lot and grave plantings, and grave
decoration); memorials, regulations, procedures, and specifications,
shrine memorials, private mausoleums, financial and management
controls (operating revenue, expenditures, accounting, planning and
controlling, cost of labor, office records, care funds).

1526 Knowles, Clayton. "City May End Hart Island Ferry. " New
      York Times cxvi(39, 819):45 (Jan. 31, 1967).
         New York City may stop ferry runs to Hart Island where
Potter's Field is located.

1527 "Land Use for the Living and the Dead. " The Director 42:
      12 (Jan. 1972).

Shortage of land; land use for burial; updated information on ecology and mausolea given by the NFDA and the ACA; discussion of high rise mausoleums; the amount of air one tree or small plots of grass purify.

1528 Lapin, H. I. "Golden Hills and Meadows of the Tax-Exempt Cemetery." Taxes 44:744-61 (Nov. 1966).

1529 "Law Curbs Cemetery Fraud." New York Times cxxii (42, 239):95 (Sept. 16, 1973).
New Jersey law forbids the removal of grave markers without owner's permission unless it is a safety hazard. New Jersey Cemetery Board can audit financial records, revoke taxes on maintenance charges, and allow for cemetery expansion.

1530 "Law Preserving Cemeteries Upheld." New York Times cxxiii(42, 371):66 (Jan. 26, 1974).
Appellate Division of New Jersey Superior Court upholds 1971 state law which regulates funds established to preserve gravesites and cemetery grounds.

1531 "Legislative Notes: Cemetery Investigation Urged." New York Times cxxii(41, 945):106 (Nov. 26, 1972).
New Jersey Legislature urges investigation of the state's cemeteries.

1532 Lichtenstein, Grace. "Pact Is Reached by Gravediggers." New York Times cxix(40, 952):1, 34 (March 9, 1970).
New York City gravediggers' strike. See entries 1499, 1540, 1600, 1601.

1533 Lieberman, Gerald. "Cemeteries Are Urged to Fight Vandalism." New York Times cxxiii(43, 302):128 (Nov. 18, 1973). Photo.

1534 "Light Up Your Landscape." American Cemetery 46(2):18-21 (1973). Illus.
Value and use of after-dark lighting of cemetery grounds. When and how to use fluorescent and incandescent lights either separately or in combination; use of colored lights on features and foliage. Sequel in 46(3):22-25 describes varied fixtures available and specific results obtainable from each.

1535 "List of National Cemetery Installations Having Available Gravesites." Pamphlet. Available from the U.S. Army Memorial Affairs Agency(A), Dept. of the Army, Temporary Bldg., 2nd and T Sts., S.W., Washington, DC 20315.

1536 Little, W. T. "Hunting Ghosts in a Ghost Town Out West." New York Times cxvi(40, 020): sect. X, p. 119 (Aug. 20, 1967).
Unexplained light flickers on Silver Cliff, CO, cemetery tombstones.

1537 "The Living Flock to a Town of the Dead." New York Times
cxxi(41, 763):67 (May 28, 1972).
East Hanover Township, N. J. --location of many cemeteries.

1538 "A Look to the Future ... Vestal Hills." National Cremation
Magazine, July-Aug. -Sept. 1974, p. 7. Photos.
One-page photo essay on Vestal Hills Memorial Park in
Vestal, N. Y.

1539 "Louisiana Cemeteries Association Gains Passage of Comprehensive Cemetery Act." The Cemeterian Nov. 1974, p. 27-
29.
The Legislative Action Committee of the Louisiana Cemeteries Assoc. outlines and explains how the new, comprehensive cemetery act was passed in Louisiana. The act updates old rules, incor-
porates new features of cemetery management, and recodifies among
other aspects of cemetery law: Terminology, care fund and mausoleum regulations, licensing, and undeveloped land control. Step-by-
step route to passage explained, the first and second drafts, getting
funeral directors' support, and strategy in getting the law passed.

1540 Lubasch, Arnold H. "Gravediggers Vow to Defy Compulsory
Arbitration." New York Times cxix(40, 949):18 (March 16,
1970).
New York City strike. See entries 1499, 1532, 1600,
1601.

1541 McCampbell, James D. "Flower Vases Are Help in Building
Public Relations." Casket & Sunnyside 105(5):46-47 (May
1975).
Fed up with theft and damage to vases, a group of Midwest cemeteries banned their sale, but lifted restrictions when plot
sales decreased. The proper vase, however, can minimize problems. Review of the advantages and disadvantages of the three
classifications of permanent lawn vases--ground level in the open
position, half exposed in the open position, and fully exposed in the
open position (all are ground level when in closed position). Cheapest from standpoint of maintenance is the ground level variety.
Reasons given.

1542 MacCloskey, Monro. Hallowed Ground: Our National Cemeteries. New York: Richards Rosen Press, 1968. 192pp.,
illus.
The history of U. S. military and veterans associations
towards burial, including the history of the National Cemetery System from its origin in 1862 to 1967, by a retired general. Over-
crowding and land scarcity has forced policy changes. Much of the
remaining usable space is committed. Offers cremation as an immediate solution and alternative long-range suggestions. Believes
20th-century practices wasteful. Complete listing of National Cemetery installations in each state, those with and without available
grave space; interment practices and detailed regulations of the U. S.

at home and abroad, rules concerning stone inscriptions, size of
memorial markers, decoration, eligibility; chapter on the Arlington
National Cemetery and the unknown soldiers of World Wars I and II
and Korea.

>   McCracken, Joseph L. "A View of the Present and Future of
>   the Funeral." See entry 1187.

1543 Maddox, William H. Jr. "Concrete Vault Association--A His-
      tory of Hard Work." Casket & Sunnyside 99(8):24-25 (1969).
          Personal view of the industry's creation and early prob-
lems presented by the governor of District 2, National Concrete
Vault Assoc., at group's 1969 convention. See also entry 1481.

1544 _____. "What Was the Most Important Contribution That
      Was Made to Funeral Service by the Concrete Burial Vault
      Industry in the Past 100 Years?" Casket & Sunnyside 102
      (5):50 (1972).
          Sketch of the concrete burial vault industry--its history,
early hardships pioneers had to overcome, development of quality
products which meet public needs, efforts to keep up with the times,
creation of the National Concrete Burial Vault Assoc. in 1930 to insure industry uniformity, and aids to allied organizations.

1545 Maidenberg, H. J. "Personal Finance: Speculating in Ceme-
      tery Plots Called 'Unwise' by Better Business Bureau."
      New York Times cxvi(40, 017):49, 53 (Aug. 17, 1967).

>   Maisel, Albert Q. "Facts You Should Know About Funerals."
>   See entry 1122.

1546 Malcolm, Andrew. "Cemeteries Open Gates to Recreation
      Pursuits." New York Times cxxii(41, 959):76 (Dec. 10,
      1972).

1547 Mano, D. Keith. "Burials--I." National Review 25(31):844-
      45 (Aug. 3, 1973). Drawing.
          Hartsdale Pet Cemetery analyzed, with a jaundiced eye.

1548 _____. "Burials--II." National Review 25(33):896-97
      (1973). Drawing.
          An irreverent analysis of high-rise mausoleums.

1549 "Mayor Rejects Park Plan for Brooklyn Cemetery." New York
      Times cxviii(40, 744):40 (Aug. 13, 1969).
          Holy Cross Cemetery, Brooklyn, N.Y.

1550 Medders, O. L. "Financial Plan for a Successful Cemetery."
      The Cemeterian Nov. 1974), p. 31-32.
          President of the Anniston (Ala.) Memorial Gardens out-
lines the responsibilities of the cemeterian to lot owners and visitors
(to keep shrubbery and grass trimmed, roads in good repair, graves
filled, etc.); to the bank (to pay on time); to the Trust Fund (to invest

money well); to employees (to pay on time, provide proper equipment); to the cemetery industry (support, financial and otherwise);
to the local community (support, civic services and participation,
etc.).

1551 "Mikveh Israel Cemetery Now a National Landmark." Ameri-
        can Funeral Director 94(9):46-48 (1971).
        Federal Government designates this historic Jewish
cemetery in Philadelphia as a national landmark, offering protection against damage or destruction. Haym Salomon, Revolutionary
War financier who raised funds on Yom Kippur for George Washington, is buried there.

1552 Milne, J. C. "Greenwood Riverside Master Plan." Available
        from the ACA. 16pp., illus., charts, plans.
        The plan for the Greenwood Riverside Cemetery in Spo-
kane, WA, prepared by J. C. Milne of Milne Co., in Portland, OR.
The master plan concept considers the total cemetery, its present
and future, utilizing land to its best future advantage. Considered
are topography, construction, buildings, roads, drainage, esthetics,
careful measurements. Present conditions and proposals are described and illustrated.

1553 _____. "Woodlawn Master Plan." Available from the
        ACA. Illus., charts, plans.
        Proposed master plan for the Woodlawn Cemetery in
Bronx, N.Y. Area included is 12 acres of rocky, wet, steep, or
otherwise difficult ground for development as burial areas. Goal
is to continue Woodlawn as a first class cemetery, preserving as
much of the open areas and greenery as necessary to maintain its
present beauty by introducing vault entombment, cremation, and
underground vaults.

1554 "More Money to Ease Crowding of Cemeteries." U.S. News
        & World Report 75(2):57 (July 9, 1973). Photo.
        National Cemetery Act allows $150 for burial of wartime
veterans in non-national cemetery in addition to the $250 already
allowed. $800 is also allowed for death from service-connected dis-
ability. The Veterans Administration acquires jurisdiction over 82
national cemeteries and is planning new sites.

        Morgan, Al. "The Bier Barons." See entry 996.

1555 "Mortuary Humor Gets a Cold Reception." Business Week
        no. 2327, p. 42-43 (April 20, 1974). Photo.
        Forest Lawn radio ads go too far and are canceled be-
cause of public outcry. Humorous ads seen as tasteless. Detailed
look at the Forest Lawn-Pierce Bros. Los Angeles competition.

1556 "Mother of Black G.I. Slain in War Vows Burial in White
        Cemetery." New York Times cxix(41,119):3 (Aug. 23, 1970).
        Hillcrest Memorial Gardens in Ft. Pierce, Fla., seeks
to bar burial of Black veteran. See entries 1422, 1423, 1495.

1557 "A 'Mountain Man' to Get Last Wish." New York Times cxxii
    (42, 504):29 (June 8, 1974).
        John (Jeremiah) Johnson to be reburied. See also entry
1588.

1558 "Mourners' Tears." New York Times cxxi(41, 532): sect IV,
    p. 5 (Oct. 10, 1971).
        San Francisco cemetery strike.

1559 "Move Over, Forest Lawn!" Christian Century 86(36):1149
    (Sept. 3, 1969).
        Thoughts on cemetery promotion and plastic tombstones.

1560 Mucklow, Walter. Cemetery Accounts. New York: American
    Institute Pub., 1935. 208pp.

    Mulholland, John F. "Borthwick's in Honolulu." See entry
    679.

1561 National Catholic Cemetery Conference. The Catholic Ceme-
    tery Subject Index. Available from the NCCC, 1975.
        Complete subject index of all issues of Catholic Cemetery
magazine.

1562 _____. Cemetery Care Leaflet. Available from the NCCC,
    Item #607.
        Cemetery care, emphasizing the need for lot owner co-
operation in providing funds for care of older cemeteries. To be
used alone or with other literature (as counter pamphlet or mailing
stuffer, distribution to parishioners or the general public).

1563 _____. The Law and Catholic Cemeteries. Available from
    the NCCC, Item #601.
        Summary of statutes and court decisions of several states
that affect the administration and maintenance of Catholic cemeteries.
Useful to cemetery administrators. Prepared by the Legal Dept. of
National Catholic Welfare Council.

1564 _____. Looking After God's Acre. Available from the
    NCCC. Item #201.
        Brochure explaining the Conference's purpose and serv-
ices provided members.

1565 _____. Parish Cemetery Handbook. Available from the
    NCCC, Item #612.
        Three volume loose-leaf bound handbook for cemetery
administrators: I (1968): canon and diocesan law, civil law and
legislation, development, administrative and office procedures; II
(1969): buildings, equipment, landscaping, operations; III (1975):
memorial and shrine, personnel, sales, service, counseling, mausoleums and garden crypts.

1566 _____. Pre-Need Handbook. Available from the NCCC,
    Item #617. 100+pp.

Designed to assist cemetery administrators sell graves--
how to set up service and counseling programs.   Loose-leaf bound.

1567 _____.   Pre-Need Leaflet.   Available from the NCCC,
        Item #610.   Up to 1000/$. 05 each; 1000 to 4, 999/$. 04
        each; 5, 000 and over/$. 03 each.
        Reviews the advantages of choosing a family burial place
before it's needed.   To be used by itself or as a companion leaflet
with other literature, forms, letters, or programs.

_____.   Rite of Burial Book.   See entry 334.

_____.   Rite of Burial Leaflet.   See entry 335.

1568 National Catholic Welfare Conference.   The Law and Catholic
        Cemeteries.   Des Plaines, IL: National Catholic Cemetery
        Conference, 1956.   39pp.

1569 "National Cemetery at Gettysburg Halting Burials. "   New York
        Times cxxii(41, 924):100 (Nov. 5, 1972).
        Gettysburg cemetery filled to capacity.

1570 "National Cemetery Plans Expansion. " New York Times
        cxxiii(42, 464):55 (April 29, 1974).
        National Cemetery at Arlington, Va. expands.

National Funeral Directors Association.   Considerations Con-
        cerning Cremation.   See entry 1697.

1571 "NCCC Opposes Growth of U.S. Cemeteries. "   American Fu-
        neral Director 98(7):6-7 (July 1975).
        Quotations of the National Catholic Cemetery Conference's
statement to Congressional subcommittees on proposed expansion of
the national cemeteries programs.   The NCCC recognizes the need
to honor veterans but does not believe a continued expansion and pro-
liferation of national cemeteries programs is the way to meet this
need.   Its solution is "the upgrading of the established program of
burial allowances or allotments which will serve all veterans equally,
without doing violence to justice, to equity or to religious considerations. "

1572 "Negro Buys a Plot in White Cemetery. "   New York Times
        cxxi(41, 518):58 (Sept. 26, 1971).
        Dade City Cemetery in Dade City, Fla.

1573 "Negro G. I. 's Wife Sues Cemetery. "   New York Times cxviii
        (40, 726):3 (July 26, 1969).
        Wife of Pvt. Henry Terry, Jr. , sues Elmwood Cemetery
in Birmingham, Ala. , for refusing to bury him.

1574 "Neighbors Dig All Graves in Small Rural Cemetery. "   Casket
        & Sunnyside 105(6):16 (June 1975).
        When someone dies in Keller, a rural Illinois hamlet,

funeral director Paul Warner calls cemetery owner Bob Keele and Keele calls up some friends.

1575 Nichols, Charles H. "The Psychology of Selling Vaults. "
      The Vault Merchandizer, April 1956.

1576 "9 Cited in Michigan in Veteran's Bilking. " New York Times
      cxxi(41, 670):9 (Feb. 25, 1972).
      Crestwood Memorial Gardens, Grand Blanc.

1577 "O'Dwyer and Leone at Odds Over Proposed Funds for Ceme-
      tery in Canarsie. " New York Times cxxiv(42, 652):124
      (Nov. 3, 1974).

1578 "The Original Ecologists: That's Us !" The Cemeterian spe-
      cial ecology edition, Nov. 1971, p. 1ff(3pp.).
          The cemetery contributes to good environment by provid-
ing trees, grass, open space, habitat for wild life--all necessary to
maintain the world's ecological balance. The cemeterian set aside
areas for preservation long before ecology became an issue and
should continue to promote ecology vigorously, "tell the public about
it, " and never exclude living people from the cemetery environment.
Environmental facts: 50 x 50 feet of green grass provides the daily
oxygen supply for a family of four; a line of trees and bushes can
reduce noise up to 60%. Incorporating ecological principles into
cemetery design is sound financial investment and benefits the general community. Tips on how to tell the ecology story, what your
cemetery is doing to help, clubs to join or speak at, and how to
publicize your programs with help from the ACA.

          Pace, Eric. "A Boom in Tomb-Building Brings Good Cheer
          to Cairo's City of the Dead. " See entry 1347.

1579 Parker, James L. "Many New Laws Restrict Cemetery Sales
      Methods. " American Cemetery 46(2):32+ (1973).
          List of the 42 bills which were enacted in 1972 affecting
cemeteries. Predicts another 300 will be enacted in 1973.

1580 _____. "Survey of 1974 Cemetery Laws. " The Catholic
      Cemetery 15(7):16-18 (March 1975).
          Review of bills pertaining to cemeteries enacted into law
in 1974, with special mention of Michigan's law which makes cemetery vandalism a felony, punishable by a $2500 fine and maximum
five years imprisonment. Cemeterians in other states are considering similar legislation to deter against theft and vandalism in their
cemeteries.

1581 "Pennsylvania Unit Bars Cemetery Bias. " New York Times
      cxv(39, 578):24 (June 24, 1966).
          Pennsylvania Human Rights Commission orders Whitemarsh
Memorial Park Cemeteries Co. to bury non-whites.

1582 "Pentagon Restricts Burials in Arlington. " New York Times
      cxvi(39, 830):1, 7 (Feb. 11, 1967).

Arlington National Cemetery will allow burial of only those veterans who served in high government posts.

1583   Perlmutter, Emanuel.   "Effects of Gravediggers' Strike Wor-
       rying City Health Officials." New York Times cxvi(39, 806):
       28 (Jan. 18, 1967).
       New York City strike.

1584   "Pet Cemetery Boom--A Token of Owner's Devotion." New
       York Times 15, Dec. 31, 1972, p. 15.
       Patricia Blosser (Paw Print Gardens, 27 W 150 North
Ave., West, Chicago 60185), president of the National Assoc. of
Pet Cemeteries.   Hoegh Pet Casket Co., Gladstone, Mich.

1585   "Pinelawn Denies State Charge That Too Much Goes for
       'Frills'." New York Times cxv(39, 565):60 (May 22, 1966).
       Pinelawn Memorial Park in Farmingdale, N.Y., charged
with shorting funds for maintenance.

Plumb, J. H.   "De Mortuis."   See entry 1006.

Polson, Cyril, et al.   Disposal of the Dead.   See entry 348.

1586   Pullins, Jerald L.   "Cemeteries--Their Future and Their
       Past."   Casket & Sunnyside 101(13[centennial issue]):72-74
       (1972).   Photos.
       Municipalities generally owned and operated American
cemeteries up until 1900; private development became popular in the
20th century because land was considered unlimited and its profit
potential was great; the Depression spurred installment purchasing;
accummulated cash and commodity scarcity of the 1940's spurred
pre-need sales.   For the future: increasing land scarcity and rising
real estate costs, public awareness will dictate new solutions, like
mausoleums, multiple below ground burial, and cremation.

1587   "Queens Cemetery to Be Restored After a Long Search for
       Owner." New York Times cxiii(38, 601):31 (Oct. 1, 1963).
       Lawrence Family Cemetery, Bayside, Queens, N.Y.

1588   "Reburial Protested." New York Times cxxiii(42, 504):29 (June
       8, 1974).
       Veterans of Foreign Wars protest "Jeremiah" Johnson
reburial.   See also entry 1557.

"Rector Puts Curse on Vandals...."   See entry 1357.

1589   "Requium for Arlington?" Newsweek 75(23):29 (June 8, 1970).
       Photo.
       Overcrowding at Arlington National Cemetery, Va., has
forced acquisition of new land, changes in rules, and new efforts
from Congress.

1590   Richards, John L., Jr.   "Appraisal of Cemetery Lands."
       Appraisal Journal 37:394-400 (July 1969).

1591 "School Officials Asked to Aid Drive on Cemetery Vandals."
New York Times cxxiii(42, 341):35 (Dec. 27, 1973).

1592 Schuchat, T. "National Cemeteries Running Out of Space."
Retirement Living 13(4):9 (April 1973).
Forty of the 84 U.S. National cemeteries have no sites
left. Congress passed V.A. study bill, but Nixon vetoed it. Benefits for veterans listed.

1593 Shipler, David K. "Proposal for Park in Cemetery Assailed
as 'Ghoulish' by Stark." New York Times cxviii(40, 737):
31 (Aug. 6, 1969).
Holy Cross Cemetery, Brooklyn, N.Y., considers opening
gates as park, too.

1594 "A Sign of Changing Times: Coast Statue Sheds Figleaf."
New York Times cxviii(40, 720):32 (July 20, 1969).
Forest Lawn's reproduction of Michelangelo's "David"
unveils.

1595 Sinclair, John J. "Vases in Markers Creating Serious Maintenance Problems." The Cemeterian p. 25-26, Nov. 1974.
President of three cemeteries installs all markers with
a separate vase to reduce the cemeteries' future liabilities. Vases
which are placed in the marker are easily damaged by equipment
and frost. Damage to a vase that is separate from the marker,
however, does not effect the marker.

1596 "Sixty-six Mournful Acres; New York's Desolate Island of
the Forgotten Dead." American Funeral Director 10(97):
86-87 (Oct. 1974).
History and description of Potter's Field on New York
City's Hart Island where over 650, 000 people are buried. In 1973,
4193 pine boxes were dispatched there, containing 1131 adults, 2182
babies, and 880 amputated limbs. About a quarter of all adults
are unknown. Rikers Island prisoners do the digging. Corpses are
unembalmed. Boxes are stacked into the ground three deep for
adults, seven deep for infants. Public programs pay generally only
up to $250 for a private funeral and the minimum cost in New York
City is $700. The city buries an adult for $75, a child for $29.

1597 Spiegel, Irving. "Burials Stalled As Gravediggers Strike."
New York Times cxix(40, 897):36 (Jan. 13, 1970). Photo.
New York City strike.

1598 St. Johns, Adela Rogers. First Step Up Toward Heaven:
Hubert Eaton and Forest Lawn. New York: Prentice Hall,
1959. 293pp., photos.
More flattering picture of Eaton and Forest Lawn than
Al Morgan's "The Bier Barons" (entry 996) or E. Cockrell's "O
Death, Where is Thy Sting?" (entry 926). Straight sympathetic biog-
raphy of the mining engineer turned cemetery entrepreneur and his
"unsurpassed" cemetery. St. Johns is a committee member of the
Forest Lawn Foundation.

1599 Stanton, Son. "Labor Relations. " Casket & Sunnyside 102
      (2):52 (1972).
      Experienced vault industry member discusses whipsawing
in labor negotiations, wages, competitive pricing, hourly wages and
overtime costs, vacations, sick pay, profit sharing, hospital and
medical insurance benefits, bonuses, etc.

1600 Stetson, Damon. "Gravediggers Ratify New Pact with 18%
      Weekly Pay Increase. " New York Times cxix(40, 953):47
      (March 10, 1970).
      New York City strike.   See entries 1499, 1532, 1540,
1601.

1601 _____. "Strike Is Started by Gravediggers. " New York
      Times cxvi(39, 792):45 (Jan. 4, 1967).
      New York City strike.   See entries 1499, 1532, 1540,
1600.

1602 "The Story of a Cemetery Strike. " The Director 41(3):6-7
      (1971).
      Illinois Funeral Directors Assoc. helped end cemetery
strike by taking immediate action and a logical position, not taking
sides but considering the public's interest over the profession's.
Strength of the mediator, Mayor Daley, also a factor.

1603 Street, Arthur L. H.   American Cemetery Law; A Digest of
      the Cemetery Laws of All the States and Important Court
      Decisions. Madison, WI: Park and Cemetery, 1922.
      532pp.
      Two part reference; 1: exhumation, cemetery trust funds,
taxes, zoning, memorials, perpetual upkeep, and the laws that pertain to each; 2: digest of the laws of each of the 48 states and their
special provisions.

1604 "Strike at Two Cemeteries. " New York Times cxix(42, 974):
      16 (March 31, 1970).
      Cemetery strikes in Brookline, Mass.

1605 "Strike Is Averted at 39 Cemeteries. " New York Times cxiii
      (38, 698):31 (Jan. 6, 1964).
      Terms set for New York City Cemetery Workers Union.

      Stueve, Thomas F. H. Mortuary Law. See entry 1088.
      Cemetery laws and regulations.

1606 Sullivan, Ronald. "'Shock' Sales Laid to Cemetery Men. "
      New York Times cxv(39, 639):35 (Aug. 4, 1966).
      Cemetery owners accused of preying on grief of the
survivors.

1607 Tebb, William, and Vollum, E. P. Premature Burial, and
      How Prevented. New York: New Amsterdam, c. 1902.

1608 Thomas, Jack W. , and Dixon, Ronald A. "Cemetery Ecology." Natural History 82(3):60-7 (March 1973). Photos, charts.

Greater Boston cemeteries used also as wildlife habitats, natural science laboratories, and recreation; attitudes of cemetery managers about present and future use of cemeteries; good suggestions for coping with multiple use problems.

1609 "Threaten Couple to Remove Negro in White Cemetery." New York Times cxxi(41, 515):49 (Sept. 23, 1971).

Area residents threaten to remove Negro buried in Dade City Cemetery, Fla.

1610 "Traffic Woes Vexed Old-Time Funerals." American Funeral Director 10(97):109 (Oct. 1974).

Woodlawn Cemetery, to the north of New York City, was created largely because of traffic in the city. It could be reached by steam cars and railway. Problems of city traffic included a lack of signal lights, wheel-to-wheel horsedrawn drays and cabs, shouting to compensate for the not-yet-invented horn--all of which contributed to the frayed nerves of mourners.

1611 "Unified Cemetery System for Veterans Is Proposed." New York Times cxv(39, 532):19 (April 19, 1966).

1612 United States. General Land Office. U.S. Laws and Regulations Relating to Townsites, Parks, and Cemeteries. Washington, DC: Superintendent of Documents, 1909.

1613 "U.S. Backs Suit to Drop Cemetery's Racial Bar." New York Times cxix(41, 121):5 (Aug. 25, 1970).

U.S. Government joins suit against Hillcrest Memorial Gardens, Ft. Pierce, Fla.

1614 "Valley Forge Cemetery Pleas." New York Times cxxiii (42, 402):18 (Feb. 26, 1974).

Proposal to create a national cemetery at Valley Forge, Pa.

1615 "Vandalism Termed a Growing Problem in City Cemeteries." New York Times cxxiii(42, 296):37 (Nov. 12, 1973).

1616 Vittur, Paul L. How to Sell Cemetery Lots. Jamestown, NY: The Author, 1932. 60pp.

1617 "Volunteers Restore Old Cemetery." New York Times cxxi (41, 721):60 (April 16, 1972).

Southside Burial Ground, Ozone Park, N.Y.

1618 Wall, Jerry. "Forest Lawn Cemetery Erects New Mortuary in Beaumont." Casket & Sunnyside 103(3):58+ (1973). Photos, plans.

Forest Lawn Memorial Park President Charles B. Locke completes a two-year study on cemetery-mortuary operations and decides to build a mortuary adjacent to his cemetery. Special features outlined in text; illustrations.

1619 Walsh, Edward R. "Cemeteries: Recreations New Space Frontier." Parks and Recreation No. 6, p. 28-29, 53-54, June 1975.
Review of need in cities for open recreation space; examples of cemetery land use for parks.

Watkins, E. S. Law of Burials and Burial Grounds. See entry 1393.

1620 Weed, Howard E. Modern Park Cemeteries. Chicago: R. J. Haight, 1912. 145pp. Illus.

1621 "Where All Are Heroes." American Cemetery 46(6):16-18 (1973).

1622 "White Cemetery Burial Cleared for Negro G. I." New York Times cxix(40, 877):23 (Dec. 24, 1969).
Pfc. William H. Terry, Jr., permitted burial in Elmwood Cemetery, Birmingham, Ala.

1623 Willatt, N. "Pay Now, Go Later; Cemeteries Have Found Installment Credit Good Public Relations and Good Business." Barrons 43:5 (Nov. 18, 1963).

1624 Wilson, William S. Improvement and Care of Rural Cemeteries. Raleigh: North Carolina Legislative Reference Library, n.d.

1625 "Wisconsin Society Cares for Cemeteries." American Funeral Director 95(7):22 (1972).
Wisconsin State Old Cemetery Assoc., formed in 1971, encourages restoration, maintenance, and preservation of small cemeteries in the state.

1626 Wooten, James T. "Black Soldier Buried Among Whites." New York Times p. 57 (Jan 4, 1970). Photo.
Bill Terry buried in all-white Birmingham, Ala., cemetery.

B. CREMATION

1627 Adams, James F. A. "Cremation and Burial; An Examination of their Relative Advantages." The Sixth Annual Report of the Massachusetts State Board of Health, pp. 241-325. Boston: Wright & Potter, 1875.
Reprint of a review published in the pamphlet collection of the Cremation Society, Vol. 2, p. 267. Quoted in Wilson & Levy's Burial Reform and Funeral Costs.

1628 Advice Concerning Cremation as a Part of Christian Burial. London: SPCK, 1960. (Pamphlet.)
Pamphlet authorized by the Archbishops of York and Canterbury, explaining the participation of the Church of England in cremation ceremonies.

1629 Auckland Cremation Society. Cremation Versus Earth-Burial. Auckland: Brett Printing and Publishing, 1905. 30pp.
Arguments for and against both.

1630 Barnard, Howard F. "Beware of What You Cremate" [editorial). Casket & Sunnyside 105(6):6 (June 1975).
Editor warns against burning caskets with plastics incorporated in any form such as polyvinyl chloride trim or lining as well as caskets made entirely of plastic. The public health hazard of burning such caskets has been noted by the Casket Manufacturers Assoc. of America, the Cremation Assoc. of America, the British National Funeral Directors Assoc., and the Monsanto Chemical Corp. They pollute the atmosphere with black smoke and poisonous fumes and coat the crematory retorts with residue and may cause explosions. Barnard advises that casket manufacturers label caskets made with plastics and funeral directors to specify non-plastic caskets in their orders for cremation purposes.

Basevi, William H. F. The Burial of the Dead. See entry 9.

1631 Berg, William. "Cremations Continue to Increase." Mortuary Management 57(1):18 (1970).
Number of cremations rising at a faster rate than the number of deaths in the U.S.: up 18% between 1963 and 1968, the greatest increase in the Mountain states (114.9%) and in the South Atlantic states (58.6%).

1632 Bermingham, Edward J. The Disposal of the Dead; A Plea
for Cremation. New York: Bermingham & Co. , 1881.
89pp.
Early arguments for cremation in America.

1633 Blind, Karl. Fire Burial Among Our Germanic Forefathers:
A Record of the Poetry and the History of Teutonic Cremation. London: Longmans, 1875. 24pp.

Blosser, John H. "The Witness of the Dead. " See entry
1750.

"The Body After Death. " See entry 1751.

1634 Bonnell, Henry Houston. Cremation: Scientifically and Relig-
iously Considered. Philadelphia: Press of D. C. Chalfant,
1885. 13pp.
Historical review of cremation practice and values for
modern society. Arguments against it implied in the early modern
period.

1635 "Bulletin Cites Danger of Cremating Polystyrene. " Casket &
Sunnyside 105(7):43 (July 1975).
NFDA announces that caskets made with polystyrene emit
black smoke and are not completely combusted in present crematoria
facilities. "In addition, " the article quotes, "inadequate air and
fuel mixing facilities inside a cremation chamber allow hydrocarbon
concentrations to develop in pockets that could result in explosions
inside the chamber. " In order to cremate caskets made of this
material, chambers must be built with larger exhaust systems, higher temperature capacity, and allowing greater air flow.

1636 Cassels, Louis. "Christians Accepting Practice of Cremation."
Northeast Funeral Director 21(7):15 (1972).
Protestants and Catholics leaning towards increased acceptance of cremation because it is less expensive than earth burial
and it eliminates the need for the traditional funeral service where
attention is focused on the corpse.

1637 _____. "Some Cremation Practices Creating New Attitudes
Among Some Clergymen. " Northeast Funeral Director 22
(5):4 (1973).
Most clergymen's initial reaction was that cremation was
impious. Now some feel it is spiritually educational, helping to replace childish interpretation of resurrection with that of Saint Paul's.
Other points in cremation's favor: it reduces costs of disposal and
eliminates the need for the conventional funeral service.

1638 Catlin, George B. "Cremation in Michigan. " Michigan History Magazine. Vol. 14, p. 59, 1930.

1639 Chadwick, James R. The Cremation of the Dead. Boston:
G. H. Ellis, 1905. 20pp.

1640 Charles, C. F. "Increased Cremations Reported." <u>Casket</u>
    <u>& Sunnyside</u> 102(9):23 (1972).
        American Cremation Assoc. President Howard Clark re-
ports at the 1972 annual convention 4000 more cremations in 1971
than 1970. The Portland Memorial Mausoleum-Columbarium, the
first crematory in the northwest, built in 1901 and recipient of over
50,000 inurnments or entombments. Now being expanded to accom-
modate 2000 more crypts.

1641 "Cheap Cremation Wins a Lease on Life." <u>Business Week</u>
    2241:31 (Aug. 12, 1972). Photo.
        Profile of the Telophase Society, a California cremation
society. Legislature bill putting the society under the State Board
of Funeral Directors meets strong consumer opposition.

    Cobb, Augustus G. <u>Earth Burial and Cremation</u>. See entry
    1278.

1642 Cobb, John Storer. <u>A Quarter-Century of Cremation in North</u>
    <u>America</u>. Boston: Knight & Millet, 1901. 189pp., illus.
        Historical account of the first years of the modern cre-
mation movement. Foundation of cremation societies; crematoriums;
the forces behind the cremation movement.

    "A Comparison of NFDA Statistics and Those of the United
    States Government." See entry 1157.

1643 Comyns, Mary B. <u>A Plea for Cremation</u>. Boston: Ellis,
    1892. 31pp.

1644 "Continent's Oldest Crematory ... A Program in Progress."
    <u>National Cremation Magazine</u> July-Aug.-Sept. 1974, p. 10-11.
    Illus.
        Outline of the history of American crematoria beginnings
and failures until the establishment of the crematory at Fresh Pond
or Middle Village in Queens Borough, N.Y. in 1895. Operations of
Fresh Pond, owned by the United States Cremation Co., is outlined;
a description of the property; listing of staff.

1645 Conway, Bertrand Louis. <u>Ethics and History of Cremation</u>.
    New York: Paulist, 1923. 28pp.

1646 Cook, William S. "Cremation: From Ancient Cultures to
    Modern Usage." <u>Casket & Sunnyside</u> 103(1):42+ (1973).
        History from Stone Age Slavic tribes who sought to purify
the remains with fire through various ancient cultures to modern
times; the Danish invasion of England when cremation was brought
to the island in 787; formation of the Cremation Society of England
in 1874; the pre-Columbian American Indian practice of cremation;
Col. Henry Laurens, the first American to be cremated in 1792;
the first U.S. crematory, built by Dr. E. J. LeMoyne; Pope Paul
VII's approval of cremation for Catholics in July 1963; cost of cremation and memorialization.

1647 Cope, Michael. "Britons Quietly Push to Discourage Burial."
     Northeast Funeral Director 22(1):8 (1973).
          Trends in Great Britain: cremation, which authorities
favor, and reclamation of cemeteries as public parks. Only 44%
of the British in 1973 preferred earth burial.

     Covarrubias, Miguel. Island of Bali. See entry 48.

1648 "Cremation." The Catholic Encyclopedia vol. 4 (1908), pp. 481-
     483.
          Catholic Church's attitude toward cremation from early
times through canon law prohibition in the late 19th century.

1649 "Cremation." Encyclopaedia Britannica, 11th ed., vol. 7
     (1911), pp. 403-406; 14th ed., vol. 6 (1964), pp. 721-22.
          Historical development of cremation in various cultures.

1650 "Cremation." Jewish Encyclopedia vol. 4 (1903), pp. 342-344.
          Background in rabbinical and scriptural sources.

1651 Cremation Assoc. of America. Answers to the Questions Most
     Often Asked About Cremation (pamphlet). Available to CAA
     members from the National Cremation Magazine.
          Available to CAA members. Straightforward answers to
questions about cremation: to what state does it reduce the body;
costs; memorialization and what types are available; columbarium;
urn and urn garden; necessity of caskets; funeral directors; embalming; pre-arrangements and final disposition of remains. Written by
the staff of the National Cremation Magazine and edited by the CAA.

1652 _____. Proceedings of the Conventions of the Cremation
     Association of America. Published annually by the CAA,
     with transcripts of addresses and business sessions. Pro-
     ceedings of the first national convention were published by
     the CAA in Detroit, 1913.

1653 Cremation; By an Eyewitness. New York: Barnes, 1880.
     31pp.

1654 "Cremation in the Continental United States." Northeast Fu-
     neral Director 20(3):6 (1971).
          Arguments for and against cremation; numbers cremated
in the nine northeastern states; table of the numbers cremated compared to the number of deaths in America, New England, and the
Middle Atlantic states.

1655 "Cremation: Permissible." Time 85 (June 12, 1964).
          Pope Paul issues a statement that eases the early Roman
Catholic Church's prohibition of cremation; his reasons and how his
decision affects Catholics the world over.

1656 "Cremation Report Shows Increase." American Funeral Direc-
     tor 95(11):46 (1971).

Cremation Assoc. of America report. Cremations increased from 1969 to 1970 by about 1. 5% in the United States and Canada.

1657 The Cremation Society. Eighty Years of Cremation in Great Britain (1874-1954). London: Cremation Society, 1954.
Brief historical overview of modern cremation development.

1658 _____. Facts About Cremation. London: Cremation Society, 1965.
Procedure for arranging cremation. Urges membership in the Society.

1659 _____. Why Cremation? London: The Cremation Society, n. d.
Pamphlet promoting cremation in England.

1660 Cremation Society of Tacoma. Cremation. Tacoma, WA: Cremation Society of Tacoma, 1915. 32pp.

1661 "Cremations in 1974 Totaled 119, 224. " American Funeral Director 98(7):36 (July 1975).
The Cremation Assoc. of America reports that cremations in the United States in 1974 increased by almost 7000. Increases were noted in all regions and in Canada.

Daly, Margaret. "Death in the Family: How to Be Financially Ready. " See entry 1106.

Dincauze, D. Cremation Cemeteries in Eastern Masachusetts. See entry 1472.

1662 Doty, Robert C. "Ban on Cremation Is Relaxed by Pope. " New York Times cxiii(38, 850):1, 3 (June 6, 1964).
Catholics who chose cremation are no longer regarded as "public sinners. "

Dowd, Quincy Lamartine. Funeral Management and Costs; A World Survey of Burial and Cremation. See entry 934.

1663 Eassie, William. Cremation of the Dead: Its History and Bearings Upon Public Health. London: Smith, Elder & Co. , 1875. 132pp. , illus.

1664 Education and Information Committee of the Cremation Assoc. of America. Cremation ... The Way of Nature (pamphlet). Available from the CAA.
Answers questions about cremation. Available also at many crematoriums.

1665 "EPA Proposes Rules for Sea Burial. " American Funeral Director 98(4):53 (April 1975).

The Environmental Protection Agency proposes rules for the burial of cremated and uncremated remains at sea. These include allowable distances from shore and materials of accompanying burial objects like wreaths, which must be made of materials readily decomposed in sea water.

1666 Erichsen, Hugo. The Cremation of the Dead, Considered from an Esthetic, Sanitary, Religious, Historical, Medico-Legal, and Economical Standpoint. Detroit: D. O. Haynes & Co., 1887. 264pp., plans.
    History of cremation by the founder of the Cremation Society of America, one of the first supporters in the United States.

1667 _____. Cremation Versus Burial. Louisville, KY: Morton, 1886. 46pp.

1668 Eusebius. "The Church History of Eusebius." Book V, Chap. 1, in Select Library of Nicene and Post-Nicene Fathers, Philip Schaff and Henry Wace, eds. New York: Scribner's, 1905.
    During the early persecutions of the Christian Church, cremation was used as a repressive measure.

1669 Fidler, Florence G. Cremation. London: Williams & Norgate, 1930. 80pp., biblio.

    Fitzgerald, Edward R. "Immediate Disposition--Fancy or Fact?" See entry 1163.

1670 Flanner, Frank B. Cremation and the Funeral Director. Indianapolis, 1915. 13pp.

1671 Fraser, James W. Cremation: Is It Christian? Neptune, NJ; Loizeaux Bros., 1965. (Paper.)
    The 19th-century arguments against cremation: a literal interpretation of the Bible and conservative evangelical theology.

1672 Frazer, Persifor, Jr. Merits of Cremation. Philadelphia: American Academy of Political and Social Science, 1910.

1673 Freehof, Solomon B. Reform Jewish Practice and Its Rabbinic Background. Cincinnati: Hebrew Union College Press, 1944.
    Treats cremation from the vantage of Orthodox and Reform Jewish traditions. Scriptural and talmudic documentation.

1674 Freeman, Albert C. Antiquity of Cremation and Curious Funeral Customs. London: Undertakers' Journal, 1909. 104pp.

    Gold, Gerald. "Wide Range of Funeral Prices Found Here in Consumer Study." See entry 961.

Grollman, Dr. Earl A., ed. Concerning Death: A Practical Guide for the Living. See entry 1117.

1675 Habenstein, Robert W. A Sociological Study of the Cremation Movement in America. Unpublished MA thesis, Dept. of Sociology, University of Chicago, 1949.
Chapters 1-4 give a detailed account of the cremation prac-tice in the U. S. and England and its relation to the sanitation movement.

Harmer, Ruth M. "Embalming, Burial, and Cremation." See entry 442.

1676 Haweis, Hugh R. Ashes to Ashes; A Cremation Prelude. London: Daldy, Isbister, 1875. 260pp.

1677 Henderson, Howard A. M. Cremation: A Rational Method of Disposing of the Dead. Cincinnati: G. P. Houston, 1890. 46pp.

1678 "Henry Laurens ... the First to Choose Cremation in U. S." National Cremation Magazine 10(2):6-7 (April-May-June, 1974).
On his request, Henry Laurens's body, upon his death Dec. 9, 1792, was enfolded in 12 yards of tow-cloth and burned until it "was entirely consumed." The ashes were collected in an urn and placed in the family gravesite. Profile of this influential South Carolinian and reason he selected cremation.

1679 Holder, William. Cremation Versus Burial; An Appeal to Reason Against Prejudice. Hudson, NY: A. Brown, 1891. 45pp.

1680 Holland, P. H. "Burial or Cremation." The Contemporary Review, 1878.
The medical inspector of burials in England denies that cremation is necessary for public health reasons. An answer to Sir Henry Thompson's article, in the same issue that advocates the modern emphasis of cremation in Great Britain. See entry 1718.

1681 Holliday, Kate, and Mitford, Jessica. "Two Conflicting Views on Cremation." Good Housekeeping 166(2):76-7, 182-86 (Feb. 1968). Illus.
Holliday, against cremation, argues at the very least the body should be at the funeral. Mitford, answering Holliday, cites the history of cremation, the non-guarantee of cemetery permanence, and the high cost of interment.

1682 International Cremation Congress, Prague, 1936. Report, Decisions, Resolutions. Prague: Krematorium Society, 1936. 62pp.

1683 "International Cremation Survey." Funeral Service Journal 74 (Oct. 15, 1959).

1684 Irion, Paul E. Cremation. Philadelphia: Fortress Press, 1968. 152pp., index, biblio. Available from the NFDA (in paper).
Three-fold purpose to encourage discussion, provide information, and foster community and church climate where people will be able to chose cremation as a means of final disposition. Historical review from prehistoric times through the Greeks, Romans, Jews, Christians, Eastern and Western world compared; the modern cremation movement in Italy, Germany, England, and the U.S. Changing motivations in prehistoric times, the 19th century, and the present. Modern processes: the crematorium, management, regulations relationship with funeral directors, disposition of ashes, memorialization, economic factors, psychological factors, theological considerations (Catholic, Protestant and Jewish); legal considerations. The thinking of the ministry and the congregation. The funeral service and committal, memorial service after cremation. Question self-evaluation guide to better understand one's own feelings about cremation.

_____. The Funeral: Vestige or Value? See entry 1173.

1685 _____. "To Cremate or Not." In: A Practical Guide for the Living, ed. by Earl A. Grollman. Boston: Beacon Press, 1974. pp. 241-52.

1686 Jones, P. Herbert and Noble, George A. Cremation in Great Britain, 3d ed. London: Pharos Press, 1945.
Crematoriums in Great Britain, cremation laws in England and Scotland, and history of cremation and contemporary developments.

Kurtz, Donna C. and Boardman, John. Greek Burial Customs. See entry 116.

1687 Lange, Louis. Church, Women, and Cremation. New York: U.S. Cremation Co., 1901. 26pp.

1688 Leonard, Walter, and Leonard, Phyllis. "Greenwood Retains Leadership Through Innovative Practices." Casket & Sunnyside 105(6):34-40 (June 1975).
Pictorial essay of the Greenwood Memorial Park in Phoenix, Ariz., one of the largest and most complete places of interment in the Southwest. Owners attribute its success to anticipating future trends and adopting innovative techniques. Sketch of past innovations, present facilities (including a unique two-chamber crematory built in 1974), and managerial techniques.

1689 "Llwydcoed Crematorium." American Cemetery 46(4):22-24 (1973). Illus.
Pictorial essay on Wales municipal crematorium. Emphasizes the popularity of cremation throughout Great Britain, a trend expected to gain even more favor as the younger generation matures.

1690 Marble, John O. Cremation in Its Sanitary Aspects. Boston: Clapp, 1885. 35pp.

1691 Michigan Cremation Assoc. The Michigan Cremation Association, Detroit, Michigan Presents for Your Consideration Incineration. Detroit, MI: Michigan Cremation Association, 1911. 49pp.

1692 Mistak, Leo. "Mistak Spoke: Everyone Listened." National Cremation Magazine, Oct. -Nov. -Dec. 1974, p. 5-6. (Orig. a speech, entitled "How to Make a Speech on Cremation.")
         Brief history of cremation, the process, psychological and religious considerations, and answers to some of the most often asked questions. Emphasizes that the motivation for cremation in early times was religious; now it is public health, conservation of land, and economics. Discussion of costs, memorialization, the importance of considering personal feelings of mourners in deciding whether to cremate. Most common personal reasons include costs, desire for simplicity, dualistic concept of man (the spirit is more important and the body should be disposed of quickly in order to set the spirit free), or fear or aversion to the grave. Since 1963 the Catholic Church accepts cremation for reasons of health, costs, or land conservation. The majority of Protestants who once opposed it because Jesus was buried now favor it. Reform Jews find it acceptable; Orthodox and Conservatives do not. Cremains can be legally disposed of at will as they do not propose a health problem.

1693 Mose, H. E., ed. A List of Books, Pamphlets and Articles on Cremation, including the Cremation Association of America collection. Chicago: John Crerar Library, 1940, 65pp.
         Bibliography, including most of the writings on cremation in English, French, and German.

1694 Mount Royal Cemetery Co. Cremation, Its History, Practice and Advantages. Montreal: Mount Royal Cemetery Co., 1902. 33pp.

1695 "A Move to Embalm 'Cremation Clubs'." Business Week no. 2349:89 (Sept. 21, 1974).
         Details California cremation societies and the State Senate's efforts to regulate them; the Telophase Society.

1696 National Cremation Magazine. Answers to the Questions Most Often Asked About Cremation. Available from the magazine.

1967 National Funeral Directors Assoc. Considerations Concerning Cremation. Milwaukee, WI: NFDA, 1974. (Pamphlet.)
         What it is, what's involved (if desired, all of the customs associated with the traditional funeral, with the exception of interment, are maintained--visitation, viewing, etc.); options for final disposition discussed: burial of cremains, scattering, or keeping the remains in an urn at home, along with columbaria, the economic advantages to cremation, and sources of further information.

1698 New England Society. Information Regarding Cremation As a Method of Disposing of the Bodies of the Dead. Boston: New England Cremation Society, 1899. 43pp.

1699 Newton, Frances. Light, Like the Sun. New York: Dodd, Mead, 1937. 25pp.

1700 "NFDA Reports Cremation Statistics for 1970." Casket & Sunnyside 102(1):28 (1972).
    Cremation Assoc. of America statistics reveal increase in cremations: 85,683 in 1969 and 88,105 in 1970.

1701 Nock, Arthur D. "Cremation and Burial in the Roman Empire." The Harvard Theological Review 25:321-60 (Oct. 1932).

1702 Oakland Cremation Assoc. Cremation. Oakland, CA: Oakland Cremation Society, 1904. 36pp.

1703 Odd Fellows' Cemetery Assoc., San Francisco. Cremation. San Francisco: Winterburn, 1899. 52pp.

1704 Opinions on Cremation. New York: New York Cremation Society, 1889. 55pp. Illus.

1705 Parker, William T. Inhumation Versus Cremation. Northampton, MA: The Author, 1921.

1706 Peirce, C. N. Sanitary Disposal of the Dead. Philadelphia: Philadelphia Cremation Society, 1891. 64pp.

    Polson, Cyril J., et al. Disposal of the Dead. See entry 348.

1707 Portland Crematorium. Portland Crematorium. Portland, OR, 1922. 32pp.

1708 Richardson, Aubrey. The Law of Cremation: An Outline of the Law Relating to Cremation Ancient and Modern ... with the Rules and Regulations of Various Cremation Societies at Home and Abroad. London: Reeves & Turner, 1893. 187pp.

1709 Roberts, Steven V. "Cremation Gaining Favor in U.S." New York Times cxx(41,224):1,73 (Dec. 6, 1970). Photo, graph.
    Survey of cremation preferences.

1710 Robinson, Ken. "Cremation--How It Began--Why It Spreads." Casket & Sunnyside 101(1):24+ (1971).
    Cremator manufacturer reviews history of cremation in the U.S. and other countries; rationale for its practice; guides for funeral director interested in installing crematorium.

1711 _____. ''A Short History of Cremation.'' Mortuary Management 58(3):25+ (1971).
Development of cremation in America, comparing U. S. methods with those in other countries. Facts, figures, and data on ownership and operation of a crematory.

Robinson, William. Cremation and Urn-burial; or, The Cemeteries of the Future. See entry 1360.

1712 Smith, Donald K. Why Not Cremation? Philadelphia: Dorrance, 1970, 46pp. Appendix.
American funeral customs have fallen behind technology. The population explosion forces other means of final disposition than burial; land is too valuable. Survey of burial, cremation, embalming, coffin use, average cost, customs and use of religious programs at the grave; cemetery land problems: availability and "perpetual" care; argues for cremation as a solution to the land problem, citing the grossness of a rotting body compared to clean cremating; cost of cremation; ash disposal alternatives and cost; "selfishness" of keeping body elements from re-entering the ecosphere; the Chinese recycle old cemeteries, grinding bones for fertilizer.

1713 Spencer, Thomas E. "Cremation; An Expression of Life Style." Journal of Individual Psychology 28:60-66 (May 1973). Refs.
How well-known people who were cremated lived and their reasons for choosing to be cremated.

1714 "Statistical Report for Years 1963-1973." National Cremation Magazine, July-Aug.-Sept., 1974, p. 8. Chart.
Yearly total of cremations between 1963 and 1973 for each region in the U. S. and Canada. Cremations rose in the U. S. from 67,330 to 112,298 in the ten-year period and in Canada from 5792 to 14,881.

1715 Sutherland-Gower, Ronald. Cleanliness vs. Corruption. London: Longmans, 1910. 56pp., illus.
Arguments for cremation.

1716 "Ten Year Cremation Increase." Casket & Sunnyside 101(11): 20 (1971).
Between 1959 and 1969 cremations increased in the U.S. 44% and in Canada 105%.

1717 Thompson, Edward J. Suttee; A Historical and Philosophical Enquiry into the Hindu Rite of Widow-Burning. Boston: Houghton Mifflin, 1928. 165pp.

1718 Thompson, Sir Henry. Article advocating cremation in Great Britain in the Contemporary Review, 1878.

1719 _____. Cremation; The Treatment of the Body After Death. London: Smith, Elder, 1884. 70pp.

Inspired the revival of interest in cremation in Europe and America. Written by Queen Victoria's surgeon, who also organized the Cremation Society of England with Anthony Trollope, Sir John Tenniel, and other outspoken critics of contemporary burial practices in England.

1720 _____. Modern Cremation. New York: Scribner's, 1901.

1721 United States Cremation Co. Cremation; 1908. New York: Press of the Kalkhoff Co., 1908. 24pp., illus.

1722 _____. Modern Thought on Modern Cremation. New York: U.S. Cremation Co., 1895, 1899. 40pp., illus.

1723 _____. Modern Thought on Modern Cremation: Selections from "The Urn." New York: U.S. Cremation Co., 1903. 40pp., illus.

1724 _____. The Urn. New York: U.S. Cremation Co., 1899. 40pp.
Thoughts on cremation.

1724a Williams, R. E. Cremation and Other Modes of Sepulture. Philadelphia: Lippincott, 1884.

C. CRYONICS

1725 Agnew, Irene. "Will Freezing Preserve Life?" Science Digest 72(6):84-85 (Dec. 1972).
Three examples: a Russian man; the experiment with the body of James Bedford in Los Angeles; and a Japanese cat brain experiment.

1726 "Can Death Be Evaded Via Cryonics?" Casket & Sunnyside 101(13[centennial issue]):84-85 (1972).
Dr. Paul Ruegsegger, director of Project Icelife of the XXV Century Foundation, Biotronics Division, assisted in the writing of this article. Time is the only barrier to successful freezing and revival of human beings. The funeral director's participation in cryonics could "strongly influence its future." The price now (1971) for freezing is from $15,000 to $20,000; for the capsule $4,000; and maintenance $300 per year.

1727 Chevalier, Lois R. "No, Thank You, I'd Rather Not Live Twice." Ladies Home Journal 86(3):70-72 (March 1969). Photo.
Reviews the cryonics movement.

1728 "Cryonic Suspension of Steven J. Mandell." Cryonics Reports 3(9):162-166 (1968).
Detailed description of cryonic suspension technique, especially as it was applied to the first body to be "frozen." The body is now in a receiving vault at Washington Memorial Park, Coram, Long Island. See also Cryonics Reports 3(10), Oct. 1968.

1729 Ettinger, Robert C. W. "Cryonics and the Purpose of Life." Christian Century 84(40):1250-53 (Oct. 5, 1967). Discussion: 84:1656-58 (Dec. 27, 1967).
A cryonics spokesman comments on the implications of movement vis-à-vis religions. Especially concerned with cryonics' relation to the "purpose of life."

1730 _____. The Prospect of Immortality. Garden City, NY: Doubleday, 1964. Refs.
Recommends refrigeration by emersion in liquid helium or nitrogen on the assumption that in the future scientists will be able to repair the tissue damage done by freezing. Argues that immortality (or, rather, indefinitely extended life) is technically attainable for our descendents and ourselves; it is practically feasible

and does not raise any insurmountable new problems; it is desirable from both the individual's and society's standpoint. Chapters cover the future and present options of suspended life and suspended death; the effects of freezing and cooling; repair and rejuvenation; alternative methods possible today; freezing in relation to religion, law, economics, individual identify, and society.

1731 "The Freezing of Human Bodies." The Director 43(1):5 (1973).
     American Medical Assoc. states there is little hope for resuscitating bodies frozen by cryonic preservation at a future date and advises patients against "purchasing at high prices false hope...."

1732 "Frozen Corpse." New York Times cxvii(40, 368):34 (Aug. 2, 1968).
     Bronx resident Steven Jay Mandell has body frozen until medicine learns to cure his illness (intestinal ailment) and, of course, thaw him out. Body stored at minus 320° in a $4000 capsule of liquid nitrogen at the Washington Memorial Park Cemetery in Coram, N.Y. The $175 per month cost of maintaining the frozen vault is shared by the Cryonic Interment Co. of Santa Monica, Ca., and donations from cryonic groups in New York, Michigan and California. The Cryonics Society of Michigan is one of the chief sponsors of the experiment.

1733 Hones, William. "Deep-Freezing Bodies? Well, No." The Director 41:6 (Dec. 1971).
     Reprint of Chicago-Sun Times article; three cryobiologist reports at the Society of Cryobiology. Cost of maintaining a body runs from between $4000 and $8000 per year; 13 bodies are deep frozen in the U.S. as of the article's publication; despite hopes for cryonics, there has never been a successful freezing and thawing of any higher animal vertebrates.

1734 Horn, F. "Cryonics: Challenge to the Funeral Industry." Casket & Sunnyside 99(9):34-35, 60-62 (1969).
     Paper by licensed funeral director and embalmer to annual Cryonics Conference, University of Michigan, April 11, 1969 describing the techniques used in actual cryonic interment by Horn and colleagues. Refutes widely held view that cryonics is a threat to funeral directors since "patient" has to be certified dead, legally, and medically, before frozen. Funeral director, however, must prepare for cryonic techniques as it will become popular.

1735 Malinin, Theodore I. "Freezing of Human Bodies." Journal of American Medical Association 221(6):589 (1972).
     Advises doctors to warn families of extreme expense of cryonics and the fact that there has never been a successful freeze preservation of large mammalians. Structural damage through freezing affects all tissues, organs, and vital systems.

1736 Montgomery, J. W. "Cryonics and Orthodoxy." Christianity Today 12:48 (May 10, 1968).

1737 "Most Recent News on Cryogenic Treatment. " The Director
        XLV(4):9 (April 1975).
        Review of Chicago Tribune article, April 6, which quotes
Robert Ettinger (see entry 1729) on the number of "dead" frozen since
cryogenic interment was initiated a decade ago.   Costs (initial about
$15, 000 with a yearly maintenance approximately $1800).   NFDA
emphasizes that restoration is based on assumption the body is not
dead but in a state of suspended animation.

1738 "Never Say Die. " Newsweek 73(12):16 (March 24, 1968).
        Photo.
        Update on body of James Bedford, cryonically preserved.
Prospects for success doubted by experts.   See entries 1739, 1746.

1739 "Never Say Die. " Time 89(5):57 (Feb. 3, 1967).   Photos.
        Details the freezing of James Bedford's body.   Explains
why freezing won't work.   See entries 1738, 1746.

1740 Ross, Nancy L.   "Can the Dead Live Again?" Northeast
        Funeral Director 21(10):4+ (1972).
        Underlying philosophy and history of cryonics since R.
C. W. Ettinger's The Prospect of Immortality (entry 1729), was
published in 1964.   Process and equipment utilized; costs; sketch
of the 15 people whose bodies have been placed in cryonic suspension.   Survivors of three of these have had them unfrozen.

1741 "Scientists Disfavor Cryonic Interment. " American Funeral
        Director 94(10):48+ (1971).
        Presently known methods preclude eventual restoration.

1742 Scott, R. B.   Cryonic Engineering.   New York: Van Nos-
        trand, 1959.

1743 "Soul on Ice: S. Mandell of New York. " Newsweek 72(7):29
        (Aug. 12, 1968).   Photos.
        Steven Jay Mandell, 24, has body frozen until time when
science can cure the intestinal disease that killed him.   Reposes in
Cryo-Capsule at a cost of $200 a day.   Expense shared by the Cry-
onics Society of New York.

1744 Tuccille, Jerome.   Here Comes Immortality.   New York:
        Stein & Day, 1973.

1745 _____.   "Man Into Superman. " Nation 215:155-56 (Sept. 4,
        1972).
        Review of Ettinger's book of that title, plus other litera-
ture relating to cryonic preservation.

1746 Wainwright, Loundon.   "Cold Way to New Life. " Life 62(4):
        16 (Jan. 27, 1967).
        Cryonics procedure and the "freezing" of James H. Bed-
ford.   See entries 1738, 1739.

1747 Wiley, John P., and Serman, J. K. "Immortality and the
Freezing of Human Bodies." Natural History 80:12-18 (Dec.
1971).
Pros and cons of cryonic preservation and policies of
the Cryonic Societies. Proponents argue freezing human bodies in
liquid nitrogen offers nothing to lose and maybe a lot to gain; critics
believe it's hopelessly premature; present knowledge is inadequate,
even concerning the injury potential of freezing, storing, and thaw-
ing. Costs, arrangement process, and mechanics of freezing method
outlined.

1748 [No entry.]

D. MISCELLANEOUS

1749   Black, Lindsay. Burial Trees; Being the First of a Series on the Aboriginal Customs of the Darling Valley and Central New South Wales. Melbourne, Australia: Robertson & Mullens, 1941. 38pp.

1750   Blosser, John H. "The Witness of the Dead." The Director 39(2):16-17 (1969).
      Missionary tells of his observations in India: cremation, exposure of the corpse to scavenger birds, and interment as methods of disposing of the dead. Cremation and the funeral pyre which suggest annihilation lead to neglect of gravesites while Christian belief in resurrection promotes better care of Christian graves.

1751   "The Body After Death." American Funeral Director 98(5):43 (May 1975).
      Reprint of article that originally appeared in the Norwich, N. Y. Semi-Weekly Telegraph, Feb. 12, 1887. In lieu of inhumation, determined to be unsanitary by modern science, four methods are proposed: cremation where the body is reduced to ashes by intense heat; coking where the body is reduced to a "hard, brittle substance" by flameless heat; cementation where the coffin is hermetically sealed in cement; and electro-plating which "transforms the corpse into a beautiful statue ... face and figure are covered with a shining veil, through which the familiar lineaments appear."

1752   Castel, J. G. "Some Legal Aspects of Human Organ Transplantation in Canada." 46 Can. Bar Rev. 345.

1753   "Concerning the Ultimate Question." America 116(8):274-75 (Feb. 25, 1967).
      Embalming procedures, funeral and legal requirements for Catholics wishing to donate bodies for medical research.

1754   "The Deep Six." Newsweek 79(2):43 (Jan. 10, 1972). Photo.
      Sea burial and ash scattering over the ocean from a plane. California groups mentioned. 1965 state legislature permitted cremated remains to be dropped in ocean from aircraft beyond the 3-mile limit; 1970 law amended to permit the ashes to be dropped from ships; in 1971 more than 4400 burials at sea; as of Nov. 1971 a coffin is no longer required for cremation in California.

1755   Diamond, E. "Are We Ready to Leave Our Bodies to the

Next Generation?" New York Times cxviii(40, 265): sect.
VI, p. 26-27, 114-120 (April 21, 1968). Photos, drawings.
Thorough discussion of the transplant issue; material on
the changing attitudes towards dead bodies.

"EPA Proposes Rules for Sea Burial." See entry 1665.

1756 Gerrits, G. J. M. "Burial-Canoes and Canoe-burial in the
Trobriand and Marshall Islands." Anthropos 69(1-2), 224-
32, 1974.

1757 Green, Charles. Sutton Hoo: The Excavation of a Royal
Ship Burial, 2d ed. New York: Barnes & Noble, 1968.
Illus.

1758 Grohskopf, Bernice. Treasure of Sutton Hoo: Ship-Burial
for an Anglo-Saxon King. New York: Atheneum, 1970.

Grollman, Dr. Earl A., ed. Concerning Death: A Practical
Guide for the Living. See entry 1117.

1759 Human Parts Banks of Canada. Human Parts Banks Are
Coming. Available from the Memorial Society Assoc. of
Canada or the Human Parts Banks of Canada, Box 34367,
Vancouver 9, BC or 5326 Ada Blvd., Edmonton, Alta.
T5W 4N7.
Human parts banks do not yet exist although there are
eye banks. The purpose of establishing human parts banks is to
prevent separate banks proliferating and competing with each other
for parts. The comprehensive center would "harvest," store, and
distribute various human parts for transplant purposes such as eye
corneas, skin, pituitary glands, temporal bones, and other tissues
and organs. Operation of bank explained, how parts could be distributed. Universal Donor Card attached which permits a person to
donate body parts at time of death legally.

1760 "Human Tissue Act: Progress Towards Reform." Canadian
Medical Association Journal, June 1973.

1761 "Loved Ones' Ashes Cast to the Sea." Northeast Funeral
Director 21(1):7 (1972).
Growing trend in California of scattering cremated ashes
from planes over the sea. The involvement of the Flying Funeral
Directors of America mentioned.

1762 Lublin, Joann S. "As Burial Costs Go Up, So Does the Popularity of Scattering Ashes." Wall Street Journal clxxxii
(60):1 (Sept. 25, 1973).
Statistics on rising number of cremations and increased
trend in scattering the remains, especially over oceans. Pilot
Michael Todd of Portland, OR, performs scattering for $35; J. L.
Searles of Progress Industries Diversified in St. Paul, MN, for
$49.95; Los Angeles mortician and pilot cremates and scatters for

$327 as opposed to the Telophase Society of San Diego whose package deal costs $265 (scattering from a boat). Some traditionalists in funeral service allege ash scattering lacks sentiment or is contrary to American religious beliefs. Jessica Mitford counters that the only thing cremation and scattering conflicts with is mortician and crematorium profits which derive mainly from the sale of products like caskets, vaults, urns, and niches.

McCracken, Harold. George Catlin and the Old Frontier. See entry 130.

1763 Menough, E. M. "Funeral Director Participation in Iowa Eye Enucleation Program Acclaimed." The Director 39(10): 2-4 (1969).
Successful program set up at the University of Iowa in the technique of eye enucleation from dead bodies in preparation for use of the cornea in corneal transplants. Twenty-five funeral directors certified to perform eye enucleation. Number of available corneas for transplants has greatly increased as a result of the program.

1764 Meyers, David W. The Human Body and the Law. Chicago: Aldine, 1970. 203pp., index. notes.
Brief discussions of the laws of transplants, donation, and definition of dead.

1765 _____. "Organ Transplantation and the Law." Impact of Science in Society 21(3):225 (1971).

1766 National Funeral Directors Assoc. Organ and Tissue Transplantation and Body Donation. Available from the NFDA, n.d.

1767 Olender, Jack H. "Donation of Dead Bodies and Parts Thereof for Medical Use." University of Pittsburgh Law Review 21:523 (1960).

Packel, Israel. "Spare Parts for the Human Engine." See entry 1068.

1768 Public Affairs Pamphlet. The Challenge of Transplantation. Available from the NFDA.

1769 Radcliff, J. D. "Let the Dead Teach the Living." Reader's Digest 79(472):87-90 (Aug. 1961).
Arguments for bequeathing remains to medical schools.

Smith, Donald K. Why Not Cremation? See entry 1712. Alternate means of final disposition.

1770 Stason, E. Blyth, et al. "The Uniform Anatomical Gift Act (A Model for Reform)." Journal of the American Medical Association 206:2501-03 (1968).

1771 Strub, Clarence G. "Bodies for Medical Science." Mid-Continent Mortician 44:12-15 (1968).
     Medical schools need bodies. Suggests funeral directors may be buying welfare recipients in violation of regulations or without need. These could be better used by schools. Asks cooperation from funeral business.

1772 "The Towers of Silence." Time, April 1, 1974.
     The Parsis (descendants of the Persians), bring their dead to the Towers of Silence or "Dokhmas" where they are exposed to vultures who pick their flesh. When the bones are clean, they are buried. Recently the vultures have stopped feeding, necessitating new ways to dispose of bodies safely. Parsis who have emigrated to America cremate their dead.

1773 "Will Tomorrow's Surgeons Utilize 'Neomort Farms'?" American Funeral Director 98(4):39-40 (April 1975).
     Dr. William Gaylin, president of the Institute of Society, Ethics, and the Life Sciences in Hastings-on-Hudson, N.Y., proposes "harvesting" organs from "neomorts" (i.e., bodies legally and psychologically dead--no more brain function--but biologically alive). They could be used for organ transplants, medical student practice, intern practice, intern practice of difficult or "exotic procedures," drug tests, new instrument tests, and scientific experimentation. Gaylin then asks, after the benefits, lifesaving potentials, humanitarian purposes, and the costs are justified, "how are we to reconcile our emotions?" Hans Jonas in Philosophical Essays insists there must be "the maximum definition of death ... brain death plus heart death plus any other indication that may be pertinent--before final violence is allowed to be done." Gaylin, too, states there is a common feeling of "the sanctity of the human body and the unknowability of the borderline between life and death."

III. MEMORIALIZATION

A. HISTORICAL AND FOREIGN

1774 Adams, James Truslow. Memorials of Old Bridgehampton. Washington, NY: Ira J. Friedman, 1962. 399pp.

1775 Alden, Timothy. Collection of American Epitaphs and Inscriptions with Occasional Notes. New York: S. Marks Printer, 1814. 5 vols.

1776 Andrews, Frank D. Inscriptions in the First "Old Cohansey" Burying Ground, Hopewell, Cumberland Co., New Jersey, with a Historical Sketch. Vineland, NJ: Privately Printed, 1911. 2pp.

1777 _____. Inscriptions on the Early Gravestones in the Baptist Burying Ground at Dividing Creek, N.J., with a Historical Sketch. Vineland, NJ: Privately Printed, 1916. 2pp.

1778 _____. Inscriptions on the Gravestones in the Old "New England Town" Burying Ground, Fairton, Fairfield Township, Cumberland County, New Jersey, with an Historical Sketch. Vineland, NJ: Privately Printed, 1919. 18pp.

1779 _____. Tombstone Inscriptions in the Old Presbyterian Burying Ground at Greenwich, New Jersey, with a Historical Sketch. Vineland, NJ: The Author, 1915. 50pp.

1780 Andrews, William. Curious Epitaphs; Collected and Edited with Notes. London: W. Andrews, 1899. 241pp.

1781 Archibald, John. English Churchyard Memorials. London: Mineral Publications, 1939.

1782 Association for the Preservation of Virginia Antiquities. Epitaphs of Gloucester and Mathews Counties in Tidewater Virginia, through 1865. Richmond: Virginia State Library, 1959. 168pp., maps, paper.

1783 "The Bangs Memorial." American Funeral Director 98(7): 26 (July 1975). Photo.

The memorial to George S. Bangs, general superintendent of the Railway Mail Service, in Rosehill Cemetery, Chicago. Crafted in the then (1877) popular "dead tree" motive, it is one of the largest and most intricately structured of its kind. Beside the tree is a sculptured limestone carving of an RPO car--the American Railway Post Office railway car which Bangs designed.

1784   Batsford, Herbert. English Mural Monuments and Tombstones; A Collection of Eighty-four Photographs. New York: Scribner's, 1916. 13pp., illus.

1785   Beable, William H. Epitaphs; Graveyard Humor and Eulogy. London: Simpkin, Marshall, 1925, 246pp.; Detroit: Singing Tree, 1971, 246pp.

1786   Berliner, David C. "Rubbings from Tombstones." New York Times cxxiii(42, 519):96 (June 23, 1974). Photo.
       Details the rising interest in gravestone rubbings.

1787   Bertram, Jerome. Brasses and Brass Rubbing in England. Great Albion, 1972 (dist. by A. S. Barnes, Cranbury, NJ). Illus.
       English memorial brasses and illustrations of rubbings.

1788   Blackman, M. B. "Totems to Tombstones: Culture Change as Viewed Through the Haida Mortuary Complex 1877-1971." Ethnology 12:47-56 (Jan. 1973). Biblio.

1789   Bliss, Harry A. Memorial Art, Ancient and Modern; Illustrations and Descriptions of the World's Most Notable Examples of Cemetery Memorials. Buffalo, NY: The Author, 1912. 240pp.

1790   _____. Memorial Markers and Headstones. Buffalo, NY: The Author, 1920. 89pp.

1791   _____. Modern Tablets and Sarcophagi. Buffalo, NY: The Author, 1923.

1792   _____. Symbols Wrought in Somber Stone. Buffalo, NY: The Author, 1925.

1793   Bowden, John. The Epitaph-Writer; Consisting of Upwards of Six Hundred Original Epitaphs, Moral, Admonitory, Humorous, and Satirical. Chester, England: J. Fletcher, 1791. 160pp.

1794   Bowman, George E. Gravestone Records in Ancient Cemetery and Woodside Cemetery, Yarmouth, Mass. Boston: Massachusetts Society of Mayflower Descendants, 1906.

1795   Brash, Richard H. Ogam Inscribed Monuments of the Gaedhil in the British Islands. London: G. Bill, 1879. 425pp.

1796 Brewster, Ethel H. Roman Craftsmen and Tradesmen of the
Early Empire. Menasha, WI: George Banta, 1917.

1797 Bridgman, Thomas. Inscriptions on the Gravestones in the
Graveyards of Northampton and of Other Towns in the Val-
ley of the Connecticut, as Springfield, Amherst, Hadley,
Hatfield, Deerfield, etc. Northampton, MA: Hopkins,
Bridgman, 1850. 227pp.

1798 _____. Memorials of the Dead in Boston, Containing an
Exact Transcript from Inscriptions, Epitaphs and Records
on the Monuments and Tombstones in Copp's Hill Burying
Ground, in the City of Boston. Boston: Monroe and Francis, 1852. 252pp.

1799 _____. Memorials of the Dead in Boston, Containing Exact
Transcripts of Inscriptions on the Sepulchral Monuments in
the King's Chapel Burial Ground in the City of Boston.
Boston: B. B. Massey, 1853. 339pp.

1800 Brindley, William. Ancient Sepulchral Monuments; Containing
Illustrations of Over Six Hundred Examples from Various
Countries and from the Earliest Periods Down to the End
of the 18th Century. London: V. Brooks Day and Son,
1887. 24pp. 212 plates.

1801 Brown, J. Epitaphs and Monumental Inscriptions in Greyfriars
Churchyards. Edinburgh, 1867.

1802 Bryant, E. "Rediscovery: the Mayfield Monuments." Art
in America 56:94-99 (July 1968). Illus.
Old American sepulchral monuments.

1803 Bunhill Fields. Bunhill Fields Burial Ground Proceedings in
Reference to Its Preservation with Inscriptions on the Tombs.
London: Hamilton, Adams, 1867. 88pp.

1804 Busby, Richard B. Beginner's Guide to Brass Rubbing. Levittown, NY: Transatlantic, 1970.

1805 Cansick, Frederick T. Collection of Curious and Interesting
Epitaphs Copied from the Monuments of Distinguished and
Noted Characters in the Ancient Church and Burial Ground
of Saint Pancras, Middlesex. London: J. R. Smith, 1869-
1872. 2 vols.

1806 Carnochan, Janet. Inscriptions and Graves in the Niagara
Peninsula. Niagara, Ontario: The Times, 1902, 72pp.;
1910, 126pp.; 1929, 147pp.

1807 Caulkins, Frances M. Stone Records of Groton, ed. by E. S.
Gilman. New London County (Conn.) Historical Society,
n.d.

1808 Chancellor, Frederic. Ancient Sepulchral Monuments of Essex; A Record of Interesting Tombs in Essex Churches and Some Account of the Persons and Families Connected With Them. Chelmsford, England: E. Durant, 1890. 418pp.

1809 Clarity, James F. "Tombstones Are Traded in Leningrad." New York Times cxviii(40, 741):22 (Aug. 10, 1969).
        Famous Russians' headstones are sold.

1810 Clark, E. L. Record of the Inscriptions in the Burial Grounds of Christ Church, Philadelphia. 1864.

1811 Clarke, George K. Epitaphs from Graveyards in Wellesley (Formerly West-Needham), North Natick, and Saint Mary's Churchyard in Newton Lower Falls, Massachusetts. Boston: T. R. Marvin & Son, 1900. 236pp.

1812 Clarke, Richard S. J. Gravestone Inscriptions; Vol. 7, County Down: Baronies of Dufferin and Lecale. Belfast, Ireland: Ulster-Scot Historical Foundation, 1972. 100pp., illus. (paper).

1813 Cohen, Kathleen Rogers. Metamorphosis of a Death Symbol: The Changing Meaning of the Transi Tomb in 15th and 16th Century Europe. Los Angeles: University of California Press, 1974. (California Studies in the History of Art, XV.)

1814 Comic Epitaphs. Mount Vernon, NY: Peter Pauper, 1974.

1815 Connor, A. B. Monumental Brasses in Somerset. West Orange, NJ: Saifer, 1970. Illus.

1816 Crossley, Fred H. English Church Monuments, A.D. 1150-1550; An Introduction to the Study of Tombs, and Effigies of the Mediaeval Period. New York: Scribner, 1921. 274pp.

1817 Daughters of the American Revolution, Conn. Abigail Wolcott Ellsworth Chapter, Windsor. Cemetery Inscriptions in Windsor, Connecticut. Windsor, CT: A. E. Morgan, 1929. 178pp.

1818 David, Cecil T. Monumental Brasses of Gloucestershire. West Orange, NJ: Saifer, 1970. Illus.

1819 Deetz, James, and Dethlefsen, Edwin S. "Death's Head, Cherub, Urn, and Willow." Natural History 76(3):28-37 (March 1967).
        Development of tombstone design in New England, the transition from death's hand to cherub to urn and willow design; the early carvers.

1820 Dingley, Thomas. History from Marble. New York: AMS Press, 1974 (orig. pub., 2 vols., 1867-1868).

1821 _____. History from Marble Comp. in the Reign of Charles Second. New York: Johnson Repr., 1974 (orig. pub., 2 vols., 1867-1868).

1822 Drew, Benjamin. Burial Hill, Plymouth, Massachusetts; Its Monuments and Gravestones Numbered and Briefly Described, and the Inscriptions and Epitaphs Thereon Carefully Copied. Plymouth, MA: D. W. Andres, 1894. 177pp.

1823 Drew, Thomas Bradford. Death Records from the Ancient Burial Ground at Kingston, Massachusetts. Boston: Massachusetts Society of Mayflower Descendants, 1905.

1824 Dunkin, Edwin H. Monumental Brasses of Cornwall. West Orange, NJ: Saifer, 1970.

1825 Elwell, Levi H. Gravestone Inscriptions of Rupert, Bennington County, Vermont, Copied and Verified 1911-1912. New Haven, CT: Tuttle, 1913. 79pp.

1826 _____. Gravestone Records of Shaftsbury, Bennington, Vermont. Copied and Verified 1908-1910. New Haven, CT: Tuttle, 1911. 76pp.

      Elzas, Barnett A. Old Jewish Cemeteries at Charleston, S.C.; A Transcript of the Inscriptions on their Tombstones, 1792-1903. See entry 1287.

1827 Epitaphs from the Old Burying Ground in Dorchester, Massachusetts. Boston Highlands, 1869. 21pp.

1828 Epitaphs of Castleton Churchyard. Castleton, VT, 1887. 48pp.

1829 Esdaile, Katharine A. English Church Monuments, 1510 to 1840; with an Introduction by Sacheverell Sitwell. London: Batsford, 1947. 144pp.

1830 _____. English Monumental Sculpture Since the Renaissance. New York: Macmillan, 1927. 179pp.

1831 Evans, Rella, and Thompson, S. P. Tombstone Records of Boone County, Missouri, 1821-1870. Columbia, MO: The Authors, 1933. 102pp.

1832 Fairley, William. Epitaphiana; or, The Curiosities of Churchyard Literature. London: S. Tinsley, 1873. 171pp.

1833 Florin, Lambert. Tales the Western Tombstones Tell. Seattle, WA: Superior, 1967. 191pp., illus.

1834 Forbes, Harriette M. Gravestones of Early New England and the Men Who Made Them, 1653-1800. Boston: Houghton, 1927. 141pp. Repr., New York: Da Capo, 1967; Totowa, NJ: Pyne Press, 1973 (dist. by Scribner's).

1835 [No entry.]

1836 Gardner, Percy. Sculptured Tombs of Hellas. Washington, DC: McGrath, 1971 (repr. of 1896 ed.). 259pp., illus.

Garstang, John. Burial Customs of Ancient Egypt.... See entry 74.

1837 Gillon, Edmund V. Early New England Gravestone Rubbings. New York: Dover, 1966; Gloucester, MA: Peter Smith, 1974. Illus. (paper).

1838 _____. Victorian Cemetery Art. Gloucester, MA: Peter Smith, 1974. Illus.

1839 Gravestone Inscriptions and Records of Tomb Burials in the Granary Burying Ground, Boston, Massachusetts. Hanover, NH: Essex Inst., 1918 (repr. by the University Press of New England).

1840 Green, Kensal. Premature Epitaphs; Most Written in Malice. London: Cecil Palmer, 1929.

1841 Greenlaw, Lucy H. Inscriptions from the Old Cemetery at Sudbury, Massachusetts. Sudbury, MA: The Author, 1906.

1842 Gresham, C. A. Medieval Stone Carving in North Wales: Sepulchral Slabs and Effigies of the 13th and 14th Century. Mystic, CT: Verry, 1968.

1843 Hackett, John. Select and Remarkable Epitaphs on Illustrious and Other Persons in Several Parts of Europe. London: T. Osborne and T. Shipton, 1757. 2 vols.

1844 Haines, Herbert. Manual of Monumental Brasses. Atlantic Highlands, NJ: Humanities, 1970 (repr. of 1861 ed.). Illus.

1845 Halberstam, David. "Tombstones Bring Poles High Profit." New York Times cxiv(39,152):9 (April 4, 1965).
    Stone cutters make big money in Poland. One of the few private enterprises left.

1846 Hall, Alonzo C. Grave Humor: A Collection of Humorous Epitaphs, illustr. by Dave Morrah. Charlotte, NC: Heritage Printers, 1961. 102pp. (also in paper).

1847 Hampton, William J. Presidential Shrines from Washington to Coolidge. Santa Barbara, CA: Christopher, 1928. 267pp.

1848 Hanigan, Maureen W. "The Rising Grave." Northeast Funeral Director 21(7):18+ (1972).
History and brief sketches of the interesting and unusual
markers in the Springfield, Mass., cemetery; profiles of the famous
persons buried there. Ends with a suspense story--an incident that
happened when the author was walking through the cemetery: a movement among the flowers at the foot of a fresh grave, the spreading
of the movement and the surprise ending explaining what it was.

1849 [No entry.]

1850 Holdcraft, Jacob M. Names in Stone--Seventy-Five Thousand
Cemetery Inscriptions from Frederick County, MD. Red-
wood City, CA: Monocacy Book Co., 1972 (repr. of 1966
ed.). 2 vols.

1851 Hotz, R. "Cosmic Spirit; Final Resting Place of Three Soviet
Spacemen." Aviation Week 89:11 (Aug. 26, 1968).

1852 Howe, W. H. Curious Epitaphs. New York: New Amsterdam
Book Co., 1900.

1853 _____. Here Lies, Collection of Ancient and Modern Inscriptions from Tombstones. New York: New Amsterdam
Book Co., 1901.

1854 Hudson, J. P. "Knight's Tombstone at Jamestown, Virginia."
Antiques 91:760-61 (June 1967).

1855 Hughes-Clark, Arthur W. Monumental Inscriptions in the
Church and Churchyard of St. Mary's, Wimbledon; Trans-
cribed and Annotated. London: Mitchell, Hughes, and
Clarke, 1934. 160pp.

1856 Hunt, Cecil. Here I Lie. London: J. Cape, 1932. 111pp.

1857 _____. More Last Words; A Collection of Singular Authentic Epitaphs. London: Low, 1946. 69pp.

Hurst, Sidney C. Silent Cities, An Illustrated Guide to the
War Cemeteries and Memorials to the Missing in France
and Flanders, 1914-1918. See entry 1313.

1858 Irish Medieval Figure Sculpture 1200-1600: A Study of Irish
Tombs with Notes on Costume Armour, 2. Totowa, NJ:
Sotheby Park Bernet, 1974. Illus.

1859 Jackson, Ada. Narrow Homes: A Collection of Epitaphs.
Birmingham, England: Cornish Bros., 1938. 48pp.

1860 Jacobs, G. W. Stranger Step & Cast an Eye, 3d ed. Brattleboro, VT: Greene, 1973. Illus.
Sepulchral monuments.

1861 Jervey, Clare. Inscriptions on Tablets and Gravestones in St. Michael's Church and Churchyard. Charleston, SC: State Company, 1906.

1862 Johnson, Stanley C. The Book of Proverbs and Epitaphs, 2d ed. London: Foulsham, 1963. 119pp.

1863 Kajanto, Iiro. A Study: The Greek Epitaphs of Rome. Helsinki: Academic Bookstore, 1963. 47pp.

1864 Kinnersley, Thomas. A Selection of Sepulchral Curiosities; With a Biographical Sketch on Human Longevity. Containing the Most Sublime, Singular and Authentic Epitaphs That Were Ever Before Collected. New York: T. Kinnersley, 1823. 352pp.

1865 Kippax, John R. Churchyard Literature; A Choice Collection of American Epitaphs with Remarks on Monumental Inscriptions and the Obsequies of Various Nations. Chicago, IL: S. C. Greggs, 1877. 213pp.; Detroit, MI: Singing Tree, 1969. 213pp.

1866 Krleza, Miroslav. "The Funerary Art of the Bogomils." UNESCO Courier 24:17-22 (May 1971). Illus.
       Tombs of "stetchaks" dating back to the 10th century in Yugoslavia. Bogomils were an heretical Christian sect that migrated to Yugoslavia.

1867 Laas, William. Monuments in Your History. New York: Popular Library, 1972. 149pp., illus., index, photos (paper).
       An introduction to American monuments which the author believes transcend the "purely practical ... and are closely intertwined with the heritage of our country." Traces the birth of the American monument tradition to the Bunker Hill Monument in Charlestown, Mass.; stories of other famous U.S. monuments; monuments of the great and unknown, old memorial customs, monuments in the Near East, the first churchyards, Puritan churchyards of New England, epitaphs, sculpture, list of burial places of U.S. Presidents, brief guide to memorial symbols, ancient, Old Testament, and Christian emblems and insignia, of how stone monuments are made, how to select a cemetery and a memorial, and the various memorial forms and designs.

1868 Lattimore, Richard A. Themes in Greek and Latin Epitaphs. Urbana: University of Illinois Press, 1942. 354pp. (also a 1962 paper ed.).

1869 Le Strange, Richard. Complete Descriptive Guide to British Monumental Brasses. Levittown, NY: Transatlantic, 1972.

       Lindley, Kenneth A. Of Graves and Epitaphs. See entry 1327.

1870 Loaring, Henry J. Epitaphs; Quaint, Curious, and Elegant, with Remarks on the Obsequies of Various Nations. London: W. Tegg, 1873. 262pp.

1871 Locke, Arthur H. Portsmouth and Newcastle, New Hampshire, Cemetery Inscriptions. Portsmouth, NH: The Author, 1907. 44pp.

1872 Ludwig, Allan I. Graven Images: New England Stonecarving and Its Symbols. Middletown, CT: Wesleyan University Press, 1966. Illus.

1873 McBride, David N., and McBride, Jane N. Cemetery Inscriptions of Highland County, Ohio. Hillsboro, OH: The Author, 1954. 547pp (paper).

1874 Macdonald, A. J. Monuments, Grave Stones, Burying Grounds, Cemeteries, Temples, etc. Albany, NY: J. Munsell, 1848. 22pp.

McWhirter, "Taj Mahal: Its Beauty Veils a Mogul's Ruthless Whim." See entry 1332.

Madden, Richard R. Shrines and Sepulchres of the Old and New World ... Including Notices of the Funeral Customs of the Principal Nations, Ancient and Modern. See entry 133.

1875 Mann, Thomas C., and Green, Janet C. Over Their Dead Bodies: Yankee Epitaphs and History, illus. by George Daly. Brattleboro, VT: Stephen Greene, 1962. 103pp., illus.

1876 _____, and _____. Sudden and Awful: American Epitaphs and the Finger of God, illus. by Robert MacLean. Brattleboro, VT: Stephen Greene, 1968. 99pp.

1877 Michelsen, Kaj Christian Bang. They Died for Us; In Memory of Allied Airmen Who Lost Their Lives in Denmark During the Second World War. Copenhagen: Scandinavian Pub. Co., 1946. 86pp.

1878 "Midwest Historical Societies Study Gravestone Genealogy." Monument Builder News, April 1975, p. 25.
   The Minnesota Historical Society, the Central Minnesota Regional Center, and the Stearns County Historical Society hold program at St. Cloud State College, one of the objects of which is to locate cemeteries in the area "whose existence is not known to public records." The program is considered a valuable community service since vital statistics were not kept in the area before 1900 and the monuments are often the only record left of a person's existence.

1879 Mitchell, John F., and Mitchell, Sheila. Monumental Inscrip-

tions (Pre-1855) in West Stirlingshire. Edinburgh: Scottish
Genealogy Society, 1973. 218pp., illus. (paper).

1880 _____, and _____. Monumental Inscriptions (pre-1855)
in West Lothian. Edinburgh: Scottish Genealogy Society,
1969. 178pp. (paper).

1881 Mogridge, George. Churchyard Lyrist; Consisting of Five
Hundred Original Inscriptions to Commemorate the Dead With
a Suitable Selection of Appropriate Texts of Scripture. London: Houlston & Stoneman, 1832. 201pp.

1882 "Monumental Inscriptions in Missouri Cemeteries; First paper,
on Monuments Erected by the General Assembly, Jefferson
City, Missouri." Missouri Historical Review, Oct. 1910,
p. 43-52.

Morley, John. Death, Heaven and the Victorians. See entry
148.

1883 Neal, Avon. "Graven Images: Sermons in Stone." American
Heritage 21:18-29 (Aug. 1970). Illus.
Collection of gravestone inscriptions from 19th-century
New England graves; many illustrations of artwork on gravestones
and monuments; study of epitaphs as source of information for his-
torians, sociologists, medical researchers and folklore students.

1884 Newberry, Percy W. Funerary Statuettes and Model Sarcophagi.
London: Quaritch, fasc. 1, 1930, 304pp.; fasc. 2, 1938,
100pp.

1885 Newman, H. "Porcelain Warming Urns." Antiques 93:660-63
(May 1968).
Urns.

1886 Noma, Seiroku. Haniwa. New York: Asia House Gallery,
1960 (dist. by New York Graphic Society, Greenwich, CT).

1887 Norfolk, Horatio E. (ed.). Gleanings in Graveyards; A Collection of Curious Epitaphs. London: J. R. Smith, 1866.
208pp.

1888 Northend, Charles. Churchyard Literature; or, Light Reading
on Grave Subjects; Being a Collection of Amusing, Quaint,
and Curious Epitaphs. New York: Coast City Publishing,
1886. 192pp.

1889 Nunn, Henry P. V. Christian Inscriptions. New York:
Philosophical Library, 1952. 72pp.

1890 Panofsky, Erwin. Tomb Sculpture. New York: Abrams,
1969 (repr. of 1964 ed.). (Giant Art series.) Illus. (paper).

1891 Parkinson, Sarah W. Memories of Carlisle's Old Graveyard;
      Containing a List of the Inscriptions on All the Stones in the
      Enclosure in 1898 and Describing a Walk Through a Part
      of the Graveyard. Carlisle, PA: M. K. Lamberton, 1930.
      259pp.

1892 Pasternak, B. "Chinese Tale-Telling Tombs." Ethnology
      12:259-73 (July 1973). Biblio.

1893 Payne, Charles T. Litchfield and Morris Inscriptions; A Rec-
      ord of Inscriptions Upon the Tombstones in the Towns of
      Litchfield and Morris, Connecticut. Litchfield, CT: D. C.
      Kilbourne, 1905. 304pp.

1894 Pettigrew, Thomas J. Chronicles of the Tombs; A Select
      Collection of Epitaphs Preceded by an Essay on Epitaphs and
      Other Monumental Inscriptions with Incidental Observation on
      Sepulchral Antiquities. London: H. G. Bohn, 1857, 529pp.,
      New York: AMS Press, 1968, 529pp., illus.

1895 Pike, Robert E. Granite Laughter and Marble Tears; Epitaphs
      of Old New England. Brattleboro, VT: Daye, 1938. 80pp.

1896 Pool, Wellington. Graveyard Inscriptions, Dodge's Row. Sal-
      em, MA: Essex Institute, n. d.

1897 _____. Inscriptions from Gravestones in the Old Burying
      Ground in Wenham. Salem, MA: Essex Institute, 1887.
      28pp.

1898 Porter, George S. Inscriptions from Gravestones in the Old
      Burying Ground, Norwich Town, Connecticut. Norwich, CT:
      Bulletin Press, 1933. 177pp.

1899 _____. Norwich, Connecticut, Epitaphs. Albany, NY:
      Joel Munsell, 1906.

1900 Potter, Gail. Stories Behind the Stones. Cranbury, NJ:
      A. S. Barnes, 1969. 244pp., illus.

1901 Poucher, John W., and Reynolds, R. W. (eds.). Old Grave-
      stones of Ulster County, New York; Twenty-two Thousand
      Inscriptions. Poughkeepsie, NY: J. W. Poucher, 1931.
      407pp.

1901a Praise on Tombs; Eulogies, Epitaphs, Inscriptions and His-
      torical Facts of America's Struggle for Independence. Ports-
      mouth, NH: The Author, 1932. 38pp.

1902 Pulleyn, William. Churchyard Gleanings, and Epigrammatic
      Scraps; Being a Collection of Remarkable Epitaphs and Epi-
      grams. London: S. Maunder, 1830. 264pp.

1903 Reder, Philip. Epitaphs, illus. by Andrew Dodds. London: Michael Joseph, 1969. 124pp.

1904 Rice, Franklin P. Marborough, Massachusetts, Burial Ground Inscriptions. Worcester, MA: The Author, 1908. 218pp.

1905 Richings, Benjamin. A General Volume of Epitaphs, Original and Selected; With Large Selection of Striking and Appropriate Texts of Scripture. London: J. W. Parker, 1840. 165pp.

1906 _____. Voices from the Tombs; or, Epitaphs, Original and Selected. London: Seeley, Jackson, and Holliday, 1858. 337pp.

1907 Richter, Gisela. Archaic Gravestones of Attica. New York: Phaidon, 1961.

1908 Ridgely, Helen W., ed. Historic Graves of Maryland and the District of Columbia, with the Inscriptions Appearing on the Tombstones in Most of the Counties of the State and in Washington and Georgetown. New York: Brafton Press, 1908, 296pp., illus.; Baltimore: Genealogical Books, 1967, 296pp., illus.

1909 Robinson, Joseph B. Cemeteriana; A Series of Designs for Monuments, Headstones, series 1-2. London: Derby, 1872.

1910 _____. Cemetery and Churchyard Memorials. London: Derby, 1856-1860. 2 vols.

1911 _____. The Cemetery Mason's Useful Book of Designs for Headstones, Crosses, Alphabets.... London: Derby, 1868.

1912 _____. Designs for Gravestones, Crosses, etc. London: Derby, 1865.

1913 _____. In Memoriam; A Series of Designs for Monuments, Tombs, Gravestones. London: Derby, 1862.

1914 _____. In Remembrance; A Series of Designs for Monuments, Tombs, Gravestones.... London: Derby, 1865.

1915 _____. The Sculptor's and Cemetery Mason's Portfolio of Designs for Monuments, Tombs, Crosses, etc., with Detailed Plans. London: Derby, 1869.

1916 _____. A Series of Designs for Carved Panels for Headstones, Crosses, etc. London: Derby, 1868. 2 parts.

1917 _____. Trade Secrets; A Collection of Practical Receipts for the Use of Sculptors, Modellers, Stone Masons. London: Derby, 1862.

1918 Rogers, Charles. Monuments and Monumental Inscriptions in
      Scotland. London: Griffin & Co., 1871, 1872. 2 vols.

1919 Safford, Susan D. Quaint Epitaphs. Boston: A Mudge, 1898.
      57pp.

1920 Schott, Siegfried. Wall Scenes from the Mortuary Chapel of
      the Mayor Paser at Medinet Habu, trans. by Elizabeth P.
      Hauser. Chicago: University of Chicago Press, 1957.

1921 Shilstone, Eustace M. Monumental Inscriptions in the Burial
      Ground of the Jewish Synagogue of Bridgetown, Barbados;
      Transcribed with an Introduction. London: Jewish Histori-
      cal Society, 1958. 205pp., illus.

1922 Smaridge, Norah. "Tombstones, Manhole Covers and the An-
      cient Art of Rubbing." New York Times (Leisure Section),
      July 27, 1975.
          The modern revival of the ancient art of transferring em-
      bossed or engraved designs from tombstones onto sheets of paper.

1923 Spiegl, Fritz. Small Book of Grave Humour. New York:
      Arco (Arc Books), 1974. (Paper.)

1924 Spofford, Charles B. Gravestone Records: From the Ancient
      Cemeteries in the Town of Claremont, New Hampshire. Al-
      bany, NY: Joel Munsell, 1896. 86pp.

1925 Suffling, Ernest R. English Church Brasses from the 13th to
      the 17th Century, a Manual for Antiquaries, Archaeologists,
      and Collectors. Baltimore: Genealogical Pub. Co., 1970
      (repr. of 1910 ed.). Illus.

1926 Tashjian, Dickran, and Tashjian, Ann. Memorials for Chil-
      dren of Change: The Art of Early New England Stonecarv-
      ing. Middletown, CT: Wesleyan University Press, 1974.
      309pp., illus.

1927 Tegg, William. Epitaphs, Witty, Grotesque, Elegant, etc.,
      etc., Together with a Selection of Epigrams. London: W.
      Tegg, 1875. 112pp.

1928 "Their Very Last Words." American Funeral Director 93(9):
      38 (1970). Illus.
          Pictorial article of epitaphs collected by Dr. Robert Pike
      of Eatontown, NJ.

1929 Thompson, Stephen. Sepulchral Monuments of Italy, Mediaeval
      and Renaissance. London: Arundel Society, 1883. 8 parts.

1930 Tissington, Silvester. Collections of Epitaphs and Monumental
      Inscriptions on the Most Illustrious Persons of All Ages and
      Countries. London: Simpkin, Marshall, 1857. 517pp.

1931 Trendall, Edward W. Monuments, Cenotaphs, Tombs, Tablets, etc., etc., with Their Details Drawn to a Large Scale. London: Atchley & Co., 1850. 30 plates.

1932 Unger, Frederic W. Epitaphs; A Unique Collection of Post Mortem Comment, Obituary Wit, Quaint and Gruesome Fancy. Philadelphia: Penn Publishing, 1904. 169pp.

1933 Wagenseller, George W. Tombstone Inscriptions of Snyder County, Pennsylvania. Middleburg, PA: The Author, 1904. 279pp.

1934 Wallis, Charles L. Epitaphs Grave and Humorous. Gloucester, MA: Peter Smith, 1974. Illus. (Orig. title: Stories on Stone: A Book of American Epitaphs, New York: Oxford, 1954, 272pp., drawings, biblio., indices; repr. New York: Dover, 1973 [paper].)
   A collection of epitaphs covering presidents, military heroes, sailors, Indians, pioneers, ex-slaves, ministers, atheists, doctors and patients, victims of chance, criminals, tradesmen, lovers, mothers, children, lodge members, writers, pets, plus additional misprints and unusual epitaphs.

1935 Wasserman, Emily. Gravestone Designs. New York: Dover, 1972. Illus. (paper).

1936 _____. Gravestone Designs: Rubbings and Photographs from Early New York and New Jersey. Gloucester, MA: Peter Smith, 1974.

1937 Waters, John C. A. Crosses of Sacrifice; The Story of the Empire's Million War Dead and Australia's 60,000. Sydney: Angus, 1932. 130pp.

1938 Watson, Margaret. Tombstone Inscriptions from Family Graveyards in Greenwood County, South Carolina. Greenwood, SC: Attic Press, 1972. (Paper.)

1939 Weaver, Sir Lawrence. Memorials and Monuments Old and New: Two Hundred Subjects Chosen from Seven Centuries. New York: Scribner's, 1915. 479pp., biblio.

1940 Webb, F. New Select Collection of Epitaphs ... Including the Most Remarkable Inscriptions in the Collections of Flacket, Jones, and Todervy; Together with One Thousand Epitaphs Never Before Published. London: S. Bladon, 1775. 2 vols.

1941 Weever, John. Ancient Funerall Monuments within the United Monarchie of Great Britain, Ireland, and the Islands Adiacent.... London: T. Harper, 1631, 871pp.; London: W. Tooke, 1767, 606pp.; New York: AMS Press, n. d.

1942 Whittlick, Arnold. History of Cemetery Sculputure; From the Monuments of Primitive Times and of the Oldest Civilisations to Early Christian Monuments in England. London: Mineral Publications, 1938. 120pp.

1943 Wilcox, Dorvil M. Gravestone Inscriptions, Lee, Massachusetts, Including All Extant of the Quarter Century, 1801-1825. Boston: Everett Pub. Co., 1901. 36pp.

1944 _____. Gravestone Inscriptions, Lee, Massachusetts, Including All Extant of the Quarter Century 1826-1850. Lee, MA: Berkshire Gleaner, 1910. 95pp.

1945 Wilkes, Peter. "Here Rest the Lords of Belvoir and Their Ladies." American Funeral Director 95(1):34-39 (1972).
Effigies of members of the Belvoir family in Church of St. Mary the Virgin, Bottesford in Leicestershire County, England. Family lived from 1285-1679. Monuments portray history of this interesting, influential family.

1946 Williams, Melvin G. The Last Word: The Lure and Lore of Early New England Graveyards. Available from Oldstone Enterprises, Publication Dept., 77 Summer St., Boston, MA 02110. Illus., biblio., directory.
English professor at American International College in Springfield, Mass., and one of the foremost authorities on early New England gravestones covers the histories in stone of the famous and the obscure, symbolic carvings that tell of life, death, and time. Fold-out map locates hundreds of old graveyards. (Also available from Educational Perspectives Associates, P.O. Box 213, Dekalb, IL 60115), free with Early American Cemeteries sound filmstrip Program. See Part IV, Audio-Visual Material.

1947 Wright, J. S. Brasses of Westminster Abbey. Atlantic Highlands, NJ: Humanities, 1970. (Paper.)

1948 Wright, Philip. Monumental Inscriptions of Jamaica. London: Society of Genealogists, 1966. 361pp. (paper).

B. CONTEMPORARY AMERICAN

1949 American Cemetery Assoc. , Monument Builders of America,
       and American Monument Assoc. A Joint Declaration of
       Principles and Objectives with Recommended Specifications
       for Memorial Work. Available from the AMA, MBA, and
       AMA. 12pp. (brochure).
       The results of a year's study by the three organizations
undertaken in order to form principles, objectives, and specifications
for memorial work. The Boards of Directors of all three approve
its contents and recommend it for study and consideration by its
members as a practical guide for planning cemetery memorials.

1950 "American Memorials and Overseas Military Cemeteries. "
       Mortuary Management 59(12):8 (1972).
       The American Battle Commission manages 34 memorials
and monuments overseas. Facts, figures and history of the memorials and the Commisssion.

1951 American Monument Assoc. Memorial Symbolism, Epitaphs
       and Design Types. Orlean, NY: American Monument Assoc. ,
       1947. 65pp. , illus. , index, biblio.
       Concise, convenient manual for general information on
symbols, epitaphs, and the principal types of memorials. Text and
illustrations by recognized authorities retained by the AMA.

       _____. Planning for Tomorrow. See entry 1410.

1952 Application for Headstone and Marker--Dod Form 1330. (pamph-
       let). Available from U. S. Army Memorial Affairs Agency
       (A), Dept. of the Army, Temporary Bldg, 2nd and T Streets,
       S. W. , Washington DC 20315.

1953 Barnard, Howard F. "Cathedral of the Pines. " American
       Funeral Director 93(5):39-42 (1970).
       Located on a hill overlooking a lake in Ringe, N. H. :
near the "Altar of the Nations, " the Cathedral of the Pines is an
outdoor worship area honoring all slain American servicemen. Place
for burial of cremated remains provided.

1954 Brown, Raymond L. A Book of Epitaphs; Cover Design and
       Line Whimsies by Ernest Petts. New York: Taplinger,
       1968. 126pp.

1955 _____. A New Book of Epitaphs. Newcastle-Upon-Tyne, England: Frank Graham, 1973. 116pp., illus.

Clark, Thomas H. "Court Restricts Sale of Markers by Cemetery." See entry 1460.

1956 Deacy, William H. Memorials Today for Tomorrow. Tate, GA: Georgia Marble Co., 1928. 74pp.

1957 Dianis, John E. "The Past Is Prologue." Monument Builder News April 1975, p. 51-52.
Speech delivered at the membership meeting during the 1975 Monument Builders of North America convention by its executive vice-president. A look at the MBNA's past, growth, present and future including new services it provides such as Workmen's compensation safety insurance, the design course, consultant staff in many areas of the monument business--management, personnel, law, and tax-estate planning.

1958 Dixon, J. M. The Spiritual Meaning of "In Memoriam." Philadelphia: Richard West, 1974 (repr. of 1920 ed.).

Edmands, Michael J. "Young Entrepreneurs Have Brought New Vigor to Funeral Parlors." See entry 629.

1959 Farber, Julius B. "Netherlands to Restore Tombstone Treasures." New York Times cxviii(40,447): sect. X, p. 23, (Oct. 20, 1968). Photos.
Restoration of Ouderkerk Sephardic Jewish Cemetery.

1960 Forest Lawn Memorial-Park Association. Art Guide of Forest Lawn, 1956.

1961 Gapay, Les. "Tombstone Industry Is Facing a Future That's, Well, Grave," Northeast Funeral Director 20(1):15 (1971) (repr. from the Wall Street Journal, Dec. 1, 1970).
Summary of factors clouding the tombstone industry horizon including increasing use of cremation, growth of memorial parks forbidding tombstones, changing cemetery practices such as restricting size of memorials, permitting multiple burials, popularity of garden mausoleums with caskets entombed five or six high in crypts, general inflation, and population mobility.

1962 "Gravestone Dealer Accused of Scheme to Bilk Bereaved." New York Times cxxiii(42,285):10 (Nov. 1, 1973). See entry 1963.

1963 "Gravestone Dealer Is Fined $13,000 on Fraud Charges." New York Times cxxii(42,045):88 (March 6, 1973).
Garden State Monument Co., New Jersey's largest. See entry 1962.

Grollman, Dr. Earl A., ed. Concerning Death: A Practical Guide for the Living. See entry 1117.

1964 Hopkins, Henry P. Sources of Memorial Ornamentation.
     Proctor, VT: Vermont Marble Co., 1924. 44pp.

     Houghton, Albert A. Concrete Monuments, Mausoleums and
     Burial Vaults. See entry 1509.

     Jabine, William. "The Law Says...." See entry 1519.

1965 Knox, Sanka. "Tombstone Gets Erosion Shield." New York
     Times cxvii(40,369):26 (Aug. 3, 1968).
          Protection fluid being tested will, hopefully, prevent de-
     cay of tombstones.

     Laas, William. Monuments in Your History. See entry 1867.

1966 Marshall, Gen. George C. "Our War Memorials Abroad: A
     Faith Kept." The National Geographic Magazine 111(6):731-
     68 (June 1957). Photos, map.
          Photo-essay by Marshall, then chairman of the American
     Battle Monuments Commission. Monuments abroad are a tribute to
     the dead and "a most solemn obligation to the living." Recently
     dedicated memorials; anecdotes supporting author's belief that "the
     excellent care given our cemeteries, and the distinguished memori-
     als erected, are not enough." Public must visit. Examples of re-
     cent tributes at Normandy, the southern Italian campaigns, and other
     battles.

1967 Monument Builders of North America. Basic Elements of
     Memorial Design. Available from MBNA.

1968 _____. Basic Style of Lettering. Available from MBNA.

1969 _____. Fundamentals of Salesmanship. Available from
     MBNA.

1970 _____. Memorial Symbolism, Epitaphs, and Design Types.
     Available from MBNA.

1971 _____. Ornamentation for Memorialization. Available
     from MBNA.

1972 _____. A Treasury of Religious Texts. Available from
     MBNA.

     "Move Over, Forest Lawn!" See entry 1559.
     Plastic tombstones.

     National Catholic Cemetery Conference. Parish Cemetery
     Handbook. See entry 1565.

1973 _____. Treasury of Religious Texts. Available from the
     NCCC, Item #603.
          Hardbound book for use in designing cemetery memorials

and furnishing catechetical and devotional inscriptions on religious shrines. Includes a pamphlet of texts for monument inscriptions.

1974   "New Sculpturnment from Jas. H. Matthews." National Cremation Magazine, July-Aug.-Sept., 1974, p. 19.   Photo.
    Sculpturnment is a new concept in memorialization, featuring cast bronze busts and "integral urns in the likeness of those to be remembered." Bust can be modeled in advance or after death from photographs and in three styles described as "realistic, impressionistic-light, and impressionistic-bold," where the artist freely expresses what he feels to be the subject's character.   Jas. H. Matthews & Co. is located at 1315 W. Liberty Ave., Pittsburgh, PA 15226.

1975   Office of Chief of Support Services, Dept. of the Army.   "Information Pertaining to Government Headstones and Markers." The Director 42:6-7 (Jan. 1972).
    Where and how to order monuments and markers, eligibility to use them, relatives eligible to apply, DoD Form 1330, how to fill it out, countersignatures required from cemetery official, and inscription details.

1976   Page-Phillips, John (ed.).   Macklin's Monumental Brasses. New York: Praeger, 1969.   Illus.

1977   Parker, William M.   "The Arizona Memorial." American Funeral Director 93(9):34-36 (1970).
    The battleship Arizona hit by the Japanese, Dec. 7, 1941, at Pearl Harbor.   Memorial commemorates all American fighting men killed during the attack.

    Planning for Tomorrow.   Dist. by the American Monument Assoc.   See entry 1410.

1978   Reed, Roy.   "Deterioration of Quaint Old Tombs Provokes New Orleans Controversy." New York Times cxxiv(42,756): 36 (Feb. 15, 1975).

1979   "State Seeks to Curb Gravestone Seller." New York Times cxxi(41,842):39 (Aug. 15, 1972).
    New York state seeks to curtail operations of McDonnell Memorials, Valhalla, N.Y.

1980   "State Sues Headstone Engraver." New York Times cxxi (41,774):51 (June 18, 1972).
    New York sues Paul Saracino, Office of Cemetery Services, North Arlington, N.J. for unethical practices.

1981   "V.A. Busy with Requests for Cemetery Markers." New York Times cxxiii(42,274):37 (Oct. 21, 1973).

1982   "Washington: For the Record Sept. 2, 1970: The President."

New York Times cxix(41, 130):17 (Sept. 3, 1970).
President signs bill giving Medal of Honor winners a free headstone. Also provides a flag for parents and spouse of deceased.

IV.   AUDIO-VISUAL MATERIAL

Organizations through which films and cassettes can be purchased or leased; and selections presently available. For further information contact the organizations, at the addresses and telephone numbers listed below.

The ALLIED MEMORIAL COUNCIL.   Box 30112 Wallingford Sta., Seattle, WA 98103 (206) 633-3510.

"Dialogue on Death": a half-hour video series produced for television stations, cable-tv stations, school closed-circuit systems.   All are in color and available in 3/4-inch videocassette and 1/2-inch reel-to-reel.   Programs 2, 5, and 8 are also available in 16mm film.

1.   Psycho-Social Aspects of Death.
     Discussion by Dr. Robert Fulton, author of Death and Identity, director of the Center for Death Education and Research, University of Minnesota.
2.   American Attitudes Toward Death and Funerals.
     Dr. Roger Blackwell and Dr. Wayne Talarzyk, marketing professors at Ohio State University, discuss the findings of their nation-wide poll.
3.   Memorialization.
     John Dianis of the Monument Builders of North America and F. Don Wahlstrom of the Pacific Northwest Monument Builders discuss the history and present trends.
4.   The Cemetery.
     John Danglade of the American Cemetery Assoc. discusses history, development, ecological contribution and management of American cemeteries.
5.   Explaining Death to Children.
     Rabbi Dr. Earl A. Grollman, author and lecturer tells how to explain death to children.
6.   Widowhood.
     Author and counselor Robert Buchanan, a widow, and a widower discuss widowhood, problems, available help, how people "can relate to the newly-widowed."
7.   Grief and the Funeral.
     Dr. Edgar N. Jackson, author, on "the nature of grief, what role the funeral plays and how clergy can be effective in assisting newly bereaved persons."
8.   Death Education.
     George Daugherty, producer of courses in death education (see

below) discusses the various courses that have been developed, their implementation in elementary and secondary schools.

Early American Cemeteries: Clues to a Nation's Heritage.
Sound filmstrip which traces "early American cemeteries and their unique forms of memorialization." Recommended for use by cemeterians and memorialists, especially during the Bicentennial.

Help When It Is Needed
20-minute slide presentation, following a family as it contacts funeral home, selects cemetery, makes flower and memorialization arrangements, contacts clergy and lawyer. Emphasis on pre-arrangement. Recommended for all groups.

In My Memory
15-minute film (16mm, color/sound) exploring the thoughts of a pre-teenage girl when her grandmother dies. Recommended for junior high school and Sunday School use.

Our Busy People
17-minute, 16mm, color film (1970). Winner of 1st place, 1973 Northwest Motion Picture Seminar awards. The functions and purposes of funerals, cemeteries, flowers and memorialization. Recommended for all age groups.

Perspectives on Death
2-part sound filmstrips taken from the Berg-Daugherty high school course (see under EDUCATIONAL PERSPECTIVES....). World funeral customs and how death has influenced art in history. Recommended for high school age and over.

Too Personal to Be Private
Half-hour color film showing the funeral and its values. Recommended for use by funeral directors.

Understanding Death
Four programs for elementary grades, one for parents and children pointing out why childrens' attitudes towards death are important. The child-oriented sound filmstrips are: "Life/Death," "Exploring the Cemetery," "Facts About Funerals," and "A Taste of Blackberries."

Vestige or Value?
30-minute, color film produced by the Religious Broadcasting Commission, featuring two clergymen, Lynn Melby and Clifton Anderson. Recommended for church sessions and clergy groups.

BARRE GRANITE ASSOC. 51 Church St., Barre, VT (802) 476-4131.

The Stone Whistle
30-minute, 16mm, color film featuring John Forsythe. While pursuing his hobby of gravestone rubbing, Forsythe meets

Melissa, a small girl. They admire the stone marking her great grandfather's grave then tour the rest of the cemetery, the Barre quarries, manufacturing plants, learning all about memorialization. Surprise ending.

CANADIAN BROADCASTING CORP., Foreign Relations and Export Sales Dept., P.O. Box 500, Sta. A, TORONTO

Tulip Garden
    30-minute tape of a radio play. An old farmer brings his wife's body home to their farm for burial. His daughter and friends pressure him to hire a funeral director to provide a "decent burial." The farmer prevails; he buries his wife simply, as she'd requested, in her tulip garden. $30/rental

ECCENTRIC CIRCLE CINEMA WORKSHOP. Box 1481, Evanston, IL 60204 (312) 864-0020.

How Could I Not Be Among You?
    28-minute, 16mm, color film. Portrait of a young poet who is dying. Shows the affirmation of life through the acceptance of death. Recommended as acceptable to all religious denominations. Award winner at the American, New York, and Flaherty Film Festivals. For rental and sale. (Study guide available. Contact Evanston office for Canadian distributor.)

EDUCATIONAL PERSPECTIVES ASSOCIATES. P.O. Box 213, Dekalb, IL 60115 (815) 895-9337).

Early American Cemeteries: Clues to a Nation's Heritage
    Sound filmstrip program on the changing attitudes towards life and death in Colonial America; the graveyard as art and history museum; symbols and images of death; how to make gravestone rubbings; death as a community ritual and individual experience; graveyards as an historical primary source. Purchase includes free copy of The Last Word: The Lure and Lore of Early New England Graveyards. (Available on 15-day approval if order submitted on school purchase form.)

"Perspectives on Death": a series developed by George Daugherty and David Berg, consisting of a six-week mini course or thematic teaching unit which can either be offered as a special course or as part of an existing high school English or social studies class. Consists of four components, which can be purchased separately: (1) an audio-visual package of two color-sound filmstrips and two separate tape cassette presentations (see below); (2) an anthology of readings entitled The Individual, Society and Death (see entry 767); (3) a student activity book (see entry 768); and (4) a Teacher's Resource Book (see entry 769).
(a) Death Themes in Literature
    20-minute tape cassette presentation showing how authors, poets, and dramatists attempt to face death. Includes

exerpts from Shakespeare, Poe, London, Wilder, Richard Armour, and Dorothy Parker.

(b) Death Themes in Music
18-minute tape cassette with selections from classical, jazz, folk, and modern music showing how composers express how they feel about death in music.

(c) Death Through the Eyes of the Artist
87-frame color filmstrip with tape cassette narration, showing how the artist tries to make death understandable through color, style, subject and symbolism.

(d) Funeral Customs Around the World
110-frame color filmstrip with tape cassette narration describing American and other nationalities' funeral customs.

"Understanding Death": a series developed in 1974 by David W. Berg and George G. Daugherty. Full color sound filmstrips with tape cassette narrations for middle school children and accompanying color filmstrip and cassette narration for parents and teachers. Designed to help children "develop affectively and cognitively by exploring values and attitudes toward life and death." Included are teachers' guides giving purposes and object of each strip, scripts, questions for discussions, and suggested class activities.

Children and Death
Cartoon strip which answers how to tell children about death, why it's necessary to help them understand, what should be said and not said, whether to allow a child to attend the funeral, and how to respond to the death of a pet. Recommended for in-service, PTA, and community groups.

Exploring the Cemetery
Photo-story of a boy who goes to a cemetery to prove he's not scared. Manager gives him tour, replacing the boy's fears with facts and understanding. Learns cemetery is an historical resource, the employee's responsibilities, cemetery's function, burials, memorialization, cremation, symbols, and cemetery regulations.

Facts About Funerals
Inquiry approach stressed. Boy visits a funeral home, asks questions, then reports to his school class what he's learned about funerals, funeral directing, steps in the funeral process and why they are taken. Photographs.

Life/Death
Photos and cartoons combined, showing what happens after someone dies: grief, sadness, modern and historical funeral customs, attitudes towards death, the major causes of death.

A Taste of Blackberries
Cartoons adapted from book by Doris Buchanan Smith. Boy learns to accept his grief at his best friend's death. Feelings of denial, anger, guilt, and final acceptance traced.

MASS MEDIA ASSOC., INC. 1724 Chouteau, St. Louis, MO 63104 (314) 436-0418.

The Great American Funeral
55-minute, CBS documentary, produced in 1965, but still relevant. All aspects of funeral industry; interviews with funeral directors, religious leaders, memorial society representatives, and Jessica Mitford. Greatly in demand.

MENTAL HEALTH TRAINING FILM PROGRAM. 33 Fenwood Rd., Boston, MA 02115.

Widows
43-minute, black and white film, made in 1972. Study of bereavement and need to express sorrow. Series of interviews with widows and their children. For rental and for sale.

MODERN TALKING PICTURE SERVICE. 3 E. 54th St., New York, NY 10022.

The Wondrous World of Sight (an Eye-Bank Film)
28-minute, 16mm, color film. Detailed description of how the eye works. Free loan. Specify No. 2235.

MONUMENT BUILDERS OF NORTH AMERICA. 1612 Central St., Evanston, IL 60201 (312) 869-2031.

Ask for the Order	Overcoming Objections
Closing the Sale	Pour It On
Developing Your Sales Personality	The Power of Enthusiasm
How to Sell Creatively	The Professional
Make It Happen	Second Effort
Making the Sale	Think Win
Opening the Sale	Your Price Is Right

Films designed to help industry members increase sales.

NATIONAL FUNERAL DIRECTORS ASSOC. 135 W. Wells St., Milwaukee, WI 53203 (414) 276-2500.

Advocating Understanding
32-minute, 16mm, color film featuring the Rev. Paul E. Irion.

A Bibliography on Death, Grief and Bereavement 1845-1973
3d rev. ed., compiled by Robert Fulton. Hardbound book for rent.

Through Death to Life
Cassette compiled by Father Joseph M. Champlin. For purchase.

The Florida Showcase
30-minute, 16mm, color film featuring William G. Hardy, Jr.

The Funeral: A Vehicle for the Recognition and Resolution of Grief
20 slides and manuscript. For purchase and for rental.

The Funeral--From Ancient Egypt to Present Day America
35-minute; 12 slides and manuscript. For purchase and for
rental.

The Funeral Gap
23-minute, 16mm film.

Funeral Service--A Heritage, A Challenge, A Future
35-minute slide (16 slides) and manuscript. For purchase.

Future Shock
45-minute, 16mm, color film.

A Humanist Funeral Service
15-minute, 16mm, color film.

The Interest in Dying and Death As It Relates to the Funeral
43-minute, 16mm, color film featuring NFDA Executive Director Howard C. Raether.

The Last Full Measure of Devotion
27-1/2-minute, 16mm, color film.

A Life Has Been Lived: A Contemporary Funeral Service
16-minute, 16mm color film.

Living With Death
45-minute, 16mm film.

Of Life and Death
The New Catholic Burial Rite film. 27-1/2-minute, 16mm
color.

Perspectives on Death
Berg and Daughtery course (see also entry 758). For purchase.

Someone You Love Has Died
15-minute, 16mm, color film featuring NFDA Executive Director Howard C. Raether.

Sunrise Semester
30-minute, 16mm, color film featuring Dr. James Carse and
Howard C. Raether.

Through Death to Life
Cassette by Father Joseph M. Champlin. For purchase.

Too Personal to Be Private
28-1/2-minute, 16mm, color film.

To Serve the Living
27-1/2-minute, 16mm, film.

Update--Yesterday--Today--Tomorrow
52-minute, 16mm, color film featuring Howard C. Raether.

NEW LIFE FILMS. P.O. Box 2008, Kansas City, KS 66110

A Time to Die
20-minute film on recurrent cycles of life and death from a
non-sectarian Christian view. Designed to stimulate discussion
in church and study classes. For purchase.

SAN DIEGO HUMAN RESOURCE CENTER. P.O. Box 5322, San
Diego, CA 92105.

A Last and Lasting Gift
26-minute, 16mm, color and sound film. Urges people to bequeath their bodies to science and education. Explains how tissues are used to help living persons; recommends memorial
services.

TRANS TIME, Inc. Dept. KB, 1122 Spruce St., Berkeley, CA
94707.

Cryonic Suspension of Two Patients
65 slides and 11 pages of text showing step-by-step preparation
for long-term storage: protective chemical perfusion, temporary
storage with dry ice, and encapsulation in liquid nitrogen.

UNIVERSITY OF IOWA, Division of Extension and University Services,
Audio-Visual Center. Iowa City, IA 52240.

An Investment in Sight (an Eye-Bank Film).
13-minute, 16mm, color film. A boy with impaired vision gets
corneal transplant and eyesight improves (specify U-6143).

VIDEO NURSING, Inc. 2834 Central St., Evanston, IL 60201 (312)
866-6460.

Until I Die
30-minute color film produced by WTTW-TV, Chicago. Dr.
Elizabeth Kubler-Ross explains her work with the terminally ill,
the five stages they progress through when aware they will die.
Designed for people who attend dying patients and interested
laymen. Winner of five awards. For purchase and rental.

V. APPENDICES

1. BRIEF GLOSSARY (some common terms are omitted)

ADAPTIVE FUNERAL   Encompasses much of the humanist funeral (see below), but includes religious though untraditional practices, such as Quaker funerals where funeral directors are not hired.

CALCINATION   Reduction of body to ashes through the action of inert heat, without flame.

CANOPIC JARS   Vases used to hold vital organs of embalmed bodies or ashes of the dead.   See URN.

CASKET   Rectangular, rigid burial receptacle, usually made of wood or metal and lined with fabric.   Compare with COFFIN. See VAULT.

CATACOMBS   Underground cemetery with tunnels and recessed rooms dug out for tombs and coffins.

CATAFALQUE   Raised, flat structure on which corpse is laid or carried.

CERECLOTHS   During the Middle Ages, strips of fabric saturated with wax and wrapped about the corpse to preserve it.

COFFIN   Eight-sided burial receptacle shaped to fit the human body.   Rarely used in the U. S. any more.   Compare with CASKET.

COLUMBARIUM   Vault or similar structure with recessed niches in the walls for storing the ashes of the dead.   In modern facilities, the niches are faced with protective glass, bronze, or marble.   See VAULT.

CO-OPERATIVE   Consumer-owned and operated mortuary.

CREMAINS   Cremated remains.

CRYONICS   The freezing at an extremely low temperature of a human who has died of a disease, in hopes that the body may be resuscitated by the advanced science of the future.

CRYPT   Subterranean vault or chamber, often beneath the floor of a church, for burial.

GRAVE   An excavation for burial of a body.

HUMANIST FUNERAL   Takes into account the wishes of the deceased, often contrary to religious or common social customs; focus is on the positive processes of life rather than death.

INHUMATION   Interment of the body in the earth or crypt, tomb, or other shelter.

INTERMENT RECEPTACLES   Repositories for the body and coffin including vaults, concrete units, or boxes.   American cemeteries usually require them to prevent the earth from caving in over the grave.   European countries rarely do, although they wait to put up marker or tombstone until the ground has settled.   See VAULT.

INTERN   Resident trainee or apprentice who trains for a specified period with a licensed practitioner before applying for a director's or embalmer's license.

MAUSOLEUM   Above-ground structure, usually of stone, with places for emtombment of the dead.

MEMORIAL PARK   Cemetery where graves are marked with markers that are flush to the ground as opposed to monuments or gravestones.

MEMORIAL SOCIETY   Voluntary group dedicated to providing members inexpensive, dignified funerals through pre-arrangement.

MEMORIALIZATION   Marking of permanent placement of body or cremated remains; usually of stone, bronze, or marble.

OSSUARY   Depository--vault, chamber, or just an urn--for the bones of the dead.

PARTIAL ADULT FUNERAL   Services, equipment, facilities provided for one funeral by more than one funeral director, usually when one director prepares corpse and then ships it to a funeral director in another city for final disposition.   See TOTAL ADULT FUNERAL; WELFARE ADULT FUNERAL.

PRICE QUOTING METHODS for Service and Merchandise   Single Unit Method (Unit Pricing): A single price is quoted which covers funeral director's services, casket, and use of funeral home facilities.   Bi-Unit Method: Two figures are given: (1) for funeral director's services and use of the funeral home facilities; (2) for the casket.   Tri-Unit Method: Three figures are quoted: (1) for the director's services; (2) for the use of the funeral home facilities; (3) for the casket.   Multi-Unit Itemization (Functional Pricing): All services and merchandise are listed and separate costs are noted for each. Miscellaneous items such as burial clothes, limosine, flowers, clergyman's honorarium, cremation, urn or interment receptacle, etc., are extra and in all cases listed separately.

SARCOPHAGUS   Stone coffin, usually inscribed and adorned with sculptured figures.

SEPULCHER   Tomb, grave, or burial place.

SEPULTURE   Burial.

SINGLE LICENSE   Combined funeral director's and embalmer's license offered by some states.

STANDARD FUNERAL SERVICE PACKAGE   Includes, but is not necessarily limited to, transporting the body to the funeral home; casket; preparing the body for viewing; using the funeral homes' facilities for viewing and funeral service; arranging of death notices, church service, documents for burial, hearse, funeral benefits from Social Security or elsewhere, flowers, and pallbearers; and other funeral staff services.

TOMB   Excavation for burial of a corpse; a structure or vault, below or above ground, for interment.

TOTAL ADULT FUNERAL   All professional funeral services--including use of funeral home facilities, casket, etc.--provided by one funeral director.   Persons over fifteen are considered adult. See PARTIAL ADULT FUNERAL; WELFARE FUNERAL.

TRADITIONAL FUNERAL   In modern usage, usually involves use of a funeral director's services, viewing, and burial.

TROCAR   Long hollow needle which embalmers use to remove cavity fluid from the body.

VAULT   Burial structure or chamber, often arched, usually of stone; also a prefabricated receptacle into which casket and contents is put, made generally of steel, concrete, fiberglass, or copper (said to prevent ground from caving in and to protect casket from earth and water).

WAKE   Watch near the body before burial.

WELFARE FUNERAL   Body preparation and service for welfare recipients; the cost is paid in part or totally by the Government.

2. ACRONYMS OF PROFESSIONAL ORGANIZATIONS

ABFSE	American Board of Funeral Service Education
ACA	American Cemetery Association, Inc.
AFDS	Associated Funeral Directors Service
AFS	American Funeral Supply Corporation
AICA	American Institute of Commemorative Art
AMA	American Monument Association, Inc.
AMC	Allied Memorial Council
CAA	Cremation Association of America
CAFMS	Continental Association of Funeral and Memorial Societies, Inc.
CMA	Casket Manufacturers of America
ECMA	Embalming Chemical Manufacturers Association
FCI	Financial Corporation International
FFD of A	Federated Funeral Directors of America
FFDA	Flying Funeral Directors of America
FIAT	Fédération Internationale des Associations de Thanatopraxie (see IFAT)
GAFD	Guild of American Funeral Directors
IFAT	International Federation of Thanatopractic Associations
IFS	International Funeral Service, Inc.
JFDA	Jewish Funeral Directors of America
MBA	Monument Builders of America, Inc.
MBNA	Monument Builders of North America
MSAC	Memorial Society Association of Canada
NAAM	National Association of Approved Morticians
NAC	National Association of Cemeteries
NCCC	National Catholic Cemetery Conference
NFDA	National Funeral Directors Association
NFFS	National Foundation of Funeral Service

NSM	National Selected Morticians
OGR	Order of the Golden Rule
PIAA	Pre-Arrangement Interment Association of America
SCI	Service Corporation International
SOS	Special Organizational Services

3. PROFESSIONAL FUNERAL ORGANIZATIONS

ALLIED MEMORIAL COUNCIL
Box 30112 Wallingford Station
Seattle, WA 98103
(206) 633-3510
    Lynn L. Melby, exec. dir., founded in 1963. Nonprofit research
    and consumer affairs organization comprising funeral directors,
    florists, cemeterians, memorial firms and related manufacturer
    and supplier firms; approximately 800 member firms; operates
    mainly in the Pacific northwest; main purposes concern educa-
    tional materials, consumer attitude research, handling consumer
    complaints; conducts seminars for members, clergy, educators.
    Publications: Dead Is a Four Letter Word, by Lynn Melby;
    slide and filmstrips; films and videotapes; monthly magazine;
    "Understanding for the Future" (brochure).

AMERICAN BOARD OF FUNERAL SERVICE EDUCATION
201 Columbia Street
Fairmont, WV 26554
(304) 366-2403
    Cooperates with groups and agencies concerned with advancing
    mortuary education principles and standards. Dedicated to
    furthering education in funeral service and allied fields, formu-
    lating standards of funeral service education, and accrediting
    qualified mortuary science schools and colleges. For scholar-
    ships up to $500 for study in funeral service apply to ABFSE
    at above address.

AMERICAN CERTIFIED MORTICIANS ASSOCIATION
35 N. Arroyo Parkway
Pasadena, CA
(213) 796-2262

ASSOCIATED FUNERAL DIRECTORS SERVICE
P.O. Box 20038
St. Louis, MO 63144
(314) 781-2060
    2511-member association of shipping specialists, international

in scope, founded in 1939 to handle the shipment of human remains between cities and states on a fair, cooperative basis. A franchise-membership is granted to one funeral home in a community to serve the other area funeral directors. Services provided members include advertising and public relations programs and cooperative purchasing packages.

Publications: Bulletin and Roster, both quarterly.

CASKET MANUFACTURERS OF AMERICA
708 Church St.
Evanston, IL 60201
(312) 866-8383

Founded in 1912; a 200-member, non-profit trade association dedicated to advancing its members' professionalism and business, improving funeral service in ways that promote the public interest, and serving as a clearing house of information affecting the profession's business conditions. Members include manufacturers and distributors of burial caskets and other funeral supplies.

Publications: Bulletin of Accounts Placed for Collection, monthly; Newsletter, monthly; manuals on marketing, safety and public relations and "Facts and Figures" on the funeral industry; Management Letter; Sales Letter; Washington Wire; Summary of Sales to Funeral Directors, quarterly; Transportation Bulletin.

CENTER FOR DEATH EDUCATION AND RESEARCH
1167 Social Science Building
University of Minnesota
Minneapolis, MN 55455
(612) 373-2851 (main university number)

CONTINENTAL ASSOCIATION OF FUNERAL AND MEMORIAL
  SOCIETIES, Inc.
Suite 1100, 1828 L St., N.W.
Washington, DC 20036
(202) 293-4821

National association of memorial associations dedicated to providing to members simple, inexpensive, dignified funerals through pre-arrangements.

Publications: CAFMS News Bulletin, monthly; CAFMS Newsletter, quarterly; Directory of Memorial Associations; Manual of Simple Burial; and Handbook for Memorial Societies.

COUNCIL OF BETTER BUSINESS BUREAUS, Inc.
Consumer Information Dept.
1150 17th St., N.W.
Washington, DC 20036
(202) 467-5338

Publication: "Comparing Costs Can Cut Funeral Expense"

EDUCATIONAL PERSPECTIVES ASSOCIATES
P.O. Box 213
Dekalb, IL 60115
(815) 895-9337

David W. Berg and George G. Daugherty, assoc. directors.
Publications: The Understanding Death series, color filmstrips with tape cassette narrative; Perspectives on Death, multi-media teaching unit; Early America Cemeteries: Clues to a Nation's Heritage sound filmstrip program (see Author Index for other publications).

EMBALMING CHEMICAL MANUFACTURERS ASSOCIATION
165 Rindge Ave. Ext.
Cambridge, MA 02140
(617) 661-0500
Publication: Embalming: Ancient Art/Modern Science (see entry 419).

FEDERATED FUNERAL DIRECTORS OF AMERICA
1622 S. MacArthur Blvd.
Springfield, IL 62709
(217) 525-1712
Wendell W. Hahn, pres., founded in 1925, 1100 members. An accounting, tax and business management organization for funeral homes; provides management counsel, accounting and other business services to members, compiles statistical data on services and costs with the NFDA and affiliated state associations' cooperation.

FLYING FUNERAL DIRECTORS OF AMERICA
811 Grant St.
Akron, OH 44311
Founded in 1961; a 150-member organization of U.S. and Canadian licensed funeral directors and embalmers who have a valid flying license. Formed in order to "unite men in the funeral industry, interested in flying, whereby they may unite and give aid on a regional or national level in case of a disaster." Disseminates information on flying related to transporting human remains; seeks to improve such transportation, exchange information on methods and equipment; formulates group insurance plans; helps members in cross-country operations. Pilots in allied industries accepted as associated members.
Publications: Crosswind; Membership Roster.

GUILD OF AMERICAN FUNERAL DIRECTORS
30112 Silver Spur Rd.
San Juan Capistrano, CA 92675
(714) 830-5723
Founded in 1963; 150-member professional association of selected funeral directors throughout the Western world. Encourages the exchange of information on professional problems, management, merchandising, and public relations.
Publication: The Guide, 6 issues per year.

The INTERNATIONAL COOPERATIVE ALLIANCE (headquarters)
11 Upper Grosvenor St.
London W1
England W2X 9PA

INTERNATIONAL FEDERATION OF THANATOPRACTIC ASSOCIATIONS
(Federation Internationale des Associations de Thanatopraxie)
62, av. du Capitaine-Glarner
93-Saint-Ouen-France
(1) 255-40-34
    Jacques Marette, gen. sec.   Founded in 1970; 16 countries rep-
    resented in its 266 members, among whom are individuals,
    firms, professional associations and federations interested in
    the funeral business.   Dedicated to the research and study of
    legal, social, moral and technical and scientific problems re-
    lating to thanatopractic; helps coordinate institutions "as regards
    the teaching, practice and diffusion of the profession."   Manages
    the European Center of Teaching of Thanatopractic.
    Publication: Bulletin, quarterly.

INTERNATIONAL FUNERAL SERVICE, Inc.
Des Moines, IA
(515) 282-0423
    Paul G. Hamilton, pres. and founder.

JEWISH FUNERAL DIRECTORS OF AMERICA, Inc.
3501 14th St., N.W.
Washington, DC 20010
(202) 232-3501
    Herman Goldberg, sec.   Founded in 1929; 175 members; pro-
    fessional society of Jewish funeral directors dedicated to pre-
    serving the traditions and customs of Jewish funeral service as
    it is recognized and practiced by those of the Jewish faith, pro-
    moting the highest professional ideals, and working for the mu-
    tual benefit of its members through professional cooperation.
    Publication: Jewish Funeral Director, quarterly.

MEMORIAL SOCIETY ASSOCIATION OF CANADA
5326 Ada Blvd.
Edmonton, Alberta T5W 4N7
(403) 477-6864
    National association of memorial societies dedicated to provid-
    ing members simple, dignified, economic means of body dispos-
    al by earth burial, cremation, donation to science or medical
    research.   (See Appendex 6.)
    Publications: "How to Beat the High Cost of Dying," by Tam
    Deachman; "Church Comment on Funerals"; "Human Parts Banks
    Are Coming"; "The Positive Role of Grief," by Myra Sable; Di-
    rectory of Canadian Memorial Societies.

M. K. BATES & ASSOCIATES
31322 S.W. Parkway Ave.
Wilsonville, OR 97070
(503) 638-5407
    Contemporary funeral service consultants.   Bates trains direc-
    tors to arrange the adaptive funeral as a "meaningful alternative
    or addition to traditional service" and also increase profits.
    Methods have been developed in conjunction with leading university

psychologists and gerontologists and are proven and documented in presentations to families. Workships are given periodically. Call collect or write for costs and further information.

NATIONAL ASSOCIATION OF CORONERS AND MEDICAL EXAMINERS
2121 Adelbert Rd.
Cleveland, OH 44106

NATIONAL FOUNDATION OF FUNERAL SERVICE
1600-1628 Central St.
Evanston, IL 60201
(312) DA 8-6545
Dr. Charles H. Nichols, dir. Founded in 1945; a non-profit educational trust dedicated to providing a "forthright program of education for funeral service and the public" and to ensure the industry's future growth and high standing. Supported by the industry; there is no membership. Programs include management training for funeral service and allied fields through the School of Management and Extension Courses; collection and preservation of funeral service literature in its 4000-volume library; demonstrations to improve merchandizing; public education through surveys, research and dissemination of information; museum of Funeral Service Artifacts featuring historical items.

NATIONAL FUNERAL DIRECTORS AND MORTICIANS ASSOCIATION
734 W. 79th St.
Chicago, IL 60620
Publications: National Funeral Director and Embalmer, monthly; National Green Book, biennial.

NATIONAL FUNERAL DIRECTORS ASSOCIATION OF THE U.S., Inc.
135 W. Wells St.
Milwaukee, WI 53202
(414) 276-2500
Howard C. Raether, exec. dir. Founded in 1882; 14,000 members. Professional society of funeral directors; presents annual awards; maintains a 300-volume library with films related to death, dying, and bereavement; special committees include Editorial, Education, Insurance and Pension, Hospital and Pathology, Emergency Preparedness and Disaster, Exhibit and Manufacturers Liaison.
Publications: The Director, monthly; Directory of Members, annual; Special State Officers' Bulletin; Regular State Officers' Bulletin.

NATIONAL SELECTED MORTICIANS
1616 Central St.
Evanston, IL 60201
(312) 475-3414
Founded in 1917; international society of 851 leading independent funeral directors dedicated to create and uphold the highest standards of funeral practice, provide members with widest "spectrum of knowledge, experience, and skills on behalf of the

public they serve." Membership is by invitation after careful screening.

Publications: Bulletin, quarterly; 1974 Social Security Benefits; What Every Woman Should Know; The Code of Good Funeral Practice; Pre-Planning the Funeral; You Can Cry at My Funeral; NSM Ailgram: A Newsletter of Ideas and Activities.

The ORDER OF THE GOLDEN RULE
P.O. Box 579
726 South College St.
Springfield, IL 62704
(217) 544-7428

Roger B. Ytterberg, exec. dir. Organization of funeral directors; operates the International Order of the Golden Rule for public relations, educational and advertising purposes.

SERVICE CORPORATION INTERNATIONAL
22 Waugh Dr.
Houston, TX
(713) 869-8421

SOCIETY OF AMERICAN FLORISTS
901 N. Washington St.
Alexandria, VA 22314
(703) 836-8700

S.O.S., Inc. [Special Organizational Services]
P.O. Box S.O.S.
Athens, TX 75751

Free personal service offered by banks through specially trained S.O.S. advisors. They help families of the deceased (at no cost) notify proper authorities, determine what must be done, locate necessary documents, see to Social Security and VA, railroad or other insurance benefits. Purely an organizing service and does not replace the need for accountants, lawyers, or insurance agents.

4. CEMETERY AND MONUMENT ASSOCIATIONS

National Organizations

AMERICAN CEMETERY ASSOCIATION
250 E. Broad St.
Columbus, OH 43215
(614) 221-6829
> Founded in 1887; 1100-member national trade group made up of administrators, superintendents, and owners of American and Canadian cemeteries, and other cemeterians. Concerned with the improvement of U. S. cemeteries, their operation, and management. Collects and disseminates information concerned with improvements, maintenance and operation. Surveys and evaluates the cemetery industry in order to strengthen its satisfactory aspects and correct or replace ineffective ones.
> Publications: ACA Cemeterian, monthly; ACA Register, annual; American Directory of Cemeteries, triennial; International Cemetery Directory; ACA Convention Proceedings; ACA Membership Register and Proceedings.

AMERICAN INSTITUTE OF COMMEMORATIVE ART
P. O. Box 145
Valhalla, NY 10595
(212) 753-8181
> Founded 1951; 40 members; association of memorial and cemetery monument retailers.

AMERICAN MONUMENT ASSOCIATION
147 North Union St.
P. O. Box 523
Olean, NY 14760
(716) 372-6627
> Founded in 1894; 153 members; association of "quarriers, manufacturers and wholesalers of granite and marble used in fabrication of cemetery memorials. Provides credit information and maintains collection service. "
> Publications: Claims Bulletin, monthly; Executive Digest, monthly; Monumental News Review, monthly; Past Due Accounts Bulletin, monthly; Memorial Red Book, annual; books for public distribution on cemetery planning, monument merchandising, memorial symbolism, epitaphs, and design types and pamphlets for retail merchants.

CONFERENCE OF STATE CEMETERY ASSOCIATION SECRETARIES
Riverside Cemetery
611 N. Center Street
Marshalltown, IA 50158
(515) 753-7891
Wallace E. Loft, chairman.

CEMETERY SUPPLY ASSOCIATION
Grinit-Bronz, Inc.
Cold Springs, MN 56320
(612) 685-3621

The CREMATION ASSOCIATION OF AMERICA
Chapel of Light
1620 W. Belmont Ave.
Fresno, CA 93728
(209) 233-6254
Founded in 1913 to promote cremation by means of publications, meetings, and lectures, improve methods, and advance the interests of the Association and its members. Fosters association between crematories, columbaria, and other memorial industries; distributes information, develops, improves, and evaluates standards of cremation and memorialization and urges the establishment of care funds to insure maintenance of memorial facilities.
Publications: National Cremation Magazine, quarterly; Roster.

MONUMENT BUILDERS OF NORTH AMERICA
1612 Central St.
Evanston, IL 60201
(312) 869-2031
Founded 1962; 806 members; an international association of memorialists established to promote knowledge and appreciation of memorialization; provides sales, advertising and management information to members; conducts sales institute and national management school; develops religious and modern memorial designs; holds design competitions. It encourages growth and expansion of traditional cemeteries, allowing lot owners freedom of choice of type and source of memorials, constructive relations among all segments of memorial industry and cemeteries, fair competitive practices, equitable and uniform tax treatment at all industry levels, and high business, professional and ethical standards.
Publications: OSHA Safety Manual; Membership Roster, annual; Monument Builder News, monthly; direct mail, management, and public relations publications (cost available on request) and films (no charge).

NATIONAL ASSOCIATION OF CEMETERIES
Suite 409, Rosslyn Bldg. North
1911 N. Fort Myer Dr.
Arlington, VA 22209
(703) 525-8774
Founded 1929; 1500 members.

NATIONAL ASSOCIATION OF PET CEMETERIES
27 West 150 N Ave.
West Chicago, IL 60185
(312) 231-1117
    Patricia Blosser, pres.

NATIONAL CATHOLIC CEMETERY CONFERENCE
710 N. River Road
Des Plaines, IL 60016
(312) 824-8131
    Publications: The Catholic Cemetery, monthly; the Catholic
    Cemetery Subject Index; The Parish Cemetery Handbook; Looking
    After God's Acre; Treasury of Religious Texts; Pre-Need leaflet;
    The Law and Catholic Cemeteries.

NATIONAL CONCRETE BURIAL VAULT ASSOCIATION
P.O. Box 1031
Battle Creek, MI 49016
(616) 963-1554
    Founded in 1929; 350 members; concrete burial vault manufac-
    turers dedicated to advancing the Association's interests, more
    effective publicity and advertising techniques, close cooperation
    with other branches of the funeral service industry, improving
    the quality of concrete vaults, and working for greater acceptance
    of them.

PRE-ARRANGEMENT INTERMENT ASSOCIATION OF AMERICA, Inc.
P.O. Box 7250
Fort Wayne, IN 46807
(219) 432-4748
    Founded in 1956; 250 members; association of cemeteries, fu-
    neral homes and sales companies promoting burial and funeral
    pre-arrangement; conducts National Lot Exchange Program;
    sponsors PIAA Research and Educational Foundation.
    Publications: Forward, monthly; PIAA Administration, month-
    ly; PIAA Sales, monthly; Membership Directory, annual; PIAA
    Public Relations.

Regional Associations

Central States Cemetery Assoc.
    Resthaven Memorial Park
    P.O. Box 278
    Shawnee, OK 74801
    (405) 273-3345

New England Cemetery Assoc.
    Linwood Cemetery
    Mill Street
    Haverhill, MA 08132
    (617) 374-4191

Northeastern Cemetery Assoc.
    Rose Hill Memorial Park
    P.O. Box 297
    Rocky Hill, CT 06067
    (203) 529-3381

Southern Cemetery Assoc.
    Gardens of Memory
    P.O. Box 4436
    Winston Salem, NC 27105
    (919) 725-8530

Western Cemetery Alliance
925 L Street
Sacramento, CA 95814
(916) 441-4533

State Associations

Alabama Cemetery Assoc.
Pine View Memorial Gardens,
Inc.
P. O. Box 177
Wetumpka, AL 36092
(205) 567-6226 or (in Mont-
gomery) (205) 272-6344

Arizona Cemetery Assoc.
Evergreen Cemetery
P. O. Box 5158
Tucson, AZ 85703
(602) 88-0860

Arkansas Cemeteries Assocs.
Roselawn Memorial Park
2801 Asher Ave.
Little Rock, AR 72204
(501) 663-0248

Interment Assoc. of California
Park Executive Bldg., Suite
315
925 L. Street
Sacramento, CA 95814
(916) 441-4533

Colorado Assoc. of Cemeteries
The Fairmount Cemetery
E. Alameda & Quebec St.
Denver, CO 80231
(303) 399-0692

Connecticut Cemetery Assoc.
Fountain Hill Cemetery
P.O. Box 157
Deep River, CT 06417
(203) 526-5337

Florida Cemetery Assoc.
Osceola Memorial Gardens
P. O. Box 174
Kissimmee, FL 32741
(305) 847-2494

Georgia Cemetery Assoc.
Forest Hills Memorial Park
722 Conley Rd.
Forest Park, GA 30050
(404) 366-1221

Hawaii Interment Assoc.
Hawaiian Memorial Park
P. O. Box 457
Kaneohe, HI 96744
(808) 247-6675

Illinois Cemetery Assoc.
Park Hill Cemetery
P. O. Box 246
Bloomington, IL 61701
(309) 828-8424

Indiana Cemetery Assoc.
Cresthaven Memory Gardens
R. R. #1
Bedford, IN 47421
(812) 275-6886

Assoc. of Iowa Cemeteries
Riverside Cemetery
611 N. Center St.
Marshalltown, IA 50158
(515) 753-7891

Kansas Cemetery Assoc.
Memorial Park Cemetery
3616 W. 6th St.
Topeka, KS 66606
(913) 234-6605

Kentucky Cemetery Assoc.
Sunset Memorial Gardens
Rt. 3, Versailles Rd.
Frankfort, KY 40601
(502) 223-3571

Louisiana Cemeteries Assoc.
Resthaven Gardens of Memory
P. O. Box 15009, Broadview
Sta.
Baton Rouge, LA 70815
(504) 937-1440

Maine Cemetery Assoc.
Brooklawn Memorial Park
2002 Congress St.
Portland, ME 04102
(207) 773-7679

Cemetery Assoc. of Maryland
and District of Columbia
George Washington Cemetery,
Inc.
9500 Riggs Rd.
Adelphi, MD 20783
(301) 434-4640

Free State [Maryland] Cemetery
Assoc.
Holly Hill Memorial Gardens
10201 Bird River Rd.
Baltimore, MD 21220
(301) 335-5300

Massachusetts Cemetery Assoc.
Milton Cemetery
211 Centre St.
Milton, MA 02186
(617) 698-0200

Associated Cemeteries of Michigan
Mission Hills Memorial Gardens
P. O. Box 294A, Hagar Shores
Niles/Dowagiac, MI 49039
(616) 683-8333

Michigan Assoc. of Municipal
Cemeteries
Oakwood Cemetery
City Hall
Adrian, MI 49221
(313) 263-2161

Michigan Cemetery Assoc.
Memorial Gardens Assoc., Inc.
24392 Crocker Blvd.
Mt. Clemens, MI 48043
(313) 465-1841

Minnesota Assoc. of Cemetery
Officials
Catholic Cemeteries
244 Dayton Ave.
St. Paul, MN 55102
(612) 227-6543

Mississippi Cemetery Assoc.
Coahoma County Memorial
Gardens
P. O. Box 643
Clarksdale, MS 38614
(601) 624-8951

Associated Cemeteries of Missouri
Valhalla Cemetery
7600 St. Charles Rd.
St. Louis, MO 64133
(314) 721-4900

Montana Cemetery Assoc.
Sunset Memorial Gardens
P. O. Box 666
Lewiston, MT 59457
(408) 538-9281

Nebraska Cemetery Assoc.
Hillcrest Memorial Park
5701 Center St.
Omaha, NB 68106
(402) 556-2500

New Hampshire Cemetery Assoc.
Mrs. James Donovan
Exeter, NH 03833
(603) 772-2133

New Jersey Cemetery Assoc.
Eglington Cemetery Memorial
Gardens
P. O. Box 75
Clarksboro, NJ 08020
(609) 423-0165

New Mexico Cemetery Assoc.
Gate of Heaven Cemetery
7500 Los Angeles Blvd., N. E.
Albuquerque, NM 87113
(505) 898-4600

New York State Assoc. of Cemeteries
101 Park Ave.
New York, NY 10017
(212) 685-5917

Cemetery Assoc. of Western New
York
White Haven Memorial Park
210 Marsh Rd.
Pittsford, NY 14534
(716) 586-5250

North Carolina Cemetery Assoc.
Carolina Memorial Park
P. O. Box 3257, Wilmar Park
Concord, NC 28035
(704) 786-2161

Central Ohio Cemetery Assoc.
Green Lawn Cemetery Assoc.
P. O. Box 23071, Central
Point Sta.
Columbus, OH 43223
(614) 444-1123

Ohio Assoc. of Cemetery Superintendents and Officials
Cedar Hill Cemetery
275 N. Cedar St.
Newark, OH 43055
(614) 345-4310

Ohio Assoc. of Cemeteries
Mansfield Memorial Park
1507 Park Ave., W.
Mansfield, OH 44906
(419) 529-4433

Ohio Cemetery Executives Assoc.
Crown Hill Cemetery Assoc.
8592 Darrow Rd.
Twinsburg, OH 44087
(216) 524-3511

Oklahoma Cemeteries Assoc.
Resthaven Memorial Gardens
P. O. Box 278
Shawnee, OK 74801
(405) 273-3345

Oregon Cemetery Assoc.
Lincoln Memorial Park
10500 S. E. Mt. Scott Blvd.
Portland, OR 97266
(503) 771-1117

Cemetery Assoc. of Pennsylvania
Resurrection Cemetery
Rt. #3, P. O. Box 38

Harrisburg, PA 17112
(717) 545-4205

Keystone States [Pennsylvania]
Assoc. of Cemeteries
George Washington Memorial
Park
Stenton Ave. & Butler Pike
Plymouth Meeting, PA 19462
(215) 828-1417

South Carolina Cemetery Assoc.,
Inc.
Mount Pleasant Memorial
Gardens
P. O. Box 218
Mount Pleasant, SC 29464
(803) 884-9041 or 884-9544

Cemetery Assoc. of Tennessee
Lynnhurst Cemetery
P. O. Box 5324
Knoxville, TN 37918
(615) 689-2120

Texas Cemeteries Assoc.
Restland Memorial Park
P. O. Box 31000
Dallas, TX 75231
(214) 235-7111

Utah State Cemetery and Memorial Park Assoc.
Provo City Cemetery
610 S. State St.
Provo, UT 84601
(801) 373-9599

Virginia Cemetery Assoc.
Princess Anne Memorial Park
1110 Great Neck Rd.
Virginia Beach, VA 23454
(703) 340-7311

Washington Interment Assoc.
Sunset Memorial Gardens
P. O. Box 90
Richland, WA 99352
(509) 943-1114

West Virginia Cemetery Assoc.
Forest Lawn Cemetery
P. O. Box 268
Logan, WV 25601
(304) 752-7225

Assoc. of Southeastern Wisconsin Cemetery Officials
Pinelawn Memorial Park
10700 W. Capitol Dr.
Milwaukee, WI 53222
(312) 562-3812

Wisconsin Cemetery Officials
Riverside Cemetery
712 N. Owaissa St.
Appleton, WI 54911
(414) 733-5629

Metropolitan Cemeteries

Metropolitan Chicago Cemetery
 Officials
John J. Neimeyer
301 Chicago Ave.
Evanston, IL 60202

Greater Cincinnati Assoc. of
 Cemetery Superintendents
 and Officials
Oak Hill Cemetery
11200 Princeton Pike
Cincinnati, OH 45246
(513) 771-7681

Greater Cleveland Cemetery
 Assoc.
Brooklyn Heights Cemetery
4700 Broadview Rd.
Cleveland, OH 44109
(216) 351-1476

Greater Detroit Metropolitan
 Cemetery Assoc.
Forest Lawn Cemetery
11851 Van Dyke Ave.
Detroit, MI 42834
(313) 921-6960

Assoc. of Cemetery Officials of
 Metropolitan District of
 New York City
Washington Cemetery
Bay Parkway and McDonald
 Ave.
Brooklyn, NY 11230
(212) ES 7-8690

Cemetery Assoc. of Philadelphia
 and Vicinity
Northwood Cemetery
15th and Haines St.
Philadelphia, PA 19126
(215) HA 4-4996

Cemetery Management Assoc. of
 Greater St. Louis
Valhalla Cemetery
7600 St. Charles Rd.
St. Louis, MO 63133
(314) 721-4900

Twin City Cemetery Assoc.
 [Minneapolis and St. Paul]
Crystal Lake Cemetery
Penn and Dowling Aves., N.
Minneapolis, MN 55412
(612) 521-7619

Canada

Cemetery Assoc. of British
 Columbia
Gardens of Gethsemani
15800 - 32nd Avenue
Surrey, B.C. V4B 4Z5
(604) 531-2141

Ontario Assoc. of Cemeteries
 and Crematoria
York Cemetery
101 Senlac Rd.
Willowdale, Ont. M2N 5S7
(416) 221-3334

5. TRADE JOURNALS

ACMA Coordinator
American Certified Morticians Assoc.
35 N. Arroyo Parkway
Pasadena, CA
(213) 796-2262
Monthly

AFDS Bulletin
Associated Funeral Directors Service
7405 Manchester Blvd.
St. Louis, MO 63143
(314) 781-2060
Quarterly

The American Cemetery
Paramount Bldg.
1501 Broadway
New York, NY 10036
(212) 279-3322
Monthly; ed. by Charles Kates, on all aspects of cemetery management including pre-need sales.

American Funeral Director
Kates-Boylston Publications, Inc.
1501 Broadway
New York, NY 10036
(212) 279-3322
Monthly; of interest to funeral directors and people in allied fields, including funeral supplies manufacturers. $8/year; $1/single copies.

The Bulletin
National Selected Morticians
1616 Central St.
Evanston, IL 60201
(312) GR 5-3414
Quarterly; three of the four annual issues contain original articles on subjects relating to funeral service and reprints of speeches made at NSM meetings. The fourth pre-convention issue contains articles and detailed information on the annual meeting program.

CAFMS News Bulletin
    Continental Association of Funeral and Memorial Societies
    Suite 1100, 1828 L St., N.W.
    Washington, DC 20036
    (202) 293-4821
        Bimonthly news of member memorial societies, the funeral
        industry, the reform movement, new ideas and announcements
        of meetings. Free to members.

CAFMS Newsletter
    Continental Association of Funeral and Memorial Societies
    Suite 1100, 1828 L. St., N.W.
    Washington, DC 20036
    (202) 293-4821
        Quarterly

California Co-op Leadership
    Associated Cooperatives
    4801 Central Ave.
    Richmond, CA 94804
    (414) 526-0440
        Monthly, Oct. through May; ed. by Fred Nora.

Canadian Funeral Director
    1658 Victoria Park Ave., Suite 4
    Scarboro, Ont. M1R 1P7
    (416) 755-7050
        Published monthly, except August, by Peter Perry, editor/
        publisher. 1700 readers. $10/year; $12/year U.S. and
        foreign. Technical articles on all phases of funeral service;
        association and general Canadian news and recent trends in
        other countries.

Casket & Sunnyside
    [as of 1975 known as C & S]
    274 Madison Ave.
    New York, NY 10016
    (212) 685-8310
        104-year-old publication; billed as the authority of the funeral
        service/cemetery industry, treating all aspects of both pro-
        fessions; feature articles of interest to directors, embalmers
        and cemeterians with special focus on business, legal, and
        technical problems, planning new funeral homes, redesigning
        present facilities, new trends and past histories of embalm-
        ing and restorative art, public relations, the opening of new
        cemeteries, building of mausoleums, office buildings, chapels.
        Quarterly listing of concrete vault manufacturers. $10/year;
        $10.50/year Canada; $15/year foreign.

The Catholic Cemetery
    National Catholic Cemetery Conference
    710 N. River Rd.
    Des Plaines, IL 60016
    (312) 824-8131

Monthly; informative, detailed articles, relative to all phases
of cemetery administration and operation, contributed by members of the conference. Subscription by membership only;
price included in annual dues. Complete index of all issues
available on request for $.25.

The Cemeterian
Journal of the American Cemetery Assoc.
250 E. Broad St.
Columbus, OH 43215
(614) 221-6829
Monthly; all phases of cemetery management, including tips
on service, sales, maintenance, office management, recommended record keeping, forms, legislation, new products and
services.

Champion Expanding Encyclopedia of Mortuary Practice
The Champion Co.
400 Harrison
Springfield, OH 45501
(513) 324-5681

CMA Newsletter
Casket Manufacturers Assoc. of America
708 Church St.
Evanston, IL 60201
(312) 866-8383
Monthly

Concrete Vault Directory
c/o Casket & Sunnyside
274 Madison Ave.
New York, NY 10016
(212) 685-8310
Directory is inserted in four issues (Feb., May, Aug., and
Nov.) of C & S each year.

Crosswind
Curt DeBaun, Jr., editor
1729 South Eighth St.
Terre Haute, IN 47802
Monthly; official publication of the Flying Funeral Directors
of America. Articles of special interest to members, announce-
ments of upcoming events, and "a clearing house of information and a forum for exchange of opinion and ideas."

Cryonics Reports
Cryonics Society of New York
306 Washington Ave.
Brooklyn, NY 11205
(212) 638-5797

De-Ce-Co Magazine

Dodge Chemical Co.
165 Rindge Ave. Ext.
Cambridge, MA 02140
(617) 661-0500

The Director
National Funeral Directors Assoc.
135 West Wells St.
Milwaukee, WI 53202
(414) 276-2500
Monthly; official publication of the NFDA, containing news
and educational articles on funeral service and business aspects
of the profession.

The Dodge Magazine
Dodge Chemical Co.
165 Rindge Ave. Ext.
Cambridge, MA 02140
(617) 661-0500
Dedicated to "professional progress in funeral service"; con-
tributing editors are specialists in embalming, cosmetology,
preparation room planning, research, advertising, and grief
therapy and counseling.

Funeral Director
57 Doughty St.
London W. C. 1
01-242-9388
Official review of the National Association of Funeral Directors, London, England.

Funeral Service
Trade Periodical Co.
434 S. Wabash Ave.
Chicago, IL 60605
(312) 922-8167
Bi-monthly; business aspects of funeral service with features
on how to solve problems; advancement; modernization; and
growth.

Funeral Service Abstracts
Renamed Thanatology Abstracts (q. v.) in 1975.

Funeral Service Journal
Hillingdon Press
Uxbridge, Middlesex
England

The Guide
Guild of American Funeral Directors
P. O. Box 456
San Juan Capistrano, CA 92675
(714) 830-5723
Six per year

Ideas Today: A Journal of Contemporary Funeral Service Management
   Techniques
   Technical and Professional Services, Inc.
   P. O. Box 5547
   Kansas City, MO 64109
   (816) 753-4943
      Bi-monthly; professional interest material including everything
      from embalming chemistry to professional management advice.

IFTA Bulletin
   International Federation of Thanatopractic Associations
   62, av. du Capitaine-Glarner
   93-Saint-Ouen-France
   (1) 255-40-34
   Quarterly

The Jewish Funeral Director
   1668 Beacon St.
   Brookline, MA 02146
   (617) 232-9300
      Quarterly; official publication of the Jewish Funeral Directors
      of America, Inc., published in "the interests of all Jewish
      funeral directors in the United States and Canada." Articles
      and features on contemporary news, reprints of trade interest.

Journal of Thanatology
   Foundation of Thanatology
   630 W. 168th St.
   New York, NY 10032
   Six issues per year. $12/US; $13.50/Canada; $16/all other.

Mid-Continent Mortician
   6700 Penn Ave. South
   Minneapolis, MN 55423
   (612) 861-3403
      Monthly; local, regional, and national news and articles on
      funeral service in mid-America.

The Modern Crematist
   Lancaster, PA
      Published by M. L. Davis and W. U. Hensel, 1886-89. One
      of the early pro-cremation journals; good arguments for and
      good rebuttals to those against.

Monument Builder News
   Monument Builders of North America
   1612 Central St.
   Evanston, IL 60201
   (312) 869-2031
      Montly; published in the interest of finer monuments and public
      memorials; treats all aspects of the memorial industry with
      features and articles on contemporary news; special reference
      to retail, wholesale, manufacturing, and supply aspects. $10/
      year; free to members of the MBNA.

Monumental News-Review
   147-1/2 N. Union St.
   Olean, NY 14760
   (716) 372-6627
      Monthly; national directory for monument and related industries,
      including regular features such as obituary record, classified
      advertising, index to advertisers, letters to editor, index to
      directory, monument industry directory, calendar of State and
      district meetings, and features and articles of special interest
      to quarriers, manufacturers, and suppliers.

Morticians of the Southwest
   Katherine Farrell, editor/publisher
   3700 Executive Blvd.
   Mesquite, TX 75149
   (214) 285-4062

Mortuary Management
   R. A. Ebeling, man. dir.
   810 S. Robertson Blvd.
   Los Angeles, CA 90035
   (213) 655-9344
      Monthly (except July); business magazine for funeral directors
      and associated manufacturers and jobbers of funeral products,
      supplies, and mortuary equipment. $8/year; $10/Canada
      and foreign, $.85 single copies.

National Cremation Magazine
   15300 Ventura Blvd., Suite 302
   Sherman Oaks, CA 91403
   (213) 981-7272
      Quarterly; official publication of the Cremation Association
      of America since 1965. Current trade news plus special
      interest articles, some historical features, announcements of
      conventions, etc. $4.50/year.

National Funeral Director and Embalmer
   734 W. 79th St.
   Chicago, IL 60620
      Official publication of the National Funeral Directors and
      Morticians Assoc.

National Funeral Service Journal
   210 E. Ohio St.
   Chicago, IL

National Selected Morticians Bulletin
   1616 Central St.
   Evanston, IL 60201
   (312) 475-3414

The New England Funeral Director
    Massachusetts Funeral Directors Assoc.
    Suite 1006, 294 Washington St.
    Boston, MA 02108
    (617) 426-2670
        Published in conjunction with the Maine, New Hampshire,
        Vermont, Connecticut, and Rhode Island Funeral Directors
        Associations. $2/annual for members, included in annual
        dues; $7/non-member; $1 single issue.

Northeast Funeral Director
    Leonard M. Ashenbrand, man. ed.
    919 Eastern Ave.
    Malden, MA 02148
    (617) 324-5022
        Monthly; personal, association, and trade news of interest
        to funeral directors and industry people.

Omega
    Greenwood Press, Inc.
    51 Riverside Ave.
    Westport, CT 06880
    (203) 226-3571
        Quarterly; international journal for the study of dying, be-
        reavement, suicide and other "deadly behavior." $20/year.

Pharos
    The Cremation Society
    London
        Official publication of the cremation movement in England
        and abroad, 1934- .

Professional Embalmer
    The Undertakers Glove and Specialty Co.
    7609 W. Adison
    Chicago, IL
    (312) 625-5175

Southern Cemetery
    John W. Yopp, Jr., ed.
    P.O. Box 7368
    Atlanta, GA 30309
    (404) 881-9780
        Six per year

The Southern Funeral Director
    John W. Yopp, Jr., ed./pub.
    P.O. Box 7368
    Atlanta, GA 30309
    (404) 881-9780
        Monthly

Thanatology Abstracts
   Alan R. Liss
   150 Fifth Ave.
   New York, NY
   (212) 924-5440
      Formerly: <u>Funeral Service Abstracts</u> (name changed in 1975).
   Summarizes selected periodical entries. Annual since 1965.

6. MEMORIAL SOCIETIES (see also Appendix 7)

Memorial societies or associations are voluntary groups of people who have joined in order to obtain simple, economic funerals for members by helping them to make pre-need arrangements with crematoria, funeral homes or organizations accepting body donations. They are not in funeral service and do not conduct funerals. Their activities include screening member societies; publishing and disseminating information to the general public on methods of reducing funeral costs and to bequeath bodies for medical, educational, or scientific purposes; providing guidance to members to achieve their purposes; encouraging the formation of new societies and reciprocity and an exchange of information between member societies.

The national societies in the U.S. and Canada work closely together and their membership is reciprocal:

Continental Assoc. of Funeral &
  Memorial Societies, Inc.
Suite 1100
1828 L Street, N.W.
Washington, DC 20036
(202) 293-4821

Memorial Society Assoc. of
  Canada
5326 Ada Blvd.
Edmonton, Alberta T5W 4N7

Member societies in the U.S. and Canada are listed below. Membership fees range generally from $10 to $15; in some societies $5 or $20. Minimum costs for immediate cremation with funeral home services in Canada range from $125 to $175 in most cases; $175 to $250 in larger cities. In the U.S. the cost is generally higher, the majority in the $180 to $250 range. For specific information, contact nearest society or the national association. New England states are represented by societies within each state as well as by the Memorial Society of New England, which is listed under Massachusetts.

United States

ALASKA

Cook Inlet Memorial Society
P.O. Box 2414
Anchorage 99510

ARIZONA

Memorial Society of Prescott
P. O. Box 199
Prescott 86301
(579) 969-2252 or (602) 445-7794

Valley Memorial Society
6808 N. 10th Pl.
Scottsdale 85014
(602) 274-8416 or 949-8857

Tucson Memorial Society
P. O. Box 4566
Tucson 85717
(602) 326-9341 or 793-1121

ARKANSAS

Northwest Arkansas Memorial
    Society
1227 S. Maxwell
Fayetteville 72701
(501) 442-5580
(50-mile radius)

CALIFORNIA

Humboldt Funeral Society
666 Eleventh St.
Arcata 95521
(707) 822-1321

Bay Area Funeral Society
P. O. Box 264
Berkeley 94701
(415) 841-6653
(Alameda, Contra Costa, Marin,
Napa, San Francisco, Sonoma
counties)

Kern Memorial Society
Box 5674
China Lake 93555
(805) 399-7291 (Bakersfield)
(714) 446-4408 (Ridgecrest)
(Kern, Southern Inyo, Northern
Los Angeles counties)

Valley Memorial Society
Box 1823
Fresno 93717
(209) 227-3168

(Fresno, Kings, Madera, Mersed,
Mariposa, Tulare counties

Tri-County Memorial Funeral
    Society
Box 114
Midway City 92655
(714) 962-1917
(Orange, Riverside, San Bernar-
dino counties; not presently member of Continental Assoc.)

Los Angeles Funeral Society
P. O. Box 9456
North Hollywood 91609
(213) 663-5005 or 877-1474
(Los Angeles County)

Peninsula Funeral Society
168 California Ave.
Palo Alto 94306
(415) 321-2109
(San Mateo, Santa Clara, Santa
Cruz, Monterey counties)

Sacramento Valley Memorial
    Society, Inc.
P. O. Box 502
Sacramento 95803
(916) 451-4641
(Nevada, Placer, Sacramento,
San Joaquin, El Dorado, Glenn,
Shasta, Solano, Stanislaus, Teha-
ma, Trinity, Amador, Butte,
Calaveras, Colusa, Yolo, Yuba
counties)

San Diego Memorial Society
P. O. Box 16336
San Diego 92116
(714) 284-1465
(San Diego County)

Central Coast Memorial Society,
    Inc.
P. O. Box 679
San Luis Obispo 93406
(805) 543-5451
(San Luis Obispo, N. Santa
Barbara counties)

Channel Cities Memorial Society
P. O. Box 424

Santa Barbara 93102
(805) 962-4794
(Santa Barbara, Ventura
counties)

COLORADO

The Rocky Mountain Memorial
Society, Inc.
4101 E. Hampden
Denver 80222
(303) 757-3832

CONNECTICUT

Greater New Haven Memorial
Society, Inc.
177 W. Rock Ave.
New Haven 06515
(203) 288-6436 or 387-3353

Council Memorial Society
20 Forest Street
Stamford 06902
(203) 348-2800
(Stamford, Darien, New Canaan,
Greenwich)

Memorial Society of Southwest
Connecticut
71 Hillandale Rd.
Westport 06880
(203) 227-2728

Memorial Society of New England
See under Massachusetts

DELAWARE

Memorial Society of Wilmington
19 Fithian Dr.
New Castle 19720
(302) 328-7110
(not presently member of Continental Assoc.)

DISTRICT OF COLUMBIA

Memorial Society of Metropolitan Washington
16th and Harvard Sts., N.W.
Washington 20009
(703) 532-3345

FLORIDA

Memorial Society of S.W. Florida
P.O. Box 1953
Ft. Meyers 33902
(813) 995-6649 or 334-4272
(50-mile radius)

Memorial Society of Alachua
County
P.O. Box 13677
Gainesville 32604
(904) 376-5890 or 376-7073
(and adjacent counties)

Memorial Society of Jacksonville
6915 Holiday Rd. North
Jacksonville 32216
(904) 724-3766

Tampa Memorial Society, Inc.
Rt. 1 Box 253
Land O'Lakes 33539
(813) 996-3034
(100-mile radius)

Community Funeral Society
P.O. Box 7422
Ludlam Branch
Miami 33155
(305) 667-3697
(Dade County)

Orange County Memorial Society
2121 Mt. Vernon St.
Orlando 32803
(305) 894-7029
(Brevard, Osceola, Seminole, and
Orange counties)

Memorial Society of Sarasota
P.O. 5683
Sarasota 33579
(813) 958-1684

Suncoast-Tampa Bay Memorial
Society
P.O. Box 12231
St. Petersburg 33733
(813) 958-2896

Funeral and Memorial Society of
Leon County
Rt. 9, Box 981
Tallahassee 32303

Palm Beach Funeral Society
P. O. Box 2065
West Palm Beach 33402
(305) 833-8936 or 732-0825
(Palm Beach, Martin, St.
Lucie, Indian River counties)

GEORGIA

Memorial Society of Georgia
1911 Cliff Valley Way, N. E.
Atlanta 30329
(404) 634-2896

HAWAII

Honolulu Funeral and Memorial
Society of Hawaii
P. O. Box 11131
Honolulu 96814
(808) 595-6681
(entire state)

ILLINOIS

Carbondale Area Memorial
Society
c/o Lyman Dennis
Ten Oaks, Apt. 29, Rt. 2
Cartersville 62918
(618) 985-6636

Champaign County Memorial
Society
309 W. Green St.
Champaign 61801
(217) 328-3337

Chicago Memorial Association
59 E. Van Buren St.
Chicago 60605
(312) 939-0678
(most of Illinois and northwestern
Indiana)

    McLean County Branch
    1613 E. Emerson
    Bloomington 61701
    (309) 828-0235

Fox Valley Funeral Association
785 W. Highland
Elgin 60120

(312) 695-5265
(not presently member of Continental Assoc.)

Northern Illinois Memorial Society
1721 Cumberland St.
Rockford 61103
(815) 968-5554

INDIANA

Bloomington Memorial Society
2120 North Fee Lane
Bloomington 47401
(812) 332-3695

Northeastern Indiana Memorial
Society
306 West Rudisill Blvd.
Ft. Wayne 46807
(219) 745-4756 or 456-3858

Indianapolis Memorial Society
5805 E. 56th St.
Indianapolis   46226
(317) 545-6005

Greater Lafayette Memorial
Society
P. O. Box 2155
W. Lafayette 47906
(317) 463-5634

IOWA

Burlington Memorial Society
625 N. 6th St.
Burlington 52601
(317) 463-5634

Blackhawk Memorial Society
3707 Eastern Ave.
Davenport 52807
(319) 326-0479
(Rock Island, Moline, Ill. , also)

KENTUCKY

Lexington Memorial Society
3121 Lamar Dr.
Lexington 40502
(606) 266-0648
(Greater Lexington)

Greater Louisville Funeral Society
805 S. 4th St.
Louisville 40203
(502) 585-5119 or 543-6513

LOUISIANA

Memorial Society of Greater
Baton Rouge
8470 Goodwood Ave.
Baton Rouge 70806
(504) 926-2291

MAINE

Memorial Society of the Pine
Tree State
425 Congress St.
Portland 04111
(not presently member of Continental Assoc.)

Memorial Society of New England
See under Massachusetts

MARYLAND

Greater Baltimore Memorial
Society
16 Cross Kings Rd. Apt. C
Baltimore 21210
(301) 685-2330 or 363-1087

Howard Country Memorial
Foundation
Interfaith Center at Wilde Lake
Village Green
Columbia 21043
(301) 730-7920 or 730-7566

Maryland Suburban Memorial
Society
c/o Bruce Bowman
Laurel Hill 20770
(301) 474-6468

Rossmoor Memorial Society of
Silver Spring
3389 S. Leisure World Blvd.
Silver Spring 20906
(301) 598-6177

Greater Baltimore Memorial
Society
709 Thornwood Ct.
Towson 21204
(301) 828-7009

MASSACHUSETTS

Memorial Society of New England
25 Monmouth St.
Brookline 02146
(617) 731-2073
(serves all New England)

Quincy Preplanned Funeral Society
1479 Hampshire St.
Quincy 62301
(617) 885-3375

Springfield Memorial Society, Inc.
P. O. Box 2821
Springfield 01101
(413) 567-7618

MICHIGAN

Memorial Advisory & Planning
Service
2023 W. Stadium Blvd.
Ann Arbor 48103
(313) 769-9830

Greater Detroit Memorial Society
4605 Cass Ave.
Detroit 48201
(313) 833-9107 and 341-4505
(Macomb, Oakland, Wayne
counties)

Greater Kalamazoo Memorial
Society
c/o First Baptist Church
315 W. Michigan
Kalamazoo 49006
(616) 345-2195

Lansing Area Memorial Planning
Society
855 Grove St.
E. Lansing 48823
(517) 489-5482 or 351-4081

Manistee Area Memorial and
Co-op Society
P. O. Box 276
Manistee 49660
(not presently member of Con-
tinental Assoc.)

MINNESOTA

Minnesota Memorial Society
900 Mt. Curve Ave.
Minneapolis 55403
(612) 824-2440
(entire state)

MISSOURI

Greater Kansas City Memorial
Society
4500 Warwick Blvd.
Kansas City 64111
(816) 531-1740
(100-mile radius)

Memorial & Planned Funeral
Society
5007 Waterman Blvd.
St. Louis 63108
(314) 361-0595

MONTANA

Memorial Society of Montana
P. O. Box 2084
Billings 59102
(406) 656-6512

Five Valleys Burial-Memorial
Assoc.
401 University Ave.
Missoula 59801
(406) 549-5034

NEBRASKA

Midland Memorial Society
3114 Harney St.
Omaha 68131
(402) 345-6800 or 345-3039

NEVADA

Western Nevada Funeral Society

Box 8413 University Sta.
Reno 89507
(Reno, Sparks, Carson City,
vicinity)

NEW HAMPSHIRE

Memorial Society of New Hampshire
274 Pleasant St.
Concord 03301
(603) 224-0291

NEW JERSEY

Raritan Valley Memorial Society
176 Tices Lane
East Brunswick 08816
(201) 246-9620 or 572-1470
(Middlesex County, adjacent areas
in Somerset County)

Memorial Association of Monmouth County
1475 W. Front St.
Lincroft 07738
(201) 741-8092
(Monmouth, Ocean counties)

Suburban Memorial Society
516 Prospect St.
Maplewood 07040
(201) 694-0920
(10-mile radius in Essex County)

Memorial Society of Essex
67 Church St.
Montclair 07042
(201) 746-9352

Morris Memorial Society
153 Farbes Hill Rd.
Boonton 07005
(201) 539-5340
(Morris, Sussex, Warren
counties)

Central Memorial Society
156 Forest Ave.
Paramus 07652
(201) 265-5910
(Bergen, Hudson, Passaic, Sussex, Warren counties)

Memorial Society of Plainfield
P. O. Box 307
Plainfield 07061
(Somerset and Union counties)

Princeton Memorial Association
P. O. Box 1154
Princeton 08540
(609) 924-1604 or 924-5525
(Atlantic, Burlington, Camden,
Cape May, Cumberland, Glou-
cester, Hunterdon, Mercer,
Salem counties)

NEW MEXICO

Memorial Association of Central
    New Mexico
P. O. Box 11143
Albuquerque 87112
(505) 345-1801

Northern New Mexico Funeral
    and Memorial Society
P. O. Box 178
Los Alamos 87544
(505) 662-9420 or 662-2346

NEW YORK

Albany Area Memorial Society
405 Washington Ave.
Albany 12206
(518) 463-7135
(Albany, Schenectady, Rensselaer
counties)

Southern Tier Memorial Society,
    Inc.
183 Riverside Dr.
Binghamton 13905
(607) 729-1641

Brooklyn Memorial Society
124 Henry St.
Brooklyn 11201
(212) 624-3770
(and surrounding areas)

Greater Buffalo Memorial
    Society
695 Elmwood Ave.
Buffalo 14222

(716) 885-2136 or 884-1221
(Erie County)

Queens Memorial Society
Box 53
College Union, Queens College
Flushing 11307

Ithaca Memorial Society, Inc.
P. O. Box 134
Ithaca 14850
(607) 272-5476 or 273-1161
(Chemung, Chenango, Cortland,
Delaware, Otsego, Schyler,
Steuben, Tioga, Tompkins coun-
ties)

The Community Funeral Society
40 East 35th St.
New York 10016
(212) 683-4988
(all five boroughs)

Consumers Memorial Society,
    Inc.
465 Grand St.
New York 10002
(212) 673-3900

Memorial Society of the River-
    side Church
490 Riverside Dr.
New York 10027
(212) 749-7000
(50-mile radius)

Memorial Society of Greater
    Oneonta
12 Ford Ave.
Oneonta 13820
(607) 432-3491

Rockland County Memorial Society
Box 461
Pamona 10970
(914) 354-2917 or 634-7167

Memorial Society of Long Island
Box 303
Port Washington 11050
(516) 334-5104 or 767-6026
(Long Island, outside Brooklyn)

Mid-Hudson Memorial Society
P.O. Box 362
Poughkeepsie 12602
(914) 454-4164 or 454-4506
(Putnam, Dutchess, Columbia,
Greene, Ulster, Orange Sul-
livan counties)

Rochester Memorial Society, Inc.
220 Winton Rd. South
Rochester 14610
(716) 271-9070 or 473-0778
(Genesee, Livingston, Monroe,
Ontario, Orleans, Seneca, Wayne,
Yales counties)

Syracuse Memorial Society, Inc.
P.O. Box 67
Syracuse 13214
(315) 474-6496
(Onondaga, Cayuga, Cortland,
Madison, Oswego counties)

The Funeral Planning Association
of Westchester
Rosedale Ave. and Sycamore Lane
White Plains 10605
(914) 946-1660
(Westchester County)

NORTH CAROLINA

The Blue Ridge Memorial Society
P.O. Box 2601
Asheville 28801
(704) 645-7330 or 254-7255
(Western N.C.)

Triangle Memorial & Funeral
Society
P.O. Box 1223
Chapel Hill 27514
(919) 942-4994
(Chapel Hill, Durham, Raleigh)

Charlotte Memorial Society
234 N. Sharon Amity
Charlotte 28211
(704) 597-2346

Piedmont Memorial & Funeral
Society
Box 16192
Greensboro 27406

(919) 732-8605

OHIO

Scotland Country Funeral & Memorial Society
Rt. 1, Box M-46
Laurinburg 28352
(919) 276-6240

Canton Akron Memorial Society
3300 Morewood Rd.
Akron 44313
(216) 492-3850 or 836-2206

Greater Cincinnati Memorial
Society
536 Linton St.
Cincinnati 45219
(513) 281-1564 or 761-2552
(and northern Ky.)

Cleveland Memorial Society
21600 Shaker Blvd.
Cleveland 44122
(216) 751-5515
(30-mile radius)

Memorial Society of the Columbus Area
93 W. Weisheimer Rd.
Columbus 43214
(614) 267-4946 or 888-4894

Dayton Memorial Society
665 Salem Ave.
Dayton 45406
(513) 274-5890 or 256-3355

Memorial Society of Northwest
Ohio
2210 Collingwood Blvd.
Toledo 43620
(419) 475-4812

Funeral & Memorial Society of
SW Ohio
66 North Mulburry St.
Wilmington 45117
(513) 382-2349

Yellow Springs Branch Memorial
Society of Columbus Area
250 Orton Dr.

Yellow Springs 45387
(513) 767-2011

OKLAHOMA

Memorial Society of Eastern
    Oklahoma
2952 S. Peoria
Tulsa 74114
(918) 743-3194

OREGON

Oregon Memorial Association
6815 Southeast 122nd Dr.
Portland 97236
(503) 285-1187 or 761-1246
(and southern Wash.)

PENNSYLVANIA

Lehigh Valley Memorial Society
701 Lechauweki Ave.
Bethlehem 18015
(215) 866-7652

The Thanatopsis Society of Erie
P. O. Box 3495
Erie 16508
(814) 864-9300 or 725-4208

Memorial Society of Greater
    Harrisburg
1280 Clover Lane
Harrisburg 17113
(717) 564-4761 or 545-8406
(central Pa.)

Memorial Society of Greater
    Philadelphia
2125 Chestnut
Philadelphia 19103
(215) 563-3980 or 742-3764
(southeastern Pa. , southern
N. J.)

Pittsburgh Memorial Society
605 Morewood Ave.
Pittsburgh 15213
(412) 621-8008

RHODE ISLAND

Memorial Society of New England

See under Massachusetts

SOUTH CAROLINA

Memorial Society of Charleston
2319 Bluefish Circle
Charleston 29412
(803) 795-4429

Clemson Funeral Society
P. O. Box 1132
Clemson 29631
(Pickens, Oconee, Anderson
counties)

TENNESSEE

East Tennessee Memorial Society
P. O. Box 10507
Knoxville 37919
(615) 523-2326
(Knoxville, Oak Ridge, adjacent
areas)

Memphis Memorial Society
P. O. Box 17590
Memphis 38117
(901) 526-8631
(Shelby County; not presently
member of Continental Assoc.)

The Middle Tennessee Memorial
    Society
1808 Woodmont Blvd.
Nashville 37215
(615) 322-2136

TEXAS

Austin Memorial & Burial Information Society
5410 Aurora Dr.
Austin 78756
(512) 452-6168

Dallas Area Memorial Society
4015 Normandy
Dallas 75205
(214) 528-3990 or 351-4807
(Dallas, Ft. Worth, surrounding
areas)

Lubbock Area Memorial Society
2412 13th St.
Lubbock 79401
(806) 763-4391

San Antonio Memorial Society
516 Maverick Bldg.
San Antonio 78205

UTAH

Utah Memorial Association
580 W. 13th St.
Salt Lake City 84115
(801) 484-7671 or 363-4541

VERMONT

Memorial Society of New England
See under Massachusetts

VIRGINIA

Mt. Vernon Memorial Society
1909 Windmill Lane
Alexandria 22307
(703) 765-5950 or (301) 474-6988

Memorial Society of Arlington
4444 Arlington Blvd.
Arlington 22204
(703) 892-6524

Memorial Planning Society of the Piedmont
717 Rugby Rd.
Charlottesville 22903
(703) 293-3323 or 293-3133
(west-central Va.)

Fairfax Memorial Society
P. O. Box 128
Oakton 22124
(703) 281-4230
(Fairfax County)

WASHINGTON

People's Memorial Association
2366 Eastlake Ave. East
Seattle 98102
(206) 325-0489
(western Wash.)

Spokane Memorial Association, Inc.
P. O. Box 14701
Spokane 99214
(509) 926-2933

Tacoma Memorial Society
5210 South Alder
Tacoma 98409
(206) 472-9442
(not presently member of Continental Assoc.)

WISCONSIN

Madison Memorial Society
P. O. Box 4033
Madison 53711
(608) 271-7508 or 271-4052
(south-central Wis.)

Planned Funeral Society of Wisconsin
P. O. Box 4444
Milwaukee 53207
(414) 771-3797

Funeral & Memorial Society of Racine & Kenosha
625 College Ave.
Racine 53403
(414) 634-0659

Regional Memorial Federations

California Federation of Memorial and Funeral Societies
P. O. Box 502
Sacramento 95803
(916) 451-4641

Funeral and Memorial Societies
of Greater Washington
16th and Harvard Sts., N.W.
Washington, D.C. 20009
(202) 332-5266

Canadian Memorial Societies

ALBERTA

Calgary Co-op Memorial Society
P. O. Box 6443
Sta. D.
Calgary T2P 2E1
(403) 243-5088 or 289-1944

Memorial Society of Edmonton
& District
5326 Ada Blvd.
Edmonton T5W 4N7
(403) 477-6864 or 479-3488

Memorial Society of Grande
Prairie
P. O. Box 471
Grande Prairie T8V 3A7

Memorial Society of Southern
Alberta
634 15th St. S
Lethbridge T1J 2Z8
(403) 328-6335

BRITISH COLUMBIA

Memorial Society of British
Columbia
Rm. 410, 207 W. Hastings
Vancouver V6B 1J3
(604) 688-6256

MANITOBA

Funeral Planning & Memorial
Society of Manitoba
c/o Dr. J. D. Campbell
183 Brock St.
Winnipeg R3N 0Y7
(204) 452-6007

NEWFOUNDLAND

Memorial & Funeral Planning
Association of Newfoundland
P. O. Box 9183
St. Johns A1A 2X9

NOVA SCOTIA

Greater Halifax Memorial Society
P. O. Box 291, Armdale
Halifax B3L 4K1

ONTARIO

Memorial Society of Guelph
c/o Mrs. Tamara Puthon
51 Franklin Ave.
Guelph N1E 4M6
(519) 822-7430

Hamilton Memorial Society
Box 164
Hamilton L8N 3A2
(416) 549-6385

Memorial Society of Kingston
Box 1081
Kingston K7L 4Y5

Kitchener-Waterloo Memorial
Society
Box 113
Kitchener N2G 3W9
(519) 745-6219

Memorial Society of London
P. O. Box 4595, Sta. C.
London N5W 5J5
(519) 451-7050

Ottawa Memorial Society
P.O. Box 5251
Ottawa K2C 3H5
(613) 825-1594

Toronto Memorial Society
14 Sinton Court
Downsview M3M 1P4
(416) 241-6274

Memorial Society of Thunder
   Bay
Box 501, Sta. F
Thunder Bay P7C 4W4
(807) 683-3051

Memorial Society of Windsor &
   District
P.O. Box 481
Windsor
(519) 969-2252

QUEBEC

Memorial Association of Montreal
P.O. Box 85
Dorison-Vaudreuil J7V 5V8
(514) 455-4670

SASKATCHEWAN

Lloydminster, Vermilion and
   Districts Memorial Society
4729-45th St.
Lloydminster S9V 0H6
(accepted tentatively, awaiting
annual meeting confirmation by
Memorial Society Assoc. of
Canada)

Memorial Society of Saskatchewan
P.O. Box 1846
Saskatoon S7K 3S2

Non-Member Societies (Canadian)

Memorial Society of British
   Columbia
410, 207 West Hastings St.
Vancouver, B.C. V6B 1J3

   Victoria Branch
   Box 685
   Victoria, B.C. V8W 2P9

   Nanaimo Branch
   Box 177
   Nanaimo, B.C.

Niagra Peninsula Memorial So-
   ciety
P.O. Box 181
St. Catharines
Ontario L2R 6S4

7. CO-OP FUNERAL HOMES

Consumer owned and operated burial associations, or mortuaries, with licensed personnel, serve members and non-members. Members receive patronage refunds.

Winneshiek Co-op Burial Assoc.
Decorah, IA 52101

Eddyville Co-op Burial Assoc.
Eddyville, IA 52553

Fremont Co-op Burial Assoc.
Freemont, IA 52561

Co-op Funeral Home
133 S. Main
Sioux Center, IA 51250
(319) 722-0791

Benton & Adjoining Counties
    Co-op Burial Assoc.
Keystone, IA 52249
(319) 442-3315

Garden Chapel Funeral Home
Pella, IA 50219

Sanborn Funeral Home
Box B
Sanborn, IA 51248

Pella Co-op Funeral Home
Sully, IA 50251

Iowa State Federation of Co-op
    Burial Assocs.
c/o Schakel, President
Pella, IA 50219

Freeborn County Funeral Assoc.
Albert Lea, MN

Northland Co-op Mortuary
Cloquet, MN 55720
(218) 879-7184

Sunset Burial Assoc.
Echo, MN 56237
(507) 925-4145

Greenwood Prairie Burial Assoc.
Elgin, MN 55932

Mesabi Funeral Chapel
Hibbing, MN

Kandiyohi-Meeker Co-op Funeral
    Assoc.
Lake Lillian, MN 56253

Minnesota Valley Funeral Home
New Ulm, MN 56073

Tri-County Burial Assoc.
Prinsburg, MN 56281
(612) 978-6805

Range Funeral Home
Virginia, MN 55792
(218) 741-1481

Co-op Funeral Assoc.
311 West Ave.
Tallmadge, OH 44278

Minnehaha Funeral Home
Baltic, SD 17003
(605) 529-5411

Community Funeral Home
Clark, SD 57225

Reedsville Co-op Funeral Assoc.
Reedsville, WI 54230

Fraternal Burial Assoc.
Viborg, SD 57070

The Telophase Society

Removes body, sees to legal details, cremation, and if desired provides a memorial service, for total cost of $250. Operations approved by the Cal. State Attorney General. Membership is $25 for individuals, $40 for couples, $15 for senior citizens and $25 for senior citizen couples. For information, contact:

The Telophase Society
3525 5th Ave.
San Diego, CA 92103
(714) 299-0805

8. BODY DONATION ASSOCIATIONS

As an option to burial or cremation, individuals can donate their bodies to scientific research and their organs for transplants. (Diseased as well as healthy bodies are needed for research.) See Ernest Morgan's Manual of Death Education and Simple Burial (entry 1126) for how to arrange bequeathals; names, addresses, and phone numbers of organizations in need of specific organs; American and Canadian eye-banks; and medical schools which accept bodies, their addresses, phone numbers, degree of need, and distances from which they will pay transportation costs. All medical schools arrange for final disposal; some on request will return the remains or arrange cremation and return ashes.

Eye Bank Association of America
3195 Maplewood Ave.
Winston-Salem, NC 27103
(919) 765-0932
    A network of American eyebanks acts as clearinghouse for matching people needing corneal transplants and donors. Write central agency above for further information

Human Parts Banks of Canada
    Headquarters: 5326 Ada Blvd., Edmunton, Alta T5W 4N7
    Public Relations: Box 34367, Vancouver 9, B.C.

Kidney Foundation of Canada
P.O. Box 422
Montreal 379, Canada
    Volunteer organization seeking donors.

National Kidney Foundation
116 East 27th St.
New York, NY 10016
(212) 889-2210
    Under the Uniform Anatomical Gift Act individuals may donate specified organs for transplants or research without going through difficult legal procedures. Write above for further information.

New England Eye Bank
243 Charles St.
Boston, MA 02114
(617) 523-7900

Though it is not body donation in the sense meant in the organizations immediately above, there is another group with whom one can arrange disposition in the interests of science:

Cryonics Society of New York
306 Washington Ave.
Brooklyn, NY 11205
(212) 638-5797

9. ACCREDITED FUNERAL SERVICE COLLEGES

Following is a list of colleges of funeral service and mortuary science accredited (May 1975) by the Commission of Schools of the American Board of Funeral Service Education, Inc., an agency recognized by the U.S. Commissioner of Education.

American Academy McCallister
    Institute of Funeral Service
229 Park Avenue South
New York, NY 10003
(212) 260-2900
John McAllister, pres.

California College of Mortuary
    Science
1920 Marengo St.
Los Angeles, CA 90033
(213) 221-2144
Melvin D. Hilgenfeld, pres.

Catonsville Community College/
    Mortuary Science Program
800 South Rolling Rd.
Catonsville, MD 21228
(301) 747-3200
William C. Gonce, coord.

Central State University
Department of Funeral Service
    Education
Edmond, OK 73034
(405) 341-2890
John H. Cage, dir.

Cincinnati College of Mortuary
    Science
3200 Reading Road
Cincinnati, OH 45229
(513) 861-3240
George M. Sleichter, dir.

Commonwealth College of
    Sciences

215 Dennis at Baldwin
Houston, TX 77006
(713) 529-3471
Austin Winter, pres.

Dallas Institute of Mortuary
    Science
(and Gupton Jones)
3906 Worth St.
Dallas, TX 75210
(214) 823-6159
Robert P. Kite, pres.

Fayetteville Technical Institute
Funeral Service Education De-
    partment
P.O. Box 5236
Fayetteville, NC 28303
(919) 484-4121
Walter L. Crox, chairman

Forest Park Community College
Dept. of Funeral Service Educa-
    tion
5600 Oakland Ave.
St. Louis, MO 63110
(314) 644-3300
Charles E. Murrell, dir.

Gupton-Jones College of Mortuary
    Science
280 Mt. Zion Rd.
Atlanta, GA 30354
(404) 761-3118
Russell M. Millison, pres.

Hudson Valley Community College
Mortuary Science Program
80 Vanderburgh Ave.
Troy, NY 12180
(518) 283-1100
David Fitzsimmons, mgr.

Indiana College of Mortuary Science
5815 East 38th St.
Indianapolis, IN 46218
(317) 545-5294
Ronald E. Smith, dean

John A. Gupton College
2507 West End Ave.
Nashville, TN 37203
(615) 327-3927
John A. Gupton, pres.

John Tyler Community College
Mortuary Science Program
Chester, VA 23831
(804) 748-6481
John W. Scocklee, dir.

Kentucky School of Mortuary Science
1103 South Second St.
Louisville, KY 40203
(502) 587-1381
John R. Braboy, pres.

McNeese State University
Mortuary Science Curriculum
Lake Charles, LA 70601
(318) 477-2520
William F. Matthews, coord.

Miami-Dade Community College
Dept. of Mortuary Science
11380 N.W. 27th Ave.
Miami, FL 33167
(305) 685-4441
John A. Chew, dir.

Milwaukee Area Technical College
Funeral Service Dept.
1015 N. Sixth St.
Milwaukee, WI 53203
(414) 278-6600

W. E. Breese, dean, business Div.

Mt. Hood Community College
Dept. of Funeral Service Education
26000 S.E. Stark St.
Gresham, OR 97030
(503) 666-1561
Walter K. Thorsell, dir.

New England Institute of Anatomy, Sanitary Science, Embalming and Funeral Directing
656 Beacon St.
Boston, MA 02215
(617) 536-6970
William H. Crawford, dean

Pittsburgh Institute of Mortuary Science
3337 Forbes Ave.
Pittsburgh, PA 15213
(412) 682-0334
William J. Musmanno, dean

San Antonio College
Dept. of Mortuary Science
1300 San Pedro Ave.
San Antonio, TX 78212
(512) 734-7311
J. Byron Starr, dir.

San Francisco College of Mortuary Science
1450 Post St.
San Francisco, CA 94109
(415) 567-0674
Dale W. Sly, pres.

Simmons School of Embalming and Mortuary Science, Inc.
2201 S. Salina St.
Syracuse, NY 13205
(315) 475-5142
Charles F. Hite, dean

Southern Illinois University
Mortuary Science Program
Carbondale, IL 62901
(618) 453-2121
Donald Hertz, faculty supervisor

State University of New York
Agricultural and Technical

College
Div. of Health and Social Science
Dept. of Mortuary Science
Farmingdale, NY 11735
(516) 420-2000
John M. Lieblang, chairman

State University of New York
    Agricultural and Technical
    College
Mortuary Science Dept.
Canton, NY 13617
(315) 386-7011
Boyd Simmons, dir.

University of Minnesota
Dept. of Mortuary Science
114 Vincent Hall
Minneapolis, MN 55455
(612) 373-2851
Robert C. Slater, dir.

Wayne State University
Dept. of Mortuary Science
627 West Alexandrine
Detroit, MI 48201
(313) 577-2424
Walter D. Pool, coord.

Worsham College of Mortuary
    Science, Inc.
515 North Dearborn St.
Chicago, IL 60610
(312) 527-5756
Erwin H. Greenberg, pres.

10. STATE EMBALMING REQUIREMENTS (Dec. 1975)

Alabama	Not required if destination reached within 30 hours, if decomposition precludes it, or if shipment is not by common carrier.
Alaska	Not required.
Arizona	Required if body will cross state lines.
Arkansas	Not required.
California	Required if shipped by common carrier.
Colorado	Required if shipped by common carrier; if body deterioration precludes it, case receptacle must be hermetically sealed.
Connecticut	Required if shipped by common carrier.
Delaware	Not required; if shipped, must be in metal or metal-lined permanently sealed receptacle.
District of Columbia	Requirements of common carriers and state to which the body is shipped prevail.
Florida	Required if shipped by common carrier unless condition prohibits; then in sealed or metal-lined containers.
Georgia	Not required.
Hawaii	Not required.
Idaho	Required if shipped by common carrier.
Illinois	Not required if destination reached within 24 hours.
Indiana	Not required unless death caused by plague, smallpox, leprosy or other specified diseases.
Iowa	Required for shipment unless destination is the anatomical department of school or hospital.

Kansas	Required if shipped by common carrier; not required for private transit within specified distances.
Kentucky	Required if shipped by common carrier unless condition precludes it, then in tightly sealed receptacle.
Louisiana	Not required; hermetically sealed receptacle if death by typhus, plague, smallpox, Asiatic cholera, or yellow fever.
Maine	Required if condition permits; if not, in hermetically sealed container.
Maryland	As per regulations of the State Board of Health and Hygiene.
Massachusetts	Required if death by virulent disease; otherwise, air-tight, sealed container.
Michigan	Required if death by virulent disease; not required if destination reached within 48 hours or if addressed to a medical college.
Minnesota	Required if death by virulent disease; not required if destination reached within 18 hours.
Mississippi	Required if death by virulent disease, shipped out of state, or if disposition is not within 24 hours.
Missouri	Not required if death by non-virulent, non-contagious disease and destination reached within 24 hours.
Montana	Not required if death from non-virulent disease and destination is reached within 24 hours.
Nebraska	Required if death by communicable disease; if condition prohibits, must be sealed in proper container.
Nevada	Not required; hermetically sealed container required if death by dangerous disease.
New Hampshire	Not specified in regulations.
New Jersey	Not required if destination reached within 24 hours.
New Mexico	Required if shipped out of state or if death by specified diseases.

New York   Not specified in regulations.

North Carolina   Required unless condition prohibits; then in
                        sealed outer container.

North Dakota   Not required if destination reached within 24
                        hours, unless death by virulent disease.

Ohio   Not required if destination is a medical col-
                        lege and is reached within 60 hours; if
                        death is not by virulent disease; and des-
                        tination is reached within 24 hours.

Oklahoma   Required.

Oregon   Not required if destination within state reached
                        within 24 hours and death is not by virulent
                        disease.

Pennsylvania   Not required if destination reached within 24
                        hours and death is not by virulent disease.

Rhode Island   Not required if destination reached within 24
                        hours and death is not by virulent disease.

South Carolina   Required if shipped by common carrier unless
                        condition prohibits; then sealed outer case
                        required.

South Dakota   Not specified in regulations.

Tennessee   Required if shipped by common carrier unless
                        condition prohibits; then in hermetically
                        sealed container.

Texas   Required if shipped by common carrier unless
                        condition prohibits; then in hermetically
                        sealed container.

Utah   Required if shipped by common carrier unless
                        condition prohibits; then in hermetically
                        sealed container.

Vermont   Regulations of common carriers prevail.

Virginia   Required if shipped by common carrier unless
                        condition prohibits; then sealed outer case
                        required.

Washington   Not required if final disposition is within 24
                        hours.

Wisconsin   Required if shipped by common carrier unless condition prohibits; then sealed outer case required. Exception: if destination is medical college and is reached within 60 hours.

Wyoming   Not specified in regulations.

11. INDUSTRY CODES OF ETHICS AND PRACTICES

<u>Code of Ethics</u>, National Funeral Directors' Association of the United
States, Inc.

I

As funeral directors, we herewith fully acknowledge our
individual and collective obligations to the public, especially
to those we serve, and our mutual responsibilities for the
proper welfare of the funeral service profession.

II

To the public we pledge: vigilant support of public health
laws; proper legal regulations for the members of our
profession; devotion to high moral and service standards;
conduct befitting good citizens; honesty in all offerings
of service and merchandise, and in all business transactions.

III

To those we serve we pledge: confidential business and
professional relationships; cooperation with the customs of
all religions and creeds; observance of all respect due the
deceased; high standards of competence and dignity in the
conduct of all services; truthful representation of all services and merchandise.

IV

To our profession we pledge: support of high educational
standards and proper licensing laws; encouragement of
scientific research; adherence to sound business practices;
adoption of improved techniques; observance of all rules
of fair competition; maintenance of favorable personnel
relations.

<u>Code of Professional Practices for Funeral Directors</u>, NFDA (origi-
nally adopted Nov. 1965; revised in 1969 and in 1972)

When a death occurs a survivor in the immediate family
or the person or persons who will be responsible for the
funeral of the deceased should be advised to contact their
family funeral director or should direct that said funeral
director be notified. This should be done regardless of

where or when death takes place. The funeral director
then becomes the representative of the family for the
purpose of the funeral arrangements.

When once a funeral director is called by the family or
their representative and as a result of such call removes
the body, he shall provide the necessary services and
merchandise in keeping with the wishes and finances of
the family or their representative.

Before any funeral arrangements are made the funeral
director should determine, if he does not know, who is
the minister, priest or rabbi of the deceased and/or of
the family. The funeral director should ascertain if
such clergyman has been notified of the death. If this
has not been done the funeral director should suggest it
be done and should offer to do so for the family.

Before the specifics as to any and all aspects of the
religious part of the funeral are decided, they should be
discussed and cleared with the clergyman. This can be
done either by the family or the funeral director as their
representative or by both.

Before the family selects the funeral service, the funeral
director should explain the various aspects of the funeral
and the costs thereof as to the services and the merchandise he provides and as to that obtained from others such
as cemeteries, florists and so forth. This should be
done before the family goes into the casket selection room.
In such explanation the funeral director should make clear
the range of prices of funerals he has available. Also
the funeral director should welcome any questions or discussions as to that which is or is not required by laws
and/or regulations to such laws.
    The funeral director should review for the family the
various death benefits and/or burial allowances that may
be available to them such as those involving Social Security, the Veterans Administration, labor unions, fraternal
and other organizations. He will assist in the preparation
and filing of the necessary forms to secure these benefits
and allowances for the family. Where further professional
assistance is required he should suggest that the families
seek the advice of other professionals.

Because the price of the funeral as to the funeral director
is related to the casket selection, there should be a card
or brochure in each casket in the selection room. Such
card or brochure should outline the services offered by
the funeral home. Services and merchandise not included
where a unit price method is used should be listed on the
card or brochure as separate items.

Representations of the funeral director with respect to caskets should be as to material, construction, design, hardware, mattressing and interior. The use of an outside receptacle in which the casketed body is placed should be fully explained. Facts should be given regarding the requirements of cemeteries as to such receptacles where they exist. The various kinds of receptacles and their materials, construction and design should be reviewed.

When a family decides on the kind of service desired the funeral director should provide a memorandum or agreement for the family to approve or sign showing (1) the price of the service that the family has selected and what is included therein; (2) the price of each of the supplemental items of service and/or merchandise requested; (3) the amount involved for each of the items for which the funeral director will advance monies as an accommodation to the family; and (4) the method of payment agreed upon by the family and the funeral director.

When death occurs in a place other than where the funeral and/or burial are to take place, most times the services of two funeral directors are necessary. Under such circumstances the family should not pay for a complete service both where death occurred and also where the burial or cremation is held.

The forwarding funeral director should make an allowance or adjustment for those of his services not required and should notify the receiving funeral director thereof. Likewise the receiving funeral director should not charge the family for the services already provided by the forwarding funeral director unless there is a duplication thereof desired by the family.

The family should pay for only one complete service plus any additional charges incurred because the place of death and the place of final disposition require the services of two funeral firms.

As soon as the details and schedule in the transporting of remains are known to the forwarding funeral director, he shall immediately notify the receiving funeral director thereof.

It is suggested that when a body is transported a report made out by the person who did the embalming should accompany the remains. Such a report could be of assistance to the receiving funeral director in the event additional professional work is required on the body.

Where burial is at a point distant from where the funeral service is to be conducted and a concrete or metal burial vault is to be used, the funeral director called for the service should suggest the funeral director who will be responsible for the interment provide said vault for a number of reasons including the saving to the family of the added cost of handling and transporting the vault to the place of burial.

When a funeral service is conducted in a place other than the church of the clergyman, his wishes and desires should be considered to whatever extent possible.

In the matter of the honorarium or the stipend the personal wishes of the clergyman should be respected. If the family is a member of the clergyman's church or parish it is a personal matter between the family and the clergyman. When the funeral director assumes the responsibility for the honorarium at the direction of the family, it is desirable to use a check for the transaction for record keeping purposes. If the clergyman does not accept honoraria, the family should be so informed in order that they may express their appreciation in other ways. When the family has no choice of a clergyman and the funeral director makes arrangements for one, the matter of the honorarium becomes the responsibility of the funeral director and a cash advance for the family.

When conducting a funeral in a church the polity, rules and regulations of that church must serve as the guide to the conduct of the service. Any exceptions to such procedures requested by the family should be cleared with the clergyman or proper authority well in advance of the time of their actual performance.

The funeral director should remain alert to the needs of the families he serves and when the need for religious or pastoral counseling is indicated he should make proper referrals whenever possible.

Funeral directors should be available to discuss with anyone all matters relative to the conduct of a funeral. Whenever possible the funeral director should assume active leadership in seminars or discussions which will bring a deeper understanding to all concerned about death, the funeral and bereavement.

The Code of Good Funeral Practice, National Selected Morticians

As funeral directors, our calling imposes upon us special responsibilities to those we serve and to the public at large. Chief among them is the obligation to inform the public so that everyone can make knowledgeable decisions about funerals and funeral directors.

In acceptance of our responsibilities, and as a condition of our membership in National Selected Morticians, we affirm the following standards of good funeral practice and hereby pledge:

1. To provide the public with information about funerals, including prices, and about the functions, services and responsibilities of funeral directors.

2. To afford a continuing opportunity to all persons to discuss or arrange funerals in advance.

3. To make funerals available in as wide a range of price categories as necessary to meet the need of all segments of the community, and affirmatively to extend to everyone the right of inspecting and freely considering all of them.

4. To quote conspicuously in writing the charges for every funeral offered; to identify clearly the services, facilities, equipment and merchandise included in such quotations; and to follow a policy of reasonable adjustment when less than the quoted offering is utilized.

5. To furnish to each family at the time funeral arrangements are made, a written memorandum of charges and to make no additional charge without the approval of the purchaser.

6. To make no representation, written or oral, which may be false or misleading, and to apply a standard of total honesty in all dealings.

7. To respect all faiths, creeds and customs, and to give full effect to the role of the clergy.

8. To maintain a qualified and competent staff, complete facilities and suitable equipment required for comprehensive funeral service.

9. To assure those we serve the right of personal choice and decision in making funeral arrangements.

10. To be responsive to the needs of the poor, serving them within their means.

We pledge to conduct ourselves in every way and at all times in such a manner as to deserve the public trust, and to place a copy of this Code of Good Funeral Practice in the possession of a representative of all parties with whom we arrange funerals.

AUTHOR INDEX

TITLE INDEX
(Periodical Articles in Quotation Marks)

"Accord Is Reached in Funeral Talks" 573
"Accounting for Morticians" 652
"Accounting Method Introduced at Professional Conferences" 574
"The Achievement of the Committee on Necropsies of the Institute of Medicine of Chicago" 835
Acts of Incorporation and By-laws of the Proprietors of the Cemetery of Mount Auburn 1340
Acute Grief and the Funeral 318
Address of the Appleton Clergymen's Assoc. 304
Addresses of the Dead; Date of Death, Burial and Location of Burial of Prominent and Celebrated People 1334
"Ads to Tell What to Expect from Funeral Directors" 575
"Advertising a Funeral Plan" 623
"Advertising Facts--Newspaper Ads That Sell" 607
Advice Concerning Cremation as a Part of Christian Burial 1628
"Aeneas and Turnus on Late Etruscan Funerary Urns" 1377
"Air Shipping Human Remains" 899
"Airlines Give Continually Greater Mortuary Service" 896
The Akenham Burial Case 68
"Alaskan Mortuary Makes First Call at 60 Degrees Below Zero" 120

"Alden Whitman--Master of a Neglected Art" 262
Alexander's Hebrew Ritual, and Doctrinal Explanation of the Whole Ceremonial Law, Oral and Traditional of the Jewish Community in England and Foreign Parts 3
Alishar Huyuk, Seasons of 1930-32, pt. 2 1387; ... of 1928-1929, pt. 1 1367; ... of 1927, pt. 2 1389
Allegheny Cemetery; Historical Account of Incidents and Events Connected with its Establishment ... Reports of 1848 and 1857 ... 1251
Allegheny Cemetery, Pittsburgh, Pa., 1844-1934 1252
Allegheny Cemetery, Pittsburgh, Pa., Its Origin and Early History, Also a Report ... 1900 to ... 1910 1253
"Allied Memorial Council Gets It All Together" 847
"Allowance for Funerals of Servicemen Raised" 265
"Ambulance Drivers Under Wages Law" 875
Amer. Attitudes Toward Death and Funerals (Blackwell & Talarzyk) 1151
Amer. Attitudes Toward Death and Funerals (CMA) 926
Amer. Blue Book of Funeral Directors 1975 836; Directors 1972-1973 836
Amer. Cemetery Assoc. Convention Proceedings 1407
Amer. Cemetery Assoc. Membership Register and Proceed-